IN DEFENSE OF THE
CONSTITUTION:
ENDING AMERICA'S OCCUPATION

IN DEFENSE OF THE
CONSTITUTION:
ENDING AMERICA'S OCCUPATION

An Analysis of the Constitution to Stop the Cultural
Genocide of America

Reg. B. Two Stones
Registered Native American

Research Specialist/Muckraking Reporter

authorHOUSE®

AuthorHouse™
1663 Liberty Drive
Bloomington, IN 47403
www.authorhouse.com
Phone: 1 (800) 839-8640

Published by AuthorHouse 04/22/2019

ISBN: 978-1-4918-5047-3 (sc)
ISBN: 978-1-4918-5046-6 (hc)
ISBN: 978-1-4918-5045-9 (e)

Library of Congress Control Number: 2014903962

Print information available on the last page.

*Any people depicted in stock imagery provided by Getty Images are models,
and such images are being used for illustrative purposes only.
Certain stock imagery © Getty Images.*

This book is printed on acid-free paper.

*Because of the dynamic nature of the Internet, any web addresses or links contained in
this book may have changed since publication and may no longer be valid. The views
expressed in this work are solely those of the author and do not necessarily reflect the
views of the publisher, and the publisher hereby disclaims any responsibility for them.*

RE-DEDICATION

Dedicated to Dr, Seuss and his book <u>Thidwick the Big-Hearted Moose</u> for inspiring me to revise, update, edit, and republish my book because as Thidwick's friends said to him, we need to "Get rid of those pests"; my mother Mary for always believing in me (RIP), my father Vic a legal immigrant who dubbed me his egg head (RIP), and my generation's Heroes on the Black Nam Wall in DC. Finally, I thank Jesus Christ for guiding me, helping me, and making sure I completed this book to save his "ordained" nation when I was ready to quit, and the United States of America may it always be known as God's Country.

Contents

In Defense of the Constitution: Ending America's Occupation

An Analysis of the Constitution to Stop the
Cultural Genocide of America

Polished – Updated – Revised for 2019 US Politics

Reg B Two Stones "Nah-Kee-Teesh"
Registered Native American

Research Specialist/Muckraking Reporter

In all human relationships a revolutionary change is necessary. But to be permanent and effective in solving man's problems, it must start at the root source of the infection... We live in the most revolutionary period of human history. Campus disorders have assumed epidemic proportions! Not only turbulent Berkeley, but also staid Harvard, has staggered under the blows and strikes of the dissidents and militants... Leaders of the "Establishment" work around the clock in their attempt to find band-aids large enough for the festering wounds [that are ripping America apart and pushing it towards a final epic End].

Bill Bright, PhD

What They're Saying About "In Defense of the Constitution: Ending America's Occupation" and Its Author on the Book's Facebook.com Page:

K.A. Hawaii: Our Country is being stolen from us so a handful of jerks can stay in their elected positions.

I.D. Texas: Thank you for your research and information I hope Justice will prevail

R.K.: Wow California is one big corrupt political conspiracy.

R.W. Minnesota: Excellent.

B.H. Arizona: Nice work

S.E. Minnesota: You should run for state senate

I.B. Georgia: A must read.

D.D. Michigan: Excellent digging and investigation, In Defense of the Constitution ...thank you...lets hope before long some of these things will begin to be brought out into the sunshine...this needs to be out there!

C.C. California: A certain Native American needs to run for President.

This book was written in 2014. It was rushed to print with limited editing because the first draft disappeared from the office of the publisher for four weeks and could not be found. The author later learned the contents of the book had been given to the U.S. Government before it went to press. This event led to some strange events that happened to the author and his family. The Author wishes to thank his reader's loyalty for buying the book anyway. For those with copies of the first edition of this book, I hope you think of them as signed collectibles because these are now limited editions that were rushed to print to avoid the suppression of this book and to stop what he felt was the American Judicial System's and politicians' lawless, criminal, and un-Constitutional power grab that was not within their powers: An example is the immigration law ex-President Obama wrote and passed during his tenure which the US Constitution (The Law of the Land in America) says only Congress has the power to write and pass. The Author feels President Obama should have been impeached for his alleged dictator type power grab and use of unwritten presidential powers he created to sign these laws into power which the author feels are non-binding and illegal immigration laws. I say this because president Obama used his self appointed executive powers as he warned America he would in November of 2014 on Network News. What you're holding here is the third installment of this book with updates, re-editing, and re-visions that couldn't be completed the first time for fear of having the book stopped before it went to press. The updates introduce this book to the public under a new light with the same message that I feel fathered the underground Citizen's revolution of 2016 that Democrats are now trying erase with tactics that were once only used in third world and communist controlled nations.

"No system invented by people will ever be safe enough, secure enough, free enough, or good enough to justify placing our confidence and hope in it... Beware the false security of Walden Pond.

Kendra Olson (Founder Magazine 2018)

"Whenever any Form of Government becomes destructive . . . it is the Right of the People to alter or to abolish it, and to institute new Government" (US Declaration of Independence)

"The only thing necessary for the triumph of evil is for good men to do nothing."

"White-collar [crime] is real [crime] . . . because it is in violation of law; and the only major difference between white collar [crime] and lower class [crime] is that the former is primarily in violation of administrative law enforced by regulatory agencies while the latter is primarily in violation of statutory law enforced by the criminal justice system."

(Edwin Hardin Sutherland)

"Question Authority"
(Reg. B. Two Stones)

Introduction

"No man who has the truth to tell and the power to tell it can long remain hiding it from fear or even from despair without ignominy. To release the truth against whatever odds, even if so doing can no longer help the Common Wealth is a necessity of the soul."

(Hilaire Belloc, author)

(Note: The cover was purposely printed out of focus because the author believes America's Judges and Government are practicing fuzzy law to betray the Republic and allow the world's citizens to invade America.)

I am starting my introduction to his book, with one of my heroes, Hilaire Belloc, a writer who wrote and published over 100 books during his lifetime. In the first Semester of my journalism classes, I was introduced to many great writers including Hilarie Belloc. As I studied Hilaire Belloc, I learned he was more than just a writer because he was also a Muckraker who was bold enough to champion other Muckrakers and their works. In fact, he not only championed them but he also praised their investigative works and articles that they wrote to protect and serve the average man and woman on the street. These Muckrakers that I also once studied in high school were so bold they even took on the rich and powerful business giants of American industry. And! During the Industrial revolution, they exposed the poor and dangerous working conditions of their factories, their illegal labor and business practices, and how America's children were being sold into factory work bondage where they would often get killed and maimed with the permission of their parents who sold them into this type of slave work.

Unfortunately for Americans from the mid 20th Century to the early 21st Century, Corporate America learned from their mistakes and according to Belloc, "'Big Business' and their owners got smart and started buying up all of America's 'News Papers' and other 'Media' companies," or what Belloc called the Fourth Estate. By owning all of these media companies, Big Business knew they would control the messengers and the messages that came out of America's Fourth Estate. When we fast forward to 2016 (thanks to the Presidential election), we now see that all of the major News and Media companies are now owned and controlled by only three or four US Corporations who allegedly, according to the sources I discuss in this book, control and edit the content of all news to their specifications before it's released to the American public. If my readers will think back, this information makes America's news appear to be more like propaganda than news. I should note that Viacom and the Walt Disney Corporation both own TV Networks, and that Disney's Network controls "The View" an extreme left wing talk show that appears to enjoy defending and championing past President Obama's Administration (and during the 2016 election pushed Mrs. Clinton's Presidential campaign) and attacking President Trump and his Administration any time they get a chance to do it.

Now that my readers understand the power Big Business now has by owning the Fourth Estate, I hope all of America is shocked and understands why I decided to write this book. Since I am a journalist and a self-appointed muckraker, I feel it my duty to challenge Corporate America's spin centers so I can stop the Fourth Estates' endless support (when they get the chance) of the left and President's like Obama and his Administration's "Amnesty" plans for millions of Mexico's lawless invading trespassers and other acts that go against America's laws. I also hope to stop their Championing of ex-Presidents like Obama who at the time of publication of this book was attempting to sign into power a law that reformed or ended America's immigration laws, as they had been written by Congress. This law that past President Obama was trying to pass was meant to weaken America's immigration laws to the point that I felt there would be no need to have a Border Patrol or a border (Thanks to Trump's election it never happened.). This bad law, if it had gone into power, would very likely have caused a tidal wave of illegal Mexican Nationals so big that I believe this tidal wave would have overwhelmed America's Border Patrol and our Southwestern States' peace officers and sovereignty (Note: At the end of 2018, American news reported that thousands of so called illegal refugees from South and Central America had arrived on the Mexican/US border and were demanding to be allowed to enter and live in America—The left and America's rogue US Supreme Court appear to be ready to let them in and force President Trump to break his promise to close America's borders by ignoring US Immigration and Constitutional law.).

Since my fellow Americans now know that President Obama and Congress' pending immigration reform was never passed, I do hope my fellow Americans know that if this law had passed it would have ended America's control of its own sovereign nation status and weakened the US Constitution's "law of the land" status (As we can see from the swarm of so called new refugees from America's Southern Border). If it had passed, it also would have hastened the decline of English as America's language and would have hastened the decline and end of America's Christian based Western Culture. How do I know the passing of this law would have been so bad? To answer this question, I want to remind my fellow Americans that although Native Americans believed whites were a weak race and would be defeated easily when they first met them. Unfortunately for my people, history tells us that Native Americans ended up losing control of their land and their homes due to a mass invasion of settlers from the East that came like the Lord's flood. Finally to drive my point home, I want to remind Americans of some other examples that show how fast a Nation can lose control of their land and homes to an invader. The first example I want to present is Europe's Armenian's who lost their country at the end of WWII when the Muslim Turks used the end of WWII as a cover to invade Armenia. This country and her people thought they had survived WWII intact. But thanks to the Turks and Greece, they lost most of their country (Cultural genocide Wikipedia The Free Encyclopedia, Online Posting, April 2, 2012: www.http://en.wikipedia.org/wiki/ Cultural Genocide): By the way, history also tells us that the US did nothing to stop the Turkish invasion and the known genocide of Armenians that was carried out very much like Hitler's extermination of the Jews.

The second example I'd like to present is how fast modern day Egypt's dictator and his indigenous people lost their country when it was overrun and taken from them by Muslim refugees they'd helped or opened up their country to as a safe haven (sound familiar?). These Muslim refugees entered Egypt humbly, became citizens, joined Egypt's military, then violently demanded Muslim rights; these Muslims then started a war and thanks to President Obama's US Taxpayer dollars and US munitions these Muslims took Egypt away from Egypt's indigenous people. The news then reported to the world that these so called freedom groups stormed Egypt's Museums and started destroying Egypt's ancient artifacts like history told us they did when the took over Armenia. I would like to note here that history says that no country has survived a war when their refugees (invaders?) decide to over throw the ruling Government. And since "history has a nasty habit of repeating itself," I feel that Americans should feel vulnerable and very scared. Note: I make this observation as a Muckraking reporter, author, and card carrying and registered half-breed son of the Lipan and Mescalero Apache Nation member whose people lost their homes, lands, and cultures in the same fashion.

Note: I want to add that my father's ancestors were Portuguese-Spaniard immigrants from Europe who arrived in the port of Galveston, Texas then migrated to Mexico and Central America and then decided to return to America so they applied and waited five years for their turn to get their US immigration "green cards" (like immigrants are supposed to do to be called immigrants) to return to the US. My father loved living in America and being an American so much that he always reminded his children that they were American citizens first and foremost and they should be proud of that fact. My father also taught us that, "We speak English in this house because you're American born citizens and live in America." I want to note that one of my father's favorite quotes was that since his homeland of Portugal and for a short time Mexico and Central America (He was an immigrant in Mexico for a few years.) had not given him a chance to earn a real living and a good life, he owed his allegiance to America for allowing him to become a success. These standards, my fellow Americans, are what real immigrants believe (or should believe) when they come to America to live and start a new life. I feel I can make this statement because my father was a real American loving immigrant who loved being an American citizen.

Because, as I just wrote in past paragraphs, I'm a proud muckraker and American Compatriot who is very worried that America is about to fall, I have decided to not "sell-out" and write this book. And like my hero Belloc, who never sold-out, I've decided not to compromise or sell my integrity for fame, fortune, or a job as a professor whose loyalty would have to be to a union instead of my country. I'm also afraid I can't be a part of what I believe is ex-President Obama's and the American Government's new socialist direction for America. This new America appears to include changing America into a borderless country that doesn't need immigration laws or Border Patrol Officers because the country is being sold out for a world government, overseas oil, and financial profits.

I now want to move on and point out the money that is being made overseas is not the only problem because the real problem is the fact that America's jobs and factories are being sent overseas and creating jobs in other countries while Americans continue to lose their factory jobs that are being replaced by menial service jobs. And while America's factory jobs continue to be sent overseas by rich CEOs, our military personnel are being asked to protect the lives of the CEOs of these companies who continue to live safe in America, who evidently don't care if these soldiers have jobs to come home to after they have served their country and protected the interest of these CEOs and their corporations. I now want to point out that I feel America is headed towards a Socialist Democrat controlled country (many Democrats are calling themselves "Socialist Democrats). I want to further note this new Socialist/ Communist State that appears to be slowly taking shape in America appears to be giving birth to a group of modernist Americans (who I've decided to call "Alienating Modernist of this Century," or AMOCs for short) who appear to want to put an end to American Sovereignty; an end to the border between Mexico and America; an end to civility, morality, and Christianity; and an end to America's great Constitution. These AMOC's are so anti-US Christian Republic that they seem to want to force all Americans to accept a hedonistic life style and then force all Americans to accept it as a social norm. AMOCs also appear to want to force foreign religious beliefs on Americans even as I write this book. These forceful acts mean the US Government appears to have decided to force some handpicked religions on America's citizens and give these religions power over America's legal citizens and their Christian Values.

Since I'm an American Compatriot, and not an "AMOC, " I've decided I can't live in ex-President Obama's "Modernist/Hedonistic America," or an America whose hedonistic life style appears to be ready to allow the United Nations, or any other foreign nation's laws, to trump American citizens' Constitutional law and then give AMOC Modernists the power to stop at nothing to push their "anything goes" modernist life style on Americans: I want to note this life style that's being pushed on America's citizens appears to be something like a Sodom and Gomorrah life style that ended up costing these cities' their citizens' lives because they were blown off the face of the earth by God (as the Old Testament says in Gen. Xiii 10). I also feel these people appear to have an agenda to push a God is dead or doesn't exist religious belief agenda on America's citizens. The irony of their "God is dead" or doesn't exist religious belief is that in the same breath these AMOCs seem to idolize and watch a TV show that has American youths believing that vampires are real.

I want to note one more fact that I find interesting about these AMOCs. The fact I found was that these new AMOC groups appear to enjoy defending any law that says flying the American flag is against the law if it insults or offends these refugee Mexicans or Muslims now living in America and/or any foreigner living on US Sovereign soil illegally. If my readers think I'm making this up, I want to point out that this year (2013) the city of Porterville had a Freedom Fest on June 29 instead of a Fourth Of July celebration because the Gays in Porterville wanted to have a Gay Rights Celebration during the 4th of July celebration (which I found very un-American) and the Mexican Colonist Invaders didn't like celebrating or attending the Fourth of July celebration (Because they'd rather Boo and Hiss at America's flag, as my readers will soon read here.). This appears to be the real reason the city Porterville had stopped having Fourth of July fireworks shows. I want to note that up until this year the city kept telling America's legal Porterville residents that the city didn't allegedly have the money to have a Fourth of July fireworks show (like they'd always had for over 80s years). But miraculously, this year (2012) the City of Porterville decided it did have the money to have a Freedom Fest party on June 29 (2012), a day that all of these none July 4 supporters would be happy to celebrate a none American holiday. I want to note that for the past five or six years the city has kept telling its citizens it didn't have the money to pay for fireworks; however, for this non-fourth of July party, the city fathers miraculously got the money together and even paid for Entertainment, Food, Live Music, and a huge fireworks display. If this none-Fourth of July celebration does not show my readers who our local government entities are pandering to in California, then it doesn't snow in Alaska. To learn more, I suggest my readers keep reading this book and be ready to fight for America against America's rogue Politicians, Judges, and Government.

Having pointed out the facts above, I want to remind Americans that "they" control America's government. So, I hope this self help book will inspire America's Compatriots to keep reading till they learn, from this book, how to defend the principle that says America's citizens are the heart of the Republic and not judges or government; so therefore, America's citizens have the power and right to decide how to repel all of America's trespassers as they see fit and they have the power to control American sovereignty and not some rich fat-cat politician or rogue judge who is paid off to keep America's borders open.

Because America is a Christian nation, I want to also remind my fellow Americans that they have the right to decide what's morally best for their country and children. After all, America's faith has always been at the core of their decisions during crises in the past so it should come as no surprise that Americans have always prayed to God for strength during hard times: I want to note this fact is known as the American way. To prove this statement, I want to add that during our Nation's darkest historical hours American History tells us that American Presidents like Lincoln (civil war), Hoover (great depression of 1929), and Roosevelt (World War II) asked us to pray with them and to look to God for guidance and strength for our nation during these times of need. So Now, as a fellow American and a Red, White, and Blue All-American Patriot who loves his flag and his Country, I ask my fellow Americans to pray to God that he will helps us throw off the yoke of oppression from these foreign invaders and the American Leaders who are empowering them by illegally giving them US Citizen powers that do not apply to these illegal foreigners.

Finally, I searched the web to see if I could find President Obama sitting or pictured in any Christian Church service throughout his presidency, and I'm sorry to say, I couldn't find one because either I didn't look in the right place or none have ever been posted. I did find a post where it was written that President Obama attended services at St John's Episcopal Church to hear Dr Ziad Asali, M.D. the founder and president of the American Task Force on Palestine who was the guest speaker. This man is described "as 'a long time activist on Middle East issues' who has testified to both chambers of Congress about Palestine interests, increased U.S. aid to the Palestine Authority, and criticized 'Israel's disproportionate use of force' in Gaza," online page written by GOPUSA.COM (GOPUSA.COM, Online Posting: November 2, 2010, www.http://gopusa.com/fresh-ink/2010/9/so-obama-went-to-church-last-sunday.php#ixzz10HrlCmpu

In closing, I want to add that America's humble Christian values, faith in God, and faith in Prayer that our leaders and parents taught us to-turn-to when things looked grim or bad for America helped me keep writing this book when I wanted to quit. I almost quit because I lost most of the use of my right arm and hand and it was hard to keep typing this book. Yes that's right, "good, old humble Christian values" are why I decided I couldn't quit, brush my love for my country and Old Glory aside, or give in to what I feel is an emerging World that's full of lawless Nations whose decadent morals are coming home to live in President Obama's "New Modernist Controlled" America. By taking this stand, I feel I'm in good company: "The world's morals," say the Directors of the IHS Press, "don't cut mustard, and "most aspects of modernity stand condemned in one way or another in the face of evidence presented by the religious, rational, and moral sense" (Belloc, Hilaire. The Free Press, IHS Press: Norfolk, VA. 2002.7-8.). Read on American Patriots, so this book and the information in it can show you how to take back America from the world's special interests groups and Socialist Democrats who will soon wrest away your Nation and Constitutional rights if things don't change.

Chapter One

Apologia for Border Closure, Immigration Repeal, and Dr. Seuss' Allegory

(To Glorify the Father)

"Government is not wholly made up of constitutions and laws, but of customs as well. These customs, in a way, also form part of our social inheritance.
                                        William Bennett Munro

It is with sorrow that I begin to write this book that will hopefully save the All-American Western Culture that created this great Nation and this All-American, God Fearing, Old Glory waving Ethnic Minority Male that's writing this book. As a self described "All-American male, I want to add that this book is not being written to champion the millions of law breaking invaders or squatters that currently live and continue to enter America's sovereign soil illegally at an alarming rate (with the blessings of America's elected politicians, US Judicial System, and the Mexican Government); however, I am writing this book to defend America's Constitution for her Compatriots, legal citizens, and US Officials who continue to demand and fight for the enforcement of America's Immigration Laws (These laws are not broken or out of date, as we're lead to believe.), criminal laws, and Constitutional laws that are known "as the law of the Land."

To the brave Americans and Patriotic souls who continue to defend America and her European Christian Culture, I offer this scholarly research and legitimate weapon of righteousness and US Laws so they can use them to go "toe-to-toe" with any "Open Border" proponent including President Obama, Hillary Clinton, Mexico's special interest lobbyists, Pro-Amnesty US Politician, American Farm Corporation Giants, American or foreign Corporation Lobbyist who uses favors to buy votes from Congress, and finally the ACLU or American Civil Liberties Union. I should add here that I read recently read that the ACLU is allegedly said to be the enemy of America's Constitution because their lawyers are great a twisting the Civil Rights laws of the 60s to apply to foreigners and illegal aliens by ignoring the rest of the words of the American Constitution. And, unfortunately for the ACLU, this minority American male feels sad to the ACLU twist and miss use America's Civil Right's laws because he grew up dealing with real racism and the ACLU was never around, so I do not trust the ACLU to be pro America or its Constitution. The reason I feel this way is because my country, flag, and Western Christian culture come first before my heritage (right or wrong) because I live in America and I love my country.

Up till now, Anti-Open Border proponents have been fighting a losing battle against pro open-border politicians which was accentuated by what was very likely an illegal use of presidential executive power by ex-President Obama (something Obama appeared to enjoy doing during his tenure as US President) when he illegally (I prove this fact later in this book.) gave thousands of illegal men and women under the age of 30 amnesty. Since I know the Constitution says that only Congress has the power to create or write immigration laws, I want to add that when President Obama used his executive power to grant these people amnesty, he broke both Constitutional and US Immigration laws. Don't worry my fellow Americans I will prove this fact later in this chapter.

Before I move on, I want to point out that President Obama appeared to be very adept at breaking Constitutional law during his tenure. I say this because I also found a story where he was evidently found guilty of over reaching his powers on January 25, 2012, when the US Court of Appeals ruled President Obama "breached his constitutional authority by making recess appointments to the National Labor Relations Board on January 4, 2012" ("Court says recess appointments to NLRB are unconstitutional." On Campus 32.4 March-April 2013: 11.). Reading that this president broke laws and helped Mexico's Invaders sums up why America's citizens keep demanding that their borders be closed and all of the Invaders sent back to their place of origin. The problem is that America's citizens keep losing the fight to stop the erosion of their Constitutional rights and privileges and are seeing the destruction of their Western Christian culture right before their eyes. I should add that instead of passing these kinds of destructive and illegal laws Presidents like Obama and America's politicians should be passing laws like the ones that Japan's Government uses to protect the citizens and Republic of Japan: These Japan immigration laws include laws that state "All foreign workers, like your author who worked overseas, have to carry a card that foreign workers have to have in their possession at "all" times. And, if these American or foreign workers are asked for it by the police, a clerk at hotel, a rental agency, or the immigration officer when they leave Japan, they have to provide it while living in Japan or return it before they leave Japan. These laws are used in Japan are not profiling because Japan's Government is only just making sure these foreigners are legally in Japan and have permission to work and live Japan. I want to note here that I never felt this was a racist law because I knew I was a guest in these people's country.

I want to point out that not one US politician has ever said anything about US Farm Corporations signing any kind of immigration sponsorship law that would make them financially responsible for any, and all, Mexican invading workers they hire and are allowed to enter the US to work on their farms (or production or manufacturing plants). But! These same US politicians do rant and rave for ignoring US Immigration laws and keeping US Borders open granting to any all illegal alien law breakers. If the US Government did the right thing, these large farming giants (and manufacturing plants) would have to be responsible for all of the illegal workers they hire till the workers leave the US and return to Mexico, or some other nation. This action would make sure Mexico's workers (and other workers) would never become a burden on America's taxpayers.

When I worked and lived in countries like Japan and China, my Japanese or Chinese (or what ever country I was working in) employers had to pay for my work permit, pay a sponsors fee, and paid my salary during the time my permit was active. When the job ended or contract ended, I had to leave the country, get another sponsor, get deported, or go to jail for breaking immigration laws. I believe this kind of law should apply to all US businesses that hire both illegal and legal foreign workers in the US because they are the ones who are benefiting from these invading/colonizing scab workers (or legally carded scab workers hat are called "Gaijin" [foreigner] in Japan). To make it fair and completely right for America's citizens, the moment one of these farm corporations hires one of these trespassers or colonizers, I believe these companies should be forced to become their sponsors and have to pay a sponsor fee, their medical insurance, and keep them employed until either a year or six months passes. After this time, they would have to tell America's Immigration Department they are not going to need them so they want them sent home because they will not be renewing their work permit. This kind of law would prevent these invading colonizers from staying in America permanently.

To prove these illegal invaders/scabs are being prodded to cross our border illegally by US businesses, US farm Bureaus and their white collar large farming coop advisory committees, I'd like to point out that in a recent Tulare County Farm Bureau Newspaper I discovered two articles that urged their members to call or write the members of Congress and demand America's government allow even more invaders from Mexico and to change current immigration policies (To me, these kinds of remarks are code for gut the US Immigration laws.). To quote Patricia Stever Blattler, executive director of the Tulare County Farm Bureau in Central California (TCFB), "I hope you (farmers/members of TCFB) take advantage of these weeks (weeks when their local reps come home to visit their constituents) to visit with some of our elected officials . . . We know our leaders understand the importance of this issue (immigration reform to benefit farmers' pocket books) to agriculture, but they also need support and ammunition for taking on the opposing team (anti-illegal immigration and pro US law groups) on this issue too." And to quote Kevin Rogers, a fourth generation farmer who chimed in by adding, "[We need] to advance realistic labor and immigration reforms supported by united agricultural groups and interests. Put simply, we need reform that works for all of agriculture (Blattler S. Patricia and Rogers, Kevin. "Speak out Now on Immigration: A Spark of Optimism for Ag Labor Reform," Tulare County Farm Labor News. Visalia. April 2013; Pp. 2 - 12). I should note that Mr. Rogers didn't say anything about keeping America a land of laws and/or what is good or works for all Americans!

Now, because "Anti-Open Border" Proponents have been on the losing end of America's propaganda wars with the rich and powerful and well-financed Open Border supporters, this book promises "not" to use any of the old arguments or over used and out dated terms that are often used by overwhelmed Americans when they battle the powerful political "Open Border Amnesty Machine" that I'm going to call OBAM. In my new American Citizens' offensive to fight OBAM supporters, this author is going to introduce many new terms, research findings, and fact filled arguments to start the offensive to finally win the propaganda wars and keep America sovereign. With this new offensive, I hope to show

America's Patriots how to finally defeat groups like the Mexican Government, the American Civil Liberties Union, the National Council of La Raza, the League of United Latin American Citizens, La Casa, SEIU and AFT teachers unions, Service Employees International Union, National Immigration Forum, American oil companies, the Labor Council for Latin American Advancement, and believe it or not the Arizona and California Farm Bureau and leaders like Patricia Stever Blattler who is the executive director of the Tulare County Farm Bureau. I want to note these are just a few of the hundreds of groups that keep pouring money into the election campaign coffers of "open border" supporting American Politicians and the Democrat Party (I should note this includes both Republicans and Democrats).

To fight these groups that do not appear to care about what is best for America or her legal and law abiding citizens, I offer this book that defends US Constitutional law, US Immigration laws, and criminal laws by providing offensive facts and tactics based on US Constitutional law, literary analytical facts, historical facts, and arguments that provide new terms and concepts that I feel will end the erosion of America's sovereignty and end the occupation of America. But before I begin my presentation and the discussion of the facts and arguments that I know will end the occupation of America, I feel there is a need to define and dismiss many of the confusions that might come from the use of these new words and expressions that I will introduce and use in this book.

One important point I want to make here is that I have decided to label the growing numbers of Mexican reprobates on American soil as "invaders," and their continued stay in America as an **"occupation"** because, as my fellow Americans shall learn later in this book, calling law breaking and colonizing invaders of America "illegal immigrants" is like calling the German invaders who entered Austria to occupy it during World War II peace keepers or immigrants because they needed very little fire power when they marched into this peaceful nation that had a small army (Note:

Think "The Sound of Music."). But, maybe the "open border's" definition is correct and the occupying German soldiers who invaded Austria were there as immigrants (or peace keepers) and that's why the US Government didn't raise a political fuss over Germany's invasion? Well, America did finally raise a fuss after Germany decided to invade Poland, Sweden, France and other European Nations, and when Japan finally attacked America's Pearl Harbor (which we all know started WWII). I think this act of war was what finally woke up America's slow thinking political leaders and generals that were isolating America from world events during this era.

From the invasion example in the last paragraph, Americans should learn that an invasion of a country by an invader doesn't require shooting at first or killing to be called an invasion or war attrition, but eventually the trespassers or invaders begin to make demands and take control of the conquered or invaded nation and then it is often too late for the host. The conclusion I reach at the start of this paragraph should help America's citizens understand the dangers of allowing another country to enter a host country without controls or resistance. To make things worse and more dangerous for Americans, I discovered in 2012 that Mexico's military or special armed forces (known as "Juaristas" by illegal Mexican citizens who were willing to confirm our discovery) is operating in the state of California and might have received permission from either America's or California's Government to operate in California.

This overt invasion of American soil by Mexico's military is bad, but I feel this invasion of US soil has been in the works since November 5, 1974 and I am going to prove it in this book. Why do I say it started in 1974? According to my research and the sources I found in books, newspapers, and on line sources this overt take over of California started when an alleged hand picked commission gutted California's state Constitution (note; They eliminated thousands of words and complete sections of this state's Constitution.). For example, Article 1, Section 1 was gutted down to "one" paragraph that simply reads, "All people are by nature free and independent and have inalienable rights. Among these are enjoying and defending life, liberty, acquiring, possessing, and protecting property, and pursuing and obtaining safety, happiness, and privacy." The first thing my readers should notice in this sentence is the non-use of words like "American or US" citizen to describe the people in this sentence of a US State. I feel this was done on purpose because the Preamble of California's Constitution introductory words use these very carefully selected words that Qualify just about any person on God's earth who manages to enter California to live and to be considered a citizen of this state (and a US citizen) with the rights of a US Citizen: "We, the people of the state of California, in order to secure and perpetuate its blessings, do establish this Constitution...." The key words in this sentence are the words, "the people of the State of California." On these words alone, the commission's re-write of this Constitution, allowed any person who entered California (or US soil) to live on US soil to have the rights of a US Citizen. Note, again, the lack of the needed words like US Citizens or American citizens because without these words in this section of the CA Constitution (Article 1, Section 1) "All people" appears to have been purposely left without any precedence or antecedence to clarify its definition as to who the word "people" represents in this sentence.

By now, my readers are probably wondering how I learned about these very scary and important facts and situations that appear to have been added by California's Politicians to hide the real reason they created these changes that both destroyed and hurt California's and America's Sovereignty in this state. Unfortunately for my fellow Americans, I can assure them that I didn't get this dangerous information from California's or our American Government's public relations department. In fact, I can prove a California Congressman didn't deny or confirm the fact that Mexico's military is operating in California, and I have a letter to prove it. This letter is signed by Congressman Devin Nunes who currently serves the 21st District in California. If my readers want to know how I got this information,

I have to be honest and say I was lucky because it fell into my lap, or maybe it wasn't just luck because maybe I had a little heavenly intervention.

The heavenly intervention I'm talking about above evidently appeared to me when some lucky American citizens ran into some caravans of Mexican military personal at several gas stations throughout California and a grocery store in Central California. And, one other US citizen ran into these military personnel when he was trout fishing in California's National Forests: "According to this citizen, he was confronted by several Spanish speaking military dressed men while he was fishing in the Sierra Mountains of California. As for your author, I also encountered Mexico's military when I stopped to buy gas at a service station located on a main highway in Central California that goes up to the Sierra Forest in Tulare County. Knowing I had a duty, as an American, to report this citing, I reported this sighting to my district's Congressman Devin Nunes. To my surprise, Congressman Nunes would not talk to me in person, and he instead replied in a letter that basically said this was not part of his job so he couldn't comment on the Mexican military sighting. Mr. Nunes then advised me to contact the Immigration Department who "might be interested." To prove I'm telling the truth, I am going to provide some information from the Congressman's letter in the next paragraph. I think Mr. Nunes' response is going to shock many Americans.

To begin, the letter from Congressman Nunes included an official government seal that read "United States House of Representatives and was dated June 11, 2012; some other information Nunes' letter provided (at the top) was that Devin Nunes served on the Ways and Means Committee, Health and Trade Committees; he was on the Permanent Select Committee on Intelligence, and finally the letterhead said he was the Assistant Majority Whip of his party. I want to note that I began my letter with questions that asked Congressman Nunes why some other American Citizens and I (who live in different areas of Central

California) had recently seen several Mexican military or special armed forces convoys traveling in California like they had special permission to operate in America. I then asked him why one US citizen who happened to meet these Mexican military personnel (who were armed like Marines) could be threatened by these men because he came too close to their camp while he was simply fishing and camping in California's mountains? I also asked Nunes why the Mexican military, or these special armed forces from Mexico, had permission to be in California and why the US Government had not told America's citizens or the general public about this very important development that puts America's sovereignty at risk? I want to add that Nunes' answer to my question was written and presented in the second paragraph of his letter, and the answer read as follows:

"Not knowing the specific details of your encounters with military personnel and who you reported your concerns to, I am unable to comment [on this matter]." Needless to say, I found Nunes' answer perplexing and strange because, after all, Nunes' letterhead says he serves on the US Government's Intelligence Committee. And! I had just reported to him some very disturbing facts. The other part of his answer basically told me he couldn't help me and to instead to call the US Immigration and Customs office, but "I should be warned this government department [doesn't] provide any updates for tip information." Since I worked for the Federal Government, I knew this meant that if the government didn't want us Americans to know the truth, they were going to either "deny it" or "ignore any and all requests" for information on this matter, and they were not going to offer any information even if it was true (Think Obama's personal records). Note: if our readers wish to contact Congressman Nunes on this matter, they can contact him in Washington at this number: 1-202-225-2523 or on the web at this address WWW.Nunes.House.Gov. (Note: As I was going to print, I learned today, 11/27/13, that the Federal Government had closed off access to California's Sierra Mountain range. My friends who work for the Forestry Department told me they were asked to leave and not enter till after they were called. I guess the Feds are interested in these Mexican soldiers after all.)

I want to say one more thing about the term "illegal immigrant" which I feel is really not the correct word to describe the 20 million lawless Mexican colonists who live in America or the thousands more who are pouring into America at this very moment as I complete this book. Since I proved that Americans should call any invader who enters America without authority a "criminal invader" and not an "illegal immigrant," I've decided **Not** to use the term "illegal immigrant" when I talk about these 20 million law breaking trespassers that are living on US sovereign soil with the illegal blessing of America's Democrat Party and our rogue Supreme Court. Instead of using this perverse term, I have decided to replace this term with some important crucial terms the American Thesaurus says are synonyms for the term "illegal": The terms I'm going to use are "criminal, unconstitutional, lawless, and forbidden" to name just a few of the words I found in Funk and Wagnalls English Language Thesaurus ("Laird, Charlton." Ed. "Lutz, D. William," Rev. Ed. Webster's New World Thesaurus, "Funk and Wagnalls Ed. 1985).

Thanks to the information in the last paragraph, I hope my fellow Americans learned that "open border" supporters made a critical mistake when they decided to create and use the term "illegal immigrants" because this perverted term contradicts everything they meant to say when they created the term "illegal immigrants." Although I'm sure that "open border" supporters thought they were creating the perfect term to cover up the fact that Mexico's citizens and other American border trespassers are not immigrants (because in reality they are multiple lawbreaking invaders), the facts I provide here show they failed to do their job right or completely. These "open border" supporters failed because when I analyzed the perverse term "illegal immigrants," that they created to define the trespassers they love to support, I learned these trespassing Mexican (and Central Americans and South Americans and others) invaders are really being called or described as "criminal immigrants" by their own supporters. The term **"illegal,"** as I noted in the last paragraph, translates into and also means a **"criminal, lawless, and/or and unconstitutional"** person. America wake up, there is no such person as an "illegal" immigrant" and you are being conned by your US Government and Judges. To put it bluntly my fellow Americans, this word or term smells a lot like the Cow Stuff found on US dairies.

In reality, what my Americans should learn from the last paragraph is that the supporters of these "criminal immigrants" are really calling these law-breakers "unconstitutional" and lawless people or "criminal invading colonizer." From the facts I just presented, I feel I can come to this solid conclusion because these "criminals" really ignored America's Immigration and Constitutional Laws, and when they broke these laws, they became "undesirables" in the eyes of America's immigration laws and all of America's Law Enforcement Officers. To conclude, according to America's Immigration laws when these colonizing invaders become "criminals," they lose any chance of ever getting a green card or becoming a US citizen because they become "undesirables" in the eyes of the law. The reason they become "undesirables" is because US Immigration laws say "any person who enters America that has a criminal record or that is a wanted criminal is considered an undesirable in the eyes America's immigration laws, criminal laws, and the US Department of Immigration and therefore they can NEVER be allowed to enter US soil, or apply for American Green cards or citizenship.

So why is it important that Americans know that applicants who break laws or have criminal records become undesirables in the eyes of US immigration laws? According to the Immigration officers I talked to during my research and from some books I read on the subject of immigration, US immigration laws seldom (if ever) allow any person to enter America legally if they've committed a crime, broken laws, have a criminal record, or are wanted in their homeland for crimes. What this information means to these lawless American border trespassers and colonizing invaders (as I have proved here) is that when they break the law by using fake names, stolen Social Security numbers, fake identifications, never report or pay taxes on their income, and of course enter America as invaders, they automatically become criminals or undesirables according to U.S. criminal, immigration laws, Constitutional laws, and even the Monroe Doctrine (I prove this fact later throughout this book).

America's legally and vested Compatriots should now understand why I say that ex-President Obama and Congress should (or must) have known that these Mexican and other trespassing colonizers are, or were never, really immigrants; so therefore, they needed to acknowledge that when these lawless and colonizing invaders enter US soil without permission or legal authorization they lose all chances of ever entering America legally. So, I have to ask my fellow Americans, "Why are Democrats and Congress still trying to give these criminals a free pass into America in 2019? Can't they see that I just proved these illegal aliens are really lawless and trespassing invaders in the eyes of America's laws? Having come to my conclusion, I have to wonder if America's Politicians and Congress know that by helping these lawbreakers they really become accessories to a crime.

I would like to add that according to the Federal Immigration and Nationality Act of 1952 (Still in force because ex-President Obama, the Democrats, and even many Republicans did not get their way.) "A criminal background is a reason to deny [and never allow] this person to be granted a Green Card or US Citizenship." This important part of America's great and legal immigration law evidently means little to ex-President Obama and the 2019 mid-term Democrat Congress (and other Democrat and Republican pro open border politicians) because at this very moment while this book is being written Congress (and ex-President Obama) are in the process of trying to help thousands of so called South American refugees to enter the US illegally and change America's immigration laws so they can grant 20 million Mexican lawless invaders a legal pardon (which Congress does not have the power to in act), or as they like to call it "Amnesty." Since I know these invaders don't qualify for Amnesty, if either Congress or America's Supreme Court Judges (or President Trump) ever give these illegal aliens Amnesty, I know they will be committing an act of treason against the Republic (I prove this fact in this book.). I want to point out one more fact: I'm going to now add a surprise fact about the definition of the term "Immigrant." My surprise should help me prove once and for all that the 20 million and growing Mexican and other invaders living in America are not in any way immigrants because in reality they are more like an unarmed military colonizing force that is currently invading and occupying America.

If you have read this far, you are possibly one of those Southwestern United States (especially those in California) Compatriots who's shell shocked by the daily shootings and murders being committed on your streets by Mexican gang members who occupy and roam your once quiet small American towns and cities in the Southwest. Like you, I'm shocked to wake up in the middle of the night by gun fire or ethnic music so loud our children wake up crying at 2 or 3 AM in the morning and wondering why American hometowns are looking more like Mexican cities instead of cities in the USA. Like you, I'm also shocked and suffering from depression and insomnia that is causing unexplained anger and fights with our spouses and our children. And, although recent studies show rising cases of anxiety that are being reflected in rising alcohol abuse, drugs, and child abuse in the US and California, to be politically correct, I notice no investigations or studies are being done to find the reason for the rising crimes that are called "senseless acts of "unexplained violence."

Could the reasons for this new unexplained violence happening in America be because our cities are starting to look more like third world nation cities or towns? Maybe (my degree in Social Psychology tells me) this is why so many people (both adults and kids) are getting tattoos, why bullying is now commonplace in America, mass shootings are becoming a yearly occurrence, and divorces and drug use are becoming an epidemic. After all, I read that studies by Jung and others say that when people feel they have no control of their lives, these people usually find ways to make them feel like they have some sense of control of the stress that they have no control over. What kind of stress? Well, how about the stress these violent illegal invaders have added to our lives with their illegal gun fire on holidays, illegal fireworks, rising violent family crimes and broken homes that are overwhelming California's Social Services Departments, and the growing Mexican gang wars for control of drug selling in states like California. If you're one of these lost souls, please don't feel alone or lost because I have a medical explanation for the symptoms you and I are feeling and it is called PTSD or Post Traumatic Stress Disorder. PTSD is a known medical condition that is caused by the stress of things that cause people catastrophic and overwhelming stress like losing your country or the 9-11 attack on New York's Twin Towers.

Why do I say America's problem is PTSD? Since I grew up and lived through the Vietnam War era, I learned a lot about PTSD and its causes because many of my friends came home with this mental disease. To put it bluntly, I first learned about PTSD because I wanted to help my friends and peers who were returning from Nam suffering from this disorder and our Government was not sticking around to help these men and women. So because I was around to see the ravages of PTSD and did my best to try to help any Nam Vet buddies that I came in contact with, I completely believe America's citizens who live in America's Southwestern States that are being overrun by Mexico's invaders are very likely suffering from this stress disorder. I feel I can come to this conclusion because they're experiencing overwhelming stress and shock from the changes they have no control over because the government is not listening to them. After all what could be more stressful than seeing a constant stream of unauthorized and lawless alien invaders swarming across your country's borders and into America's cities and taking them over with the help of your elected politicians who keep calling this invasion "immigration?" For those American citizens who think PTSD is only for military personal that suffer from combat fatigue, I hate to inform them but this is not the case.

According to the books I read on this disorder, PTSD can happen to any person who suffers through a stressful and overwhelming disaster like seeing America's borders and cities overrun by a foreign citizen's army of illegal and law breaking invaders, to any person who is seeing America's once quiet rural and small city streets become Mexican gang war zones, and to any person who watched in horror as Muslim terrorists attacked America's New York City "Twin Towers" (on September 11, 2001) with high jacked airliners. By the way, according to my research the only cure for PTSD is confronting the causes of the disorder and then dealing with it with head on by either fixing the problem or (and) confronting the stressful memories causing the emotional and physical pain. Unfortunately for America's citizens from what I read in my books, the healing process can only begin when America's politicians finally grow a spine and swear to end the Mexican Government's (and the world's) coordinated invasion of America, swear to punish any person or group who's helping these Mexican invading colonists (and the world's), and declare these groups enemies of the Republic because these people helping these illegal aliens should be labeled as traitors of the Republic.

By now, my readers should understand why this book is so important to millions of America's law-abiding citizens who love America's Western Christian Culture (Note: Most history books tell us it made America great and was the reason America won World War II.), cherish America's WWII vets for saving the world, accept America's Constitutional laws as the law of the land, who will defend and protect the American Constitution with their lives, and who have always pledged allegiance to America's flag known as Old Glory. I know these Americans feel this way because they love their country and put her first before their own desires for happiness.

Now you know why I believe this book will soon become very important to them and why I wrote it. I truly believe they know and understand America is a Republic in which the Supreme Power rests in America's citizens (both Native Born and Legally Naturalized) and not some lawless invading force or politicians who've appear to have sold out America's interests to the highest bidder. How can I say this? Well, after all, there is joke that goes something like this, "Politicians are like Geometry; they know all the angles and talk in circles to get what they want."

Before I move on, I'd like to thank the Lord for his guidance and everyone who helped make this book possible: My deepest gratitude goes to my family, my friends, my fellow American Compatriots, defenders of America's Sovereignty, the talented and brave writers whose works I quote in this book and who I acknowledged carefully by using the standard rules of documenting and research for scholarly and educational research, and all of the WWII Vets and Korean Vets who helped raise me in what was once a Patriotic All-American city named McFarland. These Vets influenced me to become a proud American who is always willing to defend and die for his country. And most of all, the author thanks the once great "Old" Boy Scouts of America who once taught their members to love America, to be true to the morals of the Christian faith, and always "Be Prepared" to serve and protect America and its citizens. As my readers can see from this book, I still live by this code and the words of my Scout Oath, "On my honor I will do my best to do my duty to God and my country," and especially to my God because I am "reverent" to the best of my abilities as the Scout Laws say.

Finally, I want to thank the California State University System for providing me professors like Michael Flachman and Dan McMillin, providing me a wonderful education, and giving me the skills to have the courage to write this book. As a grown man, I am here to say that I still love, respect, and the will to defend my country and fight to keep her free from those who would betray and oppress her, and that I will defend Old Glory and keep her flying to my last breath. And finally, I am willing to defend the fact that America is a Christian Nation that I feel was once blessed by God because the drafters of the Constitution wrote this fact into America's Constitution when the used the word "ordained" in America's Constitution. Since I feel America has lost the blessing of our Lord, I want to remind my readers that we Americans should promise ourselves to keep fighting to keep America a free Christian Nation because as the drafters of America's Constitution wrote in the preamble "[we]...do ordain and establish this Constitution for the United States of America," so as we can see from these words these drafters felt that America had been Ordained by God (or blessed), which means the drafters felt that America was God's country. After all, the English language dictionary says the term "ordained" means "it [(in our case America)] was said of God or predestined, and blessed by God's fate."

Chapter Two

An Account of Key Terms: Key Definitions

(To Pray in Jesus' Name)

"I hope I am over wary; but if I am not, there is, even now, something of an ill-omen amongst us. I mean the increasing disregard for law, which pervades the country; the growing disposition to substitute the wild and furious passions, in lieu of the sober judgment . . . What has this to do with the perpetuation of our political institutions? I answer it has much to do with it . . . men who love tranquility, who desire to abide by the laws, and enjoy their benefits, who would gladly spill their blood in the defense of their country; seeing their property destroyed; their families insulted; and their lives endangered; their persons injured; and seeing nothing in prospect that forebodes a change for the better; become tired of, and disgusted with, a Government that offers them no protection . . . depend on it, this Government cannot last . . . The question recurs 'how shall we fortify against it? Let every American, every lover of liberty . . . swear by the blood of the revolution, never to violate . . . the laws of the country: and never to tolerate their violation by others."

(Abraham Lincoln)

Later in this book (chapter 4), I introduce the details of a key principle I often use when I write or compose complicated or confusing sentences or prose works. And lucky for me, the principle I use is affirmed perfectly by two very special writers in their book **Logic for Argument** (New York: Random House, 1968). These two special authors that wrote the book Logic for Argument, are Jack Pitt and Russell E. Leavenworth, and the important writing principle these two writers affirm is the fact that one "[needs] to define any and all confusing and unknown words that might be used in any long, difficult, or complicated work" [like for example the US Constitution or a work of research like this book] (Pitt, Jack and Russell E. Leavenworth. Logic for Argument, P. 43-44). Now that I've introduced this key principle, I hope my readers will understand why I say this chapter is a key component of this book and why I say the next paragraph is the bearing wall of this book's argument.

To begin my argument, my readers should understand chapter "2" not only introduces and discusses many of the key words and terms they will need to understand the ideas and arguments I introduce in this book of research, but this chapter also starts an important discussion of a major problem America's citizens currently deal with on a day-to-day basis in every state of this Union, a Union (or country) that was once regarded the Holy Grail of law and order. And, thanks to America's Supreme Court and her politicians who have allowed this problem to grow and fester with their "open border policies and laissez faire invader policies," we Americans find ourselves dealing with the same type of damaging issues that President Lincoln warned the Union of in his speech that was given over a hundred years ago. Now my readers should see why I opened this chapter with a quote from President Lincoln's speech.

Now that President Lincoln has unknowingly warned us not to repeat history, I want to first note (even as America's lawlessness problems appear to be growing) not one US politician appears to be willing to risk his career to stop the growing disregard for America's Constitutional, Criminal, and Immigration laws. I am also sad to say that these US and Constitutional laws are also being disregarded by our own government, judges, politicians, Mexico's Government and her invading citizens' army of so called immigrants, naturalized foreign citizens (think Boston bombers), and even US born citizens (think America's murdering gang members). Although President Lincoln warned us about these growing problems he saw back during his time in the following quote, I found it scary to see the similarities between his time and our current developments in the 21st Century: "[There] is a growing disposition to substitute the wild and furious passions, in lieu of the sober judgment [in the Union]." By now, my readers should understand why I believe this book is crucial for the survival of the United States of America. After all, President Lincoln also warned us that if America's courts and politicians continue to refuse to enforce our laws, the results won't be good: "Depend on it," he says, "this Government cannot last."

Since America's very existence is on the line, this research book will try hard to meet its obligation of defending America's Constitution and Immigration Laws by using "hard core" analytical and research tools to interpret these American corner stones of law and prove America's politicians and judges are making illegal and dangerous choices and decisions. Then, this book will also make sure it provides the frameworks and tools that Americans need to prove this invasion is not immigration but an invasion of America's Sovereign soil. These tools will allow Americans to wave these facts in the faces of Washington's Supreme Court Judges and Politicians and have a real reason to start protesting and picketing in front of the White House Lawn, Congress's building, and the Supreme Court's chambers. I truly believe America's citizens should get the chance to tell America's political and judicial rouge leaders that they would rather die on their feet than be forced to their knees and serve some foreign power or United Nations group. Now that my fellow Americans know these judges and Politicians intentions are to allow Mexico's Government (and other foreign governments) and her colonizing and invading army to end American Sovereignty, I suggest my readers play close attention to Chapters 2, 3, and 4, because these chapters have the recipe to take back America from these Rogue Politicians and judges whose only interest appears to be to serve the interest of their benefactors and their careers as US politicians and life time Supreme Court Judges.

I would like to add that as I did my research I found the fact that neither the US Federal Government nor the US Judicial System has ever (or will acknowledge) acknowledged there is an invasion problem. Since these leaders say there is no problem, they've decided not to act on America's invasion problem that they keep labeling as "illegal immigration." In reality, I feel this so-called "illegal immigration" problem the US government refuses to act on should really be called what it is in fact: "a criminal, colonizing invasion," or act of aggression via colonization as it's written in the Monroe Doctrine. After all, this invasion is one of the major causes of the growing violence and murders in America and a major reason why California's prisons are full of Hispanic/Mexican murderers and millions of legal American citizens are leaving California every day of the year. These two key examples alone offer two key elements that prove my point. Note: I should add that when criminal gang members in Federal California Prisons can demand special and gentle treatment (for murdering and terrorizing on our American streets?) because they don't like being in prison, as they did in 2013 in California, I think this proves President Lincoln's warning is even more important to this generation than ever. These murderers should be punished instead of being treated like guests in a hotel. As US Citizens, we Americans refuse to keep paying over $48,000 per year for each one of these prisoners so they can enjoy their vacations for murder and terrorizing America. Folks. Before I close this paragraph, I have to ask my fellow Americans if they feel these criminals are being PUNISHED or rewarded for their crimes on society?

To make sure I meet the goal of providing Americans the tools of revolt (to end their government's betrayal) in this book, I've decided to begin Chapter Two by presenting information that helps me introduce and discuss terms that will be needed by my fellow American Citizens to defend their sovereign nation status and to help them protect the Republic's (America's Citizens) Constitutional laws and their American civil rights that belong to them and not law breaking foreigners or invaders. These important terms will be introduced in this book so I can introduce and discuss the key elements that prove my discoveries, defenses, and arguments I found to be true in America's Constitution as well as the definitions of key terms or words that help me prove America's judges and politicians have gone rogue. To start my analysis, I will introduce key terms to show how these words are used in "our" American Constitution and other legal American documents that were written to control any and all foreigners who enter America legally or lawlessly. Remember these laws were written so America coud protect the "rights and privileges" that belong to US legal citizens, but do not apply to law breaking or colonizing groups, Mexico's invading citizens, or the world's citizens as some US Judges would have Americans believe in their decisions that break and ignore US laws

And again, to make sure my readers of this book understand what laws "protect" or apply to US Citizens and not to foreign lawless trespassers, this book will explain, compare and contrast, and grammatically analyze key sentences of the laws or terms that I feel will help my argument and the defense of the Constitution. By taking the steps I just mentioned, I feel I can eliminate and weaken any or all arguments and disagreements that might arise from the publication of this book. Because I introduce some highly conclusive facts, quotes, and definitions for the terms being discussed, I feel I have avoided any confusion that might arise from the discussion of these laws and facts. However, since these "open border" proponents have many resources and many powerful financial backers with very deep pockets, who appear to take great joy in supporting the erosion of America's citizens' rights, erosion of Constitutional and immigration laws, and stopping the protection of America's border, I expect these illegal alien benefactors to come out in force to attack this book, its facts, and the solid and analytical research tools I used to write and complete this book.

I understand there are always two sides to any and all arguments, so I am going to make sure I force the opposition to offer their own balanced facts and research to establish some credibility to their positions or explain why they believe America is not under Mexican colonization and/or occupation. Let's take for example the most recent argument presented by "Open Borders" supporters who put out a propaganda video a few years ago. In this pro "open border" video, the supporters, who some how got the money to be able to broadcast it on national television, said that their video "A day without Mexicans in America" was created to prove what would happen if America's government sent all of the "criminal aliens" back to Mexico; some of their arguments said that our groceries would sky rocket; our crops would rot in the fields; our fruits like apples and other stone fruits would sky rocket, and the cost our stone fruit would be over $1 each (I hate to tell them but fruit like apples and oranges are already about a dollar each in most major stores like Vons.).

This video also pointed out that without these colonizing invaders there wouldn't be anyone to serve our meals and clean our tables at America's restaurants because Americans won't take or do these jobs. From my past experience, locally, I found this statement not to be true, and I will prove it in another part of this book. I want to point out that when a family (I figure they were either of Hispanic or Mexican decent.) bought our two local "golden arches" eating Restaurants, they went through and fired or didn't re-hire any of the white high school kids or adults for their restaurants, but they did replace them all with an "all" Mexican or Hispanic staff.

I want to also note that if a white owner had taken this action, I know for a fact that they would have been sued for Racism; yet! This action of reverse Racism occurred without a complaint. Sad to say, this kind of reverse Racism is starting to become a common occurrence in California. I say this because our state's legislature is top heavy with mostly Hispanic/Mexican Democrat legislators who are mostly "Dreamers" and not really US Citizens. I should add that Democrats have had a majority control over California for over 50 years so more than likely this might be the reason this state is close to going bankrupt and borrows every year to stay afloat. After all, these Democrats always get their way; don't they?

While the arguments presented in the video appeared to be valid, the information in the video, I'm sorry to say, was not complete or true. To prove my point, let's look at the statement made about the cost of food going up if there were no colonizing Mexicans in America to harvest the large farm corporations' fields. Although this argument sounds good and factual to most Americans who do not live in California, American taxpayers who live in California and the San Joaquin Valley know there are many costs these illegal Mexicans are costing them (or the American taxpayer) that aren't being reported to the public because either the US Government, America's large farm corporations, or America's corporate owned "Mass Media News Giants" (who we are supposed to trust) are either not reporting these hidden costs or they are simply ignoring them completely.

To start my rebuttal, I want to first look at an example of information that was (or is) never reported by Corporate America's Fourth Estate (remember this is America's media giants): Let's first begin by looking at America's Mexican/US border problem through the eyes of some information I found while collecting research for this book. From this research I found that America's so called "illegal immigration" has many facets and one of these facets, or problems, might really be nothing more than a "business gift" set up by four major American oil companies with the help of some American rogue politicians, and/or some stealth lobbyists that might have been paid to set up an arrangement with America's Government and corporate America to allow Mexico's bankrupt/corrupt government to dump its poverty problem on the backs of America's taxpayers. I want to note here that I will present some complete facts to prove this accusation. For this favor, I read Mexico's government allowed America's corporations a free reign to build polluting factories all along the Mexican/American border and gave some of America's large oil corporations and major banks access to all of Mexico's oil and the profits from this oil. By the way, I hope my fellow Americans will keep reading this book because this "oil deal" was well documented on the web by a Mexican Muckraking reporter. I found this post and story so well written that I decided put his information in my book so my readers could read all of his facts.

How can I say that Mexico is being allowed to dump their poor in America? Well, let's just say the clandestine oil deal put on the world wide web by a very smart/intelligent muckraking Mexican National, who stated that this deal allegedly involved an agreement between the US Government, four major US oil companies, and Mexico's Government controlled and nationalized oil company known as PEMEX. I want to add that after I read this report I felt it had too many facts to be a lie (Note: The Mexican oil revenues belong to the people but they have never seen any of the money!). To make sure I cover all the facts known about this deal, I promise to discuss it in more depth later in this chapter.

Although America's citizens will more than likely never hear their politicians discuss or describe America's "illegal immigration" problem as the act of dumping Mexico's poor on America's taxpayers, I'm going to prove this statement is true (and part of America's invasion problem) and a common fact in our Southwestern states, especially in California. And, although the US Constitution, America's immigration laws, and America's criminal laws say nothing about America's or California's taxpayers supplementing or baling out the Mexican government with their taxes or taking on Mexico's poverty problems and their poor citizens, this possibility has evidently become a reality for both America's and California's taxpayers. Don't worry; I will soon prove this fact in the following paragraphs I've written in this chapter. And since these law breaking Mexicans are being allowed to break US and State laws (Note: Frederic Bastiat warns us of this possibility when it becomes Socialist.) without repercussions, I will now prove that both federal and state officials are both breaking a California State Constitution law by giving these illegal aliens special powers of immunity from Law Enforcement and Immigration Officers. I can prove my statement because Article 1, Section 7, part b, says, "A citizen or class of citizens may not be granted privileges or immunities not granted on the same terms of all citizens. Privileges or immunities granted by the Legislature may be altered or revoked" (California Senate, The Constitution of the United States of America and the Constitution of the State of California, Sacramento: California Senate 1997-98, p 85). My fellow and legal Americans these Mexican Citizens are being given special privileges and immunity that no American citizens has ever had, which gives them the power to break federal and state criminal and immigration laws.

To begin proving my accusations, I first want to point out that California homeowners pay some of the highest homeowners' taxes in America. Next I want to remind Americans that many California cities are fast becoming 80 to 90 percent Mexican/trespassing colonizers (note: some are 96 percent). This means California public schools are now averaging anywhere from 80 to 97 percent illegal alien Mexican students that came here illegally or were born here illegally (That's right.). Yet, The education of these children is being paid for with Californian's homeowner's tax money. Finally, since California's schools are now 80 to 97 percent illegal Mexican Children and California's government brags that 60 percent of every Californian's property tax dollar is used for education, I think we can come to the conclusion that these law breaking student's education is being financed by American taxpayer dollars instead of America's large farm corporations and Mexico's Government (Which should be the case because these entities are the ones that are profiting from this arrangement.). And, I guess we know these farm corporations are the ones who benefit the most from this gift because they get cheap scab laborers so they can reap huge profits but not be financially responsible for their support while they are in America illegally.

One more important fact I should point out is that in Mexico many of these children would not get the free education they are being given in California at the expense of America's tax payers. I offer this information because from what I have learned of Mexico's education system, if these Mexican parents demanded the kind of education they're children are getting in America for their children, they would have pay for their children's education. Yes, you heard that right the only way a child gets a good education in Mexico is if the parents can afford to pay for it. So now we should see why America's free day care, quality education, free breakfast and lunches, free child care, and free after school snacks and day-care centers are such great incentives for Mexico's invaders who keep flooding across the border day-after-day. After all, if you were a poor American citizen with no money and no future, and you learned Canada offered your kids a free education, free breakfast, free lunches, after school day care and snacks for your kids, free cash assistance and medical cards just for coming to Canada to work in seasonal jobs, and would let you enjoy unemployment checks while you waited to work again, wouldn't you being running for Canada's borders too?

The funny thing about this issue is that America's Mass Media Giants and the US Government do not report this kind of information. They also don't report the fact that Mexico's invasion is being financed by American taxpayers and not the corporations who benefit from these invading colonists because they get millions of scab workers who will work for any wage they offer. Even if

Americans were willing to work in these entry-level jobs (I learned since Hispanics/Mexicans control the United Farm Workers Union they control who gets hired to work in the fields.), they would have to accept these low wages too or end up unemployed like they are now. My fellow Americans this is where the hidden unfair costs of this massive invasion or colonization of the US fall or end up. They end up on the front doors of America's taxpayers. I know I can make this bold statement because Americans are not only paying for the education of these lawless children, but they are also paying for the social services for these Mexican children (both children born to illegal parents in America and children born in Mexico), paying for these illegal children's free breakfast, lunch, and after schools snacks, and paying for after school childcare programs for these kids and their parents so the parents don't have to pay for child care (or baby sitters) during the school year. This summer I also learned these lawless invaders are also getting summer day care programs and free lunches and snacks while their parents are at work. My fellow Americans, how many of you would love to have these kind of FREE benefits?

Now let's look at some other programs that America's taxpayers are being asked to pay for so they can help these invaders and their children take over America. These programs include free job training through a program called PROTEUS—which is an adult training program for any and all invading colonizing workers from Mexico, and other nations. This taxpayer funded program helps farm workers qualify and compete for jobs that unemployed American citizens also need and want, and are competing for them in the job market. By the way, PROTEUS' mission statement makes no bones about who they were developed to serve: "Our mission is to continually improve the quality of life for farm workers and other participants through quality education, training and other services." To add salt to the wound, Americans are now being asked to pay for tuition free college educations for any law breaking and illegal young adult living in California.

The biggest problem I found with this new gift from America's taxpayers is that ex-President Obama never said if these illegal young adults had to register for the draft to qualify for their tuition free college educations; after all, America's young adults have to register to qualify for grants when they enter college and apply for loans or grants so why shouldn't these illegal dreamers not have to register for the draft? Since Obama said nothing about these young Mexican college aged students having to register for the draft, I think this proves that these young Mexican adults are not under US jurisdiction, or their parents. I also believe the point I made in the last sentence proves ex-President Obama more than likely broke the law by forcing Americans to pay for these young adult and criminal invaders' education. Unfortunately for US citizens, these financial perks are just the beginning of a long list of taxpayer paid incentives to entice illegal aliens to enter the US illegally. Unfortunately, my fellow Americans will learn more about these freebees throughout this book and the will learn about the troubling double standard that I feel has been created for these criminal aliens. This double standard, I believe, was created so America's government could provide help and services for these invaders by allowing them to use America's Department of Social Services and other US government agencies that were created to only serve America's citizens, and not some foreign nation's invaders (Note: I prove this statement hands down later in this book with the help of Frederic Bastiat who is one of the fathers of Republic like Governments and an expert of how they should be run.).

Without going into too much detail, I'll first explain how the double standard works for these Mexican invaders who apply and qualify for (No matter what our government says, these invaders qualify for many of our welfare entitlements.) AFDC, food stamps, training programs, Federal and state government jobs, low income housing programs, and medical cards to name a few of the programs the author is familiar with because he worked as an Eligibility Worker II (EWII) in California's Social Services Programs. Americans should not believe America's government when they say these invading aliens do not qualify for any type of social services in their press releases. As for the double standard (a standard that gives illegal aliens more privileges and an edge over US citizens) these lucky and pampered Mexican colonizers get to use when they apply for US Government financed (paid for by US taxpayers) social services, the first example I will discuss is AFDC, which stands for Aid For Dependent Children is offered to any family who claims an absent or unemployed father. Okay, I will now show my fellow Americans the real facts about this program:

As an EWII employee for Tulare County Social Services, my job was to grant family aid to illegal mothers and their children, even if the mother had a boyfriend and our staff knew the boyfriend was the father. As long as she signed a paper that said the father was not in the home, by law, my job was to take her word for it. Why did I have to grant? First, I was trained to understand that the Tulare County Eligibility worker's job is to grant aid (and I was reminded of this often) to who ever comes in the doors and applies for aid (I was often reminded not deny them.) because the county gets more federal aid the following year if our numbers increase. The second part of this program's rules state that since the mother signed the form, the eligibility worker couldn't ask the man to take a paternity test (The ACLU took care of this.) so the family was (and is) eligible to receive cash aid like WIC, food stamps, free medical cards, and other American taxpayer paid perks. The worst part about this welfare code or law is that the boyfriend (really the absent father) is allowed to make as much money as he wants and he gets to keep it because his money is not considered family income (and, he never has to pay child support.). Since the father is not supporting his children, America's taxpayers are saddled with his job.

By the way, in case Americans are wondering why they hear about these families not having enough money to buy their kids Christmas presents or have the money for Thanksgiving or Christmas dinners every year, I want to tell my fellow Americans the answer is quite simple. During the none holiday months, when these parents should be saving money for the holidays, the fathers can be seen (almost 90 percent of them—base on real time observations over the years) buying and drinking $30 to $40 dollars of beer just about every day of the week, and especially on weekends, so when these holidays roll around there is no money. I am sorry to say but this kind of waste of money is happening in California cities from San Diego to Yreka. How do I know this kind of waste really happens? In my city, I watch these fathers sit around and drink all day on weekends, and they don't stop during the week because every day after I watch these men buy their 18 packs of beer and sit around and drink with their buddies, who also bring their packs of beer too. These men drink so much beer they often fill up packing shed orange bins (the bins used for holding oranges usually measure about 5 ft. X 7 ft. X 7 ft.) at the rate of one every two weeks. One more pathetic act these men do that hurts their children is that although they say they can't afford to buy their kids presents, I see these same men buy and wear $100 Stetson hats, wear hundreds of dollars of Gold jewelry and watches while their kids go hungry and get nothing for Christmas.

I hate to say it but these men spend more money on themselves than they do on their children because they know America's government will always bail them out if they get into a financial bind or run out of food or money. So the next time Americans hear about giving money or food to help these poor farm labor families who don't have enough to eat or buy Christmas presents, I want them to remember these men sitting around a "treated" wood camp fire in their back yards polluting California's air. The ironic part of these men's act of polluting the air is that while these men are allowed to do as they please, California's Government is passing laws to take away or ban the legal American citizens' old hot-rods, pot belly stoves, and fire places. Why are these objects of fun and comfort being banned? They are being banned because their government says they pollute the air. But these same California legislatures don't want to stop these Mexican men from burning "treated wood" because "it's their way of life and part of their culture."

I want to note that most California taxpayers can spot these families on aid, with the so called absent fathers, because when they shop at local groceries stores and they check out, the mother pulls out her EBT card and (A debit card that looks like a credit card, so they can keep their pride; while Americans lose their homes and jobs.) pays for the groceries that include sugared name brand Colas, name brand flavored teas, name brand cereals, name brand cookies, steaks, name brand candy bars, name brand chips, top of the line cheeses, takeout meals from the deli, and beer that the father (we mean boyfriend) pays by for by pulling out a wad of 100 or 20 dollar bills because he is not responsible for his own children, and thank God the EBT card won't pay for their beers. By the way, these EBT cards can also be used to go out to dinner at any restaurant in California that accepts EBT and credit cards, and they can be used at local mom and pop corner stores by their children to buy over priced snacks and soda fountain drinks. Now my fellow Americans should see why Mexico's illegal invaders keep coming to California in never ending waves.

As for the boyfriend in the house (most often, really the father), who the children run around calling papa (father) in the store as he flashes a wad of 100 and $20 bills to pay for his beer, he usually drives around in a brand new top of the line pickup truck or SUV that he can afford because he claims so many dependents on his W-2 tax form that he never has to pay IRS taxes. But the biggest slap in the face for America's taxpayers is that at the end of the year, this same father will apply for and get child dependent tax credits which amount to thousands of dollars more of US tax dollars from the IRS because, as was reported on US news outlets last year, "checking on these dependents is "not' their (IRS) job. Oh yes, thanks to a new Federal welfare law that was created to help unemployed Americans who lost their jobs during the Wall Street and US banks created recession, illegal families can either own or buy top of the line SUV vehicles or pickup trucks and still qualify for AFDC Social Services and EBT taxpayer financed bank cards that can be used for public entertainment in California, like to buy Circus Tickets. This law is so controversial that a local news program did a special feature on it (5/13/13) because Americans were upset the cards could be used to pay for carnival rides and food in Fresno, California.

I am sad to say this American law was created to help America's legal citizens or Compatriots keep their reliable cars and still qualify for their government assistance money while they were looking for work, but this law has been perverted because it now helps, or allows, illegal colonizing families to buy new cars and trucks (who are willing to pay $500 to $700 a month car payments because they get government subsidies) and live like kings without losing their welfare benefits. I want to note the old law required those who applied for welfare, and had expensive cars, to sell them and buy an older model car and use the excess money to live on till the money was gone. After the applicant spent the money, they would then qualify for cash aid and other social services for their families.

From my experience as an EWII, I now want my fellow Americans to take a look at what would happen if a legal American family walked in and applied for the same social services and tried to pull off the same scam as the illegal family. When the mother would be asked if the man with her was the father and if she said no he's my boy friend, the man (or real father) would more than likely be asked to take a paternity test because the ACLU (or whom ever protects these lawless invaders) didn't include Americans in whatever court action they took to protect Mexico's alien colonizers from being asked to take a paternity test. This code or law that stops social services from asking illegal alien men to take a paternity test is (because it's racist and the Mexican Consulate could or more than likely would file a law suit against the US—even though they do not have this right.) just one of the many double standards that protect Mexico's and other countries' invaders in California and other Southwestern states. Another scam being played on America's taxpayers is the law that says all welfare recipients can only qualify for two years of social services at a time because at the end of two years they must have found a job because they will lose their benefits at the end of two years. Do not believe this law my fellow Americans because it does not work this way and it is a lie.

I'm sad to say that unfortunately for America's taxpayers this new "back to work" welfare law, that allegedly only allows two years of eligibility for so called financial aid, was designed with a trick up its sleeve. I feel this wrinkle or trick came to us courtesy of what I feel is our new "Federal Socialist (spread the wealth) State" being pushed by America's Socialist Democrats. The trick to this law that's been added to AFDC codes sadly and unfortunately still gives any and all so-called qualified families an endless life on welfare. If my fellow Americans want to know why I can make his claim, please allow me to explain that to continue receiving AFDC after the two years all these families have to do, according to the Federal and State Governments' welfare codes, is be willing to do 30 days of public service at any local non-profit certified organization and do jobs like hang clothes or sweep floors at a local Salvation Army Second hand Store or other non-profit business. After the family completes their 30 days of "public service," they qualify for another two years of American taxpayer paid welfare or social services financial aid, and I hate to say it but the beat goes on. To quote a famous line I've often heard, "Nice work if you can get it."

By the way, according to Newsmax.com "In 2012, The federal government spent more than $668 Billion dollars on anti-poverty programs (Who knows what it was in 2016 or Obama's last year in office—couldn't find figures) an increase of 41 percent, or more than $193 billion dollars since President Barack Obama took the office of President." I want to add this story also stated that "State and local government, [especially California known as the 'welfare state"], expenditures will amount to another $284 billion, bringing the total to nearly $1 trillion [dollars]" ("Welfare Spending Up 41

percent under Obama." Newsmax.com 23 April 2012. <u>www.http://</u>
<u>Newsmax@reply.newsmax.com</u>.).

Finally, one more way these male invaders and their families
get treated differently by America's Government is that these men
use four or five fake names while working in the US, so when they
get paid by check, they claim as many dependents as they need to
make sure they don't pay taxes. I am sad to say, the IRS will never
catch these illegal men because, although they never pay taxes, the
US government will never really know these men's real identity.
Their identities change from state to state and job-to-job, so, all
the money they make in America is usually never taxed. Is it any
wonder that most of these illegal men save enough money to buy or
open businesses in America, buy horses, land, and build apartments
while Americans lose their homes to banks and the IRS takes their
homes because they can't pay their taxes? Note: I am happy to say
that President Trump and Congress finally passed a new tax code
law that I hope will help America's middle class citizens not pay the
bulk of America's taxes.

The funny thing about US laws is that the IRS never questions
these Mexican colonizers, or so-called "financially poor illegal
aliens," about where they get (or got) the money to pay for all of
the horses, the new cars, and new businesses that sometimes takes
over $200,000.00 to buy and build the new business buildings (And
I note, the money they needed to pay for the land.) needed for these
new businesses when they claim to have little or no income: "Can
I say tax evasion, or fraud, while the IRS turns its head?" The IRS
also allows these illegal men to file fake tax returns where they
claim 10 or 15 dependents on their tax returns so they can get the
dependent child tax breaks, even if they never paid one penny into
the IRS, and again, the IRS won't question or red flag these tax
returns. All this money could fix some of the financial problems
we have in America, like for example help take the homeless of
the street, repair our pitted and rundown inner city streets, put a
line of defense on America's Southern Border, and open homes to

get our legal mentality ill Americans off the street and into safe caring environments like America did in the past. Americans might not remember but we Americans once had great state and federal hospitals that cared for our handicapped people who could not survive on their own. If Americans want to know where these handicapped people disappeared to, I suggest they look around at all of the street people living in your towns. Yes, Our government through these people out in the street because they would rather care for some other country's illegal invading army of colonizers and their children.

Okay, now I want my fellow Americans to look at another double standard that I feel is giving illegal aliens an edge over America's unemployed citizens who are currently looking for work in this tough job market. I am sure that most Americans have never heard of PROTEUS (a government-taxpayer funded so called non-profit business) and probably don't think it's a big deal, but they're wrong to think this because in California PROTEUS is training illegal alien men and women to take jobs that many US citizens are also fighting for in this down economy. If America's unemployed citizens knew these jobs were available, I'm sure they would be standing in line to apply for these jobs. However, I'm sorry to say only PROTEUS knows about these job openings before the public gets the news, so PROTEUS is the one picks and chooses who gets these jobs. Unfortunately because of these sneaky laws the jobs almost always go to Mexico's illegal colonizers who allegedly come to America to work in the fields, Americans never know these jobs ever existed or were available to the public. Does this sound like these lawless colonizers aren't taking jobs away from Americans?

During my investigation, and research, I also learned that PROTEUS is training illegal Mexican males for jobs with the US Forest Department as summer fire fighters, a job many college students who are majoring in Forestry and Fire fighting would love to have because during the summer fire season in California, these jobs allow the fire fighters to earn anywhere from $20 to $30 thousand dollars of income in as little as three or four months (if there are many fires, think California's recent rash of fires that burn all summer?) and gain paid on the job experience they can use on their resumes. How do I know so much about these firefighting jobs? When my younger brother and I were young, we were both hired to do this job on a Native American crew so we cold earn money during the summer to pay for college. Although I only did it for one summer, my brother kept returning till he got the career he really wanted. Since I feel the Department of Forestry is not using E-verify, I feel the hiring of these PROTEUS trained illegal aliens is against the law, and sad because these jobs would be great for all of those unemployed Americans who can't find a jobs in other states. I should note these jobs are high paying entry-level professional jobs that pay wages comparable to many white-collar professional jobs, and as we Americans can see, these jobs are going to Mexico's alien colonizers and not unemployed American Citizens.

But wait, I have one more job that I've discovered that PROTEUS is training Mexico's male colonizers to qualify for that many unemployed Americans would love to have in this tough economy. I've learned that PROTEUS is training Mexico's illegal invaders to work for the local California Company that takes care of US Highways and roads in California. These jobs with Caltrans (name of the company that cares for California's Highways.) are plum jobs that pay anywhere from $18 to $45 dollars per hour and they are being given to Mexico's alien invaders or colonizers while many American citizens struggle to keep their homes or work two or three jobs that pay minimum wage to make ends meet. I know a few Americans who currently work fulltime for either the Department of Forestry or Cal-trans who told me that when they showed up for some recent training classes they were told the class was going to be held only in Spanish so they could accommodate the non-English speaking Mexican alien colonizers who work for these US Government entities. Again, do I think these entities are using E-Verify? I would probably venture to say no they are not.

I want to point out one more important fact about the state of California that I recently learned. These Mexican invading colonizers are being given the power to replace America's English language with their Spanish language and I have the proof in this book. And since the Fourth Estate has not reported this new law, I feel this is a good place to tell America's Patriotic and English speaking citizens that California's Democrat and Hispanic controlled legislature has passed a "**Law**" that requires private, State, and Federal business entities to use Spanish in everything they publish, announce on radio, or telecast on television, including business advertisements. That's right; In California, everything must be done in both English and Spanish by order of Mexico's new power over California's government, and don't forget the legal California driver's licenses that California's Hispanic/Mexican impacted legislature has just given to these lawless invaders so they will have more power over Americans and America's Law Officers. The sad part is that this is just more proof that California's Pro-invasion Government is backing this lawless invasion of US sovereign soil.

The last special perk I want to point out to my fellow legal American citizens has to do with low cost housing for Mexico's lawless colonizers in California. Last year (2015), California's government (lead by Governor Brown, a Democrat, and ex-President Obama's Administration) used billions of taxpayer dollars to build condos up and down the state of California for these colonizers. These condos for so called low-income families that work in agriculture (The United Farm Workers Union is listed as one of the partners that pushed for these agriculture worker's condos), I hate to say it, turned out to be semi-gated communities that have solar panels to keep these colonizers' power bills low, covered parking spaces, swimming pools (yes, you read this right.), subsidized rents, and they were also going to have free computer rooms so they could keep in touch with their families in Mexico, but there was such an out-cry of disgust from America's local US Citizens that this perk was abandoned and now the computer room of this housing development sits empty and has a sign in the window that says, "For Lease."

I should note that by talking to local citizens I learned Porterville's citizens see this massive and expensive condo-like complex as a slap in the face of America's taxpayers. They feel this way because they know the majority of these tenants are illegal aliens and lawless colonizers who are enjoying air-conditioned homes with central heating and **a pool** while America's taxpaying citizens and neighbors lose their jobs and their homes because they can't pay their taxes, pay their mortgage payments, or find a job. To make things worse, the houses these unemployed American citizens are losing are being bought up by the city government (with Federal Funds) and then their homes are being sold to Mexico's low-income and lawless illegal aliens. How is that for a slap on the face of vested Americans! What do I think hurts these unemployed Americans more? I think the fact that these houses are being sold for $1000 down and then being financed with American taxpayer low-income HUD money is a nasty joke. Still think these illegal aliens are worth having in America to keep your grocery bill down that in reality is going up?

Now for more bad news for America's and California's taxpaying legal citizens who are already hurting, I learned that although these condos were built using taxpayer paid money, California's legal citizens were never allowed to vote on them like a Constitutional law says that I found in California's State Constitution. Yes my fellow Americans and Californians, California's State Constitution says that before any low rent housing project can be voted on, approved, or financed by California's elected officials California's taxpayers (or America's citizens living in California) must be given the right to vote on it to make sure they want to fund these projects: "Article XXXIV, Public Housing Project Law: "Approval of low Rent Housing Projects by Electors: Section 1, No low rent housing project shall hereafter be developed, constructed, or acquired in any manner by any state public body until a majority of the qualified electors of the city, town, or county, as the case may be, in which it is proposed to develop, construct, or acquire the same, voting upon such issue, approve such project by voting in favor thereof at an election to be held for that purpose, or at any general or special election" (California State Senate, The Constitution of the United States of America and the Constitution of the State of California, Sacramento: California Senate, 1997-98 p 225.). Yes my fellow Americans, since California's legal taxpaying citizens were never allowed to vote on these low-income condos, these condos were built by breaking California State Constitutional law.

My fellow Americans I hate to say it but these examples of American Government corruption are just a few of the hidden costs our government is not telling taxpayers about or allowing them to have a say on because they know America's Citizens would not allow the spending of taxpayer money this way. As my readers can see from my examples, the Government is not telling us so we Americans won't get upset at our State and local officials, and Mexico's (or the world's) illegal aliens. I want to add that evidently these American leaders are taking these actions so America's Republic will not become a problem for local, state, and federal politicians. By now, I hope many Americans now see why they should not believe the propaganda message that America's government is reporting to them through their corporate owned and controlled Fourth Estate, known as the media news giants. Now that I've introduced my readers to some of the many perks these illegal invaders are being given (that US Citizens don't qualify for even if they're on the street or living in their cars) by the US government, I want to talk about a few more perks that are being offered through WIC and PROTEUS by California's Social Services Department to provide Mexico's and the world's invading colonizers more incentives to come to America illegally.

For those Americans who don't know what WIC stands for or means, this program provides these illegal Mexican colonists checks for cash, so these Mexican colonizing and illegal mothers can qualify and buy groceries for their children, if they have just arrived in America and have their Mexican born children with them. As for the other PROTEUS benefits that are being given to Mexico's colonizing aliens, these benefits includes checks for any colonizing driver whose auto breaks down so they can go buy the part and fix their truck or car or have a mechanic fix it for them. These checks are written for just about any amount that the auto repair costs or the auto part is said to cost. Yes, that is right, America's taxpayers are being asked to pay for auto repairs when these lawless alien's autos or trucks break down in America, and as we said before, they are also being trained to take American jobs that many unemployed Americans need and would be happy to take them if they knew about them and were trained for the jobs.

Oh yes, I almost forgot one more perk; these law-breakers also get free prenatal and birth care at the American hospital of their choice. This law covers any lawbreaking, colonist female that walks into a California (or any state) hospital to have a child or get prenatal care. By the way, this hospital gift did not come from the Democrats, but from good old Republican ex-President George W. Bush's multi-million dollar grant he signed into law when he was in office. I guess having a Mexican in the family made him feel obligated. Yes! You read that right; America's taxpayers are being saddled with these illegal alien women's hospital bills every time these women walk into a hospital to have their babies. The bills these women rack up at taxpayers' expense usually have net totals of over $6000 in costs, and the women and husbands never have to pay these bills. I have to ask my fellow Americans this question, when was the last time you or your family walked into a US hospital and walked out without ever having to pay a hospital bill? These people know this law so well that in California young lawbreaking colonists think nothing of having (or getting pregnant) a child out of wed lock, not having a job, or not graduating from high school because they know all they have to do is run down the to the local welfare office and apply for government medical cards, cash aid, and food stamps. Yes, it is a way of life for these people, thanks to what appears to be the Democrat Party and the Obama Administration when it was in power.

I hope my readers now understand why I say that thanks to the Socialist Democrat's and ex President Obama's new America the cost of that alleged cheap under $1 dollar apple, or low cost food that America's Farm Bureaus and Big Farm Corporations keep bragging about really does not exist, and in reality, America's taxpayers are choking on this lie because the apple is really costing America's taxpayers anywhere from $300 to $500 per apple because of these hidden costs. Before I end this discussion, I now want to warn my fellow Americans to remember not to believe the media's news reports that say Mexico's illegal workers do not qualify for any US Social Services or welfare programs. I can honestly say I know better because, as I said before, I worked for California's Tulare County Social Services for over two years, and during my tenure, I investigated and uncovered hundreds of thousands of dollars of welfare fraud and rules that worked in favor of any person (both US Citizens and especially illegal aliens) who were willing to commit welfare fraud because they know there are very repercussions for this crime. So my fellow Americans, Don't' forget that these codes are set up to make sure these lawbreakers can qualify for America's Welfare aid, while many US citizens get denied because they play by the rules and are honest when they complete their forms.

The reason America's law-abiding citizens get denied is simple. Americans are held to higher and different standards that play on their honesty, so they usually don't qualify for the government welfare aid they need. One more important fact that America's taxpayers should not forget is that Federal Welfare cash aid and Social Services rules are set up (or "fixed," if I am blunt) to benefit lazy Americans, other nations' lawless and criminal illegal aliens, and Mexico's illegal alien and colonizing army who live in America. Before I stop discussing welfare codes, I want to note that some of the new laws or codes were given to the author by friends who have recently retired from California's welfare department because as they said, "We're fed up with the lies and pressures of this thankless job that favors people who lie and know how to break the laws without being caught." Please note that I also quit for the same reasons. Here is an example of why I quit: I discovered a two-story apartment complex on a welfare mother's property when I went out to make a surprise investigative house call to grant continuing aid to an absent parent household, but as you will soon read, I found much more than I ever expected:

Okay America's tax payers here is great example of welfare fraud: A Hispanic/Mexican family that I went to visit had been on aid for over fifteen years and no county worker had been out to learn more about the family, so as their EWII, I decided to make a house call, so I could continue giving welfare to the family. When I finally found the apartment, the first thing I noticed was that there was an Apartment complex on the welfare family's property. I then asked the mother receiving absent father cash aid when the apartment complex had been built on her property? Her response to my question was the following one: "I never noticed the apartment, and I don't know when it was built or who built it on my property." Needless to say when I got back to my office, I denied the family aid, and sure enough the mother appealed. When she came to appeal, she asked my supervisor this million-dollar question, "What are my children and I going to live on?" As for our District Supervisor, when she learned what I had discovered and that I had denied this family aid, I was reprimanded for "wasting county time and doing investigative work that was not my job." The fact that I, or an EWII, had saved the state hundreds of thousands of dollars in welfare fraud meant nothing, and the fact that the county could file welfare fraud charges against this family didn't matter to this big cheese supervisor. In my disgust and after more events like this one, I finally handed in my resignation after being on the job for three years.

Getting back to the cash savings Americans are supposed to see in their grocery bills, because America is allowing Mexico to dump their poverty problem on American taxpayers' backs, I suggest Americans not hold their breath to see them. To prove this statement, I suggest that Americans go to their favorite local grocery store and look at the cost of an Apple (or any stone fruit) in the store. The first thing they will notice is that these apples or stone fruit are selling for the cost of anywhere from .89 cents to $1.99 cents per pound. And since a good quality sized apple usually weighs anywhere from 12 to 15 ounces, my fellow Americans are going to notice they are basically paying anywhere from $1 dollar to $2 dollars for each apple or stone fruit. The next thing my fellow Americans are going to notice is that most of the fruit they are buying these days comes from Mexico and not California or other US farming areas. By the way, since I lived in Japan on several occasions, I noticed the prices of our fruit is the same price most Japanese citizens pay in Japan; however, the Japanese grocers have an excuse or reason for setting the prices on stone fruit high. Their reason is easy to explain because, after all, Japan is an island, so their fruit has to be brought in on ships as cargo and the grocers have to recover these costs.

If this is the low cost fruit Americans are supposed to be getting in exchange for allowing Mexico's Government to dump their poverty problem on the backs of America's taxpayers, then all I have say on behalf of America's taxpayers is no thanks. As far as we Americans are concerned, Washington's politicians and Mexico's government can keep Mexico's poverty problem in Mexico and we'll pay maybe $2 dollars for our apple if we have to do it. Why do I feel I am right? I am right because I think it's time America's Farm Corporations need to start paying a livable wage like they once did so Americans will want to work these farm jobs again like they did in the past. Besides, the average grocery bill in Central California for two averaged sized plastic bags of groceries currently costs about $50 to $60 dollars and our food prices in California are still going up every day. Hardly a bargain when we

Americans remember that most of the new service type jobs that were created in America during ex-President Obama's (and George W. Bush when he was in office) tenure only pay $8 to $9 per hour. Note: This book was published and written before Obama and many states passed the new law that will soon raise the minimum wage in America to $15 dollars per hour for "entry level training jobs?" Talk about a bitch slap on college graduates and other private school tech schools in America. Why go to college if you can make $15 per hour with, or without, a high school education? Think about all of those tenured employees who have been on the job for ten or more years and are currently only making $12 per hour after working all of their young lives to reach their current pay grade. How does this law help them? It doesn't and that is wrong and not fair.

Before some Pro-Obama readers throw this book into the trash,

I want to say or give President Obama (and President Reagan and Bush) credit for spending trillions of dollars on their job creation programs. Yes, President Obama did create jobs for America's infrastructure, and yes, I Agree; he did push unions and their members into new tax brackets with his first term trillion-dollar jobs creation bill. However, I'm sure I can easily prove that most of the money went to state and county government coffers, education and administration coffers, and unions' payroll bank accounts. For those Americans who don't pay attention to the details of where their hard-earned tax dollars are spent, I want to add that I can prove where their tax dollars went or were spent. Here is an example of what I just said: By the way, "Infrastructure" spending, as I've learned is code for infrastructure repairs and up-grades which mean road repairs, new highway and freeway construction, new bridges, new government buildings, new classrooms, and new gyms for grammar schools, and more than likely raises for educators like Principals who make over $180,000 or more for a 9 month school year. It also means raises for teachers who are now also making anywhere from $60,000 to $180,000 for a 9 month school year, to name just a few of the expenditures of where your tax dollars are going, or went.

The examples I offered in the last paragraph means US tax dollars mostly went to jobs for union truck drivers, heavy equipment union operators, union cement contractors, union construction workers, and union school employees to name a few. Now we see why I say that the people who profited the most from this cash cow trillion dollar jobs creation bills were union controlled blue-collar jobs and white-collar workers that own and control the Democrat party. All these wonderful rewards for teachers that only work 9 months a year, while the majority of Americans struggle to earn $9 to $13 per hour in low paying service jobs to me is wrong and very un-American in my book. I guess the next question my fellow Americans are going to ask me is why do I say that Americans are only working low paying service jobs? I say it because all of America's real high paying jobs that are once found in manufacturing jobs and technical jobs have been outsourced to Mexico, India, China, Bangladesh, and Korea to name just a few of the many countries enjoying American Corporation's jobs who are not paying taxes on the profits they are earning overseas in these countries. Why do I make this bold statement? I will explain later in this book.

As for the job creation tax dollars that went to white collar employees, as I stated above, the union workers who benefited from Obama's job creating spending spree (my research tells me) were unions like the American Federation of Teachers "AFT" and its members, that includes college professors, high school teachers, grammar school teachers; and the SEIU Union and its members that also include administration employees, grounds keeping employees, and sometimes bus transportation employees to name just a few of the blue and white collar employees that benefited from Obama's jobs creation program that in my book left our the average Joe who were not union members. I hope that our readers will note that I've just proved the jobs' creation taxpayer financed program mostly went to America's unions and their members, like the SEIU, AFT, and the AFL-CIO to name a few of the most famous ones I know of because I was a college professor in California from 1997 to 2004 (I'll let my readers look up these famous union acronyms, so I can rush this book to print).

I don't think I need to draw Americans a picture or a diagram to see why American unions, and union members voted for ex-President Obama and worked hard for his second term re-election. I'm not going to say it was payback for the jobs' creation money because as we all know this act would be against the law, right? I don't think any American President would have the nerve to spend American taxpayers' money in a way that it would only benefit one special interest group. Would they? So, I'll leave it up to the American public to decide what they want to believe in these kinds of matters, after they finish reading my book. After all, unions have a history or are known for the good they once did for Americans when they were needed back at the turn of the century.

Getting back to my discussion of Mexico's invaders, I want to add that sadly the majority of America's Compatriots are so tired of hearing about Mexico's so called "illegal immigrants" that they appear to have decided to give up and accept America's mass media giants' word who keep telling them they have no power to stop the invasion of America. After all, in this era of political correctness, the media and America's current politicians keep telling them that it is politically correct and legal to let this happen. After all, haven't Congress, the American Supreme Court, and even ex-President Obama all decide to give Mexico's illegal and colonizing invaders the same privileges and legal rights that America's Compatriots have as US Citizens (Which, again, Frederic Bastiat says can't be done—more later.)? And! I want to add that these same US Government entities are trying to, or are planning to, reward these colonizers (remember, who broke America's US Immigration and Constitutional laws.) by giving them a full pardon; I mean "amnesty" (Note: According to what I've read this is really what these entities and ex-President Obama are (or were) trying to for these law breakers, which Bastiat says breaks US law).

One more reason many Americans have given up on their country includes the fact that they evidently do not have any idea what America's immigration or Constitutional laws say or cover. Because of this fact, or facts, I have come to the conclusion that they can't defend themselves or their Constitution, so they don't care anymore. I don't believe Americans are too lazy to care, but I do believe and know that they're too busy trying to survive in America's new and depressed job market and economy to take the time to fight for America. I also believe that many have just given up because they see their high paying manufacturing jobs being sent overseas or to neighboring countries like Mexico, and they feel they can't stop America's corporations or their rogue leaders and Supreme Court Justices. I'm Sad to say these Americans might be right in many ways because America's corporations have decided to put profits above the needs of America's compatriots who have always been willing to die and protect the CEOs of these companies and the corporations' interests, the homes of these corporate leaders, their lives, and their families who almost always live in America, instead of the countries where they send American industrial and manufacturing jobs.

Although these patriotic souls are willing to die for their country and America's way of life, apparently this fact does not make America's CEOs of large corporations feel obligated to return the favor; but in the eyes of this author, their coldhearted choices do make these CEOs and their stockholders look selfish, greedy, ungrateful, and mostly unpatriotic. In fact, in the eyes of this American, these people only seem to care about daily reports from America's stock market and the reports that show the market is at an all time high and flirting with the 1500 point mark (Note: Since Trump's election, the stock market has gone over the 2,000 mark and there are more job openings in manufacturing than during the eight years ex-President Obama was in office.), which means the world, America's corporations, and their stock holders are getting richer but not America's citizens because America's economy has been left behind and the average American is surviving on a Socialist Democrat Government form of trickledown economics.

We all know it's no secret that America's jobs are being (and have been) sent overseas to other countries by greedy American corporate giants and the banks that fund their expansions; yes, I am talking about the same greedy corporations and banks who helped cause, or create, the collapse of the world's economy. And since America's factory jobs have been sent overseas and to Mexico's side of the border, American Compatriots have been left fighting each other (and thanks to PROTEUS, Mexico's invading force of scab workers, I mean Mexico's "illegal immigrants") for the few minimum wage paying jobs that have been left in America by companies to appease and support America's modern day humbled citizens. These minimum wage service jobs pay such low wages that many Americans now work two or more jobs just to make ends meet and they have no hope for retirement. I want to point out that in various ways all of the facts stated above all contributed to why so many Americans lost their life savings in the stock market crash and they will now have to work till they die on the job. I hate to say it but this scenario reminds me of what happened back in the early 1970s.

By the way, most Americans don't know this fact but those 401-Ks that were once hailed as a financial cornucopia retirement tool for middle class American's retirement dreams in realty were never meant to serve as retirement accounts. I know I can make this bold statement because I know a very rich man who told me they were really created for millionaires to use as a finance tool to hide money from the IRS. Yes my fellow Americans you heard that right the 401Ks you were told to invest in were never meant to be financial tools to create so much money that a person could retire on the returns. In fact, I believe the only people that will retire from the returns of 401Ks are the companies that control and sell these 401k retirement tools because they make a killing on the fees they charge America's investors. Oh yes, as for the stock market, a very rich man once warned me that unless I could afford to lose the money I invest in stocks or the stock market, I should think twice about putting my money in this highly volatile investment cornucopia: To make a long story short, I now give you the formula he gave me in-case I ever had the money to invest in the market: "I should invest ¼ of my money in home rentals for income, ¼ of my money in retail rental property for income, ¼ of my job's income money in safe high yield savings accounts, and finally ¼ of my money that I can afford to lose in the stock market. He added the last part because as he said, "The Stock Market is a gamble; so if you lose this money, the loss should not hurt your financial health. This formula according to my very rich friend is how rich people make themselves richer and why very rich people play the stock market. In other words, they do it because they can afford to lose this money. I now leave the choice of playing/investing in the stock market as your choice.

Since the Americans I discussed in the past few paragraphs are working two or more jobs to make ends meet, I can probably say that most of them are not aware their country is slowly being taken away from them. And even if they do have time to see their country being taken from them, I truly believe and have found that these Americans don't have the time to fight for their dying country that is being parceled, or divided into three or four mini-nations, which makes America a "House Divided." Because of the fact I just presented, I believe this fact is the reason most legal American citizens have just given up and accepted the death of their once great Western Christian Culture. Because of these facts, I have come to the following conclusion from a speech by President Lincoln. In this speech, Lincoln warned us that if America ever fell apart or was divided into sections, she would fall or fail: The title of the speech was "A house divided against itself cannot stand!" I want to point out he delivered this speech and spoke this warning on June 16, 1858, at 8 p.m. to 1,000 Republican delegates; "he wrote this speech because at the time he knew America could not defend itself against the world as a divided nation in the eyes of the world." I am now saying the same thing about America's current state because of where she is being lead by her leaders and their financial backers, which to me is a cliff (House divided speech by Abraham Lincoln, Online Post: Oct. 15, 2011, P. 1, www.http:// showcase.netins.net/ web/creative/lincolnspeeces.).

To prove my point, that America is on the verge of internal collapse because US politicians and the government are allowing various foreign groups to change America into versions of their homelands and not be a part of Americana culture, I want to point out and note that in the North East we have the Muslims who now control parts of Michigan and Ohio; and from what I've researched, these areas now look like the Middle East and their schools have no oversight as to how American taxpayer and federally funded schools are being used or what they are teaching in their religious controlled public schools; to the East in New York, we have the Puerto Ricans and other foreigners who wave the Puerto Rico flag every chance they get but never the US flag (think Little League World Series); to the Southwest, we have Mexico's colonizing invaders that we're reporting on in this book, and somewhere in the middle of this crumbling and decaying America are the remnants of the once great Western Euro Influenced Nation (and the remnants of what once the Westernized Nation known as Americana) and its citizens who've been forced by political correctness into submission:

I believe Berkeley Breathed, the creator of the comic strip, "Outland," said it best in one of his comic strips before he shut down his strip: In frame one, Opus and his human male companion walk into a pizza parlor and are asked questions by a female waitress like "Smoking or non-smoking?" They choose smoking; "And you were born male?" Correct they answer; "Euro Caucasian?" Correct and correct, they each answer; "Mortified by rap?" Correct and correct, they answer; "Ancestors kicked Butt?" Correct and Correct they each answer. In the final strip's block, we find Opus and his human pal sitting in a corner crammed onto one table with other white males with a sign in front of them that reads "Born Incorrect!" And when Opus asks an African American for "The Parmesan cheese, Please," The African American tells him to Apologize."

I'm sad to say that I believe Berkeley Breathed got it right. This is America in the 21st Century; and as a Native American minority male who doesn't believe in pay back (because only the Lord has that right), I don't like where my America is headed. This is not the America that I grew up loving and wanting to live in as an adult. America is great because we Americans of my generation all wanted to live in the America that had something special called the Americana Culture. Unfortunately in the new America, these new cultures that are invading America in the 21st Century want to destroy the Americana culture and not live in the culture that has been so successful Historians say it was the key reason America saved the world and won World War II. I want to now ask these cultures and their supporters the Democrat Socialists why they feel these illegal aliens and alleged refugees have the right to destroy America's Americana culture? I also have to ask these people this question: Isn't this culture of success why you foreigners came to America? And yet, these foreigners are demanding rights and privileges to allow them to destroy America's Americana culture (with the help of Democrat Socialists) with rights they have not had the time to earn because they aren't even legal American Citizens. What I find really disturbing is the way the left leaning lower judges and Democrat politicians feel these undocumented aliens and refugees have rights to destroy our Americana Culture and force their historically deficient and violent cultures on America's citizens. I hate to tell these people but they are so new to America that they have no idea what it means to be an American or Patriot.

Because I read several reports and interviewed and talked to many illegal Mexican currently living in California and some Muslims that I met in the Fresno area, I feel the conclusions I reached in the last paragraph are very accurate and true because of their responses to my questions. Since I'm a Native American and what is called a half-breed, many of these illegal Mexicans thought I was Hispanic/Mexican so they opened up to me and gave me their honest opinions without pulling any punches. When I talked to them, they would laughingly inform me that, "These stupid Gringos (white Americans) are so dumb and gullible that we are going to steal their country right from under their noses." They would then add that they feigned respect and allegiance to America's laws and flag when they were being watched by the media; but when the media left, they loved showing their disdain for America's flag and the English language in ugly words that I feel God does not have room for in his heaven. They often added this other point: "After all, California still belongs to Mexico and we're just here to take it back." I want to add that one more new way these invaders show their disrespect for California and America's Government: These illegal aliens show their disdain and hate by wearing hats and t-shirts with the California Bear stenciled on them in the 3 colors of the Mexican flag. I was told the message is that California is now part of Mexico again, or an independent Mexican Republic.

By the way, the hatred of these invaders for whites and our flag is only matched by their arrogance and hatred for any and all Americans and our law-abiding culture. An example of their hatred for white America often rears its head after one of these families (a California thing) has saved a sizeable grub stake of cash, from the generous programs California's Welfare System provides these illegal aliens and other families, and they use this grub stake to buy an American franchise (like the one who once had golden arches in front of their stores). This illegal alien franchise owner, thanks to America's taxpayer financed generous welfare checks and other monies, usually takes over the business and then goes in and the first thing they do is fire all of the white employees and replaces them with an all Mexican/Hispanic staff (Note: These kind of mean spirited hiring practices are becoming an occurrence more often than not in Central California.); Oh yes, one more thing I want to add is that if these same people open their own business (and don't buy a franchise) the one thing I have noticed is that their staff or employees area always all Mexican/Hispanic employees. Since these hiring practices are now very common in California, you would think Governor Brown and the California Legislature would consider this act a form of reverse racism and crack down on these hiring practices but they aren't. These new owners (that sometimes are un-documented illegal aliens) of these American based fast food famous name restaurants, I would like to add, usually also start forgetting to put up the American flag that is supposed to fly over all of these restaurant's flagpoles that the founder of these golden arches franchises felt was so important to his corporation's image when he created his chain. I truly believe that if the founder of this hamburger chain were still alive he would have taken back these restaurants and given back these people their money.

When I saw these practices started to appear in my hometown, I was so upset that I called this company's franchise department and informed them of the actions these Mexican/Hispanic owned franchises were taking. These hiring practices as far as I was concerned are nothing more than reverse racism because they were firing all of the white employees when they took over these businesses. When I called, I added that this type of racism was just as bad as any other racism in America. By the way, although reverse racism is starting to be common in California, the state government is doing nothing about it and has not even investigated the problem. I have one more Mexican/Hispanic owned major business that I want to report on that is a chain of super markets stores that has spread in the state of California. I want to talk about these stores before I end this discussion because this chain only hires Spanish speaking Mexican employees, never displays American flags in it stores, or celebrates US holidays either inside or outside of their stores. Theses stores that I refuse to mention here, because I don't want to give them free advertising, are known for the loud Mexican music they play in their stores. The music was so loud in our Porterville store that some of the neighboring businesses that share walls with these stores in shopping centers finally had to complain because it was disrupting their daily business, or they moved out of the buildings that shared the walls.

These new Mexican/Hispanic owned franchises, I would like to add, are also showing their arrogance and hatred for our country by celebrating their Mexican holidays in their franchise stores by displaying the Mexican flag and its colors, yet they never decorate for any of America's flag holidays, even though these families who own these businesses are successful because many of them participated or took advantage of America's taxpayers paid welfare programs that provided their free government grub stake that allowed them to open these businesses. I should note one more way these people show their hatred for American laws is showing up in the driving habits that they use while driving in America. When they're driving on our California streets, these illegal aliens that are driving with California Representative Alejo's California driver's licenses are often seen running traffic lights, not stopping at STOP signs (unless there is a police car around), using both lanes by driving on top of the divider line of the road (especially on curves), speeding whenever there is no police officer around, or tail gating other cars so close (even if the person in front is doing the legal speed) that one of the most common accidents in our town are rear end accidents. Because these illegal invaders are making life terrible for California's legal citizens, I hope my book you're holding in your hand will soon help Americans stop Mexico's invasion of America by forcing our government and our politicians to admit this invasion is not immigration, but that it is instead an aggressive US government sanctioned invasion and foreign colonization of America's sovereign soil.

As I stated in previous paragraphs, I pray that Americans (who are tired of seeing their country overrun by Mexico's colonizing citizens' force) will soon use this book as a weapon/tool to stop America's politicians and what appear to be some corrupt left leaning US courts and judges who appear to be intent on letting another country's citizens take over America. Having called this book a tool, I hope and pray my fellow American Patriots will take this book with them, when they finally realize that they have had enough, and march on Washington DC by the millions (like we did when we'd had enough of the Nam war) so they can put the fear of God and their power in the heart's of these American Politicians and "rogue Supreme Court Judges who need to GO! After they march on Washington, I hope they'll use their new found power to take back their country from an Alien Mexican (and other illegal nationals) force of invaders and their treacherous US Politicians who appear to have sold out America for corporate profits, cheap labor, and aliens who support the Socialist type Government these politicians appear to want to set up on US Soil. I truly hope my book is the weapon that is going to educate America's citizens on what is really happening to their country so they will care and get "mad-as-Hell" and be ready to fight America's corrupt politicians and Judges. I hope my book helps them understand they can use America's English language and the English language dictionary, which I used to correctly interpret and explain America's Constitution and its laws, to fight and take back their country from these sneaky and corrupt politicians and judges before it's too late.

After all, history teaches us that education has always been the best tool to fight leaders who would oppress the masses, or the Nation's people, and want to keep them in the dark. So, America let Freedom Ring one more time in America because this book wants the Republic and America's citizens (the ones with the real power in a Democracy) to declare their independence from Mexico's (and other countries) invading colonizers and America's insidious politicians and judges. To free them-selves from this new political oppression, all they have to do is find the courage to use the information and facts that are found in this book to take back their country's sovereignty. After all, doesn't US History teach us that sovereignty is a power that belongs to a country's citizens and not the government? To quote a famous saying that many American citizens have forgotten, and some of us might have learned in the age of typewriters (when we learned to type): "Now is the time for all good men [and women] to come to the aid of their country."

If Americans think this call to political arms and possible physical defense of America's Sovereignty (by its legal citizens) is out of line, or crazy, then why does this online post found on the world-wide-web warn Americans to prepare for war against Mexico? The author, Cypresso, says, "[the] United States is being invaded by Mexico, [and] we need to be at war [with Mexico] . . . This is my call to the American people on the border; secure your borders, as the feds will not; your lives and your future are at stake" (Cypresso. "United States is being invaded by Mexico—We need to be at war." News Public. 6 February 2011. <http://newspublic.com/index.php?).

Before I move on, I want to note the "irony" I found in the statement Cypresso published on the web. The irony of his statement is that most American citizens know, or feel, we are at war with Mexico but America's government and her politicians are in complete denial of this very open fact. I decided to reach this conclusion because I accept the fact that most Americans know this Mexican invasion has been sanctioned by America's leaders and America's Politicians. Since this "lawless colonization" consists of a daily flood of Mexican Nationals swarming across America's unprotected Southern Border, I feel I can honestly say this mass swarm of illegal Mexican and other countries' citizens does not in any way resemble, match, mirror, or look like the orderly and controlled legal process that real legal "Immigration" is described as in the eyes of the law and in the old (real) library type huge English language dictionaries that used to be found in American Libraries from Coast to Coast. Nor does this mass illegal invasion look like the orderly process that is written into current American Immigration Laws that were created to protect US Citizens and their sovereignty. Unfortunately for America's legal citizens in the know, their politicians are currently closing a blind eye to the facts I have just presented in this paragraph and our US Immigration laws. And to make matters worse, these politicians and US Court Judges continue to this day to tell Americans this criminal process is a form of "immigration." What my book proves here is that this statement is a lie and is a treasonous act.

Finally, to conclude my thought, I am going to say the information I presented in the previous paragraph speaks volumes that America's citizens and their country are not dealing with anything that looks like immigration. I say this because this massive military like swarm of uncontrolled and lawless foreign invaders that cross America's borders by the millions on any given day can-NOT be defined or defended as immigration in any logical or educated manner. The fact that this invasion looks more like a massive calculated movement of citizen troops, and a controlled lawless act of trespassing, I believe proves Americans are basically dealing with a Mexican government (and world government) controlled and declared act of re-colonization of America and its sovereign nation's Southwestern States. Doesn't America's Government find it strange that most American citizens know we are at war with Mexico and are saying it? Yet! America's Government, her Politicians, Federal and State Judges, and the so called self proclaimed protectors of America's Constitution The American Civil Liberties Union don't see it and will not acknowledge that America is being invaded because they appear to be too busy attacking America's Citizens for demanding US Immigration laws be enforced and US borders closed.

Instead of attacking US citizens, shouldn't these political leaders be protecting America's Citizens from these foreigners and fringe groups who, as we Americans can see, are intent on taking over America and destroying her Christian based Western Culture known as Americana? By the way, most 1970s and older American History Books write that America's rise to power, prominence, success, and victories in WWI and WWII were made possible because of America's Americana Culture. So I must add here, I read in a history book that the best way to destroy a country was to destroy its culture from within like the Europeans and the Early US Government did when they destroyed America's only real "Natural Citizens the Native Americans by killing off the Buffalo—their main source food, taking away their languages, their rights as owners of their lands, putting them on reservations, and finally forcing them to accept the white's man way of life, religion, and culture. If this information sounds familiar, I suggest my readers look around and ask why Spanish is being forced on US Citizens, why hundreds of other languages are being forced on US Citizens, why other culture's way of life are being forced on US Citizens, why other culture's religions are being forced on US Citizens, and why even other culture's laws like Sharia Law are being forced on US Citizens and used in US Courts to settle Muslim cases? Still think America and her Americana Culture are not under attack and in danger of being wiped out like Native America's culture was wiped of the face of old America?

To add salt to the wound, I feel one more problem America has is that many young and middle-aged Americans are too busy trying to be cool to care about stopping the end of America. So unfortunately, it seems like these Americans would rather pay more attention to buying and owning the next cool electronic gadget or having their noses buried on the screen of this gadget than to be bothered with the end of Americana's culture or the invasion of America. When one of my friends asked me why I didn't have a tablet or a smart phone so I could be "with it" and "connected," I simply answered I was "old school" and didn't need these toys to feel connected or with it, and that I was very comfortable with my own thoughts and being deep in thought at times. Since I grew looking up to people like the "Rat Pack kind of class," my idea of being with it, or "classy," is keeping a low profile, not being loud in my dress code or my manners, and basically letting my achievements speak for me. I know that in these days of wearing bling, over-the-top clothes, and pushing the envelope to get attention most people will say I am crazy and not with it because I do not stand out. But, I don't agree with their way of getting attention and being with it. I hate to say but who is to say what is right for each person? If you are unique and you know it, isn't this the best way to live your life then to just be a follower and one of the followers? Now you see why I say and feel that Americans are so busy being cool that America and Americans have lost their class. Yes, I said it in this book. I feel "Americans have no class anymore." And to tell you the truth, since I have lived in Japan, I feel the Japanese Nation has more class than America in this day and age. By the way, for those people who don't know what the term "CLASS" means, here is a brief definition: "according to sense number 9, or definition 9, class is (means) slang [for] Superiority; elegance… the more educated, or higher social classes" ("Landau." Funk and Wagnalls Standard College Dictionary, 1967 ed.).

To be more clear about the difference between "class" and "cool," let's compare a few items to make it even more clear: "Frank Sinatra and the Rat Pack" were the definition of the word or term "class," period; rappers who steal song writer's music because they don't' know how to use, half notes, full notes, pause notes, music bars, stanzas, or write music have no class, but are "cool" by today's standards. Jerry West and Bill Russell (who played by the rules found in the rules of Basketball) had class because they played basketball by the rules of real game of Basketball that can be found in the rule book of the game; today's basketball players have no class but they are considered cool and put on a great show but walking with the ball, double dribbling, standing in the key for ten seconds, and carrying the ball, but have no class because they don't play by the rules found in the basketball rule book: If our readers want an example of a rule today's BB players don't follow, here is one: "The rule says a player "can't put his hand or palm on the side the ball at a 45 degree angle, under the ball, or dribble the ball above his shoulders because this infraction is deemed to be traveling or carrying the ball; yet, today's players and the refs don't call this infraction and that is why these players look like they are great ball handlers compared to past players like Bill Russell or Jerry West but they're not because they are cheating by not obeying the rules of the game. Here is another rule in the book of basketball: When a player decides to dribble the ball the rule says he MUST put the ball down (dribble) on the court before he can take a step, otherwise, his step without the dribble is considered walking or traveling with the ball. To put it mildly, today's BB players cheat or break the rules when they do their fancy moves because they are playing according to made up street ball rules. Finally, players that use steroids (or any kind of enhancement drugs) are a joke, and so are all the players who have used these drugs or are using them to win without being caught. Now you see why I say they have "no class." If you don't believe me, I suggest you go to your library and read the book of rules of the game of Basketball.

To continue my discussion of America's problem with wanting to be cool, I also want to add that I feel too many Americans are too busy being entertained by Roman Gladiator like spectacles now called "cage fighting." I want to go on record and say this kind of fighting is such a brutal display of anger that I actually feel sorry for these fools who risk their lives for the sake of fame and to be "cool" in the eyes of these so called fans who, according to psychology studies, actually go to these spectacles in hope of some gruesome conclusion instead of just a winner of the so called fight. If my readers don't believe these studies, why do my readers think people like to slow down and look at car accidents or watch documentaries that show animals being shredded to death by another predator? I hate to say it but people in general love violence, carnage, and blood. Think about the last movie you went to and think back to how many violent scenes it had, how many shootings, how graphic the movie was, and how much you enjoyed watching it. People are obsessed with it, but don't want to hear about it or admit it because in some ways it proves humans are a little ghoulish. I find it sad that Americans will pay thousands of dollars to watch spectacles like cage fighting, baseball games, football games, and rappers who swear and tell them to hate their police, their wives, their fellow man, kill each other for turf, and disrespect women. The sad part of Rappers is that the people who buy their rap stuff (it's not music.)

makes these rappers filthy rich, and yet they are only (statistics prove this) one paycheck away from being on street, losing their homes, cars, and life, if they lose their jobs. The problem with Americans is they forget that these so called celebrities are just human beings like the rest of us. They are all going to die; they all put on their pants or clothes the same way we do; and even the women stars put on their pants one leg at time like the rest of us. Sad to say, they are going to leave this world the same way the rest of us will someday. Or, as Native Americans say, "We are born to die because life is a circle."

A. The definition of the term "IMMIGRATION"
   has "NO SHADES" of "GRAY."

As stated before in this Chapter, This book has proven current "Open Border" proponents have labeled the actions of the over 20 million colonizing invaders, and their act of staying in America without legal permission, as "Illegal Immigration." By creating this perverse, and very deceptive word, "Open Border" proponents have been able to classify these law breaking trespassers and their lawless actions with millions of "Legal Immigrants" who applied for entry under US Immigration Laws in the early 20th Century and waited in line for their chance to enter America legally. These real and legal immigrants, I want to note, arrived in an orderly and controlled manner and they presented themselves (in a legal fashion to be processed before they ever set foot on American soil) to US Immigration officers. If we compare the actions of these real immigrants to the actions of the 20 million Mexican invaders who currently ignore US immigration laws and trespass on US soil on a daily basis, I think my fellow Americans can see for themselves that there is no comparison and these trespassers are not immigrants in any shape, way, and manner. My fellow Americans should note the true and law abiding immigrants that landed on America's shores at receiving-centers, like the famous one known as "Ellis Island" in New York and the other famous one at the Port of Galveston, Texas that was known as the Ellis Island of West, so they could be processed and registered as legally processed alien immigrants who deserved the green cards they received and earned them by following the laws of America. By following America's Immigration laws, these new real immigrants that came from all over the world proved to America's citizens that they respected America's immigration, criminal, and Constitutional laws and were willing to earn the title of becoming an American citizen.

All of these "Legal Immigrants" followed American laws and presented themselves to American Law Enforcement Officers where they were registered, were processed, were checked for diseases, and if needed they were quarantined and treated for any disease they might have been carrying. I want to note these legal immigrants were always under the watchful eyes (and "Control") of the US Department of Immigration, America's Port Authorities and US Immigration doctors and nurses. I should also note these immigration check points, or stations, were implemented to see if any of these "Legal Immigrants" that were being processed had ever committed a crime or were wanted for crimes in their homeland. During this processing, if an immigration officer found an immigrant who had committed a crime or was wanted in their homeland and were wanted criminals, the immigration officer arrested the immigrant and he or she was sent back to his or her homeland for prosecution or for a trial in their own country. These days, thanks to "open borders" supporters/proponents, any and all foreign criminals who enter America via the "open border" liberal policies are never caught, so they enter America and commit crimes, murder people, and join Mexican gangs which I hate to say explains why America's prisons (especially in California) are filled to capacity and cost American tax payers about $48,000 per prisoner per year.

As my fellow Americans can see from the example in the last paragraph, when we Americans contrast the legal immigrants of the past, who entered America in an orderly manner during the early 20th Century, to the current lawless invaders (or 20 million

"Mexican colonizing invaders") of this century, we Americans find the past Obama Administration and company appeared to enjoy advocating the act of "Mob Rule Law," and the rule of a lawless society (And evidently the new Democrat Congress that was just put into office during the 2018 midterm elections). After all, ex-President Obama, Mrs. Clinton, and the Democrat Socialist Party insist on calling Mexico's law breaking trespassers "illegal immigrants" even though I have just proven over-and-over these invaders are not immigrants at all. I can say this because they break US immigration, criminal, and Constitutional laws when they enter US soil and basically thumb their noses at America's Republic and her Law Enforcement Officers. So, thanks to ex-President Obama, Clinton, and company these invaders currently continue to live in America without having to meet any standards or take the time to apply for legal entry into America so they can be processed legally. I guess this thought never crossed these lawbreakers' minds, or the politicians and Supreme Court Judges who support these lawbreaking trespassers.

Since I can see that America's current government and politicians don't appear to want to enforce any of America's laws, I am sure that we are going to see these recusants Mexican invaders continue to pour across America's borders on a daily basis and continue to break US immigration and criminal laws without fear of deportation or arrest. I guess we Americans can only wonder why these US politicians and America's Supreme Court Judges can't see that these lawless invaders are doing the complete opposite of what past legal immigrants did when they came to America. I guess my fellow Americans and I also have to wonder why these US leaders insist on ignoring these important facts, which alone prove these Mexican invaders are not immigrants. With the information I've just provided, I hope America's legal citizens can now see why these illegal trespassers should not be compared to the legal and law-abiding immigrants of the early 20th Century that included people like my father's ancestors. After all these Mexican lawbreakers enter US sovereign soil illegally, break criminal laws by carrying weapons to allegedly protect themselves, are not willing to apply for Visas or wait their turn to enter America, and never present themselves to be checked for diseases, which could trigger a pandemic disease with grave consequences for America's un-inoculated citizens. After all, We Americans should not forget how the early European Settlers' Small Pox epidemics or pandemics wiped out hundreds of North American Indian tribes because these Native Americans had no immunity to these foreigners' deceases.

I want remind our American politicians that protecting the health (and more!) of America's citizens is one of the main reasons Immigration Laws were created in the first place. In a round about way, some other reasons for immigration laws include protecting America's citizens from foreign insects and poisonous reptiles that could wreak havoc on American's lives and flora and fauna. America, where do you think the current bed bug, lice, new skin diseases, and crop-damaging bugs are coming from? Sad to say, these trespassers never even attempt to obey or follow US Immigration laws, yet they continue to receive the protection of open border supporting Presidents like Obama, America's Politicians, America's lower court Judges, Mexico's Government, and even some Supreme Court Judges who are supposed to be impartial in their decisions and not commit Embroilment. Even sadder is the fact that these so called champions of the American legal process also like to use the perverse word "illegal immigration" when they discuss or address the issue of these law breaking foreigners known as (includes Mexicans and all others) "illegal immigrants." Before I end this paragraph, I want to note that the facts in this paragraph speak volumes as to why I believe many of the childhood diseases America had defeated in the 60s and 70s are now back in America, and why Americans are suffering with bed bugs, lice, and other infestations in many Southwestern States.

To clear up the uncertainty of the words "immigration" and "immigrant" and other words and terms used to explain America's intruder problem, I have decided to present the terms used by open border groups and then include several of the (not abridged or condensed) ignored, but very important, definitions listed in English dictionaries for multi-definition words like "immigration." I want to note that the definitions I found will be used to add descriptions, or definitions, to the term "immigration and the word immigrant" to clarify how these words should be used, instead of the way they are being used by the current administration and all of the open border proponents and their allies. These added definitions will not only allow me to add new insight into the discussion of the invasion of America, but they will also allow my readers to see how the words "immigration and immigrant" were really meant to be used in the English language. I also hope that these added definitions will help show America's Supreme Court Judges, college educated officials, US Presidents, alleged educated officers of the law, and alleged educated/elected American Politicians that are supposed to be representing their Constituents, how these words/terms were really meant to be used to enforce America's Constitution and Immigration laws. I hope this information will provide the needed clarity I found in these true and exact definitions of the word "immigration." With this information, I hope my readers (and these US Officials) will be able to see the limitations found in the true definitions of the word "immigration," and to conclude the facts on this topic, I hope these facts will help my readers understand that America is "not" dealing with what is being called or labeled as "illegal immigration," but in reality America is dealing with a well coordinated non-military act of colonizing of America by Mexico's (and the world's—think the thousands of illegal aliens that arrived on Mexico's/US border this year, 2019.) citizens.

To avoid any further confusion, I now present three key definitions for the word "immigration" for your perusal: According to Funk and Wagnalls Standard College Dictionary (and even Webster's New World Dictionary of the American Language), the word "**Immigration**" has **more** than the **following** definition that is often used by open border proponents to argue their point: "1. The act of immigrating [or] . . . aliens entering a country

("Landau." Funk and Wagnalls Standard College Dictionary. 1967 ed.)." This definition is the one ex-President Obama and all Open Border advocates would have you believe is the only politically correct one for their "new-world Socialist America." They use this definition because it disregards or ignores American Immigration and Constitutional laws, and because by using this definition, they feel they can grant Mexico's lawless border crashers Amnesty so they can have millions of obligated disciples. These disciples will then become scab workers that are willing to accept the low wages offered by corporations in the new non-industrialized and welfare state called America of the 21st Century (because America's manufacturing jobs continue to be out-sourced to Mexico and the world.).

To correct the perversion being utilized by this open border confederacy that distorts the word "immigration, I want Americans to look at two other key **senses (definitions)**, as the American dictionary calls the added definitions of all words with more than one definition, that are being ignored by what I've decided to label the "Pro-Foreigner Confederacy." This open border "Confederacy," I want to add, seems to be hell-bent on ending the Euro-Caucasian Christian Culture that drafted the US Constitution and created this once great nation called the United States of America. From the results of my research, I feel this very powerful Confederacy appears to have been operating on American soil for quite some time now and appears to be heavily financed because of the success they are having in the Southwest, which is looking more and more like it is part of Mexico.

The first sense, or definition, I am going to define is often found as the second sense in many dictionaries, and the other sense or definition for the word "immigration" that I define here was listed as the 10th definition in the dictionary I used that I found in the big library dictionary of my hometown Library. I want to note this large table-top reference dictionary book I was using for my research mysteriously disappeared after a library clerk asked me if she could help me find the word I needed, and when I told her, she did not look too happy. I returned the next day to complete my research of words I was looking up and the large dictionary had disappeared from my local library. When I asked where it had gone, the library person said they had decided to get rid of them because they were falling apart. The funny (ironic funny) part about this lady's statement is that I had used the book the day before and found it to be in very good condition. Since I needed to complete my research, I then decided to go to a larger library in a larger neighboring city (in the same county) and found there book had disappeared too and the extra large dictionary had been replaced by a standard smaller version that most people have in their own homes. I then took a trip to my local university and guess what? The large dictionary had also disappeared from their floor too. In the state of California, I am now stuck with only the standard sized home dictionaries. Since I had saved my work, I decided to use my notes I kept to define the words I present in this book for discussion.

The first definition I'll discuss also comes from the 1967 edition of Funk and Wagnalls' dictionary that I found in my local Library, before it was removed, and is the second "sense" of the word "immigration." This sense says that when we use the word immigration we are describing the following action about the action of these trespassers and the meaning of the word immigration: "The total number of aliens entering a country for permanent residence **during a stated period."** What the reader must learn from this definition is that in order for an alien to be called or qualify to be called an immigrant the English language dictionary says he or she must meet the requirement that says, "In order for a person to be called an immigrant he or she must be part of a group of aliens that enters a country **'ONLY during a stated time or [controlled] period.'"** If the alien enters a country (like America) by ignoring this set period, which obviously is a means to control the number of aliens entering said country during the specified time, he or she can't be considered an "immigrant" under the standards set by the definition of the English language dictionary.

The next fact I want to point out is the definition for the word "**stated**" (as used in the sentence that defines the word immigration) has the following meanings or senses in its definition: "1) Announced or specified [period]. 2) Established or fixed [period]." Because I am trying to avoid any confusion in my discussion of this key sentence that importantly defines the word immigration, I want to make sure I point out the word "specified" (as used in this definition) has the following meaning: "state [or declare] in . . . explicit terms [to avoid confusion] ("Landau." Def. 2. Funk and Wagnalls Standard College Dictionary, Text Edition, 1967.).". So! We now learn that in order for a person to be legally called an "immigrant," under the English language dictionary, he or she must "only enter US sovereign soil "during the stated explicit time." If these people meet the written guidelines to enter America as an immigrant, they will then have earned the right to be considered/called an immigrant. Again, I want to remind my readers these people must only enter during the fixed period and under the set principles, procedures, and laws being used by the US Government to be allowed to enter the country as "immigrants." If these applicants do not follow the laws or standards set by the US Government, or the host country, these people cannot be allowed to enter the country or qualify to be considered "immigrants." Since America's current invaders should not be called immigrants, they definitely do not qualify to enter the country or qualify to be considered "immigrants." And! Since America's current invaders should not be called immigrants, or qualify to be called immigrants, they have to be put in a category that fits their actions or the way they have chosen to enter America. Because I want to make my research complete, I want to add that the only categories I found these people qualify for is being called unauthorized lawbreaking invaders or colonizers as my research proves in this paragraph.

The second sense that I found in the large library dictionary/ reference book at the Porterville, California City Library was listed as the10[th] definition or sense for the word "immigration." I want to note that when the library personnel learned that I was looking for words that defined terms like immigration, lawless entry, and the word criminal they informed me the library was about to close so I would have to come back the next day. Since I knew I would return the next day, I decided to mark my spot with a paper sticky to note where I had found it (So I would not damage the book), and I left. The next day when I returned to my library I was informed the large "old style" reference dictionary book had been removed because it was old and haggard and the head librarian had decided to discard it because it was too old and damaged. I then asked the employee if I could buy the book but they said it had already been given away/donated. The librarian then told me I could still use the smaller dictionaries they had in the Library. The problem with this choice (that I've learned from experience) is that just about all of the new "modern" smaller dictionaries now offer only one or two definitions per word and some kind of historical example to show the use of the word (They are watered down definitions with no real concrete information for serious research.). To put it mildly, I became very upset when I learned later that all of the local libraries in the surrounding area had also removed their big reference type dictionaries from their floors. So, in one swift and over night action all of the large research type dictionaries had been removed from all of my county's libraries. In the end, although I was not able to get the title of the dictionary I was using the day I was asked to leave. I want to note that I was lucky and fortunate enough to have had the for-sight to write down the definitions/senses for the word "immigration" that I had found that day.

The critical definition I found that day provided the key information I needed for the book that you now hold in your hands. I want to note again this key information I needed was found in the 10th sense of the word: "immigration": 10) "to enter a country under set controls [or laws] to settle." This definition basically says that in order for a person or group to be called immigrants, under English dictionary usage rules for this word, they must have entered the host nation by following the controls in place at the time. If they fail to follow these "set" controls, they cannot be called, or determined to be immigrants. Now that I've introduced this definition that I found in the 10th sense of the word "immigration" and my fellow Americans see how damaging this definition is to the supporters of "open borders," I feel there should be no doubt in my readers' minds as to why the large old reference type library books appear to be disappearing from the floors of America's libraries. After all, this definition (and the other one I provide in this chapter) and the information it provides about the word "immigration" does more damage to those who support "open borders" than any speech or ad that those who oppose "open borders" have ever created. Together, I believe these two definitions help destroy any argument that says Mexico's invading citizens' army are in anyway "immigrants." I also believe these two definitions help me put an end to the use of the perverse word "illegal immigrant."

After reading the two senses that I just introduced for the word "immigration in the past paragraphs, I think my readers should now understand why their fellow Americans are being kept in the dark about the many senses that apply to the use of the words "immigrant and immigration." This discovery, I believe, also helps me show Americans why there is a saying that goes something like this, "keeping the masses in the dark (and ignorant of the truth) is the most powerful weapon developed by those who would oppress the masses." Now my readers should see why in the 21st Century, I feel Americans are being duped into believing the invasion of America by Mexico's civilian colonizers is not wrong and nothing more than a "modern form of lawless immigration" that should be accepted. After all, ex-President Obama, America's politicians, the Supreme Court Judges, and Mexico's Government accept the use of the term "illegal immigration" as a term that they insist gives them the power to override America's Constitutional and US Immigration Laws. Unfortunately for these self-appointed English language word masters, the American dictionary of the English language does not agree with them. According to English language dictionaries, they do not have this power because as Albert H. Marckwardt states in Funk and Wagnalls' Preface, "It is of primary importance to find the meaning . . . of the word about which one is in doubt [before we use it, because the dictionary is] . . . a body of data about the language, deriving its authority from the care and completeness with which the facts were collected and interpreted" ("Landau." Forward. Funk and Wagnalls, Standard College Dictionary. Text Edition. 1967.VII.).

Before I close the discussion and defining the words "immigration and immigrant," I want to note that Funk and Wagnalls Edition of **Webster's New World Thesaurus** substitutes or lists the word "colonization" as one of the "other" words that should be used to replace the word "immigration" (Laird, Charlton and Lutz, D. William. Webster's New World Thesaurus: Funk and Wagnalls Edition. Simon and Schuster, Inc. New York. 1985. p 374). So, since the millions of law breaking intruders entering America from Mexico can't/shouldn't be called "immigrants" maybe my fellow Americans should insist the Supreme Court Judges, America's Politicians, and the Mexican government need to call these Mexican lawless, trespassers what they really are in the eyes of America's criminal and Constitutional laws and America's English language dictionary: "lawless colonizing invaders."

B. Ending the ABUSE of the term "ILLEGAL" by showing the Word's Definition Limitations.

I opened this chapter by proving the term "immigration" can't and shouldn't be simply applied to any person or group of persons who decide to intrude or enter another sovereign nation's soil without permission. I then helped my readers learn that in order for a group (or person) to be part of the process known as real or legal immigration the person (or group) had to enter the host nation during a "stated" or "set" time period and under "the set controls or laws" that the host country had set in its immigration laws to control the people who enter their country. These controls or laws I would like to note are the reason countries have law enforcement officers like the US Border Patrol. The job of these officers, as we know in America, is to make sure foreigners follow these laws and to enforce these laws and make sure the people who enter the country, enter in an orderly and LEGAL manner. If these people enter the host country during the set period and under the laws or controls, then these people can honestly call themselves immigrants. Now that I've set the correct and true standards for the definition of the word "immigration" (and "immigrant"), and in a logical way shown who should really be considered an immigrant, I feel I need to show my readers that there is no way the term "immigration" should ever have been coupled or joined with the term "illegal" in an attempt to work around the true meaning of the two key senses or definitions found in the word "immigration." To make my point, I will now introduce several reasons why I feel or say the terms "illegal immigration" or "illegal immigrant" should NEVER have been formed to try to convince America's Citizens that they are both proper terms that describe a sincere and sensible form of legal entry into US sovereign soil.

To prove the statement I made in the last paragraph, I feel I need start by looking in one of America's English dictionaries to learn the true, or right, definition of the term "illegal." If my readers were to look in the English dictionary, they would learn that the English language dictionary says this term is defined as follows: 1. Not legal; contrary to law; unlawful . . .—Synonym: See "criminal" (Funk and Wagnalls, Standard College Dictionary, Text Edition, 1967.). Since the dictionary added that the synonym for the term "illegal" is the word "criminal," I decided to add a few other synonyms that Webster's New World Thesaurus felt were also associated with the term "criminal." Here is what I learned when I completed this act: According to Webster, the term "criminal," which can replace the term "illegal," as a modifier has the following same meanings as the following words found in the English language dictionary: unconstitutional, unlawful, contraband, outlawed, lawless, unauthorized, taboo, forbidden criminal, and prohibited to name just a few of the many negative or anti-social terms that paint this word as "lawless, uncivilized, savage, and warlike" actions

(Laird, Charlton, and William D. Lutz. Funk and Wagnalls Edition: Webster's New World Thesaurus, 2nd ed. 1985.).

To put it kindly, the words unconstitutional, lawless, and outlawed hardly paint the picture of an honest or law-abiding person (as ex-President Obama liked to describe these invading colonizers while he was in office) or group of people that Americans would want in their country and feel safe living with them. Even if I use the perverse words "illegal immigrant or illegal immigration" to sugar coat the lawless act these illegal aliens commit when they enter America's sovereign soil, I think my fellow Americans will agree with me that these terms do not hide the fact that these perverse terms translate into the following lawless and caustic terms: "unconstitutional migration," "unconstitutional colonization," "lawless migration," "lawless colonization," "criminal migration," "unauthorized migration," and finally "prohibited migration" to name just a few of the many lawless and criminal acts the union of these two words describes in the English language. So why, I have to ask, did the Obama Administration keep pushing to have these criminal invaders be given Amnesty (or a pardon) and not be sent back or prosecuted under any US criminal law? Now that my fellow Americans have been shown the limitations of the word "immigration" are real, and English dictionary (the defender of the English language) says the term "illegal immigration or illegal immigrant" are incorrect words, I hope my fellow Americans and I can finally end this political charade and stop the use of theses perverse words that defend these illegal aliens, so we can demand that they all be sent back to their homelands.

Let's face it; when the "Pro-Open Border-Confederacy" (as I like to call them) combined the words "illegal" and "immigration" to create the word "illegal immigration," they probably did this to fool or confuse Americans into believing these lawless invaders were comparable to early European legal and law abiding immigrants. They knew this term was corrupt, incorrect, and against what America's law and lawyers call "Natural Law"; yet!

They still created this pathetic word. I want to remind my fellow Americans that by allowing these supporters to argue that it's okay for Mexico's invading and colonizing army (and other South American nation's citizens) to overwhelm America's border officers and then hide the crime by calling it immigration, these open border supporters are saying, in a round about way, that invasions like when Hitler invaded Poland back on September 1, 1939 was a form of immigration because there was little or no resistance when they entered Poland. Or, these supporters are saying that when Turkey and Greece used the end of World War II as an excuse to invade and divide up Armenia among themselves it was okay because it was a form of illegal immigration. After all, these two countries only swallowed up a weaker and neighboring country and oppressed the legal citizens and only destroyed their cultures.

To conclude this thought of using semi-military like invasions like a form of immigration, I want to add that according to Korean War Vet stories the Chinese Government used Chinese citizens armed with pitchforks, axes, and clubs to overrun American military bases during this war. So the idea of using citizen manned armies for illegal wars of invasion is not new, but in one way or another, it has been used several times in the past and as we can see it works. So, I feel I can say the idea of not needing soldiers to invade another country's sovereign soil is nothing new in this world of aggression and conquering. Evidently, or unfortunately, today's "Open Border" supporters of Mexico's (and the world's) invading colonizers don't believe that this type of war to conquer another country exists, or can happen, but they are wrong, dead wrong. Yet when North Korea invaded South Korea, the North Korean army used Chinese citizens (not military trained or part of the military but just farmers) to invade and attack US troops. I know these examples are not quite the same as our illegal aliens, but I still feel America's invasion ins many ways does look a lot like these forms of non army invasions that Mexico's " president and politicians are using to invade America and attack our border patrol officers.

Unfortunately for Americans, these examples of overt and covert acts of aggression are more than likely the reason Mexico's President keeps demanding that Mexico's citizens be allowed to enter America without permission and illegally. After all, to paraphrase Brenda Walker, "the Mexican Government [to this day] teaches their children in Mexican schools that America's South West was stolen by the US" and states like California, New Mexico, Texas, and Arizona really belong to Mexico. So I guess the fact that Mexico's government thinks that they are just trying to get their land back sits well with their supporters like America's Socialist Democrats and the party's supporters. Too bad Mexico's government seems to have forgotten the treaty of Guadalupe Hidalgo that Mexico's politicians signed, and that included an agreement to use "the Rio Grande as the boundary between Mexico and the US. By the way, this agreement also included California (including the much-desired port of San Diego) and New Mexico and it forced the US to assume 3.25 million US dollars of Mexican debt owed to US citizens, and it also paid Mexico's government $15 million dollars for all this land" [and more, that Mexico's Government keeps saying is theirs]" (Hofstadter, Richard, William Miller, and Daniel Aaron. The United States: The History of a Republic, Prentice-Hall, Inc. New Jersey: 1960.).

After reading that Mexico's schools are teaching their students that America robbed Mexico of the Southwest, I think we Americans need to understand why two of my American History teachers and Brenda Walker (editor and author of the web page "Limits to Growth") said this form of territorial claim from centuries past is often used to give [any] so called "wronged" country [the] right to claim another country's sovereign soil." My teachers liked to label these types of crude claims for territory as "Rewritten Voodoo History," while Brenda Walker labels these wild, crazy claims as, "revanchist fantasies."

On Walker's web page I found that Walker described "revanchist fantasies" as, "some vague territorial claim from centuries before [that allows one country to form a new] modern national boundary . . . She [then] adds, "China used these [revanchist fantasies] to invade Tibet in 1949" (Walker, Brenda. Limits To Growth Page, 27 August. 2012. http://www.limitstogrowth. org/WEB-text/aztlan.html.). Unfortunately for Americans, we Americans now find that Mexico is using this same type of voodoo or revanchist history to claim America's southwest, very much like Germany, Turkey, and Greece did in their conquest of their neighboring weaker nations. Unfortunately for Mexico, according to a North American Tribal saying, "North America (including the Southwest) has always been Native American Land. We like to say it this way: "America is Indian Land, always has been, and always will be."

To prove my point, my Native American people often point out that both Indian history books and US government history books always report (or write) that Mexico never conquered North America's Indian tribes in the Southwest, except California. So US history tells us that the only state that Mexico conquered was California because California's Indians were non violent and they trusted the Jesuit Priests who came to them with an olive branch, and then enslaved them, butchered them by the hundreds of thousands, and forced "Mission Indian" life on them by destroying their cultures, their names, and languages as Mexico's invaders appear intent on doing to America's Citizens using the same tactics in the 21st Century. To prove the point I am making here, I want my readers to look at a quote from one such history book: "California Indians were gentle as the climate in which they lived. The Spaniards (Mexico's Government) gave them names, established missions for them, converted and debauched them . . . taking what they wanted from the submissive Indians, debasing those whom the Spaniards had not already debased, and then systematically exterminated whole populations now long forgotten, [for example the] Chilulas, Chimarikos, Urebures, Nipewais . . . whose bones have been sealed under millions of miles of freeways, parking lots, and slabs of tract housing" (Brown, Dee. Bury My Heart at

Wounded Knee: An Indian History of The American West, Pan Books. London: 17ᵗʰ ed. 1983.).

History also shows and tells us that the reason America's Southwest very likely belongs to America is because they went to war with the American Indians and won the Indian wars by either offering the tribes treaties that the US Government never kept, or intended to keep, and/or by simply slaughtering these indigenous people after they had disarmed them: "I saw a white flag raised [by the unarmed Indians] . . . I think there were six hundred Indians in all . . . I saw one squaw lying on the bank whose leg had been broken by a shell; the [US] soldier came up to her with a drawn saber; she raised her arm to protect herself, when he struck, breaking her arm; she rolled over and raised her other arm, when he struck, breaking it, and then left her without killing her . . . There seemed to be indiscriminate slaughter of men, women, and children . . . Everyone I saw dead was scalped. I saw one squaw cut open with an unborn child, as I thought lying by her side . . . I saw the body of White Antelope with his privates cut off, and then I heard a soldier say he was going to make a tobacco pouch out of them . . . I saw one squaw whose privates had been cut out . . ." (Brown, Dee, Bury My Heart at Wounded Knee: An Indian History of The American West, Pan Books. London: 17ᵗʰ ed. 1983.).

Finally, my readers also need to remember the US won the war against Mexico for the Southwest. So unfortunately for America's Indians and the Mexican Government, as the saying states, "to the victors go the spoils of war." Besides, I want to note that Mexico's government was lucky because they were paid millions of dollars for land they never really owned, while North America's Indians only got lied to and slaughtered when they tried to defend their rights to their land, says Dee Brown in the book <u>Bury my Heart at Wounded Knee</u>.

Since this book is not about Native American history or the wars for American Indian Lands, I suggest my readers take the time to read the books I'm going to recommend here because they shed some light on two very important points I would like to make here. First of all, I'm going to cover the fact that the Southwest always belonged to Native Americans. I can make this claim because in the book <u>Bury my Heart at Wounded Knee</u>, Dee Brown writes, "In the arid Southwest were the Apaches [and the] Navajos [who] were related to the Apaches . . . In Rockies north of the Apache and Navajo country were the Utes, an aggressive mountain tribe inclined to raid their more peaceful neighbors to the South the Navajos . . . Nana in his fifties but tough as rawhide, considered the English-speaking white men no different from the Spanish Speaking Mexicans he had been fighting all of his life . . . For as long as anyone could remember, the Mexicans had been raiding Navajos to steal their young children and make slaves of them, and for as long as anyone could remember the Navajos had been retaliating with raids against the Mexicans" (Brown, Dee. <u>Bury my Heart at Wounded Knee</u>, An Indian History of the American Southwest. Great Britain: Pan Books, 1972. 10-14.).

I believe the quote, I just cited in the last paragraph, from Brown's book speaks volumes as to who really owned America and America's Southwest, and the kind of people and culture that settled in Mexico, So in reality, Mexico's alleged claim to the Southwest pretty well becomes mute when my readers learn the facts found in Brown's book. As for the Mexican peoples' penchant for stealing Indian children and entering and taking land that was not theirs, I hate to say it but history appears to be repeating itself in America, sans (without) the stealing of children for slaves, thank God (a joke to lighten up this book.). I hate to add some bad news to this joke but this statement and joke are not completely un-true, when I include the young American/Hispanic teens girls that fall for the young 21 year-old (and over) Mexican illegal male invaders who often kidnap these young girls and try to take them back to Mexico to be their wives. Thank God most of them get caught before they get into Mexico. For my readers who don't want to look up the word "sans," the term "sans" means "without," as in "without stealing children." This example, I hope, proves my point that when using difficult or vague words a writer should always define the words so the reader knows what the writer is talking about or saying in a sentence.

To conclude this section of this book, I recommend my readers find and read the following books about America's Native Americans and North America, and the land that was once theirs: <u>Comanches in the New Southwest, 1895-1908,</u> Gelo, J. Daniel and Noyes, Stanley. University of Texas, Austin. 1999. This book is filled with historical photographs of Native Americans of the Southwest and some written facts about the historical value of these photographs. And the book <u>Life Among the Apaches</u> by John C Cremony, University of Nebraska Press, Lincoln and London, 1983. This book is said to be a firsthand account of Indian history through the eyes of a white man. I should note I feel this book is a good book for anyone who wants to know the sad, bloody, facts of how America's Native people were methodically butchered, slaughtered, and pushed off their homelands so that America could be built over their ancestors' buried bodies.

If my readers don't think America's Government isn't capable of killing or harming America's citizens or the Republic's members, I want to remind my readers that this government is the same one that sent the US Military (or National Guard) to confront American citizens and students on the Kent State University campus with loaded rifles, live (or real/not blanks) ammunition, and in the process caused what the generation of the Nam War era still call the Kent State Massacre. Although I don't remember the exact date it happened, I do remember it happened in May of 1970 because I remember watching the newscast showing students putting flowers in the barrels of the Guards' rifles, leaving the room, and when I returned and sat down the broadcaster was almost yelling that students had been shot and killed by the National Guard. The broadcaster added that many students had also been wounded seriously and were running away from the National Guard in a panic. In the end, I learned that four students died on that day, and our nation came very close to (or was on the verge of) a civil war. Before I move on, I want to remind my readers that this government that murdered American Indians and sent armed soldiers to a US college campus is the same one that is now asking America's citizens to trust them in the 21st Century (again) because they are doing their best to protect their sovereignty and their nation's borders against an invading hoard or force of illegal aliens from Mexico, when in reality America's Government and her politicians and judges are opening the doors for these invaders.

C. Using the term "INVADE" to solve "AMERICA'S ENIGMA."

In the last section of this chapter, I ended the discussion of the term "illegal immigration" by replacing the term "illegal immigration" with the terms "invading, invader, and invasion" so I could correctly describe the "lawless, or unlawful act" of entering a country without legal authority in an unlawful intent to invade and colonize a host country's sovereign land. To prove this "unlawful act" is a crime against the sovereignty of any host country's people. In this case America's Compatriots, I decided to not view this crime through the rose colored lenses of what appears to be the United Nations' socialist agenda to destroy illegally America's Democratic created and established borders and sovereign nation status that are protected by America's Constitutional laws. This means that unlike "world-wide open borders" proponents, who appear to enjoy labeling "illegal immigration" as a victimless crime or small crime that doesn't hurt the host nation or its legal citizens, I am going to view this crime and this perverse term as nothing more than a sugar coated code word for the "lawless, criminal invasion, and colonization" of our established sovereign nation.

I hate to say it but, no matter how "world-wide open border" proponents sugar coat this lawless and criminal act of aggression, this lawless act of aggression is nothing more than a code word for the lawless aggressive act of invading any Republic that has a Constitution that protect its people, that are known as members of the "Republic." After all, this aggressive lawless act (and the perverse term that labels it) in reality is nothing more than a trick or excuse to allow hoards of foreign and lawless trespassers to enter a sovereign nation's land without permission, so these hoards of trespassers, who are really "criminal and unlawful invaders, can enter sovereign nations like Japan, France, or England (to name a few countries) and colonize these Democratic/Republic nations without the use or need of an army, or without the permission of the law abiding and legal citizens of any of these types of Democracies or Republics.

From my research, I learned these hoards of trespassing invaders, unfortunately for disillusioned Americans, are the Mexican Government's impoverished masses or second-class citizens that have always been a blight on Mexico's Government for hundreds of years, and now Mexico's Government has decided to get rid of this poverty problem by dumping this problem on the backs of America's taxpayers with what appears to be the blessing of America's Government. If the "open border" supporters say how dare I use the terms "invading, invader, or invasion," and even the term colonization to describe the lawless actions of these trespassers from Mexico, I simply answer how dare we not use the words invading, invader or invasion, and colonization to describe "the uncontrolled hoard of invaders whose numbers are so large they now continually "over-whelm" America's federal immigration officers on any given day. By swarming over and across America's Southern borders in a relentless flow day-after-day, these invaders know America's government is not going to stop them. And as we can see from the last sentence, these invaders are so lawless they don't ever try to acknowledge or yield to American Jurisprudence or obey any US laws.

Since I proved in the last paragraph that America's compatriots are not dealing with anything that remotely resembles the beautiful process that lawful and legal European immigrants were part of during America's 19th and early 20th Century industrial revolution, the task of this section in Chapter 2 will be to define the terms "invade," "invader," and "invasion" to prove and show these terms are the correct and more appropriate terms to chronicle the daily breaching and intrusions of America's borders by millions of foreign born invaders from Mexico and other countries who now understand America's Government does not seem to be in the business of protecting its citizens or its borders from any invader who wants to colonize American sovereign soil. By proving these terms are more appropriate to describe America's invasion problem, I'll be able to terminate the "open border" supporters' game of using the term "illegal immigration" to describe the breaching of America's borders.

My decision to use these terms that we all know are the correct terms for America's "criminal invasion problem now, allows me to look up the definition for the first term I've chosen: Okay, 1 will start with the definition for the term "invade." By looking up this word first, my readers will now learn that Funk and Wagnall's Dictionary says the senses or definitions that apply to America's border problems are found in senses 2 and 3 of this chosen word: "2. To rush or swarm into as if to occupy or overrun: Crowds invaded [businesses to loot them during the city blackout.] 3. To trespass upon; intrude upon; to invade privacy" ("Landau." Funk and Wagnalls Standard College Dictionary. Standard. Ed.1967). As my readers can all see now, both of these senses provide a better description of the actions the ex-Obama Administrations and all other open border proponents keep labeling as harmless groups of "illegal immigrants." Having proving my point, I think we can now see the crime these foreigners commit when they swarm across and overrun America's Southern border with the intent of invading and occupying US sovereign soil is a very dangerous act that is setting a very dangerous precedence for America and the world's countries' when they try to enforce and protect their borders.

Before I continue with the definitions for the terms, "invader" and "invasion," I want to remind my readers the perverse term "illegal immigrant" translates into the term "lawless or criminal immigrant." But if I use the most important synonym that was given to me by our English language thesaurus to replace the perverse term "illegal," as in "illegal immigrant," my readers and I find the most appropriate translation term to describe the lawless act of these invaders is the term "criminal," as in "criminal immigrant." Because I took the time to translate the perverse term "illegal immigrant" into two more appropriate terms that best describes what's really happening to America's citizens, I was lucky that I was able to show America's citizens that both of these terms describe people Americans would never want to welcome into their civilized nation. I make this solid and documented comment that America is a civilized nation because, as we all know, America is, and has always been, (at least when I was a boy) a country ruled by civil, criminal, and constitutional laws.

Next, I want to next note that the two synonyms I found to replace the term "illegal" not only describe Mexico's invaders better, but they both help me prove the term "invader" is the best word, or term, to describe and prove that Mexico's 20 million lawless trespassers are not immigrants at all. I can say this because the news reminds us on a daily basis that these trespassing invaders breach America's borders on a daily basis so they qualify to be called invaders or criminal trespassers as the English dictionary cites. After all, Funk and Wagnalls dictionary says the sense for the term "invader" is a "conqueror, trespasser, intruder, or a plunderer" ("Landau." Funk and Wagnalls Standard College Dictionary, Standard Ed. 1967.). As for the term "invasion," Funk and Wagnalls' dictionary uses a lot of negative terms to define this term in senses "3" and "4" of this term: Here is sense 3) "Encroachment by intrusion or trespass" and sense 4) "Entrance with intent to overrun or occupy." As my readers can see from these two senses, neither of these definitions provides a pleasant or positive description of Mexico's "citizen-invaders" because these invaders continue to overrun America's Southern borders without going through any legal channels. These occupying Mexican colonizers are hardly the law-abiding citizens ex-President Obama (and the "Open-Border" proponents) continued to champion during his presidency and also continued to ask Americans to accept his recommendation to give these people complete "amnesty."

If Obama thought Amnesty was such a good idea for Mexico's invaders, maybe he needed to read stories like the one I offer here for his edification that happened during his presidential run: In the mid 1990s, I was hired by Sun World Incorporated, a large Farming Coop located in Bakersfield, California to create a beginning English language Speaking course for their Spanish speaking employees. My job was to teach English using TEFL and TESL (Teaching English as a Foreign Language and Teaching English as a Second Language) methodology to this company's non English speaking Hispanic/Mexican employees so that Sun World could promote some of these workers from within the company. Although the students were asked to participate, they were not forced to take the course because the class was held right after work. At the beginning many students showed up because food was provided, extra pay was offered, and many seemed eager to learn English; unfortunately, their enthusiasm went down once they learned they had to work hard and study a lot to learn to speak and write the English language.

As time passed, one day, several of the students approached me (your author) and told me they would not be returning to class because they felt it was a waste of their time to learn English. After all, they all added, soon everyone in America will be speaking Spanish so you will have to learn our language. One student even took the time to confront me, and as he spoke, he pointed his finger at my chest and said, "We don't have to learn English; you need to learn to speak Spanish." With the arrogance of a conqueror, the middle aged Mexican male, that by his own acknowledgement admitted he was an illegal, stood up immediately after class was over and left the classroom and never returned.

I want to add the response of this illegal Mexican male (that had been offered a chance to become a part of the American fabric and culture), unfortunately, was not what I expected to hear or what ex-President Obama kept telling us these people were all about during his tenure. This Mexican male's response (a man who had broken the law to enter America and was being offered a chance to improve his life skills) was not an act kindness, graciousness, benevolence, or thankfulness for being allowed to break US laws and live in America without punishment; in fact, it was the opposite. I hate to say it but this man's response was more like that of a conqueror or oppressor, and in many ways foretold of the radical decree ex-President Obama made in one of his speeches during his run for president when he told Americans they needed to start learning to speak Spanish. Evidently, as we can all see now, ex-President Obama's speech was aimed at the 20 million illegal Mexican trespassers who are colonizing America and their financial supporters who more than likely helped fund President Obama's first election, and his re-election.

The last story I want to add under the discussion of the term "invasion" is the fact that Mexico's Army or Special revolutionary guard is being allowed to enter and function as a military force in the state of California, and although many sightings have been reported to California's politicians, no official response has been forthcoming from California's Government or politicians. To prove how prevalent these sightings have become, your author of this book (myself as a citizen) had two encounters of his own with this clandestine military forces that are evidently being allowed to roam the American state of California without government interference from California's Hispanic Attorney General, who on April 11, 2017 (on a local Television News Show) stated that all of Mexico's citizens should break America's Immigration law and come to California because he would protect them using the

State of California's laws to trump Federal Laws. This Mexican clandestine Military force, that as I said before, are called Juaristas by Mexico's invaders appears to be operating in Central California and is so embolden that it currently travels in military like caravans using white unmarked vans. One of these Mexican military men was so emboldened, I learned, that last year (2012), by the stand our California Government's has taken against the US Government, that he was seen wearing his Mexican Military Uniform at a local major grocery store in a Tulare County, California while he was shopping.

Before we move on to the next section, I want to add one more reason why I feel Mexico's soldiers, or special forces (and Mexico's colonizing invaders), have become so daring in California that they are willing to travel as a military caravan in broad daylight simply by using white unmarked vans. The reason for the boldness of these soldiers, I feel, appears to come from the possible fact that maybe Governor Brown and the left leaning legislature (That has been in control of the Democrats for over 40 years) gave Mexico's military permission to operate on US soil. After all, why else would these soldiers be so bold and not fear a confrontation with America's National Guard or US military? Sad to say, but I feel these soldiers might be in California to protect Mexico's Government officials who live and operate over 10 consulates in California (Note: There are small consulates in every city that has an airport that has an airline that serves Mexico to US arrivals). After all, We Californians know that California's government has quietly allowed Mexico to increase its Consulates to the recent number of over 10 consulates; remember the small ones in California airports. By the way, I've learned through research that allowing these many consulates in one US State, or as they say in Japan a prefecture, is allegedly unheard of in diplomatic circles. Most countries only allow one consulate per major city in a country's province, prefecture, or state. For example, Japan's Government has one consulate in Los Angeles and one consulate in San Francisco in the state of California not over ten and growing, and they have Japanese Citizens living in California too. One more point I want to make about foreign consulates allowed in California (or other nations) is that this land becomes a part of Mexico's land, or whatever country has a consulate on US soil. So, each time California's Democrat Controlled legislature approves another consulate for Mexico, Mexico gets another chunk of US soil to call its own.

D. OBAMA AND "amnesty" or FORGET
    "a criminal" ACT for tomorrow's VOTE.

In 2012, ex-President Obama went creatively wild formulating ways to implement immigration laws, or bills, his Executive Branch could write and pass without waiting for the Government's Legislative branch to exercise its Constitutional powers. And because ex-President Obama signed several laws he wrote into power, without going through what Americans consider the right Constitutional channels, he forced me to find information that would allow me prove that ex-President Obama did indeed appropriate some Constitutional powers that were not his to use and meant for America's Legislative Branch. Thanks to my research, I learned "the Legislative Branch has the power to write and establish rules of law for America's government, but not the president" (Grilliot, J. Harold and Schubert, A Frank, Introduction to Law and the Legal System. Houghton Mifflin Company. Boston: 1989 P 357). I also learned and discovered the "US Constitution says the Legislative Branch is the only one responsible for major changes that regulate American's lives and creates laws by enacting statutes that require Congressional approval at the federal and state level. However, even if these statute or laws pass, they can still run into various obstacles like being vetoed by the Executive Branch (a presidents real job in the law process), or being challenged in court" due to negative public opinions or demonstrations against the law (Grilliot and Schubert, Introduction to Law and the Legal System. H oughton M ifflin Company. Boston: 1989 P 355).

Now that I've shown that statutes and laws, up for approval, usually run into various obstacles during the approval process, I feel

America's legal compatriots can now figure out why ex-President Obama decided not to wait for America's legislative process to try to pass his controversial immigration law or statute that a majority of America's citizens were completely against, including this Native American author with Portuguese immigration roots. I want to note that I was against Obama's laws because unlike ex-President Obama I always put Americans first. With the information that most new laws always run into opposition, I feel America's Compatriots can now see and understand why ex-President Obama decided to not wait for Congress to write the laws he wanted and instead wrote his own laws and signed them into power by using his Presidential Executive Power. By using this controversial method of passing his immigration laws, ex-President Obama avoided taking a chance that his Amnesty law or laws, that he wrote to protect Mexico's illegal aliens (Later in this book, I show that one of the laws Obama wrote was really an illegal presidential pardon.), would be rejected by the checks and balances built into America's Constitution.

Unfortunately for Americans, ex-President Obama either didn't realize that his executive power didn't give him the right to override the Legislative Branch's powers, or he didn't care. I feel I can come to this conclusion because according to my research I found that President Obama knew exactly what he was doing when he avoided the checks-and-balances the Constitution's drafters wrote into our Constitution. And although I'm sure ex-President Obama knew he was breaking the law, I find it sad that he still went ahead and used his executive power to grant Amnesty to thousands of illegal aliens that were (and are) in reality an invading force whose act of aggression against the Republic's Sovereign Nation status is a deliberate act to colonize America. If America's citizens continue to allow these invaders to colonize their nation, I firmly believe that these invaders will someday, in the very near future, overwhelm and destroy America's Westernized Americana culture and replace it with their historically corrupt culture. Having introduced these facts, I feel America's citizens better be ready to fight for their country against their own Government in the very near future. If the US Government continues down the path that I'm disclosing on this book, I think Americans better be ready to demonstrate with massive crowds of millions Americans in front of both the White House and Congress' doorstep in the coming months and years to stop the invasion and destruction of American Sovereignty. As I close this paragraph, I can only pray that this fight will not become violent or end like it did on that fateful day of May 1970 on the Kent State Campus in Ohio.

In case my readers don't understand why ex-President Obama was willing to take the risk of breaking Constitutional law and getting caught breaking US Constitutional protocol, I feel I have the answer. I feel I can honestly say that I believe this president passed this controversial immigration law because it not only gave 800,000 Mexican invading colonizers (under the age of 30 and living in America) Amnesty, but it also created 800,000 (plus their friends and parents) alien invaders whose allegiance would, and will, always belong to ex-President Obama and the America's Socialist Democrats, and not the Republic. As I noted earlier in this book, ex-President Obama appears to be very adept at stretching Constitutional laws to his advantage, and in this case, it appears to have been to gain political points with Mexico's invading and colonizing force of lawbreakers.

Unfortunately for ex-President Obama, thanks to my research, I feel I just proved he not only disobeyed American Constitutional law, known as America's law of the land, but he also aided and abetted a group of alien aggressors of the US during his tenure by protecting Mexico's colonizing and invading force from prosecution by America's Constitutional, criminal, and Immigration laws. To back up my statement and accusations I just made, I feel this is a good time to look at the definition of the word or term "Amnesty" and discuss how the "concept of this law" was (and is being abused these days by current Supreme Court Justices and Socialist Democrat leaning politicians like Pelosi) misused by Obama to favor and appease America's Pro "Open Border" supporters like the Mexican Government (and other nations' invaders currently entering US Soil) and its 20 million (and growing) law breaking invaders.

In case you're wondering why a US president, America's Congress, and many state politicians are backing this invasion, let's just say it all goes back to a law that I proved exists in California's state Constitution. I add this statement because during my research I found out that many US universities all have chapters of something called MECHA, or Movimiento Estudiantil de Azatlan, which have been operating on US campuses since the 1960s. Although this movement or group sounds like any other college student's group, I know from personal contact and researched information that this movement is not what it appears to be on paper. Since I have a Latin or Portuguese background on my father's side of the family, I was often courted to attend the meetings of this campus group and was once given an award by this group without my knowledge to align themselves with my success as an American athletic school scholar. During the meeting I attended, I learned something interesting facts about this group (behind closed doors) that sent me running in the opposite direction: MECHA is a Chicano student movement that clings to the Azatlan ideal. This ideal basically says that the US Southwest is part of Mexico, and MECHA's job is to move into America (both legally and illegally) to reclaim Azatlan "the legendary ancestral home of the Aztec also known as the "Mexica." This new Mexica is allegedly located in what is now north of Mexico and includes the territory from Texas to Californian, which as I proved earlier in this book was bought for millions of dollars from around 1830 to 1890. I should note this group has some very notable alumnus like California's Lt. Governor Cruz Bustamante. I also want to note that this land is Indian land: "Always has been, and it will always be Indian Land."

Getting back to the word Amnesty, and before I discuss the definition of the term "Amnesty," I think Americans need to see a philosophical view of this term so they'll understand why I say ex-President Obama and ex-President Ronald Reagan both misused the "power" associated with the word Amnesty to appease Mexico's Government, America's Corporations, America's Big Farm Corporations (operating in states like California), and the Democrat's extreme left wing Political Party members. My fellow Americans should note these major American political powers appear to always support Mexico's invading colonizers so these support groups appear to not care if these invaders destroy Americana's Western Culture, her English language, or America's strong Christian bond with God's word. By the way, I am not preaching here, saying I am perfect or a man without sin because I know "none are without sin, no not one." So, I'm not preaching or selling God to those who don't believe.

Since the best place to begin (when we are defining English words) is their etymology, I want to first note that the word "Amnesty" comes from the Greek word "amnestia, which [Philosophically speaking] means literally forgetfulness. This fact leads me to point out that "Amnesty" is usually defined as a "concept of law that permits a head of state (like America's President) to overlook or forget offenses committed by "a person," or in this case a massive group of Anti-Vietnam War soldiers and US citizens who defied the draft and/or went AWOL during the Nam war, "or people against an authority [which] is customarily their government" (Dolan, F Edward, Jr. Amnesty: The American Puzzle. Franklin Watts. New York and London. 1975. p 3). Now that I have introduced a bombshell of information that basically proves these illegal aliens don't ever qualify for Amnesty, the next rational thing to do in my study of the word "Amnesty" is to answer questions like "What kind of offenses is the authority (the president) allowed to 'forgive' and whom can this authority forgive with this law's concept" (Dolan, F Edward, Jr. Amnesty: The American Puzzle. Franklin Watts. New York and London. 1975. p 3)? I am happy to say I am going to provide the answer to the questions in my last sentence of the next paragraph I present here:

Thanks to Edward F. Dolan, Jr., I've learned that "Amnesty officially 'forgets' acts that were branded as "criminal" at the time they were committed (Note the word for this act is criminal and not the word misdemeanor, as is the charge for "illegal entry into the US.), for example military deserters of the Vietnam war because they broke U.S. laws, and who did it as a political protest against the American Government's involvement in Vietnam. I should add, "Amnesty is almost always granted ONLY (my emphasis) to groups . . . and to segments of the public (This means the country's own citizens not foreigners who do not have these rights.) that rose [up] in political opposition to [their] government . . . [so] amnesty is a tool governments use to [forgive their] citizens whose offenses are based on honest opposition to laws and policies they find odious" (Dolan, F. Edward, Jr. Amnesty: The American Puzzle. Franklin Watts. New York and London. 1975. p 3-4). In the end, the problem with giving these foreigners who enter America illegally Amnesty is that Amnesty can only be given to America's legal citizens and not another country's citizens who break America's laws!

Now that I've cleared up how and when Amnesty should be used by our presidents or even our courts (if the courts had the power to grant amnesty), I feel I need to add that in reality both ex-President Reagan and ex-President Obama broke US Federal and immigration law. After all, neither President had the right or power to grant amnesty to any of Mexico's citizen invaders because none of these invaders are, or were, American citizens. So in realty, the only way these illegal invaders could have been granted Amnesty by either of these American presidents was if Mexico's invaders were (or had been) "AMERICAN" citizens who had committed crimes against America's government. What my fellow Americans should learn from this example is that neither of these presidents had (or have) the power to grant any foreigner Amnesty. In reality what these two US elected ex-Presidents really granted these foreigners was an act of wholesale Presidential Pardons that in reality were also against US laws because an American President can only use this law to pardon only a few people (Americans!) at a time:

So to summarize, unfortunately for ex-President Ronald Reagan and ex-President Obama, during their tenure neither of them had the power to grant pardons to the eight million illegal lawbreakers or to give "amnesty" to foreign law breakers of American laws, and I should add that President Obama didn't have the power to grant the 800,000 Mexican alien invaders Presidential pardons or Amnesty either. I'm sure they both knew that a pardon could only be used to . . ."forgive a guilty person's criminal offenses." In the case of Obama, he forgave the illegal intrusion or invasion of America's sovereign soil to thousands of illegal aliens and not just one of Mexico's lawless invaders or so-called illegal immigrants (Dolan, F. Edward, Jr. Amnesty: The American Puzzle, Franklin Watts: New York, 1976 P.3). Finally, no matter how we Americans look at the actions of these two rogue American presidents, they both appear to have misused laws meant to help our country's citizens and not some other countries' citizens that are on US soil trying to tell Americans they have the right to invade America and then colonize her sovereign soil because they decided to not follow or recognize America's Constitutional, Immigration, and criminal laws, or recognize America's sovereignty.

Before I move on, I want to add that I feel ex-President Obama and many so called American left wing patriots have more empathy for Mexico's mass group of lawless colonizing invaders than most Americans had in the 60s and 70s for the large group of American young men who left America to avoid the draft because they knew America's involvement in Nam was wrong. Although these young men walked away from military duty to protest the Vietnam War that divided America and pushed her to the brink of a civil war (remember Kent State's massacre), they were treated like they had committed treason. And, Less we forget, the Vietnam War cost the lives of over 57,000 young promising American men (my peers), who more than likely would have made better leaders than the ones we now have in political offices that used bogus medical excuses and their fortunate son status to avoid being drafted. This war also left America in so much debt, both financially and emotionally, that it took America and her citizens almost 20 years to recover from it both at home and in the eyes of the world. The sad and pathetic after math of this war is that Vietnam is now a Communist country, the French are back in Vietnam (The people who started this war because they were in Vietnam colonizing, and when they got in trouble, they asked America for help then left Americans holding the bag.), and America's government and her businesses are now trading with this country that was once our enemy (which is now a Communist Vietnam Government) like the war never happened. In the end, it appears the lives of all of the young American men and women were lost for nothing. In a word, they were American Politicians' political cannon fodder.

One more point I want to make as a minority male who lived through the turbulent and destructive years of the Nam war era is that I feel (as a journalists and survivor of this turbulent era) America's Government and politicians are treating Mexico's massive force of illegal lawless alien invaders (who continue to enter at alarming rate) better than they treated millions of young American men who demonstrated against their country's government (by burning their draft cards) during the Nam war era by either leaving America to avoid the draft or going AWOL from military service; however, when these young men came home after the war, they ended up being treated like animals and criminals for years before their Government finally decided to give them Amnesty. If my readers don't believe this statement, I suggest they go out and find the book on Amnesty and the Nam war titled <u>Amnesty: The American Puzzle</u> by Edward F. Dolan, Jr. and read it to see if I'm not right. If my fellow Americans don't want to bother reading the whole book, I suggest they only read Chapter 7 "The Ford Program" and see that Mexico's illegal invaders are being given Amnesty faster and easier (and illegally) than these young US Citizens were ever given Amnesty. The sad part is that these young men's only crime was that they disagreed with their government and acted on their beliefs by choosing to demonstrate, ignore, and disobey US draft laws (that I feel, as a novice historian, were used by glory seeking and higher rank seeking American life time military officers and US politicians to satisfy their egos).

For those young men too young to remember the fear of being drafted for the Vietnam war, Draft Boards, and the law that required all young men of draft age to carry their cards and present them when they were asked for them during induction, I hope these young men know how lucky they are to not have the weight of having their future plans controlled by some local Draft Board's decision. I also hope their future does not include a time when they will asked to serve in a meaningless war because they are being drafted to fight in this type of war: Note: A good possibility could be an unneeded war with Russia that many Americans feel is coming or looming on the horizon. I also want to note that if any illegal foreign young men think they will have the power to refuse to serve or just pick up and leave the country for places like Mexico, I suggest they read the back of their draft cards because, if nothing has changed, it more than likely has a statement that reads something like this... "This card should be carried with you at all times... and when asked to serve, this card must be surrendered at the time of induction... Failure to follow these laws can and will result in a fine of $10,000 (might be more in 21st Century) and/or a sentence of up to five years in a federal prison" (Note: To learn more, or inspect the new and current laws that apply to America's new draft registration guidelines, I suggest my readers contact the Federal Government's draft registration department.).

E. "COLLUSION" and the DIRTY WORD
    "treason" THAT HELPS DEFINE IT.

Why would an American President use America's military weapons that cost America's tax payers millions of dollars to support one side in four different foreign country's civil wars without the permission of Congress (needed according to war law) And, after he helped these groups win their so called wars for Democracy, why would this same president start sending millions of US tax dollars in financial aid to each one of these countries to build and fund four (at last count) Muslim controlled Nations by disposing of their so-called tyrant dictators, only to see these new countries replace the dictators with both Ayatollah Muslim Leaders and Muslim Clerics? And why, I have to ask, would an American President allow these new so called Democratic governments to put the countries under the rule of the Muslim Religion's Constitution, after he handed over control of these countries to the Muslim rulers that allegedly wanted to create Democratic Nations? And, unfortunately for the people who allegedly fought for and wanted freedom, they ended up with nothing more than another form of dictatorship that has "nothing" do with Democracy? Since these new Muslim controlled countries are not Democracies, as ex-President Obama and ex-Secretary of State Clinton promised Americans, why did the Obama Administration continue sending these countries millions of American taxpayers' dollars in financial aid during one of America's worst recessions since the "Great 1929 Depression," especially after one of these countries, Libya, allowed their Muslim faithful to overrun America's Consulate in Libya and kill four American diplomats and not one killer was ever brought to justice? What's even harder to imagine is that then President Obama never (during the time he was President) reprimanded Libya's Muslim leaders or said one cross word to any of the Libyan Muslim leaders or stopped their millions of dollars in cash aid during his tenure for not preventing this crime.

And, again, why would an American President take away our American Border Patrol Officers' military weapons that any knowledgeable American citizen would know these officers needed for self defense to confront and arrest possible terrorist entering America via the American/Mexican border? And after ex-President Obama removed their weapons, why did he order his staff to replace the Border Patrol's bullet firing weapons with bean bag firing weapons, which basically made these officers "a joke" in the eyes of Mexico's heavily armed drug cartels and hard core armed terrorists? This unforgivable act by the Obama Administration is why many

Mexican criminals were emboldened enough to follow and ambush a Border Patrol officer and shoot him dead. The worst part of this very stupid decision by a standing president was that even after the Obama Administration's actions got this officer murdered (which evidently showed a lack of knowledge by ex-President Obama of the dangers that exist on the Mexican and US border) the President decided to push even harder for a "carte blanch amnesty" for anyone entering America on this same border. I want to remind my fellow American that many Historians who study American History said that ex-President Obama's decisions would only lead to an even larger massive group of invaders entering America via the Mexican border. In closing this paragraph, I want to also remind my readers that ex-President Obama's Amnesty Bill did nothing to prevent or close America's border or stop the erosion of America's sovereignty. To prove I was right, I want to remind Americans that in December of 2018 and January 2019, a caravan of thousands of illegal aliens from Central America arrived on the Mexico/US border to demand they be allowed to enter America like Mexico's citizens are being allowed to enter. Can we say, "I told you this would happen to America?"

Although this section is going to deal with the definition and application of the words "collusion and treason," I decided to begin this section with four important questions I introduced in the last paragraph. When I wrote this book back in 2014, I hoped to entice America's citizens into asking the then Obama Administration why Obama's foreign policies (that I introduce in this book) literally favored or put the interests of other nations and their citizens above America's citizens and their safety? I asked this question because I felt the Obama Administration needed to answer these questions because all of this Administration's foreign policy decisions never achieved the results Obama told Americans they would achieve. I also want to add these policy decisions did not help Americans live in a safer world, as the current events in 2018 showed us in many news stories. After all, although then ex-President Obama said the freedom fighters were oppressed citizens fighting to topple the dictators in Libya and Egypt (to name two of the countries), when the alleged freedom fighters won the wars with the help of the Obama Administration's military intervention and American taxpayer financed support, these so-called freedom fighters ended up being mostly Muslims and Muslim Brotherhood members who put these alleged free nations under the controlled of the Muslim Religion and its leaders.

I should add here that after President Obama crushed these Muslim fighters' opposition, or dictators, these so called freedom fighters also quickly turned their new countries into Muslim Religion and Sharia law controlled nations. In the end, ex-President Obama's foreign policy not only helped build four new Muslim Nations, but his Administration's military support allowed and helped these Muslim Clerics to take control of some the world's richest oil fields in the world. This fact means that America is now at the mercy of Muslim Clerics that often call the US their mortal enemy when they don't get their way: I also want to remind my fellow Americans that at the time this book was being written (2013-14), President Obama also kept accusing Syria (Remember?), like Bush did Iraq, of using and/or having Chemical weapons because he wanted to get permission to use American tax dollars and the US military to again help another group that was being hailed as "freedom fighters" by Obama again. In reality, I hate to say but I think what ex-President Obama was really trying to do was help the Muslim Brotherhood (I mean freedom fighters) win another war so they could take control of another oil rich Nation like he did in Libya and Egypt.

I hate to say it but if America ever helps Syria's alleged freedom fighters that have been fighting a civil war in Syria to again take down another country's alleged bad dictator or president, I believe Syria will follow the same path as the other three or four countries the Obama Administration helped take down and turn into a Muslim and Cleric controlled so called Democracy. From all of the facts and results of countries like Egypt and Libya, I firmly believe they will become just another Muslim and Ayatollah controlled nation. Having made this bold statement, I believe we Americans need to ask ourselves as a country why ex-President Obama was so intent on helping create Muslim Nations in countries that the world knows has large oil deposits during his tenure as America's President? I want to add here that I have lived under many US Presidents going all the way back to when Ike was the US President, and to my recollection, ex-President Obama is the only American President that I can remember that has ever helped Muslims fight a war or used America's military and/or taxpayer dollars to fund a Muslim war against a country's government that ended up with Cleric Controlled Governments.

The other strange results that ex-President Obama's military and American taxpayer paid assistance created in these new Muslim controlled Nations appears to be a new negative and anti-democracy law movement in this part of the world that has only made the world more dangerous for US Citizens any Christian who might be living in these new Muslim controlled countries. I hate to say it but anyone with a little knowledge of Muslim law would more than likely have thought this might happen. After all, these anti-Christian (and others) results come right out of Muslim law and belief that are found in the "Muslim Constitution Law's that says, "any and all non-Muslim religious groups who also fought for freedom in these countries are now second class citizens." According to what I've read on web pages that present translations of the Muslim Koran, this edict comes from the fact that these non-Muslims have to live in the shadow of the Muslim Religion's Sharia Law. One more thing, according to revelations discussed and reported in recent news reports, this law appears to be nothing more than another kind of dictatorship which I feel many of these alleged oppressed people all fought to free themselves from and died for in this war. I am sad to say the freedom that ex-President Obama said they were all going to get was evidently a lie. The next point I want to make is that I heard our country was told in news reports by America's Fourth Estate that Americans should be thanking ex-President Obama for creating these new Muslim Nations (What?).

And less we forget, I feel the discussion of the murdered Border Patrol officer should be addressed one more time because his death came as result of ex-President Obama's decision to take away this officer's weapon and his peers. Although ex-President Obama's Homeland Security Secretary Janet Napolitano and the Obama Administration kept telling us the Mexican borders "were more secure now (when they were in power) than at any point in our History," An officer of the US Border Patrol was shot during their tenure as the leaders of this law department. Since I pointed out that ex-President Obama and his aids felt their actions were good enough to control the porous border, I have to ask this President and his staff this question: "If the statement they was true, then how and why did Border Patrol Agent Brian Terry (aged 40) get gunned down and murdered near Rio Rico, Arizona when he allegedly approached 5 suspects during his patrol of an area known for border bandits, drug smuggling, and violence?" And I have to ask again, why was this officer not armed with real ammunition on the orders of both Obama and Napolitano? Doesn't the murder of this Border Patrol Officer prove that the Obama Administration either didn't really know what was happening on Mexico's border, or they didn't care? And evidently, these two leaders never really knew (or cared) how dangerous having "open borders" was (and is) to America's citizens and its law officers during their tenure?

To close my argument, I feel I have to ask why did ex-President Obama (like ex-President Reagan) keep promising Americans that amnesty would help make the Mexican border (one of the most dangerous areas in America) safer and more secure for America's citizens if he was allowed to pass his law/bill that not only gave 800,000 illegal aliens amnesty and a free pass to stay in America, but it also opened the door for another 20 million law breakers to get a chance at amnesty in the future? Especially when I have presented facts that show the opposite results of what they said would happen if they got their way. So, I guess I can say the statements made by these two leaders in the paragraph above were not true. After all, didn't Ronald Reagan's 8 million Mexican invaders, that he gave Amnesty to during his presidency, turn into the current 20 million new illegal and lawless trespassing invaders of the 21st Century? And to make things worse, during ex-President Obama's tenure, didn't the new 20 million illegal trespassing invaders keep "demanding" that Obama use his power to pardon them, I mean, give them Amnesty (just like the 8 million illegal invaders President Reagan pardoned during his tenure)?

With all the troubling information I just presented here, I have to ask my fellow Americans they feel the billions of US taxpayer dollars that are spent to protect foreign countries and provide them with millions of US dollars in cash aid to buy favors and to get political promises from these foreign countries' leaders and religious groups (like the Muslim Brotherhood) are worth the alleged benefits that America's Citizens are supposed to get in return for their tax dollars (that are always sent overseas but in many ways never seem to materialize)? To make matters worse, I really believe that all of the money that's spent on these countries, unfortunately, never makes the world safer for Americans. And to say the least, if some benefits do appear to materialize, they never seem to be worth the high cost or sacrifices that America's taxpayers make. To prove the statement I just made, I want to show my readers some information, facts, and a few interesting contracts I found during my research that Americans do not know about. I feel these deals are worth looking into (And at the same time, I will discuss the terms "collusion" and "treason" because they apply here.) because they seem to work together, or go hand-in-hand. I also feel this information is important because, after all, these favors or deals our American Presidents and Congress make on the behalf of America's taxpayers always seem to end up costing America's taxpayers more than just their tax dollars. Some examples of these extra and unpredicted costs appear to point at the fact that America's current financial problems, America's current "open borders" and "security problems," and the current unemployment problems (or lack of American jobs being created in the US) that keep biting Americans on the butt are all connected, or related.

Continuing the line of thought I've just introduced in this section of my book, I want to point out that both present and past modern day American presidents continue to try to sell America's citizens on the idea that the only way to fix and save America's economy is by continuing to allow them to lower (sorry, I prefer the term "sell-out.") America's security standards and let the world run over US Citizens' rights and privileges that are found in America's laws and Constitution. The standards these administrations and presidents want to lower are our border protection laws, our immigration laws, and our Constitutional laws that keep America's sovereignty valid. Other quick fixes or magic elixirs that current and past American Presidents and Congress keep selling to America's citizens include asking US citizens to continue to allow (without financial penalties) America's Corporations to outsource America's manufacturing jobs to foreign countries and allowing foreigners to enter America illegally and be rewarded with the same privileges and rights as US Citizens. In return for these pro-foreign "open borders," foreign investment policies, and using American tax dollars to finance foreign countries our politicians tell us that America's corporations will get richer, pay more taxes, and create more jobs in America that will, according to US Politicians and US Administration, in turn provide more tax dollars and allegedly allow America's Government to invest in America's infrastructure, create more government jobs, and save the US. I hate to say it but doesn't this economic strategy sound a lot like ex-President Reagan's "trickle down economics" theories that, less we forget, didn't work during this 1990s. Since I'm updating this book, I want to add the Republican controlled Congress of 2018 appears to be taking a page out of Reagan's "trickle down economics," which could cost them the mid-term elections.

The job creation information (propaganda as far as I'm concerned) that I just presented (that talks about America's politicians letting America's corporations invest America's money overseas to build factories and make huge profits without paying US taxes to allegedly create more jobs in America), I'm sorry to say appears to be America's current foreign trade and jobs policy and it is not working (Note: This policy was changed in 2017 by President Trump and things are getting better.). A foreign policy that US Citizens can clearly see is not working for them, or in their best interest. And to make things worse and prove the facts I just presented here are true, I'd like to offer the following details about the kind of money these corporations are spending/investing overseas to create these jobs in foreign countries (but not America), and I want to point out the huge tax breaks these companies are getting from America's politicians and their lobbyists: On May 4, 2011, the Wall Street Journal wrote a story about how "Goodyear Tire Company was building a new tire plant worth 700 million dollars in a coastal city in Dalian, China" (Areddy, T. James. "In China, Fight Over the Secrets." The Wall Street Journal, 4, May 2011. Dow Jones and Company, final ed.: B1.). Yes, I hate to inform unemployed Americans but this huge tire plant that went up in China more than likely will provide the Chinese people thousands of jobs while Americans, again, get stabbed in the back twice. Please note that Americans get stabbed in the back by Corporate America once, because America's citizens lose more jobs overseas, and twice because Americans will more than likely be asked to pick up the check for the lost revenue by paying more taxes (think lost income tax revenues). The reason I know these US Corporations will not be paying their fare share of US taxes is reported in the next paragraph:

As for the profits and the taxes these US corporations are currently not paying this year in 2018, if Trump and Congress get away with the "DEAL" the Republican controlled house wants to pass, these American Corporations will not pay their fair share of US taxes. Having reported this key and very important fact, I want to report that Time Magazine published and reported in a story on January 14, 2013 that "America's companies are using "complex financial strategies, with nick names like "Double Irish" or "Dutch Sandwich," to transfer profits they earn overseas to other foreign countries with lower tax rates to avoid paying US taxes." With these facts on the table, I hope my fellow Americans now know the "DEAL" that Trump and Congress are trying to pass is one that would barely tax these huge profits that these American Corporations are making by sending their manufacturing plants to places like Mexico and China. I want to now ask my fellow Americans who pay their taxes every year, doesn't the hiding of earned income overseas by these corporations sound a lot like tax evasion to them? And, if these companies are committing tax evasion/fraud, why aren't these companies and their CEOs being charged with tax fraud/evasion by the Internal Revenue Services? One more key point I want to make also comes from the Time Magazine's article where it stated that according to their sources, "estimates say [America's] Corporations have some 1.7 trillion dollars stashed away in foreign countries and won't bring the money home unless America's Government won't tax this money." I want to note here that according to the Times: "Republicans have been trying to do this (Pass a "DEAL" to not tax these profits) for them for years (and now that Congress has Mr. Trump as a fall guy and possible stooge, they just might get their "DEAL.")." (Foroohar, Rana. "The Trillion-Dollar Home-coming: Giving U.S. companies a tax break on overseas profits won't help the economy." Time Magazine. 14, January 2013: 20.). After reading that America's businesses are making trillions of dollars overseas, sending jobs overseas, and not paying taxes on their windfall profits, Americans might be thinking and wondering why this kind of preferential treatment is not considered corporate tax fraud and treason against the Republic, or why America's Politicians or Government has not charged these companies with fraud and tax evasion, and why these politicians that are trying to help them have not been charged with some form of criminal offenses and collusion to avoid paying US taxes. Note: I am sure this act of not paying taxes on income is considered tax fraud and is punishable by prison sentences. After all, didn't the IRS send Al Capone to prison for not paying his taxes and for tax evasion in the 1930s?

By now my readers are probably wondering why the words "collusion" and "treason" are being included in my discussion of America' foreign and domestic financial policies and the current 20 million illegal Mexican trespassers living on American sovereign soil, let's just say I've discovered some possible monkey business deals or developments that I know I can prove were signed in clandestine fashion. And since these deals were signed in secret, they definitely reek of collusion and possibly treason by elected US officials on both sides of the political spectrum. One of these under the table deals I uncovered (thanks to a fellow muckraking journalist in Mexico) shows that America's government; Exxon-Mobil and Chevron-Texaco; Mexico's richest man, and the Mexican government all allegedly signed and approved a major oil deal that America's citizens were never informed about. As a reporter, I can only guess how much money this deal was worth to the parties who were involved and what the American Government gave up or promised Mexico in return for this oil deal: Maybe this is where America's current, and back breaking, open door policy of America's Southern Mexican border came from that allows all Mexican Nationals (and other South American countries) to enter American soil illegally and ignore US Sovereignty? Maybe this is why Mexico's Military gets a free pass to operate and live on American soil in the state of California without interference by either the US or California government?

In addition to discussing the clandestine oil deal I just mentioned, or introduced, I now want to remind my readers (recap) of the information I have about Mexico's military operating in California. I feel Americans need to know if it was the California's State Governor, the California's legislature (that's loaded with Hispanic/Mexican born (DACA children) representatives who appear to be very sympathetic to Mexico's colonizing efforts or illegal aliens), or the Obama Administration who gave Mexico's military or special forces legal (or behind closed doors) permission to operate in California in a clandestine fashion. Unfortunately for these politicians, during the past few years more than a few US citizens have reported seeing Mexico's military in California and they have all reported it to California's government (and to this reporter/ author) that, for all intensive purposes, either doesn't care or does not want to stop Mexico's military from operating in California. If this information is true, I believe these facts could lead to an armed confrontation between Mexico's military and some angry armed US patriotic citizens who might view these sightings as an invasion of their country.

The problem I see with an armed confrontation is that if ex-President Obama and the left get their way America's citizens won't have the firepower or the right weapons to defend themselves or their nation against these invaders that are living in California because of all of the new restrictions on guns ownership and gun ammo in California. After all, we Americans all know of the recent mass shootings in America by several crazy/angry persons are being used as excuses to take away any and all assault weapons away from honest and law abiding Americans. This act, I'm sure, will put US citizens at a disadvantage in a firefight with Mexico's military or any armed military that might decide to invade America in the coming years. I want to add that many of Mexico's invading males who now live in America often carry unregistered concealed weapons that include assault rifles and hand guns (with high round clips) and these people don't have US gun permits or have reported that they own these weapons. These men avoid the need for gun permits because they buy them in Mexico and bring them into America illegally. Note: On May 1, 2013, the California government passed a new law that gives them the right to confiscate any (even if the gun is registered legally) banned guns from America's citizens without due process of law, so much for Second Amendment rights.

The reason I know that Mexican illegal invaders have and carry these unregistered and concealed weapons is because they often take out their weapons on American Holidays (like New Years or Christmas) and use them to fire round after round into the air (a dangerous act because the bullets often come down and hit houses and wound citizens, as reported on local news in Fresno, CA). These lawless colonizing invaders fire so many rounds into the air that it sounds like a firefight in a war zone. Oh yes, they also use these weapons to threaten American citizens who dare to call the Police or local Sheriff on them (Note: one of my friends called local law enforcement on some of these illegal aliens and when the "officers" left these illegal aliens threatened his family with violence after the police left.) to complain about daily and constant loud Mexican Music or the illegal gun fire or illegal fireworks.

During my research gathering, I was told by several local officers that sometimes the music gets so loud the responding Sheriff's officers can hear the music from two miles away as they drive towards the house with the loud music. More often than not, these illegal Mexican men or partiers are so drunk and arrogant that they turn the music back up the moment the officers leave the premise. This means the officers have to come back again and get serious by finally threatening the partiers with disturbing the peace and legal action, or they just shut down the party. One officer told me during an interview the that Sheriff's department gets so many calls for loud Mexican music on weekend nights that they often can't respond to all them. Yes my fellow Americans, these are ex-President Obama's illegal alien trespassers that he often called law-abiding citizens on National News during his tenure as President. Note: I am going to be happy to provide more information about these Mexican lawbreakers later in this book. For Now, I want to remind my readers that America is a Republic and Democratic Society and this means the government cannot go behind the backs of America's citizens and make deals with oil companies, other countries, and rich tycoons without letting their constituents know about these deals or contracts.

I now want to say that American laws state the US Government cannot allow some other nation's military to operate on US soil without letting the Republic (American citizens) know about this situation because the Republic or people control this Nation's sovereignty and not the US Government. I also want to remind my fellow American citizens that America is both a Republic and a sovereign Nation. This fact means America's Citizens have the right to demand that the US Government has to provide them a Nation and Society that allows them live in a safe, peaceful, tranquil, moral, and law abiding Society. Now that I've established the fact (and proved it) that Americans have certain specific rights as American citizens that illegal invaders, visitors, and prisoners of wars don't have, I feel Americans need to remind America's government, politicians, and judges this means these Government Entities must use every law and guideline written into the US Constitution and Federal laws to protect these American citizens' rights. These entities also need to use any and all media out lets like television, radio, the web, public service ads, press releases, and immigration and criminal law pamphlets to educate any and all new legal visitors or immigrants that enter America. They also have a responsibility to arrest any and all persons who ignore or break US Constitution and Immigration laws when they enter US Sovereign soil.

As for the lawbreakers who enter American soil illegally, the US government has the responsibility to use any and all media outlets to inform these lawless invaders of the fines (a law that Congress should pass) their home nation will owe America's citizens, and inform them of laws of deportation for all illegal criminal aliens and undocumented illegal alien invaders who enter US sovereign soil. That's right; I feel the illegal invaders' home country should have to start paying fines for the Republic's costs of supporting these illegal aliens on American taxpayer dollars. And finally, I believe that all legal immigrants and illegal alien invaders should be educated about America's Western Christian morals and standards, her cultural standards, and her Civil Laws that make America a law abiding and civilized nation that they want to be a part of by entering US soil. These Public Service Announcements should be broadcast on all Spanish speaking TV and Radio stations that are operating on US soil and under the control of the FCC's rules and regulations (America's Federal Communications Center for licensing and broadcasting).

By fulfilling its duties, that include stopping all lawless colonizing invaders from entering US sovereign soil, America's government will not only end our border crises but it will also send a message to any future trespassers of American soil that these illegal aliens do not have the power or right to come into America and threaten, disrupt, and bully America's citizens into submission, or ignore American Constitutional and Immigration laws. The US Government also needs to make sure the corrupt Mexican Government knows (or any nation with trespassers in America) it can't protect their invading Mexican citizens by sending their military into America just because their lawbreaking citizens are living in America. After all, when Americans travel overseas to foreign countries, the US Government pays for ads that run on military controlled radio stations that constantly remind America's citizens to respect the citizens of the host country they are visiting, to obey the foreign countries' laws, and to respect the cultural standards of the country they are visiting so they won't disrupt the lives of the host country's citizens (or offend the foreign Nation's government). To conclude my suggestions I have for our US Government, I want to say that I find sad that Americas Government does not hold these lawbreaking and colonizing invaders to the same standards in America as that they expect America's citizens to live up when they are in other countries.

Finally, I want to begin this paragraph by stating that in April of 2013 I was channel surfing on TV and found a Spanish program that I'm sure America's Federal Communications Commission (FCC) would have consider an X-rated sex material program that was being broadcast during primetime on Network, non-cable, Spanish TV. What I saw was so upsetting that I took a photo of the screen as evidence to send to the FCC, and possibly publish in this book as evidence to show that the FCC is not doing its job of protecting our children when it comes to Mexican/Spanish broadcasting stations that are operating on American soil. In case my readers want to know what I saw on my TV on this day, I guess I can say that I saw a man holding a lady who had very little clothes on her body. Since this women was sitting in the man's arms and dressed in her see through night gown and panties, in a way that her baby factory and her camel toes were in full view for the TV audience, the author came to the conclusion that evidently foreign television stations were not held accountable for the content of their TV programs by America's FCC. By the way, this is the same FCC that watches US broadcasters like "a hawk watching a mouse on our San Joaquin valley floor" for any offensive material that (allegedly) America's kids might see.

As for Spanish radio stations, I have also noticed that many of the Mexican/Spanish FM "radio" stations operating in Central California usually crank up their broadcasting power higher than they're allowed to by the FCC. These radio stations pump out so much power they often interfere with the English Speaking radio station's broadcasts because the run over on the same frequency as the English Speaking radio station. Yes, even though radio stations are supposed to broadcast on different wavelengths and different broadcasting call letters, these Spanish radio stations overpower English radio stations every day of the year and nothing is done about it by the FCC. After pointing out these infractions that Spanish television and radio stations are committing on US soil, and not getting fined or stopped from broadcasting over US airwaves, I've come to the conclusion that evidently the FCC has a double standard that is more lax for Spanish radio and Mexican TV stations so as not to offend them. Maybe this double standard will end after this book is published, which I hope will help stop these pirate like Spanish station TV and radio broadcasters.

Now that I have introduced what either the American Government, the California Government, and maybe both government entities appear to be doing behind the backs of their citizens (because they apparently okay these lawless acts and deals), I think this is the perfect time to introduce one of the terms that I feel deals with these kinds of secret agreements or business deals. The definition that I feel fits the term that describes these illegal deals was found in Funk and Wagnalls Standard College Dictionary. This English dictionary states that, "collusion" means a secret [deal] that's created for a wrongful purpose, especially between persons wishing to defraud another [as in America's citizens] ("Collusion." Funk and Wagnalls Standard College Dictionary. Text: Ed. 1967.), and to which Funk and Wagnalls edition of Webster's New World Thesaurus adds this information about the term "collusion": This noun's main synonym is the term "conspiracy" (Laird, Charlton, and Wiliam D. Lutz. Webster's New World Thesaurus: Funk and Wagnalls Edition. Simon and Schuster, Inc: New Yoork, 1971.), which we Americans all know means a hidden deal between several or more persons who intend to break the law. To be more exact, Funk and Wagnalls' Thesaurus says that the term "conspiracy" is applied chiefly to major crimes, [for example] a conspiracy to betray one's country," like for example our US Government's alleged illegal deals (that I stumbled on with the help of a great reporter from Mexico) that America's citizens were never told about, and I am about to discuss in full depth in the next few paragraphs. I hate to say but instead of creating the Mueller conspiracy theory investigation of the Republican party and President Trump, I feel they should be looking in the collusion I am disclosing in this book

If America's citizens knew that some of their politicians, and evidently their government too, were illegally creating and signing secret oil deals that were signed by Mexico's President and government, Chevron-Texaco and Exxon-Mobil, and over 30 large banks and/or corporations, I have to ask would they be happy to know their Politicians were using collusion to make oil deals behind closed doors? Would America's Citizens care? Would they be happy if they knew these alleged deals included or contained possible promises that America's Government would basically turn their head and allow any, and all, of Mexico's citizen/invading colonists to enter America's sovereign soil illegally and allow Mexico's Military to operate on US soil? Would they be happy if they knew these illegal deals were worth millions of dollars to America's banks, major oil companies, and US Corporations who keep sending their manufacturing plants and American high paying jobs into Mexico, where they pay poverty like wages? After Americans read the alleged facts I am about to introduce and report here, I hope and pray that my fellow patriotic will ask for some answers and that they will get mad as hell and finally want to know why their country's real and legal immigration and Constitutional laws are being thrown under the bus in the 21st Century by every American Administration that takes power, because they all appear to have all sold out to America's oil companies and corporations. Note: I feel I can come to this conclusion because more than likely these oil companies all bankroll the election and re-election of these Presidents and their parties.

So why do I believe the US Government allegedly threw America's Constitutional and Immigration laws under the bus to help Mexico's Government appease their citizens when they learned Mexico's Government had given up the income from their Nationalized Oil fields to America's Corporations? Well, let's just say I found some information that proves a Mexican journalist caught their (Mexico's) president and their Government handing over their Nation's energy industry to both America and Spain's Governments, and I am sorry to say this critical (appears to be) secret information (of an oil deal) dates back to when America's very own President Clinton signed NAFTA into power. I hope Americans remember NAFTA because I truly believe NAFTA is one of the key reasons, or one of the corner stones, of why America now has over 20 million illegal invaders waiting around for some American President or a new Congress to give them Amnesty; and if this happens, there will be soon be a millions more illegal aliens running to the Mexican/US border so they can be next in line to get Amnesty. And if this happens, I guarantee they will destroy America's Western Christian culture within a few years, instead of in the coming years.

I want to note that in the last paragraph I introduced some accusations that I'm about to prove to be facts by using the results of my research, experience, and good old honest observations that this author and a good Mexican Muckraker and reporter discovered and published to get some help from people like me. The first fact my fellow journalist and I found in his research was the fact that all of the information pointed out that America's Government was involved in an alleged secret deal whose details were never explained or exposed to America's or Mexico's citizens. This oil deal, I'm sorry to say, appears to have been only a small part of several deals that Americans were never told about because the deals were never even reported to them by America's Fourth Estate (America's media giants that are now all over President Trump). I hate to say it but in many ways I believe we Americans can actually say this deal had all the makings of a conspiracy deal whose details evidently were never supposed to have been seen by America's citizens (or reported to them). Fortunately, thanks to the Mexican (Hero) reporter and your author's research skills, the facts of these deals are about to be reported in this book for the first time. I want to add that after reading these facts, I hope that my fellow American citizens will understand why their country is changing before their eyes and why their jobs are leaving America:

The details I am talking about, that according to Manuel Perez-Rocha, our Mexican Muckraker reporter who uncovered this deal, included the "future privatization of PEMEX, which is Mexico's National Oil Company" that has always been owned by Mexico's Citizens; however, unfortunately for Mexico's citizens, they have never seen a penny of the money. I want to note that most Mexican citizens that were against this deal believe this privatization was lead by Mexico's President Calderon because of a "promise

President Calderon made to America and Spain for putting him into power in 2008 with their money" and helping Calderon complete this oil deal . . . [with the help of some powerful business leaders] "like allegedly Carlos Slim, [who stands to benefits from these kinds of privatization schemes]." Perez Rocha, the Muckraker Reporter, then added this oil deal also allegedly helped "the . . . Mexican banking system [who was also part of this oil deal], because the deal was allegedly sold by Mexican bankers to a few U.S. and European firms (mainly Citicorp, BBVA, Santander, and HSBC), which were allegedly bailed out by the Mexican State . . . [using] funds that came from PEMEX." Perez Rocha then added, "The results [of this bail out] for these banks were an increase in earnings of 316 percent from 2000-2006" (Perez-Rocha, Manuel, "The Future of Mexico's Oil: Social Action to stop the energy grab." Online Posting: 17 March 2008.)

Now that my fellow Americans can see and understand how this clandestine oil deal went down and connects America's corporations and oil companies to it, my next step will be to show how and why America's so called moral Government is allegedly involved in a deal that, as we'll all see, involves collusion. I also want to show why America's Government helped broker this silent and secret deal. To provide this information, I will quote my fellow muckraker Manuel Perez-Rocha because as he says, "This information should have been released to Mexico's population," and as far as I'm concerned it should also have been released to America's citizens. Perez-Rocha makes this recommendation because this oil deal involves "the riches of his nation . . . [and because this] oil belongs to Mexico's citizens." "The idea or fact that this "Secretive Security and Prosperity Partnership (known as an SSP) agreement even exists, and was an arrangement between Canada, Mexico, and the US, [and the fact that it was signed] by presidents Bush, Fox, and Martin [I feel shows this contract] was nothing more than a... [a deal that was set up] to satisfy the US's oil addiction," added Perez-Rocha in his report that is posted on line at this address:

Perez,-Rocha, Manuel, "The Future of Mexico's Oil: Social Action to stop the energy grab." Online Posting: 17 March 2008.

Since this oil deal was allegedly set up to satisfy America's oil addiction, the next logical step I will take will be to disclose the major American companies that signed on to this corrupt deal that basically sucks away both the oil and money that belongs to Mexico's citizens, and sends all of Mexico's oil to American oil companies. And if my fellow Americans look closely at this clandestine deal, I feel my fellow Americans will find, according to Perez-Rocha, that " . . . the 30 companies that control and profit from the North American Competitiveness Council (NACC), a non-democratic appointed or instituted group of companies that not only control Mexico's oil but they also make decisions that affect Mexico's future. These groups, Perez-Rocha said, "includes oil giants Exxon-Mobil and Chevron-Texaco, [the NACC], and the previously mentioned companies and banks (like Citicorp) who are part of this oil grab in Mexico," and more than likely are part of the group of companies that are forcing America's politicians and Government to keep Mexico's borders open so that Mexico's citizens and their Military (that evidently might have been given permission to patrol in California by California's mostly Hispanic state legislature) can enter and live on US Sovereign soil illegally. And finally, this deal allows Mexico's Government to have all of those Mexican consulates in California so Mexico's Government can protect their citizens living illegally on US soil. All of these favors, from what I found in Mr. Perez-Rocha's article evidently might be payback for the money and oil, and "the power of dictating the rules for Mexico's oil and how Mexico's income from the oil sales will be used," says Perez-Rocha (Perez-Rocha, Manuel, "The Future of Mexico's Oil: Social Action to stop the energy grab." Online Posting: 17 March 2008.).

Before I conclude this section of chapter two, I want to remind my readers that collusion usually goes hand-in-hand with the term "treason." After all, if America's politicians are willing to be corrupt enough to allegedly make secret deals with foreign countries who use the deals to cause problems and do harm to America's legal citizens (like dumping a foreign country's poverty problems on the backs of America's taxpayers), then these politicians either don't care about their constituents, or they don't care about their honor or allegiance to America and/or where they should stand in the eyes of their fellow countrymen. And, if these US politicians are corrupt enough to make deals with other corrupt foreign politicians who use these kinds of secret deals (with US politicians) to fill their foreign pockets with US tax dollars and get special considerations for their citizens, then we should accept the fact that America's politicians have somehow, or have allegedly, decided to betray their allegiance to the Republic, which is treason. After all, doesn't the definition for the term "treason" say that treason is "an offense against the duty of allegiance; levying war against the United States . . . and giving them ([foreign governments]) aid and comfort," [which is what I just reported about these greedy and treacherous American politicians] (Grilliot, J. Harold, and Schubert, A. Frank, Introduction To Law and The Legal System. 4th Ed. Boston. 1989: P 652).

The final statement I want to make about the word "treason," as it applies to modern day politicians who appear to be busy making alleged secret deals, can be found in this sentence: "If these politicians are allegedly corrupt enough to make closed door deals with greedy and corrupt corporations who use these kinds of secret deals to earn record profits overseas, then why aren't these corporations being required to pay taxes on these profits?" The answer to this question is simple: These politicians have evidently fixed America's tax codes to favor America's corporations so they don't pay taxes on these windfall profits. And, I guess the reason politicians give these American corporations tax breaks can be summed in the following sentence: They do it because these corporations more than likely, or allegedly, helped finance their election campaigns and helped them get elected or re-elected. Which begs the question, how can these arrangements not be considered a breach or betrayal of these politicians' allegiance towards America's citizens, government, and the Republic's sovereignty? After all, the definition for treason says that it is "an offense against the duty of allegiance" (Gilliot and Schubert, Introduction to Law and The Legal System. 4th Ed. Boston. 1989: 652).

Since these kinds of alleged secret deals are often brokered by America's Politicians to help those who helped them get into office, these kinds of deal usually do not (and almost never) help or improve the quality of life for America's legal patriotic and taxpaying Citizens. Having said this, I guess I have to say that we Americans must conclude that these secret deals are not in the best interest of the American Republic. And since together, my readers and I have learned that these deals often appear to give aid and comfort to corrupt and sometimes dangerous foreign governments and their military like a colonizing and invading force of foreign citizens, I feel we Americans have to come to the conclusion that some of America's modern day politicians have decided to betray their country and their constituents and replace them with foreign citizens who will be indebted to them (and vote for them) because these politicians have made it possible for these invaders to enter America without legal immigration processing as required by America's Immigration Laws.

After all, I think we can all see that to this day Mexico's and other South American foreign citizens continue to enter America by trespassing and swarming across her borders by the thousands. And although these millions of trespassing illegal citizens have made their intentions of replacing America's Compatriots and their Western Christian Culture with their own cultures in beachhead states like California, America's politicians ignore this threat and instead keep telling America's citizens that these invaders are here to help them and to become law abiding American citizens. But, how can Americans believe these politicians when these Mexican colonizing invaders are forcing America's California citizens to use their tax dollars to print all government forms and press releases in Spanish and this even includes California's welfare applications forms? Instead of using English or learning English, these colonizing invaders are now acting like they have the right to force Spanish on Americans and have the right to fly their Mexican flag over their houses and businesses (as the photos in this book show) instead of the American Flag known as "Old Glory." In case you missed it, the act of displaying and flying the Mexican flag by these illegal Mexican citizens showed up front and center at this year, 2019, Rose Parade when a Mexican stood up and started waving a huge Mexican flag when the camera was turned in his direction. The only reason he sat down was because a Los Angeles Sheriff came over and told him to sit down and to stop waving the Mexican flag. Yes my fellow Americans and Californians, these two government entities passed a law that says Spanish must be used in California even if English is America's and our culture's language of choice. And to make things worse, during the Cinco de Mayo (May 5, 2012) Mexican holiday in our city of Porterville, California, when the US flag passed down our home town's Main Street, the local invading Mexican illegal aliens went so far as to "hiss, boo, and remain silent as America's flag and color guard went by them. But when the Mexican flag passed by these same invaders, they exploded into cheers and yelling "Viva Mexico" (Long Live Mexico).

By the way, I can prove this "un-American," Anti-America" law, or attack on Americanism would not have happened in the America I grew up in the 50 and 60s because old Social Science (History) books often state that Americans often helped the new legal immigrants of the Ellis Island era become "Americanized" after they were allowed to enter America legally. Here is what the old books stated about the act of Americanization of new immigrants through use of community involvement: "Americanization . . . is an earnest attempt that has been made both by the public educational authorities and by private organizations to **Americanize** these people [(legal immigrants)] by helping them learn the [English] language, obtain a working knowledge of American history, become [legally] naturalized, and to acquire a proper concept of American

Democracy . . . [so these foreigners can earn their place in America and like] citizens of the United States enjoy certain privileges and immunities by virtue of their citizenship which are **not extended to aliens,,,**". I want to add that we should note these civic duties were set up to insure that when America was under attack (or at war) the rule of our Democracy that basically asks its new and old citizens to serve America would be accepted by these new Americans: "It is the duty of the citizen to serve his government when he is called upon. This may take the form of military service in time of war, or service in public office, or serve on a Jury. I say this [because, after all,] it is more blessed to give then to receive" (Munro, William Bennett, Social Civics: Our Democracy in Action, The American School: Chicago, 1960. 3rd ed.). I want to end the discussion of American Ideals in this paragraph by saying that American civic duties in these book basically said foreigners should learn English, not Americans learn their languages or to ask the government to accommodate a possible invading force of illegal alien trespassers.

These trespassers or illegal aliens that are pampered by the Democratic Party and Hollywood elites, I want to note, evidently have decided that since they do not have to obey America's Constitution or Immigration laws they have the right to fly the American flag upside down (A Federal crime, unless they're a US citizen and need life and death help.) anytime they feel slighted or insulted (There are many photos to prove this statement, but I decided to not to show them because they make me too angry.), yet ex-President Obama and Congress never dared file charges against these so called "illegal immigrants" during his Administration's tenure. Finally, I want to add in the state of California these illegal trespassers have decided to wear t-shirts that declare their desire to over throw America and justify their claim to California (Note: According to statistics, for every 1000 Americans that move out of California, 2000 illegal Mexicans cross the border to replace them, so California is headed towards becoming 100 percent illegal Mexican Citizens.) because the populations in many cities in California are now almost 90 percent lawless illegal alien

Mexican colonizers. Don't worry, I've provided photos of a young Mexican and Hispanic adult wearing one of these t-shirts around town in my book for America's edification. I would like to suggest that ex-President Obama put all of the information in the last three paragraphs the next time he decides to come out of retirement and tell us American citizens how much his illegal trespassers love America.

Before I close the discussion of this topic, I'd like to add one more reason why I feel America is in financial trouble. After I completed this research, I remembered some foreign "Bullet Train" expenses that I had incurred while I was traveling and living overseas in countries like Japan, and some other foreign countries. The ticket costs for these Bullet Trains were so high that they made me wonder Why ex-President Obama and California Governor Brown (and now evidently even President Trump and the Republican controlled Congress) were both spending trillions of US tax dollars to build these types of expensive trains that have very expensive ticket prices? I also remembered learning the cost to build these trains were so high it made me wonder why Obama and Brown decided to build such expensive Bullet train systems during one of the worst American recessions/depressions in recent US history and since the Great Depression of 1929? Finally, I wondered why some other less costly trains, like commuter trains I used in Japan, were not chosen to be built instead of the more expensive Bullet train systems I have used overseas? After all, from my experience, I know for a fact that most American families will more than likely not be able to either afford the tickets to travel on these high dollar trains, or they will not want to spend this kind of money to travel on them once the Bullet trains are put into service in the future because, like in Japan, many times flying by jet is much cheaper or economical.

To prove my point, I want to present an example of a trip an average American family might decide to make to let's say visit grandmother and grandpa. Would this family pick the train or the air to travel for this visit? After all, from my personal experience, I found that it was cheaper to travel by air than train most of the time in Japan for business. I hate to say it, but for all the hype ex-President Obama and Governor Brown have released to America's Fourth Estate (also known as Network News), neither of these politicians have bothered to explain or inform Americans that their bullet train's tickets are going to be "very" pricey, or shall we say "EXPENSIVE." How does the author know this fact, when neither of these politicians has informed the public about the future costs of these train's tickets? My answer is simple: I have lived and traveled in several countries that have bullet trains so I know how much the tickets for these trains cost on a day-to-day basis. Having made this revelation, I want to now provide an example of the cost of a train ticket for one of these Bullet Trains that evidently, or possibly, neither of these spends crazy politicians have either never bothered to use when they were overseas, or since the didn't pay for the tickets, they are not aware of the costs associated to travel on these bullet trains.

To begin the discussion of my example, I'll help my fellow Americans look at some costs of train tickets to travel on Japan's bullet trains, known as the Shinkansen, from let's say Tokyo's main train station in Tokyo to Fukuoka's main train station in a Prefecture also called Fukuoka. I want to note this train trip is comparable to taking a train trip from let's say Santa Barbara to San Diego, California. This trip would take about five hours each way by bullet train in Japan and would cost around $475 US dollars for the round trip per person. In our American trip example, let's say we were going to make this trip to visit grandmother in San Diego and we were starting out from Santa Barbara as a family of four. Since we are using the $475 cost per ticket to find the net cost of our trip for our family of four, the cost I'm sad to say would add up to about $1900 total for our family of four: "$475 X 4 = $1900. Can I ask my readers how many of my readers would be willing to spend this kind of money to visit grandmother, when my readers know they could take a local jet service (like Japan Airlines in Japan that offer lower prices, or Southwest airlines in the USA) that would take them less than two hours to make the same trip each way, and the cost would more than likely be about $130 per person or (Southwest airlines in America recently offered a $69 per person one way ticket price offer) only $552 for a family of four. I can only guess, but I believe most families would take the jet over ex-President Obama's and Gov. Brown's slow and costly bullet trains, or take their own automobile. By the way, the costs I mention here are about the same in China or Europe for bullet trains. But, I want to add that the costs fluctuate during heavy travel times like the holiday season in some of these countries.

Now that I've educated Americans on the future cost of traveling on Obama's and Browns' future costly Bullet trains, I have to ask my fellow Americans who are these costly travel trains really being built for in America? After all, I recently heard from some reliable sources that Obama and Brown always knew they were going to have to use taxes, bonds, and grants to build their future cash albatrosses/money pits, I mean bullet trains. My readers should know that I found the following information hidden in a study requested and published by a Senate Select Committee on Central Valley Economic Development in California: "The Authority [(California High Speed Rail)] is considering several methods of funding the project [(high speed rail)], including a sales tax increase, motor vehicle surcharges, private investment (hasn't happened), and airport facility charges" (Umbach, W. Kenneth. "San Joaquin Valley Selected Statistics on Population, Economy, and Environment." Unpublished Essay: May 2002 Pp 47). I want to further note that nothing has ever been said about the trains providing the income or revenue needed to pay to keep these trains operating. Since I have lived in Japan, I would like to point out that many trains and railroad companies are often owned and financed by large corporations in Japan and not the government. I also want to note that the bullet trains and Japanese airlines are always competing for Japan's city-to-city travelers and foreign tourists, and if the trip takes more than 3 hours (most of the time) the Japanese traveler take the airline over the train, including me your author.

Speaking on behalf of America's taxpayers (and as a man who practically lives in Japan) who are tired of being the politician's and US Government's piggy bank, I truly believe we Americans feel we don't need this costly future "ghost train" of empty rail cars running through America or in states like California. I also believe we Americans do not want this albatross (I mean Bullet Train) hung around our necks so we can subsidize this trillion-dollar project in perpetuity. I think I can say the future does not look good because I honestly see the US and California governments handing out travel vouchers, or more than likely free tickets, to low income families and/or Mexico's lawless and colonizing invaders so Mexico's citizens living in the USA can travel on the Obama bullet train to visit their relatives. Having said this, I want to add that I might be wrong and there is a purpose for this bullet train, but I doubt it. After all, after these trains are put into service, maybe American's taxpayers won't mind helping Mexico's lawless invaders get to the Mexican border in record time to visit their relatives in Mexico courtesy of America's taxpayers and America's Politicians.

F. DEFINING "collusion" & "treason," part 2:
    "President Obama's" CONNECTION.

Now that past ex-President Obama has saddled America's taxpayers with his costly trillion dollar bullet train, saddled us with billions of dollars of debt in financial aid to help the four new Muslim Nations, and saddled us with billions of dollars in stimulus packages that are, or were, allegedly used for infrastructure improvements and repairs, I guess we will have to wait and see if America's taxpayers will continue to support ex-President Obama's tax and spend shopping spree he created to support his new Modernist America; or will they buy this book, read it and get mad as hell and finally say enough to the US Government and Presidents who think and spend like Obama? Will Americans demand that Presidents like Obama and Congress explain why they won't close the Mexican border? Will they also ask why the US Government almost granted 20 million Mexican invaders an illegal or unlawful Presidential Pardon that they keep labeling or calling Amnesty? Or will Americans have enough of this status quo and finally demand that Presidents like Obama finally explain why his administration never bothered to disclose the details of the Mexican oil deal I discussed in this book? Will Americans finally ask why ex-President Obama used America's military and money to try to build yet another Muslim Nation in Syria that might end up like Libya's Muslim controlled Government (and ask why the Trump Administration is also pushing to create another Muslim Nation in Syria?)?

Maybe it's time we use the terms "collusion" and "treason" to describe the ex-Obama Administrations' and Congress' actions (and the current Trump Administration and Republican controlled Senate) that favored Muslims and Mexico's colonizing invaders in so many ways during ex-President Obama's Administration reign. Although I can't list all of the favorable actions this administration provided these two groups, I want to assure my readers I am going to discuss a few in detail. After all, the word "collusion" appears to fit this ex-President's remarks that he made during his last year of his tenure, which was the fact that he was willing to use America's military and tax dollars, with Congress' blessings, to help the Muslim rebels in Syria again because the news kept telling us the Syrian Government might be, or had been using allegedly chemical weapons on the rebels and their allies. Since Americans have heard this "song and dance" act before (Remember when Bush sent our war machine into Iraq, and found "NO" chemical weapons?), I have to ask past President Obama and current President Trump why they are both so intent on helping these Muslim invaders or freedom rebels, as they like to call them, by using America's military and tax dollars? What is America's connection (or un-known allegiance) to these Muslim Rebels that our Presidents are willing to spend millions of US tax dollars to support these anti-American Muslim nations (think 4 dead US consulate workers) that always show their true colors the moment America's Government does something they don't agree with because it goes against their religion's standards?

To make things worse, before Obama left office, he created 20 trillion dollars of US debt, and he kept asking for permission to create more debt before he left office, which he knew he was going to leave for our children when he left office: Note, when Obama left office, he was worth 10 million dollars even though his income as the US President was only been about $400,000 per year. I find this amount strange because on his income as our President, Obama should only have left office worth, at the most, around $3.2 million dollars after eight years of being in office. If my math is correct, I have to ask the question, "Where did the extra millions of dollars in income come from? I know from reading Obama's personal history that he said his net worth, when he was elected as President, was only around $800,000. According to my math, I feel the most ex-President Obama should have been worth when he left office (even if he saved every dollar he made over 8 years in office) is about 3 million 2 hundred thousand dollars ($3,200,000.00) before taxes. Still think being an American politician doesn't pay money that Americans will never know about or where it comes from? I should add that almost all Congressmen and women leave office worth 30 to 40 million dollars or more on yearly incomes of about $185,000 per year. Must be nice to rack up 18 or even 20 trillion dollars in US tax payer's debt then leave America's taxpayers holding the debt while in office (like President Obama did), and then leave office worth 10 to 30 million dollars on incomes of $400,000 to $185,000 per year as an American Politician. And you thought these politicians really got into politics because they wanted to serve their country and countrymen. It pays to serve special interests and foreign governments while in office to serve America, doesn't it!

As I said in the last paragraph, by using American taxpayers' money and our US Military power, ex-President Obama not only helped so called freedom fighters in Libya and Egypt (etc) but he also helped create several Muslim Nations in countries that have always had massive oil deposits that are now in the control of these Muslim Cleric Governments. If these are the results that this ex-President (Obama) was shooting for in the Middle East, then the results of his expensive intervention speak for themselves. I hate to go out on a limb here but these results should really scare the crap out of Americans who love to drive their big V8 powered trucks and cars because some day in the near future we might end up with an oil embargo that will make the 1970s embargo look like a cake walk. One more fact I want to point out here, I'm sorry to say, is the fact that these new Muslim Cleric controlled Nations now control some of the world's largest oil fields and American consumers of gas and oil are now at the mercy of these Muslim Clerics.

Since ex-President Obama never appeared to be ready to reveal or release any information about America's oil deal with Mexico, or why he helped build so many Muslim controlled oil Nations, I think it's time Americans demand some answers; you know, before it's too late and he slips away into history. And maybe it's time we Americans ask this ex-President why he was so intent on keeping the US/Mexican border open during his presidency and why he kept trying to grant 20 million Mexican colonizing invaders Amnesty during his tenure? And finally, I feel I have to ask this ex-President why he was in such a hurry to make America a two-language country (Spanish and English), like Canada, during his tenure. Think about it my fellow Americans; if we go to war with Russia, as more and more scholars are saying this is a possible future, do you really think America would be able to defend itself like it did during WWII (when Americans almost all spoke English) with half of the country speaking Spanish and the other half speaking English? As I look at America in the near future, I feel America will soon be divided into three nations. I feel I can come to this conclusion because there are millions of foreigners who only speak Arab, millions of foreigners who only speak Spanish, and then we have the rest of America's original English speaking citizens. I hate to remind my fellow Americans here of what the Bible says of what happens to a "house divided." Yes, we know the answer is bad because "a house divided soon falls."

Before I continue writing my book, I want to tell my readers that I have sacrificed (both financially and personally) three years of my life doing research and writing this book so I could hopefully convince my readers to say enough to what I feel are complete acts of madness, treason, and collusion that are being committed by America's Political and Judicial leaders. I feel I can make this statement because these American leaders refuse to close our borders and insist that any foreigner who enters US soil has the same rights as America's citizens (which Frederick Bastiat says is wrong). My fellow Americans, if I could talk to these leaders face-to-face, I would tell these people that setting these kinds of precedence is crazy because as a person who has lived overseas in other countries, I have not lived in a country overseas that is willing to give illegal foreigners the same powers and rights as their legal citizens (unless it's done by an act of law). Having made this statement, I really hope my readers will take this book, internalize its content, and then march by the millions on Washington DC and demand that these politicians start protecting America's sovereignty, tax dollars, and its citizens better starting today! After my fellow Americans march on Washington, I urge them to demand that America's Government and politicians start putting Americans first when they pass US laws make decisions that will impact America's citizens and their legal rights that are found, or written, in the American Constitution, criminal laws, and Immigration laws. So, listen up America's politicians and judges; instead of putting some foreign nation's illegal citizens or refugees, like Mexico's invading illegal aliens, the new alleged Muslim refugees or their Muslim religion Koran laws first, or above the interest of America's citizens and their US Constitution's laws, you politicians and judges need to remember that you were elected or appointed to protect America's citizens and America's Constitution and their Republic, and not these illegal or alleged refugee foreigners, their religions, or their foreign government's interests and laws.

To conclude my discussion in the last paragraph, I want to say I feel the US Department of Education needs to do a complete on sight inspection and investigation of all schools that are under the control of Muslim school boards in America's states, like for example Michigan, so this American Government entity can reassure and promise America's taxpayers that their US dollars are not being used to teach some controversial teachings found in the Muslim religion's Koran that allegedly teaches Muslims and their children to use the word "Infidel" to describe any non Muslim they meet in America (including America's Christian children), or any other non-believer that does not follow or believe in their religion. And, I believe the "Free Press" (not network news) should be allowed to tape these surprise visits and/or planned investigations so they can show the findings on national television as a public service presentation to ease the minds of US citizens. Since some people may call my requests racist, I wish to add that as a registered Native American and minority American whose tax dollars are being spent on these schools, I believe I have a right to say that these curriculum checkups fall within the right of Americans that want to know how their tax dollars are being spent in America's public schools. I want to remind my fellow American that the schools these Muslim Children are attending are allegedly public schools that are being funded by US tax dollars so the all have to follow US Department of Education laws and principles as written. If these Muslim schools are privately funded, then I guess they have more leeway to teach what they feel is good for their kids.

Since I am no stranger to racism because I am often called "chief," "injun," and other names we Native Americans don't like, I feel Muslims that are living on US soil should stop using the word "infidel" so loosely and strike the word from their religious books because I hear this word too often in our state of California. In case my fellow Americans want to know why the use of the word Infidel bothers me so much, I feel the use of the word reminds me too much of the way early racist American Christian zealots, or so called "red-necks, used the "N" word to describe hard working

African American slaves and called Native Americans Prairie-Ni--ers or Injuns when I was young. I want to add that I feel the Supreme Court should ask America's Muslims to change any and all controversial anti-American/racist sounding words or sections that are found this religion's Bible-like-book that is known as the Koran. I feel this act is needed so that the Koran can be brought into the 21st Century and made to be more politically correct or civilized. This act of peace, I feel, would help these Muslim people's Koran meet America's civilized and modern standards. After all, if Muslim citizens are going to become part of America's successful culture that many historians, and US history books, tell us made America and her citizens the envy of the world, then they should be willing to learn to be open-minded about America's Euro Christian Culture (which US History books say is the heart of America and her people's success) and become a part of it.

To prove why I feel most Muslims need to be more tolerant and accepting of America's Christian mainstream culture, I want to add that when the "Book of Mormons" first came into use in mainstream America, American Christians read this religious book and found it to have scriptures that offended them because it, for example, allegedly had a verse in it that said this book believed African Americans were beasts of burden that could be bought and sold like horses and oxen. Another controversial verse that was allegedly (According to some historical books, this statement was once true and found in older Mormon Books that are no longer in print and hard to find.) found in the Book of Mormons in the older books allegedly stated that Mormon men could have more than one wife (This fact can be found in recent news stories that have aired on Network News Special Reports). To bring the Mormon religion in line with mainstream Americans and into the 20th Century, the American public demanded the removal of these very controversial scriptures from the Book of Mormons and the Mormon leaders complied and brought the religion in line with Main Stream America. Now that we've taken a look at an example of an American religion being brought into the modern era, I feel that asking the Muslim Religion to bring their Religion and their book, the Koran, into the 21st Century is not any different from the request that was made of the Mormon Church in the 20th Century. After all, America is a civilized Western Euro influenced Christian Nation, not a third world nation where those that spread fear with violence are allowed to rule others. I don't believe any church in America should be allowed to terrorize others to make others accept another religion or culture (Note: The author studied religious theology and owns some very old religious books.).

I want to point out that history now tells us the Book of Mormon "proved to be a composite of mythology and [alleged] prophesy. It gave currency to the ancient legend that the [American] Indians were descendants of the lost tribes of Israel and enjoined the followers of Joseph Smith to convert them from their heathenish ways (The irony of this task taken on by the Mormons was the fact that almost all of the Native Americans tribes believed in one great God, or Grandfather.). On the basis of this revelation, "Smith founded the Church of Jesus Christ of the Latter-Day Saints in 1830 . . . In 1839, when their settlement was thriving in Illinois . . . misfortune befell them when Joseph Smith's encouragement of plural marriages (he had received a revelation to this effect in 1843) alienated the monogamists of the sect and infuriated the non-Mormon inhabitants" (Hofstadter, Richard, William Miller, and Daniel Aaron, "The Mormons," The United States: The History of a Republic, Prentice-Hall: Englewood Cliffs. 6th ed. 1960.). We should add that according to Hofstadter, Miller, and Aaron, an "act of destruction of property by Joseph Smith and his brother of a local newspaper's printer" ended up costing the lives of both of them, when "a mob lynched them in 1844 for destroying the newspaper's printing presses" of the city of Illinois.

Because I have dealt with and I am familiar with racism, I would like to note that I feel there is a new wave, or type, of racism in America's culture and I feel that unfortunately it's connected to the population growth of Muslims and Mexicans in

America who evidently have brought their insecurities and fears of Americans (and their Western Christian Culture) with them. I can relate to racism simply because I grew up in the '50s and 60s in the Southwestern region of America where I was often called a prairie ni--er by insecure whites and because I was a half-breed Native American with long hair living in US cities that had a white majority. The other people that voiced their racist opinions were the newly arrived Mexicans people who often labeled or called me a Porshae (Sorry, don't know the spelling of this word or the meaning of it; this is what the word sounded like to me.) because they felt (or they misread my love for my Americana culture, my clothes, and my hair style) I was trying to be a white person (Note: I learned why I was being called a Porshae from one of my older "old school" Hispanic/Mexican friends.).

I'm happy to say, I never got angry at these lost souls because my father taught me at a young age that the only way to fight back against racist people is to ignore their ignorant ways and not give them the satisfaction, or a reason, to hate me more. The funny thing about racism is that the legally born American minorities that are targeted by these racist people are usually more patriotic and God loving Americans than the racist people. As for the Mexican people who think these true blue Americans minorities are trying to be white, the reality is that these minorities (including myself) just love being Americans and the ARE part of the fabric that makes up America's Americana culture. And since they say the proof is the pudding, this love for America shows up in their willingness to die for their American flag and their fellow countrymen and women of any color. In my opinion, they take this stand because they know what it means to be real Americans. With their actions, I guess we can say these American minorities have internalized what it means to be an American because they were raised this way by their parents who, like my parents, came to America to be a part of the American fabric and not use hyphens (example: Indian-American or Hispanic-American) when they described their humble new ties to America. I hope I can make this statement for many of the minorities whose parents taught them in the past to be proud to be Americans. My father and mother often told my siblings and myself to remember that "you are an American, and in this house we respect America's values," so when we got into trouble or ran into someone who tried to convince us that we were not Americans because of our heritage, we just remembered what our parents taught us. Evidently these racist Mexicans don't understand that being white has nothing to do with being an American, but US Patriotism does have everything to do with it and this is why a minority American Patriot is writing this book to save his country from them and several other invading colonizing forces:

After all, when I read some of old Civics book that were once used by America's schools when America's government was still teaching American Westernized love and values for our country and not bending over backwards to be politically correct so they could sweep America's European and Westernized Christian culture under the carpet to appease all of the new lawless and colonizing invaders that I feel are in America demanding that US courts make their religions, languages, and cultures the law of the land in America, I learned (or read) an old truth that is being swept under the rug and erased from US History books. However before I present the point I found in these old books, I want to add that I feel these lawless and invading cultures not only want their religions and cultures to be law in America, and not American law, US criminal law, or US Constitutional law but they appear to also want Americans to be treated as second class citizens in their own country and not be allowed to show their American pride like my parents (and myself) did by having a US Flag in our house 24/7. As for me, I show my pride and love by wearing clothes with the US flag all over them, I have a flag pole with big American flag flying in front my yard and you can take this fact to the bank.

Now that I've introduced some facts about how my family and past minorities feel about being Americans, I want to introduce some facts that I found in many of America's older History books that I guess would be called "old school" or "real Civics Books" in my opinion. Here is what these books said about the Basis of Patriotism: "The state and government [(The Republic, or as the Constitution says, America's citizens and their elected officials)] are the agencies through which the individual obtains rights, protection, assistance, and liberty, but neither rights nor liberty can be achieved without incurring obligations in return. More specifically we owe the duty of patriotism. Patriotism is not a mere sentiment. It is a definite expression, by thought, word, and act, of the citizen's respect for the state to which he belongs [(and if a person is enjoying the benefits of America's culture and freedoms, they do NOT have the right to ask Washington and the Supreme Courts to destroy the Republic's power or ignore any of America's laws)]. It should be based upon the recognition of the fact that without the security, the justice, and the freedom that the state (America) provides, life would not be worth living [(like it would be in Iran or Mexico for example, which is why these colonizers are in America)]. Patriotism is a mixture of pride, gratitude, and faith—pride in the community to which a man belongs, gratitude for what it is doing, and faith in what it may do for those who come after him" (Munro, William Bennett, Social Civics: Our Democracy in Action. The American School: Chicago, 3rd ed. 1958. Pp38.).

As my fellow Americans can see from the information in the previous paragraphs, I am no stranger to racism and I know the pain of being called hurtful racist names, and I know what it means to be a Patriotic American. I want to add that I also know how racist names cut like a knife when you're just a child because I had to deal with being called names (and racism) when I was between the ages of five and 18 years old very often. And, now thanks to these lawless name-calling Mexicans, and racist Mexican invaders, I am have to deal with the ignorance of racism because these people don't like Patriotic Minority Americans. The fact that I find even worse is the fact that I am seeing this racism in my home state of California.

To show how these racist attacks are meant to hurt, and to understand them better, I have selected three attacks that I feel show the new racism that is slowly taking shape in California and maybe America too. My readers should note these three racist attacks occurred in California's San Joaquin Valley in 2012 in the cities of Fresno, Porterville, and Visalia. For my readers who haven't seen these types of racism, the following information I'm going to introduce should help them understand the racist, cold hearted remark used against my fellow Americans by Mexican and Muslims are not a joke. This information should help me explain that Mexico is just as racist as any other country because it has a racist skin color Cast system in its country that its people have used on each other for centuries, and it is still alive and kicking from what I have been told by Mexico's own people. In fact, this Cast system can still be seen on many of the Spanish TV programs and movies. I can prove this cast system still exists because it still shows up in today's Spanish programs, movies, and singing stars like today's modern day minority female singers or Divas, actresses, and Spanish TV announcers on Spanish shows telecasting in America. These women are usually found on Spanish stations, and I'm sad-to say, they almost always look like white women, or minority women trying "hard" to look Anglo or white. As for the Muslims who are using racism to show their disdain for Americans, I will let their actions speak for themselves in the next few paragraphs.

The first two incidents of racism, or according to our valley's local school administrator's non-racists acts or alleged racist acts, occurred when a grammar school Muslim child used the word "infidel," or allegedly called an American child an "infidel," in what I feel was a derogatory way in the Fresno School District. Yet! According to Fresno school officials, the Muslim Child allegedly did nothing wrong that required any kind of reprimand or action from the school's principle. I should add the Fresno verbal or written attack (never made clear) upset so many parents in Central California that it even made the areas' major newspaper the Fresno Bee and created a lot of anger and discussion in Central California about Muslims using the word "infidel." In Porterville, the second verbal attack using the word "infidel," unfortunately, I want to add that it was never reported to staff by the child because the child went home and told his or her parents about being called an "infidel" by a Muslim child in school and they did nothing about it so it became an "after-the fact and mute incident so nothing was ever done about it or even reported to school officials. The reason I learned of this second incident was because my older sister's grandchild was a friend of the little girl who was called an infidel. Although I told the child's parents to tell the school of the incident, they told me they didn't want to cause any trouble for their little girl.

Before I discuss the third and final racist act, I want to say that I had not heard this racist or mean spirited word "porshae/ porche" (Sorry again, I don't know the spelling or how this word is pronounced.) since I had left Texas when I was still a very young boy and I was often called his by the Mexican kids. In fact, it had been so long since I'd heard this word that I had forgotten this word even existed. I had forgotten the word, that is, until I heard it again recently while crossing a street in Visalia, California. While crossing the street, I heard some Mexican (yelled out of their car) men call me the racist word Porche because they evidently didn't like the fact that I was with my white wife or that I didn't dress like they felt I should be dressed. Evidently, according to one of my Spanish-speaking friend, this derogatory word was used on me because of the way I was dressed and looked, and the fact that I was with my white wife. My weekend clothes included a baseball cap I wear that has an American flag on it, an Eagle feather that was given to me by my tribal elders, and pins that have many American logos or US flags on them. Although this act of hatred would not have occurred in California in the late 60s or 70s, I feel this racist type of incident that came from a group of Spanish speaking Mexican males happened in our state because California's cities are looking more and more like Mexican colonies. I hate to say it but many California cities are now averaging anywhere from 70 to 90 percent lawless and colonizing illegal aliens. And as these cities become Mexican colonies with mostly Mexican populations, according to the news, thousands of California's legal American citizens are packing up and leaving California to escape the growing lawlessness and crime that appears to be following this demographic change in California.

Because of all the new type of racist controversy I've introduced in this section, I have to wonder when Americans will finally say enough to what seems to be a corrupt rogue American Government that more than likely reaches all the way to America's Presidents (After all ex-President Obama granted 800,000 colonizing invaders Amnesty in 2012 during his tenure.). If it does reach all the way to America's President and Congress, I wonder if America's citizens will demand the resignation of these elected politicians. I also wonder when America's Compatriots will say enough to what appears to be a corrupt and renegade US Government that also includes many of its politician's and US Judges? Finally, I have to wonder which president will finally respond to the growing fears and demands for actions by America's scared citizens (Note: I think President elect Trump finally heard America's Citizens and that is why he was elected in 2016.)? Will it be the president they voted for and put into office twice (Obama) because they felt they knew him? Or! Will it be some new President in the near future?

By the way, as I did my research for this book, I did learn that President Obama could never have been the American President who would try to close her borders, enforce her immigration laws, and finally stop the crumbling respect for America's Sovereignty. I know I can say this because during my research I found I couldn't access any of Obama's personal or school records, and this included his college transcripts (Note: He had them sealed by his lawyers.), his school grades, and none of his High School or Elementary records. I guess Americans can only wonder why this man doesn't want us to know anything about his past, like for example what clubs he belonged to in high school or college. Although I have years of experience getting records and past history for articles I have written for newspapers, articles, and journals, I hate to say it but I couldn't find a way to access President Obamas' records so that I could report how young Obama paid for his expensive college education, or what jobs he held while he attended college. To tell the truth, I hope America's citizens will finally say enough and demand changes and some answers to the questions I am raising in this book. By the way, I'm not talking about the public relations bio that the Left Wing Media rolls out for their audiences whenever too many Americans demand to see Obama's records. I'm talking about the Bio that is constantly under the watch and control of Obama and his lawyer watchdogs that are hidden under lock and key for what ever reason.

The reason I, your author and muckraker, can't report on President Obama is because this ex-President won't allow myself or any other reporters (or the public) to access his school or private records. So unfortunately, we Americans have no idea which ex-President Obama will address the American public if he ever has to defend himself in publish because of controversial books like this one are published (currently being updated, edited, and republished) that demand his disclosure. Maybe it will it be the president who spent 20 plus trillion dollars (Ex-President Obama left President Trump a 20 plus trillion dollar debt to deal with during his Presidency.) during his eight years in office and single handedly created more debt than any president I have known in my life time. Or? Maybe it will be the President who has spent more time and money helping Muslims, and the Muslim Brotherhood, than any US President this author/reporter has had the pleasure of being lead by since I understood what Presidents do for America. By the way, my first President I took an interest in was the WWII hero President "Ike" Eisenhower" when I was a very young boy.

I wish I could report that I have the answers to the questions above. But like most Americans, I have no idea as to which ex-President Obama I think will address Americans after this book comes out. However, as a reporter and researcher who has written and reported on many US politicians, I have to report that can't access any information about President Obama, other than what his press releases say that he allows to be released to answer some of our many unanswered questions as American Citizens. But fret not my fellow Americans, I'm happy to report that I did find an article that young Obama wrote while he was in college that helped me (your author, reporter, researcher, and retired professor) shed some light on President Obama's college days. According to my sources, ex-President Obama wrote this article while he was at Columbia University, and oddly enough, from what I found during my research, I learned some interesting facts about young Obama from this written work that he wrote for a newspaper (I want to note that the article provided very little information about his time at Columbia, which was strange.). If my readers want an example, I found that I couldn't figure out his class level from his article, what courses or major he had, or what part-time jobs he held to pay for his education while he was at Columbia because he was very vague when it came to discussing own background in the article. This essay that young Obama wrote as an alleged college student at Columbia appears to be purposely written in a vague manner to avoid providing information about his time at Columbia University as a student.

To say that then Student Obama's published article was poorly written, truncated, and not college level writing only appears to scratch the surface of some negative personal information I learned about young Obama's abilities while he was allegedly attending Columbia University. I hope this is not why now retired ex-President Obama didn't allow us (his constituents) to see his college transcripts. I also want to add that after reading Obama's article, I wondered if young Obama held any part-time jobs like some of the jobs my college roommate and I held while we attended our California State University. The jobs we worked, I want to add, helped my roommate pay for and earn a BA and his teaching credential in 1996, and my jobs helped me pay for and earn my MA in 1996 (3.10 GPA), an AA in '79, a BS in '81, and a double BA in '83 (3.0 GPA major and 2.7 GPA overall) respectively. By the way, my roommate and I took jobs in places like JC Penney Co., a Part-time janitor job at a local Grammar school, a fellowship to do research for the Department of Anthropology at CSUB, and some part-time teaching jobs. Other means we used to earn money for college also included a job as a TV station intern, various school loans (I borrowed and paid back $30,000 in full after I graduated by working overseas as an English teacher.), sports or athletic scholarships, and various grants that we both qualified for as California residents with good high school GPAs. (Note: as our readers can see, I am proud of my college records, and I am very open about them, unlike Mr. Obama.)

Since ex-President Obama is still not open about his college years, Could it be that President Obama never wanted to talk about his days in college (or his jobs) because most Americans would find them to be out of the ordinary, offensive, anti-US Government, or maybe he had benefactors that paid for his college years that he doesn't want us to know about? As American citizens who lived through the eight years of Obama's presidency, we can only guess as to the motives or reasons that our ghost President (I like to call Obama this name) never allowed us to see his life records before he became President. I come to this conclusion because of ex-President Obama's secretive private life that he held on to like gold. Or maybe ex-President Obama never wanted to release too much information about his younger days because his constituents would learn important information about him that he didn't want us to know; for example, maybe he took a year off to think about registering for the draft before he finally decided to register and own up to his citizenship responsibility (so he could qualify for college grants). This, of course, would mean he evidently didn't register for the draft until he was 19 years old (I found this fact on the web.), maybe he made this choice because he didn't believe in the draft. I want to remind my readers that when a young American male didn't register for the draft when they turned 18, it meant he had decided to break Federal law as it says on the back of America's draft cards. I want to add that if I remember right this act is punishable "by either a $10,000 fine or 5 years in prison or both." Not knowing what young Obama was thinking when he failed to register for the draft, I guess I have to say that maybe President Obama didn't want us to learn he was a political activist who raged against America's Government and the US military and the draft. I add this information because of some information I found in the article young Obama wrote while he was allegedly attending Columbia University. I point this fact out because I feel I can prove it by using this article that he wrote in 1983 while at Columbia.

As I stated above, I was able to get a copy of the article that a very young (either 21 or 24, depending on which age you want to believe that was posted by the President on Obama's My Space page on 8-17-2009) Obama wrote and published while he was either attending Columbia University or working on Columbia's campus as a political anti-war activist, anti-draft card registration activist, or anti-nuclear power advocate for a group he championed that he said was called the ARA or Arms Race Alternative group. To analyze the article young Obama wrote while he was at Columbia, I used or applied some literary analysis tools that helped me deconstruct young President Obama's article so I could find any imbedded truths or facts that would help him me shed some light on what our young future President was up to during the time he was at Columbia from possibly '81 to '83 when he wrote his article: Obama, Barack. "Breaking the War Mentality." Sundial: The Weekly Newsmagazine. 10 March 1983: p 2-3.

Since I analyzed young Obama's prose work using textual criticism and a little deconstruction criticism, I've decided to first look at young Obama's introduction for any clues that might help my readers know young Obama better. If my readers will look at the first paragraph with me, I believe we will find that young Obama introduces himself as a student who appears to have lived in the area, or attended, Columbia University since possibly 1982. I arrived at this date ('82) because Obama's article was dated March

10, 1983. I also want to note here that young Obama's poor writing skills appeared in his article immediately after I read a sentence that appeared to say he came to Columbia two years ago, but because he did not take the time to introduce who was speaking about in his first quote in this sentence that introduces his article, and he doesn't warn his audience of a possible topic change in this paragraph, we never know if young Obama is talking about himself, about one of the men he's writing about in the article, or if he just used the few quotations he added for emphasis in this sentence. Since the paragraph doesn't introduce the speaker, I can only guess whom young Obama is talking about in the sentence and paragraph, which, I hate to say, is considered poor writing for a college level student. The next thing I learned about young Obama's writing is that (our quotations for emphasis) "young Obama, either lead a sheltered life during the Vietnam war era from 1964 to 1974, or he had not been living in America very long because he says he had never 'tasted war' in his life while living in America because the closest he had come to a war was on 'television, film, and print.'" Young Obama then added this comment in his article: "We know that wars have occurred, will occur, are occurring, but bringing such experiences down into our hearts . . . [is] a difficult task." (Obama, Barack. "Breaking the War Mentality." Sundial: The Weekly Newsmagazine. 10 March 1983: p. 2). According to young Obama, he comes to this conclusion because "his life was never touched, influenced, or impacted by the Vietnam War. I hate to say it but I found this statement by Obama to be "UNREAL." I will explain why I say this in the next paragraph.

I hope my readers are wondering why I said I found young Obama's statement about the Nam war era unreal: Well! Having grown up during this same era, or the Vietnam War era, I have to say that if young Obama was not affected by the young men who were coming home from their tours in Nam either alive and looking like the walking dead, or in flag draped caskets on a daily basis as shown on National TV News, then I guess he was hiding his head in the sand. And, if he was not affected by the death of some young man who might have been some of his friend's older brothers or cousins, and he never had any contact with any of the young American male draftees who were coming home or being drafted for Nam when he was anywhere from age 12 to 15 years old, I have to say that young Obama must not have been living in America or he was living under a rock in Hawaii or America. Does young Obama expect us to believe some of his school peers never have had an older brother get drafted, killed, or came home a mental mess? If this is what young Obama is saying, I hate to say but I feel I can honestly say I think he must have been blind because when I was a young male growing up during the Vietnam era in the early and mid sixties, I watched three of our young men that were seniors when I was in 7th grade, get drafted and very soon two of them came home in flag draped coffins, and the other came home and became an alcoholic and a was a mess for years. These young men were much older than I was but, as you can see, avoiding being touched by war in the Nam era was pretty hard to do in America during this era. To get a feel for this era, I suggest my readers watch the movie "1969." Since I was older than young Obama was during the Nam era, I can say that I "was" definitely touched by the war, more often than allegedly young Obama. I hate to say it but not being touched or torn apart by this war, even as a young boy that was not old enough to be drafted at this time was almost an impossible task during the Nam era no matter how old you were during this time.

The next thing I noticed about young Obama's article is that he said he was more interested in what was happening in the war in Guatemala and the nuclear race between Russia and America than he was in his grades or college courses (Note: I found this message inferred loud and clear in young Obama's article.). Well young Obama really didn't really say that but this is what he appeared to say to say in his article because he writes that "Paul Martin (director of Earl hall) and I discussed our interests, and (we) decided that ARA would be one of the programs we pushed" (Note: Since writers and reporters are supposed to be impartial, I found it strange that young Obama used the word "we" in this sentence.).

Although I think young Obama is quoting Don Kent, who was maybe talking about himself and Paul Martin (I think, using some grammar rules that evidently apply here), the way Obama wrote this sentence it made it look or appear like he was including himself in this sentence's time line and discussion. Unfortunately, because we weren't were there to ask him, the contents of this sentence only serve to make this sentence very confusing to the readers of that era, and today's readers that are reading it as a historical piece (Obama, Barack. "Breaking the War Mentality." Sundial: The Weekly Newsmagazine. 10 March 1983: p. 2.).

I should note in this paragraph that since I taught transfer level English both in California junior colleges and in overseas universities, I want to note this article might have earned young Obama a grade of C if he had written this for a college course (to help boost his confidence). As for myself, I might have given young Obama a D because young Obama does not use quotation marks correctly and the story line of his narrative is hard to follow. After reading this article that I felt was hard to follow and understand, and if I had been one of his professors, I think I would have suggested to young Obama that he needed to take some remedial writing courses at a local junior college to improve his writing skills.

Continuing my analysis of this work by young Obama, I feel that at times his article reads like he is talking about himself; however as I read further, I later learned, or found, that young Obama was paraphrasing without quoting the source of this statement in his work (I want to note college professors call this act plagiarism). Finally, I want to note one more important fact about students who have taken advanced university level college writing courses that is a very important key to getting passing grades. I want to note students who have taken college level courses all know that university level writing/English courses require a tremendous amount of reading, writing, and time to get a passing grade (especially if the student wants to get a high grade like an A or a B). And since young Obama appears to have devoted a lot time to these two advocate groups, I feel that young Obama was either not taking courses during the time he was helping the ARA, or he was only taking one or two courses at Columbia during the time he either wrote for or worked for ARA. Or, I can only guess that maybe he didn't want to commit to these groups for fear of being associated with these groups so he instead purposely wrote this article in this very vague manner. Again, I can only guess because of his vagueness and possible poor writing skills.

My readers should now see why having access to young Obama's college records is very important for myself and to his constituents. After all, since ex-President Obama froze his college and lower grade school records, all we Americans can do is continue to speculate as to why he took this action. And, we can only continue to speculate what young Obama was really doing while he attended Columbia University or other American colleges and universities. On the other hand, maybe ex-President Obama really didn't attend all of these schools on a full time basis and that is what he is really hiding. I want to finally point out that although Obama's article was sloppy and vague and I noted that he was "not" writing at a university level while he was attending Columbia University, I find it strange that he some how allegedly got into Columbia and other Ivy league level schools with such poor writing skills. I find this fact a problem because young Obama never tells us (his audience) if he is a member of these groups, or if he is just reporting about the groups and its members to the general public.

As stated above, in my opinion, the vagueness in Obama's written work really hurts the message of his article. So, having pointed out this fact, I want to say that I feel young Obama never really commits himself or includes himself in this article until the end when he writes the following sentence: "By adding their (ARA and SAM) energy in order to enhance the possibility of a decent world, they may help deprive us of a spectacular experience— that of war. But then, there are some things we shouldn't have to live through in order to want to avoid the experience" (Obama,

Barack. "Breaking the War Mentality." Sundial: The Weekly Newsmagazine. 10 March 1983: p. 3.). Unfortunately for us, even in this sentence, we are never told by young Obama if he believes in these causes, or if he is just saying that he is happy to be benefiting from the efforts of others.

Now that I've analyzed young Barack Obama's article and I hope my fellow Americans have learned about young Obama's college writing skills, I hope I have convinced my fellow Americans that young Obama really didn't belong in a university level setting. And since I have proven this fact, I guess the next question we have to ask ourselves is how did young Obama really get into universities like Columbia? I ask the last question on behalf of my fellow Americans because I believe we all have to wonder how a young man with such poor writing and grammar skills could get into an Ivy league school, majored in Constitutional law, received a law degree (or JD), and then ended up being a University level lecturer, when all these achievements evidently require above average writing skills and grades?

Moving on, I feel I can add that my analysis of young Obama's article surprisingly also helps me show my fellow Americans some insights into young Obama's early political philosophies and ideals because his article shows that he decided to be a part of these political groups and help them in their cause. Why do I come to this conclusion? Well, since young Obama took the time to report on these two radical anti-war and anti-government action committees known as ARA and SAM, then took the time to report about their beliefs and political opinions, and then sort of insinuated he was an active member of these groups (without saying he was a member), we Americans have to decide for ourselves if young Obama was just writing this article or saying his was an active member of these groups and supported their efforts? And since young Obama insinuates that he was a member of a group that advocated and instructed college students to "not" register for the US draft, we Americans are left to wonder if he was or was not registered with the draft when he wrote this article (Note: Records show that young Obama did "not" register for the draft till he was 19 years old— Why?), or did he possibly burn his draft card (a Federal offense) while he was attending or living on campus at Columbia, then decide this was not a good idea for his future ambitions?

Having arrived at some of my conclusions in the last paragraph, I have to ask this question: Since young Obama seemed to enjoy playing anti-war and anti-US government advocate but never appeared to commit or say he was allegedly either for these groups, or a allegedly a member of these groups, was this wishy-washy or non-committal way of thinking a (future?) part of his political thought process only used in college? Or was this thought process, that he appeared to hone in his younger years, still a part of ex-President Obama's current political ideology that he used during his eight years of service? I also have to wonder if this way of thinking, or thought process, influenced how ex-President Obama operated during his tenure as the leader of America? Sort of makes us Americans want to cringe and pray we didn't deal with a President who appeared to love riding the fence, and appeared to always let others do his dirty work for him and take the blame for him when he made mistakes. And although Obama wrote in this article that says he hated war and the draft, I find it strange that he was very quick to risk the lives of America's soldiers and use America's military to defend so-called freedom fighters that we now know were Muslim Brotherhood insurgents, Palestinian mercenaries, and a few other non-Muslim groups to defend countries like Egypt and Libya that ended up becoming Muslim Cleric controlled nations. I feel it's a shame that young Obama said he hated the draft and war when he knew he could still be drafted; but when his life was no longer on the line, he seemed to be willing to send Americans into battle to help future Muslim controlled countries and it didn't appear to bother him.

So in the end, we American are left with the thought that we had a president who allegedly never provided an "original" paper birth-certificate from Hawaii the state he was allegedly born in either in 1961 as the White House's Public Relations Department reported (when Obama was running for president, and again in 2009, when he allegedly celebrated his 48th birthday) or in 1957 as President Obama posted on his official My Space page on August 16, 2009 (Note, this page can't be taken down, but someone went on this page and covered up the post with a bucolic photo.). I hate to say it but it seems hard to believe that a man who has a law degree, lectured at Ivy league universities, and served in several offices as an American politician, can't get his birth date correct on his own web page. After all, as your author, I have to note that I have known the day and year of my birth since I was about eight or nine years old because I needed to know this for little league and other recreation sponsored sports I signed up for as youngster. And! Believe it or not, I still have my original copy of my birth certificate that was made for my parents on the day I was released from the hospital that I was taken to after I was brought into the world by a mid-wife in our home. Oh yes, my birth, I would like to note, was quite a few years before Obama was born when records were all hand typed, like Obama's would have been typed because there were NO computers back in this era. I want to add that the my mother, a woman with three years of education, kept this form safe for me till I grew up, left home, and was on my own in college. Guess what? I still have my original social security letter with my duplicate card that has my number on it and my original Catholic baptism certificate. If I (a poor kid from the Rez era) can still have all of his original life records, then I have to ask why doesn't an Ivy league graduate with a highly educated mother and grandmother not have any of his "orginal" records?

I'm not going to say anymore about Obama's birth certificate because I'm not obsessed with it and have left it in the Lord's hands; besides until ex-President Obama (if ever) allows hard-line real investigative reporters like myself to view his high school, college, and University records (so we can report the facts to the public), or until he's forced to open his school records by some real patriotic

American judge, we Americans really won't know or have all the facts about this reticent (The author prefers "cloak and dagger President" to describe the most secretive US President he has ever had the pleasure of investigating.) American President. After all, for a President who was supposed to stand behind the statement "that the buck stops here," like many past US Presidents have done before, President Obama appears to have never known what his appointed staff members or secretaries were doing while he served as our president for eight years because these people always seemed to be at fault when things went wrong and not Obama.

For my readers who might have forgotten the news stories that informed us of ex-President Obama's mistakes that always seemed to be his staff members' fault, I want to remind them that during his presidency, every time some Presidential hand-picked Obama Administration senior staff member allegedly screwed up (sorry, but I see it this way), ex-President Obama and his Public Relations staff always seemed to release a report to the public that basically said Obama didn't know about the problem or development that had allegedly implicated his presidency or administration so the President couldn't comment on the problem till he knew more about it: Some examples from Obama's era that show he allegedly felt that the statement "the buck stops here" didn't apply to his presidency (or his Presidential Staff) included sending millions of dollars in cash aid to Libya, but when these same Libyans caused the death of four patriotic American consulate officers who were murdered in Benghazi by the Libyans he supported and championed, President Obama's and his staff members released a statement that said neither he nor Secretary Hillary Clinton (his right hand) knew of the dangers in this country (and its leaders), or had not been briefed about them. Unfortunately for the American citizens who died in Benghazi and our country, this press release didn't provide any answers to the many questions that were brought up by Americans, the press, or the Congressional hearing that followed this mess. To show the last example was not a fluke, I want to now provide another example that showed ex-President Obama never liked owning up to his administrations mistakes and this blunder included the way he handled, or should I say like he allegedly never handled or knew about the back door meetings and hearings that were going in Congress during his Presidency that had to do with the secret "US/Mexico Social Security Treaty" that was going to send Social Security Checks to Mexico's citizens that were living in Mexico.

Since I am sure many Americans don't know what I am talking about here, and I bet not one American ever heard President Obama discuss this treaty in a speech, even though this treaty (if it was ever passed behind closed doors?) was written so that America would send millions of Social Security tax dollars into Mexico; the irony of this treaty is that during this same era (and even today) both Republican and Democrat US politicians kept telling us Social Security is going broke. What is even worse is that SSI disability (which is NOT Social Security retirement and is a real entitlement, that no one pays into to get it for life.) keeps giving away money to any person who walks into the doors of any US Social Security Office without ever having worked a day in America, or being a US Citizen. I should add that even America's Mass Media News Agencies never reported or investigated this treaty or has ever done a story on who is being allowed to receive and apply for SSI in America and then having their checks sent to Mexico.

Finally, the last example that our mighty allegedly "Honest Abe like" ex-President Obama (who likes to quote Lincoln) never owned up to, or ever laid claim to the famous quote "The Buck Stops Here" is the big problem that surfaced during his presidency that had to do with the IRS "blow-out." This IRS "Blow Out" was so big that for several weekend "News-Shows" discussed it on their Sunday morning shows including May 12, 2013. I want to point out that all of the Sunday News hosts and guests on these shows recommended that Washington DC and the politicians should have a full investigation to find out who ordered the US Internal Revenue Service to politically attack and audit any Republican Group (like the Tea Party and other Republican 503c non-profit groups) and hurt their chances of keeping their 503c status as non-profit groups. By the way, I should add that this "big scandal" that could (and should have) have hurt the Democrats and Obama's party died down and was literally buried by the Media Giants in less than a week and "Nothing ever came of it, and it was never mentioned on the news again." Can I/we say "COVER UP" and possible damage control on behalf of the Democrat Party and Obama's Administration?

G. "Cultural Genocide" the act and term that has the
     power to Destroy America's Western Culture.

I'm going to open this very critical section of my book with a term and definition that I feel speaks volumes as to what is wrong with America, and why America's Government is failing the Republic of America. The key term is "Cultural Genocide" and as the Free Encyclopedia (and other reference books) states, "Cultural Genocide is a "component of the term Genocide that was proposed by Raphael Lemkin, a lawyer, in 1933 which he considered was a form of [intense] "'vandalism' that includes protesting and the destruction of [a country's] **cultural heritage.**" Although the drafters of this history making 1948 Genocide Convention considered the term "cultural genocide" for discussion, the article said it was [never included in their final draft]. The legal definition of genocide [was also] left unspecific; [however, according to the members of this convention, they did attempt to define cultural genocide by saying this about the term]: " . . . It is the destruction [of a culture], with [the] intent to destroy [its] **National,** racial, **religious,** or [in some case a country's] ethnic groups ("Cultural Genocide." Wikipedia: The Free Encyclopedia, 2 April 2012. http://en.wikipedia.org/Wiki/Cultural Genocide.). If I were to use this definition of "cultural genocide" to describe what is happening to America's Western European Christian Culture and to ask why groups like Antifa are being allowed free reign to do as they like in states like California, I feel I can say that the United States Government, the US Supreme Court, and the ACLU are evidently (or seem to be) intent on destroying America's Western European

Christian Culture using "cultural genocide" so they can push America towards a Socialist State. I know my last sentence in this paragraph is bold and to some of my readers this accusation might seem a little too far fetched but before my readers stop reading my book, I want to ask my readers to look at the evidence I am about to present in the rest of this book.

Before I move on, I want to remind my readers of the definitions for the words or terms "vandal" and "vandalism" because, after all, these words were included the definition for cultural genocide, and as Funk and Wagnalls dictionary states, the act of "intense vandalism by those who would destroy a country's culture . . . a vandal is "one who willfully destroys or defaces . . . anything of beauty ([like our great nation America and its Western Euro Christian Culture]) . . . [and] "people who ravaged . . . and pillaged the city of Rome in 455"...[Finally, I want to add that] the word "vandalism" is the "willful destruction or defacement of artistic works, or of property in general" ("Landau." Funk and Wagnalls Standard College Dictionary. Standard. Ed.1967. P. 1480-1481). By the way, in California, America's legal citizens are experiencing daily culture shock because they're seeing their old English language road signs suddenly disappear and being replaced by Spanish language billboard road signs that make California look like and feel more like a part of Mexico with each passing day.

Since I am the half-breed grandchild of a North American Indian and renegade brave (my grandfather on my mother's side would not stay on his assigned reservation, so by law he was considered a "renegade Indian."), I feel my family's firsthand knowledge of how my grandfather's people, culture, and way of life were destroyed by the US government will help me show that the US government is no stranger to allowing "cultural genocide" on American soil. After all, the US Government used "cultural genocide" to destroy my grandfather's peoples language, religion, way of life, food source (deer and bison), and took away my grandfather's (and his tribe's) land by sending him and is people into exile to reservations. I should note that many American Native braves went to Canada and Mexico because they didn't want to live/die on the Reservations. Now that I've shown that the American Government is quite capable of using "genocide" to destroy a culture, I feel my readers should not be surprised to hear that I feel the US Government appears to be allowing a new form of cultural "genocide" to keep control of America so it can gain more financial wealth for its corporations and CEOs. Only this time, I feel America's Government is using "cultural genocide" on America's citizens, or the Republic's members, to push the new progressive agenda that appears to be a push towards making America into a Socialist Nation where the world's citizens have the same citizenship rights as America's citizens.

To prove the accusation I made in the last paragraph, I would now like to show some examples of what I feel are real, or recent, acts of "cultural genocide against America's citizens. Here are some of the examples: In America's Southwestern states, I feel "cultural genocide" has already started because in states like California English is being replaced by Spanish, or being forced on California's American citizens in many sectors of every day life and especially business. How can I prove what I just said? Well, in California, I found cultural genocide being pushed in the area of California's Government employees because they are being told, or required, to have all of their forms printed in both Spanish and English. I want to note this order even includes non-business forms. So what happens to the old English only forms? These English only forms are being cut up into note pads. Another area I found cultural genocide being used on America's citizens was in the state's hiring practices where I learned that almost all new California state employees have to speak some Spanish to get, or find a job; finally, one more area where I found Spanish being forced on to America's Citizens is on English TV commercials where a form of Bilingual Education (Spanish with English) is being used subliminally (Funny thing is that if I remember right in one of my college television courses I learned this act was against FCC laws.)

by companies like Target, McDonalds, and major "beer" companies who are interjecting quick Spanish words into their commercials to augment the English language (Our readers should know that I have an MA in English with an emphasis in TEFL/TESL and linguistics, and a BA in Communications with an emphasis in television, radio, and journalism, and these facts are why I know about subliminal suggestion being used in some forms of media communications.).

To conclude my discussion on Cultural Genocide, I want to point out a few more areas where I feel our state and federal governments are now using "cultural genocide" to weaken and destroy America's Western Christian Culture or Anglo European influence. But before I move on, I'd like to add that adding subliminal messages or words into television, especially commercials, is considered a form of brain washing and is considered against the law by the Federal Communications Commission to prevent businesses from adding these messages into their ads. Having said this, I can now say that this illegal act of quickly inserting Spanish words in their television commercials should be a crime in America. If my readers still think America's major media groups and the U.S. Government are not up to no good, then I have some flood-plane land I want to sell them in California. Some other areas that I found more proof of "cultural genocide" included the following examples that basically show America's government seems to be an aggressive agenda of forcing America's Christians to take a back seat to America's atheists, the Muslim religion, Islam's Constitution, Islam's followers, and the loss of the Republic's sovereignty and Constitutional Rights that are being given to both Mexico's colonizing invaders and Mexico's Government. I feel I can make this final statement because America's politicians are handing over America's citizens' Constitutional and civic rights, political power, and the power of sovereignty to Mexico's citizens and other foreigners by calling Mexico's and the other colonizing invaders immigrants, which I have proven in this book that these foreigners are not immigrants.

In case my fellow Americans are wondering what other devious acts the US Government is instituting to destroy American Citizens' power, I guess the best way to show my fellow Americans is to write about them here. First, In case my fellow Americans haven't noticed, I want to point out that our U.S. Government is ignoring Article I Section 8 which has to do with training and maintaining a militia, which was once covered by the draft lottery because it was NOT a fulltime (the military draft only required a two year commitment.) paid or permanent Government military that might end up being loyal to the U.S. Government. By the way, Article I Section 8 basically does not allow the US Government to have a standing professional army for more than two years because the drafters felt the government might decide to use these professional soldiers against it own people. But because the draft was ended and we now have an alleged all volunteer American Government paid for professional standing army, I guess Americans should be worried: Oh yes, Here is what the law says in the US Constitution: "To raise and support armies, but no appropriation of money to that use shall be for a **longer term than two years.**" This sentence means that money raised to keep an army in the United States cannot be used for this purpose for more than two years, or that the Army cannot be financed and kept active for more than two years. I want to remind Americans that up until the Vietnam War era all draftees served a "two year" mandatory military tour of duty, and it was up to the draftee to decide if he wanted to serve more time in the military. This system, I feel, was good because it made it hard for the Government to create and keep a professional military whose loyalty could end up belonging to the government, and not the people.

Because of the past courses I've taken in American History, I feel that Article I section 8 was put in the Constitution on purpose by its drafters to keep the American government from having a professional full-time army that might end up being loyal to only the U.S. Government and not the Republic. I feel I can say this because I see today's new volunteer soldiers as full time professional soldiers (mercenaries) that owe their allegiance to the Government and not the People or Republic. I say this because in many ways these new American soldiers are mercenaries that get paid to fight in wars and kill in the name of the US Government. Since I am from the Nam era, I still have not forgotten what happened, or what I saw happen on my television, on the Kent State College Campus. Having looked back at an event from my youthful era, I hope my readers will forgive me for saying that today's American military scares me. Why do I say this? I say it because I see our soldiers and military as a mercenary type professional army that gets paid to kill and fight in wars. These volunteers have no other job or career because they are full time highly paid soldiers, which is very much unlike the old days of the two-year hitch that was required of all Americans who were drafted to serve in the military, and after their two year hitch, they were free to return to civilian life. Oh yes, as for the pay during those two years, I hate to say it but the pay was very, very low, and there were NO cash cow signing bonuses.

Since I seem to be on a roll, I have decided to list a few more ways I found the US Government is using "cultural genocide" on its own citizens. I want to point out that there was a recent written report that said America's government was allowing the ACLU to separate America's God from the Republic by allowing them to sue, at will, any school district or local and state government who dares to make any kind of connection between America's past and the Christian culture that founded this great nation. For example, the ACLU "sued the Giles County School Board for adopting an 'open forum' policy, which [permitted] the display of historical documents by private individuals, or American patriotic groups... [So,] when a private group posted 11 historical documents that included the Lord's 'Ten Commandments,' [that were put up] to teach the historical foundation of America . . . " an 'offended' parent [(might have been Muslim or Atheist)] and a student . . . partnered with the ACLU to have the display of the 'Ten Commandments' removed" from the display" (Staver, Matthew. "ACLU puts Ten Commandments on Trial." Liberty Action. 4 May 2012. http://

libertyaction.com). I should add that when I was in High School our school had a wall with many historical documents like the Constitution, and it also had the 'Ten Commandments." By the way, although I was a Native American, this wall never offended me in any way. Talk about thin skinned, cream puff alleged American citizens, these people really take the cake in my book.

Continuing my discussion of the "Cultural Genocide" of America's culture, I have noticed that "cultural genocide" attacks are now being aimed at America's sports past times and youth sports programs like baseball and football that have been part of Americana since the 1800s. The first attacks I have noticed on our Americana sports is what I feel a deliberate effort to push American youth sports and professional sports like baseball, basketball, football, and even tennis to take a back seat to soccer (Think AYSO and Mexico's National sport) in America. If America's citizens want to see how deliberate the push is to replace America's sports with soccer, I suggest they pay attention to the sport that is being used on American television commercials that are advertising anything from food to sportswear, to candy, and even shoes (especially in states like California). I want to note that most of these commercials are being aimed at America's children and the mothers of these kids. As for the sport that is being pushed on these kids in these commercials? The sport you will see is soccer, but never baseball, football, or basketball like in past commercials of old Americana days. Whoever is behind this changing of our sport culture and the sports or kids play, I want to point out they are also pushing the eviscerating of America's national foods like hot dogs, hamburgers, French fries, and even the poor humble (and I might add tasty) bubbly coke by labeling them unhealthy for consumption, while these same powers push burrito wraps, tacos, and highly sugared rice and cinnamon milk waters as healthy (Note: flour tortillas have over 150 calories each with either pig lard or hydrogenated oils that are known to clog arteries, and fried tacos that have over 270 calories each that also have oils that clog arteries.) alternatives. The trouble with these food lies is that any real nutritionist or sports coach will tell you that it is not the food that's bad for you, but the eating food in excess is what is bad for you and your health. Most people with common sense know they can eat almost anything, if it is done in moderation. By the way, I want to note that my mother always reminded my brothers, my sisters, and me "that unhealthy foods like cake, candy, ice-cream, and potato chips were a treat and not a meal."

Now that I have introduced the definition for the term "cultural genocide" to my fellow American's vocabulary and their mind set, and I have introduced them to the dangers this term carries with it, I hope my fellow Americans will finally be alarmed and understand the dangers they are facing as their country's culture is slowly and methodically dismantled before their eyes by home grown anti-American groups and anti-American foreign groups who seem intent on pushing America towards a new Socialist State or Government. I hate to say it but these groups could, or might even include past and present Presidential Administrations, groups like the Democrat party, some RINO Republicans within the GOP Party, the US Supreme Court, and a majority of America's politicians. To prove my point that our own US Government appears to be part of these groups that are using "cultural genocide" to weaken America's Western Christian Culture (with the aid of American and Mexican politicians, and many Supreme Court and Lower Court Judges), I am now going to present some news events and court decisions that I feel prove America's culture is in trouble and being hurt by American institutions that are supposed to uphold and defend America's laws, language, and culture. These news events and court decisions should help me prove some U.S. institutions are helping Mexico's government (and other nations), are helping Mexico's law breaking illegal citizens, and are helping the refugee Muslims and their religious leaders to force their culture's morals, social values, languages, and the Muslim Constitution (and its religion) on America's unsuspecting citizens:

To begin my presentation of events that show the US Government is slowly allowing the destruction of America's Western Euro Christian Culture, and hiding the facts and truth, I want to first look at a very recent news event that America's news broadcasters labeled or called "The Boston Marathon Bombing." I'm sure every American knows by now that two brothers planned and executed this attack on April 15, 2013. And, like everyone else, I too was glued to my TV screen so I could learn as much as I could about the attack on America, again, by alleged "legal immigrants" (NBC, CBS affiliates, National News. 15, April 2013). But! This important information was not what caught my interest after the story broke about the bomb blasts in Boston. What caught my interest was the following fact, I noticed that ex-President Obama and his staff went to great efforts to inform the big News agencies that they felt "this attack had **NOT** been carried out by a terrorists cell in the Boston area, or that the attackers didn't appear to have any connection to Alqida." In fact, the Obama Administration went to great efforts to say that according to them, "no other act of terrorism had occurred in Boston so it appeared the brothers had acted alone." I want to also note that by making these on air statements ex-President Obama and his staff were able to make the argument that there was no reason to start an investigation of the Boston area to see if terrorist groups were operating in the Boston area. While these words may not be the exact words in the press release, I can assure my fellow Americans, that as a retired print journalist, these are the key points I was able to glean from the then in power Obama Administration's press release.

While I'm sure the news reporters who released this report thought the press release was correct and had no (shall I say) "little white lies," I feel I can prove this report was not correct, and I believe that it may have been released with these facts, or points, to misdirect Americans from the following truth. Looking back at these events, I truly believe the White House released this "white washed," or incorrect report, so Americans would not get upset at ex-President Obama and his Administration for allegedly not having advised Boston's local government officials that there might be a terrorist cell working in the area. How can I make this bold and damaging statement? I say this because feel I can prove that on October 7, 2011 a conservative web page known as http://conservativeactionalerts.com reported the following news: "Reswan Ferdaus, a Boston College grad and band drummer, 26, has been arrested and indicted on charges of plotting a terrorist attack on the U.S. Capitol Building and the Pentagon. This alleged American Citizen [(note that like the two brothers, this Muslim had become a citizen to throw off Homeland Security from flagging him)] is alleged to have intended to fly remote control airplanes into the targets. Each 'airplane' would have had explosive devices aimed at the targets to set them on fire." According to the web page http://conservativeactionalerts.com, Reswan Ferdaus had created the following plan that would unfold as the buildings were evacuated; "according to the plan, Ferdaus allegedly had hoped to fire into the crowds with assault rifles and grenades as the people ran out of the buildings." I feel that If the local government had been alerted or advised that Ferdaus might be a part of local terrorist cell by President Obama's Administration, the bombings of the Boston Marathon might have been prevented because Boston officials would have been more careful, alert, and vigilant.

Another example I found that shows America's Federal Government is evidently using a double standard, that allows a form of "cultural genocide" or "re-verse acculturation" on unsuspecting American citizens, was reported last year on February 1, 2012 by the web page "Pray in Jesus Name" that can be found at this address: http://prayinjesusname.org. This web page reported that "after four Christians [had] been arrested and jailed for simply talking about Jesus to Muslims on the street of Dearborn, Michigan who had asked them [about Jesus]"; according to this report, the Pray in Jesus name Project had gone on the offense by taking the Dearborn, Michigan Mayor and Police Chief (who are Muslims living in America—we should note that according to press releases this area is now largely Muslim and looks like the

Middle East.) to court. According to Chaplain Klingenshmitt, the web page's spokesperson, "The judge has ruled the Mayor and Police Chief violated the rights of Christians by forbidding them to distribute gospel tracts and free Bibles on the public sidewalk at **Dearbornistan's Annual Muslim Festival**" (I want to point out a very important fact here for future reference: Note the erasure of the Euro, English Christian type name of Dearborn, Michigan.). Before I end this report, I want to add that according to this report, "Dearborn has a long alleged record of this kind of illegal, heavy-handed treatment of Christians in the area…that's why the judge [allegedly] ordered them [city officials] to pay $103,000 dollars [to the Christians]," added Klingenshmitt ("Victory for Jesus in Dearborn! Judge Fines Pro-Muslim Mayor, Police Chief," The Pray in Jesus Name Project. 1 February 2012. http://prayinjesusname.org).

As hard as it may seem to my readers that in the last paragraph they read a news story telling them about American citizens being arrested for being Christian and losing their First Amendment rights in an American city, I hate to tell them but this example unfortunately is not the only Islam-controlled American city that is forcing American citizens to accept "Muslim Sharia law" on US sovereign soil. I add this information because I also found other cities that are forcing Americans to remember they're living in Muslim Sharia Law protected and controlled American cities. For example, I found a story published by the Traditional Values Coalition that reported the city of Shelbyville, Tennessee was also having troubles with Muslims; or as Fox News stated, "As America's Muslim population grows, so too does the influence of Islamic Law or Sharia law grow in life in the U.S . . . Last year, a Tyson Foods plant in Shelbyville, Tenn. replaced its traditional Labor Day holiday with paid-time-off on "Eid al-Fitr the Muslim festival." This holiday marks the end of fasting during Ramadan." A labor union (I don't know if this union is anti-American or Muslim controlled, sorry) had requested the Muslim Holiday change on behalf of hundreds of Muslim employees working at this [American] food plant—many of them were alleged immigrants from Somalia . . . and [(before I close, I want to add that)] in 2007 the University of Michigan installed ritual foot baths around an American University to accommodate an Islamic tradition religious needs" (Fox News. "Islamic Laws Influence in America a Growing Concern." Online Posting Washington DC: Traditional Values Coalition. 2013). Mind you, Labor Day is a National American Holiday that has military connections because it also celebrates the work our military men and women do every day all over the world, so the act of replacing this American Holiday with a Muslim one is really not a "culturally" sound decision, or a legally sound heritage decision, says this patriotic minority male. My fellow Americans, do you still think America's politicians and government are not pushing a "cultural genocide agenda" on America, or pushing for the demise of America's Americana culture?

Since I have a degree in Social Psychology, I want to add that in my opinion this type of social change to America's Western Culture actually hurts American's mindset and increases their PTSD stress levels and their fears of "losing control of their Nation via cultural genocide," which according to my research on PTSD is very real and very dangerous to America's future survival as a Nation. I make this bold statement because I feel this type of holiday change to a National American Holiday can, and should, be considered an attack on America's cultural fabric and that special piece of America that the world calls the Americana Culture. After all, I am an American English professor who has worked in Mainland China, Hong Kong and Japan, and although there are many Americans living in these countries, I would never go into these countries and demand they allow me to take time off for the 4th of July American Holiday, which celebrates America's Independence day, in these countries. I feel I can honestly say that if I had tried to demand this kind change in any of the overseas Nations I had contracts to work in, I know I would have been asked to pack my bags and leave Japan, China, or Hong Kong.

Before I continue showing more examples that I feel are red flag alarms to America's citizens of the dangers they face in the near future by ignoring and allowing Muslim Sharia Law and Mexico's historically violent and lawless culture to enter and influence America's Judicial system and her Supreme Court and Lower Court Judges, I feel my readers need to take a good look at a written warning that was left to us by one of America's most prolific, successful, and intelligent writers of the 20th Century. This writer not only warned us of the dangers found in the Muslim Religion, in one of his many award winning books, but he intelligently used real events in world history to explain how dangerous the Muslim Religion and its followers are to America and the world's Christian population. So without further delay, I now offer a few quotes/ citations from one of Mr. James A. Michener's famous books The Covenant that was published by Random House Publishing Company of New York in 1980:

"His triumph was Africa [(Libya, Egypt, etc.)]…He did fix Africa in the Renaissance mind, and he did spur its exploration and its conversion to Christianity . . . but the main burden of his life was the Christianizing of Africa, and that is why the year 1453 brought him such grief . . . The Muslims, those dreadful and perpetual enemies of Christ, had swarmed Constantinople, lugging their ships across land to break the defenses, and this outpost, which had long protected Christianity . . . had fallen. Since all Europe could now be invaded by the followers of Muhammad, it was more urgent than ever…to salvage it, became a Christian duty." In this now famous quote, James A Michener not only gives us a very important history lesson that we should not forget, but he also laments about the fall of Africa into Muslim hands and the cost of this lost battle. I present this key part of world history here because I feel Michener's quote includes a very important message for the people of the world in the 21st Century. After all, Isn't there a saying that says, "If mankind does not learn from history and their mistakes, they are doomed to repeat their mistakes and history" (Michener, A James. The Covenant: Volume 1. Random House. New York: 1980 p 28).

Now that history and James A. Michener have warned Americans and the world to beware of what history taught us in the past, I feel Americans and the world need to be reminded of one more history lesson that happened in 1915, when the remaining strands of the "Ottoman—Muslim controlled" empire launched an offensive against the its Eastern Turkey Armenians, "...because they allegedly were supporting a Russian Invasion; [sadly and according to history...tens of thousands of Armenian men were shot and hundreds of thousands of women and children [were] driven out of their homes and forced to march towards Syria and Iraq" (Note: When I read these words, it reminded me of the U.S. Government's forced move of Native Americans now known as the "Trail of Tears.")...According to history and records, the forced march of these Armenians included Shootings, deliberate starvation, mass burning and drowning, which meant very few [Armenians] survived [this long march]. The death Toll [was] estimated to have been a million people," writes Richard G Hovanissian, one of the contributors to the book, <u>Photos That Changed The World: The 20th Century</u>.

I want to note here that to this day, adds Hovanissian in his notes, "Turkish [Turkey is Muslim in the 21st Century)] scholars dispute what happened to the Armenians, [and] Turkey's persistent denial of the Armenian genocide worked on many leaders including Adolf Hitler in 1939." I think this last statement basically and pretty well sums up importance of the warning James A. Michener left the world in his book, <u>The Covenant</u>: Volume 1 and Horvanissian left us in the chapter: "Armenian Genocide: 1915 Ottoman Empire." <u>Photos That Changed The World: The 20th Century</u>. Ed. Peter Stepan. Munich: Prestel Verlag, 2000.). To make things worse in the 21st Century, thanks to President Obama's constant urging, cash aid, military aid, and alleged push for Democracy in countries like Libya, Syria, and other African nations, it seems Africa will soon be in the control of the World's Muslims again. How bad can Muslim rule be in these African countries? Well let's just say I don't think it is going to be pretty especially after the Christian Church burnings that happened in Egypt in August of 2013, as reported on Network News stories. To close these thoughts on Muslim rule in Africa, I can only pray for the Christians living in these new Muslim controlled countries because I don't' see it getting any better for them, "May God be with them and protect them in Jesus name."

My readers should note that I ended the last paragraph with a blessing from the Lord; I took this action because of some information that one of my peers gave me that I decided needed to be in this book. The information my peer gave me allegedly had to do with Islam's "Muslim Government Constitution" that allegedly all Muslims must swear to and live by because it is written into their Koran (or part of their religion). I want to add that although these Muslin people live in America and the U.S. Constitution is the only Constitution they should be swearing to defend and obey (because they live in America and it's now their new home), according to my peer, these new U.S. Citizens don't see it that way because of the Constitution that is allegedly written into the Muslim Religion known as Islam. The Muslim Constitution, says my peer, tells them not to obey any other Constitution or swear allegiance to any other Constitution.

What troubles me about this alleged Muslim law is that when I found a translated copy of the Muslim Constitution on the web, I found several examples that confirmed these religious rules, and here is just one example of the laws found in Islam's Constitution: The Muslim Constitution I read said in Article 172: "The State's (the Muslim State's curriculum—no matter where they live) curriculum is the only one that is allowed to be taught. Private schools are allowed [in the Muslim State] provided they are bounded by the State's Curriculum. There should be separate classes for boys and girls. Furthermore, there should be no schools based on a particular religion or a sect or a race. All schools must adopt the State's curriculum and establish themselves on the education system and accomplish the goal and policy of education set by the state" (Anonymous, Daniel. Memo to Reggie B Two Stones

Author. Visalia, CA July 21, 2012. Note: When I typed in the words needed to find this page on the web to cite it in my book, the page's name was there but the web page had been "Removed."). After reading this part of the Muslim Constitution's laws, and a few more examples my peer sent me to read, I wondered if America's Department of Education is monitoring the schools in cities like Detroit where Muslim's control the local governments and schools? Since I do not have to the time to look up the complete Muslim Constitution, I want to let my readers know they can find the Constitution on the web by typing in the words "Muslim Constitution" on their search engine (Note: I did take the time to look us this page and it has been removed in 2018).

Note: Here are a few more Articles (laws) that are allegedly found in the said translated copy that is "on line" of Islam's Koran (That bothered your author and American Patriot, if it's true?): Article 179 and 184. I say it bothers me because Article 179 allegedly teaches Muslims the following trick when dealing in politics: "Political maneuvering is necessary in foreign policy. The effectiveness of this maneuvering is dependent on concealing one's aim and disclosing one's actions" (this basically means that they can lie to the people and nations of the world); and, Article 184, section 3 and Section 4: Section 3 teaches, or starts, with these scary words: "States with whom we do not have treaties, the colonists states, such as Britain, America, and France, and those states that have ambitions in our lands, such as Russia, are considered to be potentially warlike states. All precautions must be taken against them and it is not permitted to establish diplomatic relationships with them (If this law/article found in Islam's Religion is true, I have to ask, "Why are Muslims living in America?"); and Section 4 of this same alleged Muslim Constitution that allegedly states or teaches Muslims why there can never be peace in Israel: Allegedly, the Muslim Constitution makes this statement in it: "With States that are actually belligerent states, like Israel, a state of war must be taken as the basis of all dispositions with them. They must be dealt with as if a real war existed between us, whether during cease fire or otherwise." This statement, if we read it carefully, basically tells the world that even if the Muslim Nations say they want peace with Israel, they are never going to actually do it, or mean it. Now my fellow Americans should see whey the Palestinians and the Israelites can never have peace in this region.

Now, I want to ask my fellow Americans and the world's Democracies, and other world governments this question: If the Muslim Religion hates Western Nations as much as it allegedly says in their Koran, then why are they entering Western Nations and living in Countries like England, America, France, and Russia? They surely will never be happy in these nations that live in sin in the eyes of the Muslim Religion; so, why live in these nations? Maybe, the reason they're here is to usurp the standing governments and convert them into Muslim Nations so these nations will no longer be living in sin, as it allegedly says in their religious principles. If this is not their goal, but they still hate these sinful nations, then, I suggest they move to the new Muslim controlled Democratic countries like Egypt and Libya where they can live among others that want the same principles they want to live by because of their religious beliefs (Anonymous, Daniel. Memo to Reggie B Two Stones. Author. Visalia, CA. July 21, 2012). Before I end this paragraph, I want to add some scary information that I discovered today October 18, 2018 on the web, while I was looking for the web page that my contact Daniel had provided so I could find the web page that he had used to send me the information on the Koran's alleged or embedded religious constitution. Well, the address is still on line, the page does open up, but the page is gone. I tried several times to log on to this page at this web address https:// www.scribd.com/document/140868278/The-Divine-Constitution-Explained, and guess what? The page is gone! Remember hearing the message that people who use the web should be careful what the post on the web because once it's on the "world wide web," it is there for ever? Well (Guess what?), this message was a lie. I say this because those who have the Government's power can delete any thing they want, and I have the proof because the web page I used to cite the passages from Islam's Religious Constitution is gone and not assessable. This kind of power should really scare my fellow Americans.

Although there are countless more examples like the ones I offered in the last two paragraphs, I've decided to only show two more examples of Cultural Genocide. I should add these two quotes sent a cold chill up the spine of this minority writer and Compatriot because I feel these two examples weaken America's defenses against most kinds of attacks from those who would attack America's citizens. The first of these two examples that I want to note here should have been reported before the elections that were happening on the year this event took place; unfortunately, America's Fourth Estate (allegedly now known as Corporate America's News and Propaganda Machine) didn't bother to mention it in any news report. I make this statement because I think they covered up this story because it damaged President Obama's image. The hysterically funny part about this story is that although it was never reported by America's news organizations on the evening news this story's main topic had American, National, and International Security interests written all over it. Don't worry my fellow Americans I'll soon prove my point in this book:

But before I get a head of my self, I want to report that America's legal citizens should understand that on September 11, 2012 Freedom Outpost reported it had learned "President Obama was negotiating a deal to give aid to the Muslim Brotherhood [using] more American taxpayer dollars . . . By forgiving $1 Billion dollars in debt that Egypt owed the US" (Brown, Tim. "Obama Administration Aids Muslim Brother-hood with $1Billion of Taxpayer Money for U-Boats." Online Posting. 11 Sept. 2012. http://freedomoutpost.com/2012/09/obama-administration-aids-Muslim brotherhood). After reporting that America's President was, again, attempting to help Egypt's Muslim Brotherhood controlled government, Brown added that he learned the Daily Caller (a news organization) had reported that, "President Obama's deputies were negotiating a $1 Billion dollar aid package with Egypt's [new Muslim] government, even as Egypt's cash-strapped military revealed that it was trying to buy $1 Billion dollars worth of ultra modern German submarines that could threaten and destroy Israel's fast growing offshore energy projects. . . These U-boat submarines [(latest 209 class subs)] are among the most advanced non-nuclear [(that we're sure can be made nuclear with modifications)] subs available." The unbelievable part of this deal is that even after Obama had spent over $1200 Million U.S. taxpayer dollars of weapons, ammunition, and man-power to help the Muslim Brotherhood take control of Egypt and Libya, he still wanted to give Egypt $1 Billion dollars more to help these new Middle East Muslim leaders" (Brown, Tim. "Obama Administration Aids Muslim Brotherhood with $1Billon of Taxpayer Money for U-Boats (Online Posting. 11 Sept. 2012. http://freedomoutpost.com/2012/09/ Obama-administration-aids-Muslim-brotherhood.).".

The final example of "cultural genocide I have decided to present here is found in a quotation of an article that was posted on the web by Joel McDurmon on January 13, 2012. According to McDurmon, "The U.S. State Department removed the sections covering religious freedom from the Country's [(America's)] Reports on Human Rights that it released on May 24, three months past the statutory deadline Congress set for the release of these reports." Although McDurmon doesn't say why the then Obama Administration controlled U.S. State Department took so long to release this very important report, he did note that when the report was finally released the **report was missing** "sections that discussed the status of religious freedom in these new Obama financed countries [that included Egypt and Libya], and the...human rights reports that included the period that covered the Arab Spring and its aftermath" but, without the in-depth coverage report of "what had happened to Christians and other religious minorities in these new predominantly Muslim countries of the Middle East that saw the rise of revolutionary movements in 2011...[I also want to point out that] **for the first time ever**, the State Department simply eliminated the section of religious freedom in its reports covering 2011," added McDurmon (McDurmon, Joel. "State Dept erases religious freedom section from Report, hiding Arab Spring abuses." Online Posting. 13 Jan. 2012. http://americanvisionnews.com/3752/state-dept-erasesreligious-freedom-section-from-report-hiding-arab-spring-abuses).

Stop the Presses! Sorry, I have always wanted to use this famous saying from the past. Anyway, before my book went to press, an explosion of violence erupted in Egypt again during the week of 8/11/13 to 8/17/13 because the military and anti-Muslim control groups overthrew President Mohammed Morsi, the Muslim President. According to this story of one of Obama's so-called Democracies is blowing up in flames of violence, and the violence caused over 600 deaths, which (according to the Fourth Estate of Americ) has received condemnation from the world "for the bloody crackdown on Morsi's mostly Islamist supporters, including an angry President Barack Obama…" (Michael, Maggie, "Egypt Death toll hits 638." The Fresno Bee, August 16, 2013. Front Page.). I want to note that according to the news on television and the press "scores of Christian Churches were burned and policemen shot by the angry Muslim Morsi supporters." Yet! It was reported that President Obama did not condemn these acts against Christianity, or the attacks on the Policemen trying to control the mobs. These acts against Christian and their Churches pretty well sums up who the Muslim religion loves to hate when they get a chance or an excuse to show their hatred for Christians. At the time this book was printed, I found myself asking President Obama, "Where is your voice on this matter?"

Photographs of the signs of "The Times," or "Cultural Genocide in America"

This Mexican flag is the only flag that flies over the city of Richgrove, CA 24/7. This city has a 99 percent illegal alien Mexican invader population. The only American flag that flies over this city is the school flag that comes down every day, and during the weekends.

This 70 unit Obama Government financed semi-gated community is only one of the many multifamily units that went up all over California in 2013. As we can see from the sign in the photo, this unit spared no cost to build them. By the way, the families renting these condo-like units that offer them swimming pools, covered parking, solar panels, and low-cost rents are field workers that are mostly illegal aliens from Mexico.

Mexico's lawbreaking citizens get to live in US taxpayer financed condos with swimming pools, while America's legal citizens lose their homes and get to live in their cars with the children or in shelters because the banks these taxpaying Americans bailed out now continue to foreclose on their homes without any mercy or humanity.

This very nice, black truck that belongs to one of the many Mexican, lawless invaders who run to America's taxpayer financed cash welfare programs all over the nation. Thanks to a new welfare Obama Administration law 99 percent of the Mexicans who apply for cash aid, food stamps, medical cards, and WIC checks all drive trucks or cars this new because they know America's government will always bail them out. These Mexican laugh and makes jokes about Americans and their government because they say Americans are stupid.

An example of the hundreds of large, loud, and expensive parties (cost is usually $2,000 to $5,000) that are paid for and put on by Mexico's lawless invading families who claim poverty, qualify for welfare/ social services (80 % of these families are on some kind of welfare in California), get free cell phone services, low cost housing, food stamps, free Christmas gifts, and free day care and meals for their children at California schools. Yes, these are the families the US government reports that they are living in poverty because they work for low wages for US Corporate Farm Corporations.

This broken down and crumbling stone fence, was once a work of art, and had been standing at one of Porterville's City Parks for over 50 years. Unfortunately for Porterville's American Citizens, as Porterville's population became 70 percent illegal Mexican Invaders and these lawless invaders took over the park, they destroyed it in just under six years, it had to be torn down and replaced with an iron prison like fence.

And! Yet another Mexican flag flies in California across from a city golf course. These Mexicans put up these flag because they didn't like the fact that the golf course flew an American flag every day while it was open. This building or home that housed a group of lawless Mexican invaders would often play loud music to upset the men and women who were playing golf.

"The caption of this rally poster that is worn on T-shirts, put on posters, and often quoted by Mexico's illegal invaders when they protest at rallies against US-Immigration laws and demand Open Borders, tells Americans that America belongs to Mexico's invading force, because the are working in the fields of America's farms (they ignore the fact that

Americans have worked in the fields since 1776.) Translation: "The land (or America) belongs to those who are working the fields or land."

One of the many business that left McFarland because of the growing crime in this city, and as we can see from the sprayed on message by one of the 79 Mexican gangs that live in this city of 7,000, these Mexican lawless invaders have as much respect for America's law enforcement officers as they do in Mexico for their corrupt police officers. Yes, President Obama, your lawless invaders are law-abiding citizens.

This Stop sign on a street in McFarland says it all. These Mexican lawless, invading colonists' gang members have such little respect for American laws that they are even willing to use a sign that was created to make this American city safer, as a message board to warn Americans that the end of American rule in California is near.

H. Replacing America's Western Culture with
     Mexico's Dysfunctional, Lawless Culture.

Stop

In this section of the book, I hope to provide as many answers as possible to give Americans the tools they'll need to stop "America's Open Border Supporters" who appear to be intent on destroying and taking America from her scared and angry citizens. These citizens are not only scared but they also feel helpless as they see their beloved country march to its demise, and they see it replaced by Mexico's (and the Muslim's Culture too) dysfunctional culture that to this day is mired in murders, gang cartels, government corruption, and a lawless society. So what are the fears that are keeping America's citizens awake at night, as they do your author, and are the source of American's Post Traumatic Stress Disorder? The fears that keep them awake come from reports like the one written about Detroit, Michigan by Frosty Wooldridge. According to the web page "News With Views," On October 5, 2009, Wooldridge wrote a scathing report about how his hometown Detroit, Michigan had been destroyed by "diversity" and "cultural genocide." In his report, Wooldridge wrote that his beloved city Detroit had "descended into the abyss of crime, debauchery, gun play, drugs, school truancy, car-jacking, gangs, and human depravity . . . [because] as Muslims moved in, the whites moved out. And, as the crimes became more violent, the whites fled... Finally, unlawful Mexicans moved in at a torrid pace." Wooldridge then added that, "Detroit may be one of our best examples of multiculturalism's pure dislike America, and total separation from America" (Wooldridge, Frosty. "How Immigration and Multiculturalism Destroyed Detroit." On Line Posting 5 October 2009 http://newswithviews.com).

Although Frosty Wooldridge thought he was only reporting on his beloved city's plight back East, I know he was really reporting on what's happening to American cities across this great country because American cities are systematically being destroyed and gutted by the lawlessness that President Lincoln warned us about in his speech that I used earlier in this book to introduce this chapter. I want to add that Wooldridge's report of how Multiculturalism destroyed his beloved city of Detroit is nothing more than an affirmation on what I know is happening all over America, and what I am reporting in this book as the destructive powers of "cultural genocide," "diversity," and "reverse acculturation" overrun and destroy America's Americana Culture. I want to warn Americans that these three very destructive powers are moving across this once great nation, known for its law and order, with the force and destructive power of the tornados that ravaged Oklahoma in the summer of 2013.

But if Wooldrige thinks Detroit city is the only American city that is seeing its demise, I feel he needs to come to California and the other Southwestern states where Mexico's lawless band of colonizing invaders are taking over American cities faster than American businesses and American citizens can pack their bags and leave some of America's most beautiful states in the Union to the invading swarm that is coming across Mexico's border from Mexico and the rest of South and Central America. These businesses and citizens are leaving states like California because they're tired of seeing their businesses and homes pulled down into an abyss of lawlessness, murders, and crime. Now, before I move on and discuss the lawlessness and dysfunctional culture that's engulfing America's cities, I want to add that this culture of lawlessness has always existed in Mexico and many other Latin countries that lie below Mexico's borders. And I want to add that this lawlessness has always existed in Mexico ever since it was founded back in the days of Mexico's colonization when countries like England, France, and Russia claimed land that wasn't theirs in the Americas (because they didn't pay the indigenous people that lived on these lands and owned these lands). I feel I can make this statement because this lawless culture still exists in Mexico, and it's still a part of Mexico's culture. And now, thanks to our Government's open borders policy, this lawless culture has taken root in America.

When I think of the words lawlessness and lawless cultures, I think of the days of Europe's "dark ages." For those who don't know, the dark ages were a time when self appointed kings, queens, knights, dukes, earls, and the lot used lawless powers to keep the poor and uneducated people in submission by taxing them and starving them to death without any kind of laws to protect this class of people. I also think of the days of the "Spanish Inquisition" when religious fanatic leaders and their conspirators tortured, maimed, and even crucified citizens who were falsely accused of being heretics. And finally, when I think of the terms "dysfunctional and lawlessness," I think of the days of the old west in America when fast guns, kangaroo trials, worthless Indian treaties, and lawless uneducated people passed judgment on both guilty and innocent people in the name of an alleged God fearing Anglo controlled lawless (because the law did not protect all citizens of America) Culture of the United States Government. Incase my readers are wondering why I used these examples to describe the term lawlessness, I used them because I feel these examples are very much in line with the definition of the word "lawlessness" that I found in Funk and Wagnalls College Dictionary and the synonyms I discovered in Webster's New World Thesaurus: Funk and Wagnalls Edition.

I now want to note that by defining the term "lawlessness" and later the term "dysfunctional" I feel I will be able to discuss the lawlessness that's moving into America and the dysfunctional cultures and religions that I feel are responsible for the slow demise of America's "Western Euro Influenced Christian Culture." According to Harold J. Grilliot and Frank A. Schubert the authors of Webster's New World Thesaurus: Funk and Wagnalls Edition, the term "lawlessness" has several synonyms that not only show how dangerous the act of lawlessness is to America, but also how destructive it is to those who find themselves in the way of this term's actual, physical realities. The synonyms for this word include the following words that Grilliot and Schubert list in their book: irresponsibility, terrorism, chaos; see disorder 2, [and] disturbance 2, [in the book, Webster's New World Thesaurus: Funk and Wagnalls Edition]" (Laird, Charlton, and William D. Lutz. Webster's New World Thesaurus: Funk and Wagnalls Edition. Simon and Schuster, Inc: New York, 1971.).

As for the definitions I found for the words "lawlessness and dysfunctional," Funk and Wagnalls College Dictionary tell us the term "lawlessness, which is part of the term lawless, means: "1. Not controlled by law, authority, discipline, etc. 2. Not in conformity with law; contrary to rules and regulations, etc. [and] 3. Having no law or restrictive regulations" ("lawlessness." Funk and Wagnalls Standard College Dictionary. Text: Ed. 1967.). As for the word "dysfunctional" it comes from the root word "dysfunction," which means "Deterioration of the natural action of a part [of an object or thing]; or the malfunction [of an object or thing.]" What I feel we learn from these anti-control or anti-law terms is that a "dysfunctional" culture is simply a culture that has not progressed to the standards of what Social Psychologist consider a civilized or culturally advanced culture ("dysfunctional." Funk and Wagnalls Standard College Dictionary. Text Ed: 1967.). Since this type of dysfunctional foreign culture is not considered (or defined) advanced socially, I feel I can say cultures like Mexico's (and Islam's religious Culture) culture do not possess a natural and preferred advanced civilized way of functioning as a society or cultural group (This lack of advancement culturally would show up in a country like America in various ways like not obeying American laws, social mores', cultural and social values of the US, or US social cultural norms that Americans feel are a natural part of life.) in the new host country's modern or morally advanced country. A representative sample of how lower advanced cultures act can be seen in the way Mexicans ignore their own country's driving laws and criminal laws in Mexico that are now finding there way onto America's soil, yet these people are being allowed to drive in California with their Mexican driving licenses.

The sad point I am going to make here is that these colonizing new invaders/ and alleged illegal aliens, that are now living on US Soil, are bringing their lack of respect for laws and social norms into America. Please note this conclusion is shared by Mr. Wooldridge in his article because he also says "these people [have a] lack of respect for laws in their own countries [and it] is following them into America." Note that I decided to add this last quote from Mr. Woolridge's article that he wrote about his hometown because in his article he describes what he feels has happened to his hometown of Detroit and other colonized American cities, and I can prove it has happened to my hometown in California that was once a small quiet "All-American" city. In case my readers are wondering what happened to my hometown of McFarland (that is found in Central California), it has been completely taken over by these colonizing, invaders from Mexico's lawless culture. My hometown that was once the home of mostly World War II Vets, Korean Vets, their families, and various other American family groups is now about 90 percent illegal Mexican invaders. And unfortunately for Americans, with this large contingent of Mexican illegal colonizers moving into this city, McFarland's crime rate has gone off the scale in a per capita comparison to larger cities. According to some "old timers" who are still living in this city (I was lucky enough to talk to at my last class reunion.), Gunfire can be heard in the city almost every night and the teachers that used to live in and teach in the city have now moved to Bakersfield a safer city over 40 miles away.

I want to note that this paragraph was not in my original first or second edition but I feel I need to add this information to show my readers how powerful the forces (deep state?) are that are behind this push to destroy American Sovereignty and force their Socialist type culture and Government on Americans in the 21st Century. After my book came out (was published) in 2015, I heard rumors that Walt Disney had contacted McFarland's city government about making a movie on a coach I knew well from my youth that was still living in McFarland and had achieved some high level recognition because the cross country teams he coached had won the small high school's state championship several times. In the end (to make a long story short), this information turned out to be a half-truth, or half a lie. I know I can make this statement because when the movie came out this movie did NOT have the coach's name in the title of the movie nor did it really tell his story. I say this because Disney basically didn't use the coach's name in the title of the movie or talk about his personal life. What Disney did do was title the movie "McFarland USA," and instead of keying on Coach White's accomplishments and coaching theories (which would have been a great movie especially if had been called something like "Jim White Small High School Wonder Coach," like old movies of past great coaches like "Pop Warner" or "Jim Thorpe All-American"), the movie keyed on several high school runners (whose parents were illegal aliens) that had grown up to be alleged successes in America, and it also keyed on the fact that these runners were children of illegal immigrants that had become successful because America's Government had allowed them to stay and live in America illegally.

To make sure the people who went to see this movie got the message that "open border illegal aliens are good for America, the movie also keyed on two runners Mr. White had coached and that had grown up to become a Sheriff in Kern County and a Bakersfield Police Officer. To make a long story short, this pro-open border movie ended up falling flat (I guess God or Karma caught up with Walt Disney and the open borders people.) on its face because the two ex McFarland High School runners the movie keyed on both ended up going to jail and being stripped of their officer's titles because they both committed some very serious crimes in Kern County, or the county the city of McFarland is found in. By the way, both of these ex-McFarland runners were found guilty of the crimes they each allegedly committed during the time they were officers on duty. Now you know why the movie was not pushed as a DVD to sell to the public and most smart Americans forgot about this worthless propaganda movie. If this addition to my book doesn't scare my readers, I guess these kinds of cold hard facts are not enough to wake Americans up. One more point I want to make here is that since I had described how my old high school looked like it had been changed to look more like a jail than a high school because of the crimes of high vandalism being committed on the school grounds when it was closed (by the same illegal children attending this school), Walt Disney invested over $3,000,000 (that's three million dollars) to make the school look like an All-American High School that included a college level track, football stadium, and gym, that I'm sure was done to make my book look bad, or to prove I lied about McFarland in my book. As my readers can see, this expensive cover up didn't work thanks to the runners turned cops that in the end went back to their old cultural deviant norms and became lawbreaking criminals.

Now that I've provided semi-scientific proof and examples that show why Mexico's culture is so violent to this day in America, and is a long ways from changing their cultural norms, I want to add that as this culture invades America and colonizes the Southwestern states (which by the way is not a legal act according to past treaties that America, Mexico, and the South American countries signed into power when they approved the "Good neighbor policy" and the Monroe Doctrine), the crime rates in these states are growing by leaps and bounds just like they did in the city of Detroit. I've also found that Mexico's colonizing illegal invaders, and other U.S. invading cultures, are causing great harm to America's Western European influenced Christian culture and her legal American citizens because they're importing or bringing their lawlessness and violence in to America's Sovereign soil. And since I feel I've proven my accusation(s) with real facts and citations, I want to add that Richard T. Schaefer's research and facts about cultures that are dysfunctional (and dysfunctional cultures) also confirms the facts I found in his book that he simply titled <u>Sociology.</u> I want to note that he writes in his book that "not all parts of society contribute to its (the host new country or society) stability all of the time" [because the new illegal immigrant cultures have not evolved completely]. As a reminder, I want to add that according to Richard Schaefer, "dysfunction also refers to cultural elements and other lawless and illegal acts performed by culture's [like Mexico's invading colonizing culture], or a process of society that may actually be disrupting the new social system or culture, and/or leading it to a decreased instability," [as it seems both the influx of Muslim Religion's Sharia Law Constitution and Mexico's colonizing invaders are doing to [America's society, the American Constitution, and our Western Christian Culture]" (Schaefer, T. Richard, Sociology. McGraw Hill: Boston 9 Ed 2005.).

As I continue my report of the damage being done by these invading cultures entering American Sovereign soil illegally, I think I can honestly say I feel I've proven "cultural genocide, lawlessness, and dysfunctional acts seem to go hand-in-hand with the acts of cultures that have not progressed, bothered to learn, or even tried to internalize its host (America) country's culture. To continue my presentation of real facts that show the damage being done to America's culture, I want to now show some solid examples that I feel explain how certain foreign country dysfunctional cultures (for example Mexico's, Islam's, and other, invading colonists) are impacting the cities they chose to settle in on American soil. These negative impacts that affect America's cities and citizens, I want to note, are having such a negative impact in states like California that America's citizens are giving up on these states and leaving them in record numbers:

To prove the statement I made in the last paragraph, the first example I'm going to explore for the benefit of my readers comes to us from the city of Fresno, California. Last week (5/29/13) the author watched several Fresno city television stations report that two major businesses/companies were pulling out of the city of Fresno and California because, as their CEOs said, "they were tired of the growing crime their businesses were dealing with on a daily basis in the Fresno area and they felt it was getting worse instead of better." The two TV stations that were ABC and NBC affiliates added that these two companies' decisions were not "the only businesses that had recently pulled out of California in recent years," and they then added in their news cast that businesses leaving the state of California were becoming a common trend in California cities like Fresno" (Fresno: ABC and NBC affiliates, 29 May 2013.).

Now that I've hopefully shocked my readers who are not living in Southwest states, I hope these Americans will pay close attention to the next few examples I'm going to present in this section of my book. But before I do, I'd like to put the city of Porterville, California into perspective so my readers won't think it is some huge metropolis like the city of Fresno, which is a big city. First, I want to tell my readers that Porterville, California has a population of about 55,000 or 60,000; however, the population has been growing at an uncomfortable and fast rate over the past five years because like the rest of the state of California Mexico's invading colonists continue to enter California on a daily basis and at an alarming rate (like Wooldrigdge reported in his story about Detroit city).

I wish I could say the reason Porterville's population is growing at an alarming rate is because of job growth but that would be a lie. The reason I'd be lying is that Porterville is located in Tulare county where the average income is about $16,000 per year (among the lowest in the state, or maybe the lowest), and Tulare County is known as a Welfare county in California because almost 80 percent of the county's population is on some kind of financial aid, social services, Medical Card, or Food Stamps (reported on local television news). The fact I just reported now leads me to report my next negative fact: I want to report the population in both Tulare County and it cities like Porterville are running anywhere from 70 to 90 percent lawless or colonizing Mexican illegal citizens. The reason these Mexican citizens love this country is because these invading and colonizers are being handled with "kid gloves" (or with "special regulations" that only apply to Mexico's colonizing invaders) that allow these families to apply for so-called absent father welfare cash aid with very little investigating, so the so called absent father really lives in the home and it is not questioned because of a loop hole in the law. This loophole allows these families to live on California welfare subsidized combined incomes of over $4,000 per month, instead of the $1500 per month the family reports it is living on from fieldwork. I should add that Aid For Dependant Children (AFDC) was created for American families that end up short on cash because either the father loses his job, the parents get a divorce so the father stops supporting the family (or sometimes the mother stops supporting the family) and the family has to get help. But thanks to California's Socialist like Government, this program has been expanded to the point that even illegal foreigners who have children in the home now qualify for many of the "new" various forms of Social Services or Cash Aid.

I want to add that the Welfare Subsidized incomes of these illegal aliens can sometimes get even bigger, especially if these illegal aliens have been able to get their grandparents across the border. I add this important fact because I know these grandparents (who have never worked a day on US soil) do qualify for SSI. That is right my readers; these old injured or retired people qualify for SSI even if they have "NEVER" worked in America, paid into social security, or lived in America. These grandparents can and do qualify for the current amount of about $999 per month or higher for each grandparent and for Medical cards and Food Stamps. Now you see why these illegal families often do better than most Americans living on minimum wage jobs who often have little or no chance of qualifying for these same benefits because they have to use their real names and their real social security cards when they apply for social services. I finished with the last statement because of my experience as an ex Eligibility Worker II when I worked for Tulare Country Social Services. I know these illegal alien Mexicans, or alleged immigrants, all qualify because the often usually have four of five different names and several fake identifications to go with the names, and as I was told, "our job is not to investigate these families' lies, because our jobs is to "grant them aid." Since America's left leaning leaders and their operatives working in the US Government have deemed it prudent to let these illegal aliens enter US Sovereign soil without having to follow US immigration laws to establish their real identities, I hate to say it but there is no way to know who these people are or what their backgrounds have hidden in their past, even if they are on Social Services because we don't want to offend them.

Before I get back to discussing America's lawless illegal aliens, I want to add that Social Security Disability (SSDI), unlike Social Security, has no age limits and no contribution requirements so nobody has to pay into it to qualify for this real entitlement; oh yes, I want to add one more key component of SSDI is that none of these persons who decide to enter the Social Security Office with some kind of disability and apply for American tax payer financed disability has to prove any kind of citizenship or legal status for being in America. When these illegal aliens, who more than likely were injured in their home country, get denied, they are allowed by US law to simply get an American lawyer who will take their case for a piece of their future free US taxpayer paid income. So to sum it up for my American tax payers who do not know about SSDI, SSDI rules allow any person with a permanent injury, deformity, or disability who enters an American Social Security office to apply for American disability, again whether they were born with it in their own country, injured in their own country, or are just too old to work. And the sad part about SSDI is that almost anyone qualifies for SSDI, if they can get across the American border and into the United States legally or not. That is why both lawless colonizing invaders and legal immigrants always make it a priority to bring in (or smuggle in) their aged or disabled parents and disabled children into America.

My fellow Americans, I want to go on record here and tell you that SSDI is the biggest and most expensive give away, entitlement, boondoggle, or joke that American taxpayers have ever been forced to pay without ever having been asked if they wanted to pay for any or all of the world's disabled citizens who manage to get into America legally or illegally and end up on this big entitlement.

By the way, my fellow Americans, I want to remind my fellow Americans that they will never hear (or have ever heard) that SSDI (Social Security Disability Insurance?) is going broke from any elected government representative of the US Government. On the other hand, I am sure we Americans have all heard (or will hear again in the near future) that Social Security, which is really an American citizen paid and financed retirement Insurance that almost all Americans who work pay into when they start working in America till the retire. If my fellow Americans are wondering why I say almost all Americans pay into Social Security, I remind them that private retirement programs like 401Ks (which are a joke, as the last stock market crash proved) and other private programs are now allowed to be offered by employers in America. As for why we Americans keep hearing that Social Security is going broke, well the answer is quite simple if we look behind the curtain of deception and lies that our elected representatives use to hide the truth about what is really wrong with our Social Security retirement system. If we look behind the curtain of Government lies, the first fact we find is that our Social Security retirement system has been mismanaged by the same elected officials that were supposed to take care of it, and that is why it is going broke. To tell the truth, I'm sure the mismanagement of Social Security is really our Congress' fault. I come to this conclusion because records show that Congresspersons have been using the coffers of Social Security as their piggy bank to pay for special pork barrel projects in their states by allegedly borrowing the money, but the problem is they never pay it back. The reason these Congresspersons use our Social Security money for special projects in their states is to get re-elected by their constituents in their state for being good providers of pork barrel projects. And! Although these Congresspersons all write IOUs and promise to pay, or replace/repay the money they borrow from our retirement system, to this day, the records show that none of these Congresspersons has ever kept this promise or paid back one penny.

Now that my fellow Americans see how easy it is for any foreigner to get an income for life in America from one of our entitlement programs (without ever working a day in America) and how our Congresspersons are draining their Social Security retirement coffers, I hope they are ready to help me stop this American Government give away of American cash resources to the world's citizens who are not vested US Citizens and the borrowing of money from our Social Security System's coffers. My fellow Americans, if we don't stop this craziness and we let our US Government Reps do as they please, all I can really say is the following: Is it any wonder that we have a growing influx of Mexican colonizing invaders (and other invading nationals) entering and taking over America and states like California with all of this easy money being offered to them by America's Government?

And, unfortunately for my California city of Porterville and what is left of her citizens, I feel it is too late for us because our city is looking more and more like the city of Detroit. In fact, I feel my city looks like more like what happened in Detroit because, like Wooldrige wrote about Detroit, we have a growing crime rate in our city like he wrote about his city. In fact, our city's crime rate is growing so much each day both in the number of crimes being committed and the severity of the crimes being committed by Mexican gang members, that I feel these gang members now control Porterville's streets. And! I want to remind my fellow Americans that we shouldn't forget that our fellow American Wooldridge reported that his hometown of Detroit also suffered this kind of crime growth every day before it became the lawless city he says exists there to this day. Unfortunately for my city, Porterville seems to be following in the footsteps of growing crime just like the city of Detroit reported in Wooldrige's story: In other words, as the number of crimes go up each day, and the severity of the crimes go up in Porterville each day, and the more illegal Mexican aliens move in to our city, the citizens of Porterville are seeing their town turn into a lawless society. And, as this lawlessness increases, more and more American Citizens and businesses are getting fed up with the lies of their elected politicians, and they are deciding to leave cities like Porterville and the state of California. To add salt to these American citizens' wound, a recent news report released last year (2012) said that for every 1,000 American citizens who decide to leave California (and cities like Porterville) some 2,000 illegal Mexican aliens are entering California and replacing them (Note: Newspaper story or the report did not specify if it was a monthly or yearly figure, but to Californians, it appears to be a weekly figure from the changes we are seeing in the city of Porterville area). I want to now add that this statistic basically means that in the near future the state of California will someday become 100 percent illegal aliens, and the state of California will very likely be controlled by Mexico's citizens and its government.

I hope my fellow Americans now see why I (a Minority American citizen) felt that a person of my heritage and skin color was the only person who could write this book and not be called a racist person. After all, I am a minority and a man of color so I feel I have a right to write this very controversial book. And! Because I'm a minority of Hispanic and Native American heritage, I feel this book cannot be called a racist attack, or a racist book. For the readers who have read this far in my book, I am sure my readers can tell this book has nothing to do with racism and everything to do with returning America's citizen's rights back to the right-full owners of the principles and laws found in "America's Constiution," which is what Fredric Bastiat says in his Book <u>The Law</u>. By the way, having read Fredric Bastiat's book, I can honestly say I feel that with a Minority American Patriot as the author of the book you're holding, this book cannot be labeled a racist agenda type book. So in the end, my book is not about Nationalism, as Democrats accuse us Patriotic Americans, because it is more about the Americana Culture and the true owners of the Constitution because they created and wrote the American Constitution to protect their "Individual" rights that they created and wrote for themselves from those (or any one) who might enter America illegally, or by force, and try to lay claim to the rights and laws that are written into their American Constitution and their Declaration of Independence. I also want to add that as I was writing this controversial book I felt that "Right" was on my side and God too.

I now say that I hope my fellow Americans will join me in starting the fight to take back our American Constitutional rights that according to Frederic Bastiat only belong to America's legal and real citizens. A fight that we must win, so we can start to take back both America and states like California (one of the most beautiful states in America) from falling into the hands of foreign governments like Mexico and foreign religions that have hidden Constitutions that preach for the destruction of Western countries like America. As I write this work of rebellion to take back our rights and country, or perish if we don't, I hope my readers will start paying attention to the many kinds of crimes and incidents that are presently happening in America's Southwestern states like California. I want my fellow Americans to start paying attention to these crimes that are making American citizens feel like packing up their belongings and leaving their homes, friends, and jobs to start new lives in either another state or a foreign country (Note: In the past few years, many of my friends and relatives have packed up and left California for other states and countries.). To highlight the impact of this pattern of abandonment, I want to add that my brothers and nephews have started to move out of California to other states because of the crime and drug wars being fought on the streets of our small hometowns like Porterville that is located in Central California.

Without any further delay, I'd like to take a quote from one of the many violent news stories that have appeared in our local Porterville newspaper dubbed the Porterville Recorder. This story was published on Saturday, June 1, 2010 in the weekend edition of the few English written newspapers that are still in business in Central California. I want to add that because of the demographics change that are happening in our cities, or as Central (and the state of California) California becomes or is pushed towards a 100 percent illegal Mexican population, more and more non-English reading or speaking people are becoming the norm in America's Southwest states like California. Now, to get back to the story I introduced that was published in the Porterville Recorder, the headline of this story read as follows: "Gang members sentenced in 2009 murder." I want to add the story in the Recorder said, "Ruben Juarez, 23, Alfredo Navarro, 22, and Aurelio Llamas, 21, were found guilty of the January 16, 2009 murder of Robert Santillan: "According to the Recorder, Santillan was severely beaten and stabbed in a gang related argument, then killed with a 12 gauge shotgun and a .357 handgun." The three gang members were convicted of first degree murder" (Recorder Staff, "Gang Members Sentenced in 2009 Murder," Porterville Recorder, June 1, 2010. Front Page.). I want to add that I decided to open with this story because it shows the brutality of these Mexican or Hispanic young gang members that come from a macho culture that is still a mainstay in Mexico.

For those people who might say, "How dare you say that Mexico's culture has always had a problem with violence, murder, and brutality like the three young men in the story," I answer with this sentence: The answer to their remark is not hard to come up with or defend because as I stated in this section of my book, "Mexico's culture can be classified a dysfunctional culture because through out its history, as research shows, it has always had a problem with a violent, macho based, revenge, graft, and lawless culture. I also want to add that when I was young boy my mother ran (owned) a small grocery store out of our back spare room in our home, and I remember seeing illegal Mexican men, who shopped at our store, reading Mexican tabloids and newspapers that they had brought with them from Mexico. And, as I watched them read their papers, what horrified me the most about these magazines/newspapers was that the front pages of these tabloids were always covered with gore, blood, and bodies of murdered and raped or shot victims. When I would ask the men in my broken Spanglish why there were so many murders in Mexico, they would answer that men and women in Mexico would kill to defend their honor, their sister's honor, or their mother's honor because it was the right thing to do in their country. I also want to note that they also added these people also killed to protect their personal property from bandits. These men would also add that some people also killed for money or revenge on a Police officer or local government official too, as pay back. To say the least, although I was quite young, I often found myself thinking that I was so thankful and lucky to be living in my country of America and not in Mexico.

By looking at Mexico's current and past violent culture using the results of a recent study completed by Dr Leonard D. Eron and then applying it (and some of his results on Human behavior and Sociological Behavior) to today's Mexican culture, I was able to find some parallels and identical answers to the ones Dr. Enron found in his study when I applied his methodology and results to the local Mexican/Hispanic young people (illegal and some legal) in the city of Porterville. I want to add the results Dr. Eron's research established and presented, that I found in his study, came in quite handy to study the impact these new illegal aliens' thought process is having on my city and California. These young Mexican or Hispanic students and some non-students that were my target, or research group, helped me see that there was indeed a connection between Dr Eron's study (and the results or conclusions he reached) and my study group. In fact, after weeks of research and studying my target group, I was able to duplicate and reach the same conclusions that Dr. Enron reached in his study, by applying his methodology to the young people in my study. What I learned was that the young people in my area (and throughout California) are some of the main reasons of why California's cities and America's culture are slowing feeling and looking more and more like Mexico's violent revenge based Macho culture.

To begin my discussion on my study, I want to start by showing my readers a statement made by American Psychologist Leonard D. Eron who studied and discovered that "aggressive children that come from an overly aggressive culture have certain common characteristics that I will now offer as facts: "First, they tend to be disliked by other children. Second, these children tend to indulge in active aggressive fantasies. Third, in these types of cultures, both aggressive boys and girls prefer masculine activities (and tend to blur the lines between being a boy or a girl, which might explain why many, many of the young female Mexican/Hispanic students in our local schools are dressing and defining themselves as young boys) [like fighting], talking about being aggressive, talking back to teachers or those in power and using fowl language like swearing at every opportunity they can get during their conversations. Fourth, these young people are usually low achievers in school; and Fifth, these young people enjoy watching violence on TV and often identify strongly with the violence they see on the television screen" (McConnell, V. James. "Eron's Chicago Circle Studies," Understanding Human Behavior. Holt Rinehart and Winston: New York 5 Ed 1986.). I want to add here that although I did not start taking notes of the interactions I was observing and hearing of these young people at first, I later found myself taking notes and making these young people the subjects of my study that I decided to start one day when I was forced to listen to a loud and lively discussion. I decided to start studying and keeping records of these young males and females after I found their behavior to be very much in line with the characteristics I had read about in Eron's study. As I studied these young people, I found them to be very aggressive children in both their mannerisms and their very vocal discussions in public.

I want to add that before I decided to study this young adults, teens, and students I had already started gathering information several months earlier on the growing violence in our cities and state. I also want to note that I had started to collect this information even before I had decided to write this book. In case my readers want to know why had already started to collect these facts, the answer is quite simple: I was doing it because (as a Social Psychology major with a degree in this field of study, and having done field work for my University's Anthropology Dept. during my MA studies) I had found the students' topics very violent and at the same time interesting. So! When I decided to write this book, I also decided to see if Eron's theory of violence applied to these seemingly aggressive students that I had found in my own backyard; basically, I decided to see if I could possibly apply the results of this new information to the information I had already gathered and put it in this book. As my readers can see, after I completed my research and combined all of the results of my research, I reached the conclusion that I had to include the results of this new study in this section of the book.

I decided to include the results here because I felt it helped me show how the growing violence in California cities (that is becoming common place and accepted) is probably connected to the thought process of these young adult and teen students and the adult role models of their culture, the Mexico gangs, and even their parents. I want to note that my results were reached by using the actual topics of these students' discussions. The sad part is that these students offered this information (for observation) because of their very loud boisterous discussions that anyone could listen to and hear at many of our local fast food restaurants and national coffee houses that these high school and junior college aged students use as hang outs. During the time I was in these places either having a meal or enjoying a coffee break, I would listen to these young students' loud and boisterous crude and violent conversations that were so loud it was easy (I do want to add that I think it has to do with a sense of identity crises, or the old "look at me I'm somebody syndrome.) to listen to their conversations, or audit them. Believe me, listening to them was not a hard task to accomplish, so they were never meant to be private discussions:

As to the most interesting conversations I encountered during my research, I have to say I found the discussions about "who kicked whose ass" (their words) as evidently the most important topic these young people wanted to discuss on a daily basis. I learned this fact because of a lively discussion one young lady was having with her friends. The discussion went something like this:

The young lady had confronted some other young girl in school and allegedly she had warned her she was "going to kick her ass for talking to her man"; another interesting and loud conversation I was allowed to hear in the same eating place was one that had a young man bragging that he "had pulled a gun on some guys because they had said something about his car that had pissed him off," and the final discussion that I was allowed to hear, along with the rest of people in this place of business, was a discussion between two young men who were discussing how "they were going to get even with a teacher at a local high school" and how one of the student's father "had told him to not let the teachers push him around." To show this statement of getting even with teachers evidently was no joke to these illegal people from Mexico, I want to add that in Fresno (CA) three very young Hispanic/Mexican grammar school students were arrested for the attempted poisoning of their teacher because they were upset with the teacher." So what I learned from all of these not so private, or public, conversations was that these students do actually act on their parents' advice of not letting their teachers push them around. Evidently these young grammar and high school aged Central California Valley Mexican students never got President Obama's message (that he always delivered when he had a chance to ask Americans to accept his "Amnesty plans while he was still in office) that "these people (illegal aliens) are law abiding people who only want a chance for a better life and blah, blah, blah."

As my readers can now see from these random conversations I was allowed to over hear and document at some of local students' hang outs, these young (illegal and semi-legal) Mexican or Hispanic students (both girls and boys) think nothing of fighting, assaulting, threatening, or getting even with others when they feel someone has wronged them, and these acts of violence even apply to their teachers. Now that I have shown my fellow Americans that "many" of the local Porterville Mexican/Hispanic boys and girls are willing to use violence without a second thought, I feel I can prove how easy it was for me to apply Eron's research theory of violence that he said is committed by children that come from aggressive cultures that have not developed. I believe my fellow Americans can see why Eron's theory applies quite well to the results of the research I gathered at our local young Mexican's hang outs in our area. For a good example, I want to note that when I applied Eron's theory to my research, I found Eron's conclusions that, "1. Aggressive (violent) children dislike other children, 2. Have active aggressive fantasies, and 3. Enjoy watching violence on television, all applied or were found to be part of these students every day life (as gleaned from their own discussions, and from their actual and active conversations that I recorded during my research that is now included in this book. So in the end, I found my observations matched up very well with Eron's conclusions and theories of violent cultures. I want to note one more fact here that comes from my observation of these young people. Since the parents of these children some times came to pick them up, I learned that some of these children came from parents that fathered them when the parents were still quite young because most of them were in the late 20s or 30s (Note: The parents would often come to these hang outs to pick up these young students so they wouldn't be shot by Mexican gang members.), so evidently Eron's conclusion that says that "Younger and less educated fathers [usually have] aggressive sons" definitely applies here (Note: From my recorded observations, I learned the daughters are also aggressive.) (McConnell, V. James. "Eron's Chicago Circle Studies," Understanding Human Behavior. Holt Rinehart and Winston: New York 5 Ed 1986.).

To prove that the threats made by these students were often acted on, and were not just talk, I want now offer some stories of violent acts that have become common place in the Porterville, California as more and more Mexican lawless illegal aliens move into this city. The first story of violence I want to discuss was the talk of the town in Porterville back in March of 2013. What was horrible about this story, or act of violence, is that my home is only one block away from where this act of violence by young Mexican gang members took place. This event of violence happened one day during my drive home through my local neighborhood. Although nothing seemed to be out of the ordinary during my drive, when I came around a corner, I suddenly noticed that one of my streets had been taped off with police tape that said do not enter. After slowing down and talking to the Police and neighbors, I learned that four young Hispanic/Mexican males had started yelling (in Spanish) and arguing with a couple that had been out for a bike ride with their children. When the yelling got very heated, the four young men suddenly jumped out of the truck and started attacking the young father and mother in front of the couple's children.

According to a witness, "a man and several teens in a pickup had driven by the couple and yelled something at the couple and then they suddenly jumped off the pickup bed and started attacking the couple. During the scuffle, the bike riding couple had their faces slashed multiple times by the four young Mexican/Hispanic males that had attacked them. After the attack, according to the witness, the attackers left the couple bloodied and screaming for help. Police said a local neighbor who had been watching the attack from her window had called the police. According to the Porterville Police Department, the suspects allegedly fled on foot and two bicycles, and the oldest member had driving off in the truck. Most of the local people I talked to after the attack felt this senseless attack had been a gang initiation attack; however, I want to add, this information was allegedly never confirmed. The only good that came out of this senseless attack was that within hours three of the four alleged Hispanic/Mexican (adult and teens) male suspects, or attackers, had been arrested and were in custody, and the final suspect was allegedly arrested a few days later.

As my readers can see from this eyewitness report of this act of violence, the violence in the Porterville area is scary and real; however, if my readers think this was a scary and unexpected attack on an innocent family, the next act of violence that occurred in the Porterville area is really going to make Americans think twice about what is really happening in California (or coming to California) as it heads towards a 99 to 100 percent illegal Mexican population. This incident might also have them asking themselves, "Why are these California based colonizing and invading illegal Mexican people so violent, and why doesn't someone stop the mass lawless invasion of California?" One has to wonder why these young people and their parents don't change and learn to appreciate the new life they've been given a chance to live? Or, why these people don't appreciate and take advantage of the fact that they are living in one of the most beautiful states in America, and are no longer in their drug and war torn Mexico? I'm sad to say, and point out, that the answer can be found in some of the following paragraphs that discuss Dr. Eron's research and his brave scientifically calculated conclusions that he arrived from his research.

Now that I've started to prove why the violence in California is growing (and also in the USA), I want to move on to the next story that also shows how violent this culture is that is coming from America's Southern border. According to the facts I read on 12-27-2010 in our local newspaper that is called the Porterville Recorder, the Recorder said or reported that a young couple had been held at gunpoint in their own home and had been robbed by four Mexican suspects who had entered their home by force. "The suspects," the story read, "included three men and a female who, according to Porterville Police, forced their way into the couple's home and robbed them" ("Couple Robbed at Gun Point," Porterville Recorder. 27 December 2010, Online posting http://www.recorderonline.com.) at gunpoint. Now that I've reported yet another violent crime in the Porterville area that shows the growing violence, I hope my readers are starting to see the pattern of violence that is slowly taking shape in our California's cities as the massive invasion of illegal citizens from Mexico (and other South American and foreign countries) grows in numbers. I want to add that the result of this growing violence is causing a major change in California that has America's legal and once proud citizens of California abandoning their homes, their friends, and their state for the safety they hope to find in either some other state and some other country.

By now my fellow Compatriots that don't live in the Southwest, or in California, should be starting to be aware that America's Fourth Estate is not reporting the truth to them about the growing violence that is taking over states like California as the racial and cultural demographics change because of the large influx of illegal aliens and foreign invaders that do not qualify to be called immigrants. I also want to add here that the Fourth Estate is also not telling America's Compatriots the truth about the fact that millions of Americans are leaving America's Southwest states (like California) at a record pace because they are seeing their cities and states explode in crime and violence. As my fellow Americans can see from my report, the facts I'm providing in this section of my book show that with the growing influx of Mexico's illegal alien Invaders (and other countries) in states like California are forcing Americans to decide to find relief by abandoning their homes, friends and jobs they once loved (Note: The majority of my classmates that I went to high school in Porterville have either quit their jobs, sold their businesses, or closed their businesses and have moved to states like Missouri, Alabama, Arkansas, and Tennessee in the past six years.).

If my readers think they've heard it all, I'd like to offer just a few more violent crimes that have occurred in the city of Porterville over the past few years that happened during the time I was writing this book. These crimes are the ones I learned about from my contacts with the Porterville Police Department during the time I was writing this book: 1) "Porterville officers responded to a residence where they arrested Luis Quintero age 26, Adrian Martinez age 20, Pedro Sanchez age 28, and two other suspects who were later arrested and booked for suspicion of assault with a deadly weapon and conspiracy for taking property, robbery, and intimidation of a victim witness." 2) "A young man and young woman were arrested for getting a 14 year old girl drunk and then allegedly sexually assaulting the 14 year old girl at a home in Porterville. The young man and young woman, were both arrested on suspicion of sex with a person under 18, and illicit contact with a minor with intent to commit a sexual offense and conspiracy," said the Porterville Police Department Spokesperson." I want my readers to note that although I covered this story by contacting the Porterville Police Department myself, I decided to give the Porterville Recorder credit here too because I learned they also carried this sexual assault story as one of their main stories in their publication ("Two Teens suspected of sexual assault." Porterville Recorder 19 Jan. 2011, A1.).

As my readers can see from the violent stories I decided to include in this section of my book, the state of California and cities like Porterville are fast becoming what appears to be a lawless state. Because of my research and observations, I believe this growing lawlessness is connected to the fact that California's state government (which has been under Democrat control for over four decades, 40 plus years) appears to like bending over backwards (and seems to enjoy breaking some federal and immigration laws) to help and accommodate these Mexican and other law breaking and colonizing invaders. An example of how California's government seems to constantly bend over backwards and/or side step federal immigration laws includes acts like changing the car insurance laws of the state so that Mexico's illegal aliens don't have to have a California driver's license to get insurance in California. Even worse, these drivers can carry Public Liability and Public Damage (PL and PD) at the minimum level of protection (This amount is only about $15,000 per person and $30,000 per accident), which means the person they hit will have to use their own insurance policy to pay for their hospital bills and their own auto repairs so these Mexican illegal aliens and other foreign illegal aliens will always get off scot-free, sort of like a no-fault insurance law.

Before I move on, I want to discuss some laws that I feel California's left leaning controlled government created to more than likely caudle Mexico's illegal alien invaders and any other countries' law breaking invaders that don't follow US Constitutional or Immigration laws when they enter America. I want to report what happened to me when I was in accident with one of these under insured drivers. I also should note that she was not the owner of the car. Although this driver was not driving fast, I want to report that she was sending a text and not looking where she was driving when she hit the car I was riding in as a passenger. The sad part was that my friend and I were waiting for a green light and helpless when she hit us. I later learned a valuable lesson on this day about California's new auto insurance laws. To make a long story short, when all was said and done, my insurance advised me that since the teen driver (or daughter of the car's owner) was not named in the auto insurance, and the auto was under insured, they could not do a law suit for lost wages, pain and suffering, or my emergency hospital bills. In the end, I found myself having to pay for the bills myself because of this young ladies carelessness and her parent's pathetic car insurance. As for the reason I paid my own doctor's bills, I hate to say it but my car insurance would have gone up if I had allowed my auto insurance company to pay for my losses. So, I decided to bite the bullet and take the loss by paying for all of it myself. Side note: A year later, I want to add that my auto insurance policy went up by $100 dollars per year, which I feel was caused by the fact that California's auto insurers are making us pay for all of these bad drivers that are now driving on our streets.

I hate to say it but I feel these price hikes appear to point to the fact that California's auto insurance laws are now working more like "No-Fault Auto Insurance" laws and also appear to put the burden of paying for any auto accident losses on the backs of America's higher insured drivers. I say this because the majority of America's legal citizens, who have much more to lose if they were ever sued for an auto accident, usually carry more than adequate car insurance. Need I say more as to why we feel California's state government seems to have created laws that protect Mexico's (and any other country's illegal citizens now living in California) colonizing invaders more each day, and why I say it appears that the state of California does not care if they throw America's citizens under the bus. By the way, since these Mexican illegal alien invaders are allowed to use their Mexican driver's licenses in

California (and they now get California drivers licenses thanks to the Illegal and DACA Controlled California state Legislature and Governor Brown), I feel California is now one of the most expensive and dangerous states in America to drive a car on US soil.

In the previous paragraph, I said that California had become one of the most expensive and dangerous states in America to drive a car and even a motorcycle. Having opened this paragraph with my bold statement, I guess I better prove my statement by pointing out two reasons that I feel vindicate my statement. The first reason I said California has become so expensive to drive in (as a car owner) is because when my auto insurance renewal payment came in this year (2018) the cost of my car insurance had gone up $200 dollars. I guess I can say that I was quite upset and felt I was being taken for a ride because I had not had any auto accidents, tickets, or claims in the past ten years. After the shock of the letter was gone, like any reasonable person who felt they were being taken, I decided call my agent to find out why I was paying more for my auto insurance. To my surprise, my agent informed me that the company was adding this rate increase to cover the cost of the increase in auto accidents in the state of California over the past three years. After all, added the agent, the extra costs they had incurred last year from the growing amount of auto accidents in California had to be paid by all of the drivers who were insured by this company (Note: I am no longer with this company.). As for the reason I say this state is now too dangerous to drive in, I came to this conclusion because, as I see it, the state of California has become more dangerous to drive in because the California State Legislature and Governor Brown are allowing Mexico's citizens who are living in California illegally to drive using their Mexican driver's licenses and they are also providing California licenses to these people even though statistics show that auto accidents went up when these people were given permission to drive in California.

Although my fellow Americans might think the idea of allowing foreigners to use their driver's licenses in America is not so bad, I was recently informed by two law abiding legal Hispanic/Mexican immigrants that Mexico's driver's licenses are not worth the paper they are printed on in Mexico. The reason these two legal Hispanics offered me this disturbing news was to inform me of a disturbing practice that goes on in many of Mexico's cities. The bad news they provided? According to these legal immigrants, the employees who issue Mexico's driver's license will take or accept a bribe to pass the person who is taking the driver's test if they failed the test. Why do these Mexican Government employees take bribes? I was told that they will to take a bribe because their pay is so low they have to make extra money on the side to make ends meet; so instead of making drivers in Mexico take the drivers' license test again if they fail the test, they just rubber stamp the test as passed and give these people their license for the "extra fee." Now my readers see why I worry when I am on the same road with these illegal aliens whose driving skills and driving habits are to say the least very questionable. To prove the point I just made in my last sentence, I want to point out that these illegal alien drivers usually speed up when the light turns yellow to try to make the light before it turns red, instead of slowing down and preparing to stop like the California Driver's Handbook says they are supposed to react when approaching a stop light that has turned yellow. I want to add that running red lights and not stopping at "stop" signs at four way stops or major intersections with traffic lights is now the fastest growing cause of accidents in our city of Porterville and California too. I am not joking; these illegal aliens and legal aliens often just speed up and run the red light even though they have plenty of time to stop. How do I avoid accidents on my city streets? If I am at a red light and the light turns green, I now count three seconds off (and look both ways) before I enter the intersection.

Since I can't stop Governor Brown from making California's roads and highways more dangerous than ever by passing laws that allow these illegal aliens to drive with their shady Mexican driver's licenses or the giving them California state issued California drivers' licenses (that are being offered to all of Mexico's illegal alien invaders that manage to enter California without legal permission), I guess I will just have to follow my friends who have left California and move to either another state or a new country (Note: I am seriously thinking about moving to Japan.). By the way, I am certain these new California laws that lets Mexico's illegal aliens get a California driver's license, and at the same time lets them register to vote in "all" of America's elections by mistake (wink, wink) are allowing these illegal aliens to vote. I want to add that because the laws says these illegal alien voters can't be found guilty of voter fraud (because the state of California takes the blame for these illegal aliens falsely registering and voting) I know I am seeing millions of California's illegal aliens vote in state and Federal elections. In fact, during the 2016 Presidential and local elections, there were lines of Mexican voters waiting to vote in the precinct I voted in and the local census stated that at last count our county was now over 80 percent illegal aliens. If the facts in the last sentence of this paragraph doesn't show that California's elections are being plagued by voter fraud or illegal voting, then I guess America's local, state, and federal politicians have decided it's okay for illegal foreigners to vote in US elections.

Before I move on, I want to remind my fellow Americans of the reasons why legal Americans are leaving California about as fast as the Hispanic controlled state legislature is giving away California to Mexico and other South American countries. The first Reason I want to point out, again, is the rise in auto accidents in the state of California and its cities because many of these illegal aliens now driving in California run or roll through stop signs, and they are simply not stopping at red lights too. I also want to add that these Mexican/Hispanic drivers often run red lights so blatantly that they seem to dare other drivers to pull out in front of them, even if the other driver has the green light or the right of way. These Mexico licensed or California licensed Mexican illegal alien drivers know there are not enough police officers or Highway Patrol officers on the road to see every illegal incident or act they commit, so they know they are not going to get a ticket. I should add here that these drivers break the law so often that they often smile and laugh at America's safe drivers who just let them have their way for fear of having an auto accident. I have to add here that in the past two to three weeks (8/4/2013 through 8/10/2013) Porterville has had 3 more ugly murders, and another deadly head on collision on one our local roads. I guess I can say these incidents add to the growing fears of more violence and more Post Traumatic Stress Disorders for California's legal American real citizens.

If my readers don't mind, I would like to add a little more information about the driving habits of these illegal alien Mexican licensed drivers and their supporters because I had the scary pleasure of driving in Mexico when I was a young man hanging out with my buddies from my American high school. Since I have driven in Mexico, I can honestly say from experience that these foreign Mexican drivers don't ever obey Mexico's driving laws in Mexico, so I have to ask how can California's Government, for one minute, think these illegal Mexico and California licensed drivers are going to follow our state laws? My fellow Americans, as I drive around in California on our highways and cities, I often see these so called law abiding foreign Mexican drivers speeding down our California and American city streets doing 55 miles per hour in a posted 30 mile per hour speed zone; or speeding past a grammar school that is in session doing 40 to 50 MPH (Note: These illegal drivers even do this in hospital zone that have always had a 25 MPH speed limit.) while there are children present on the school grounds. I hate to tell these lawless illegal drivers and the California State Legislature but any American licensed driver knows the speed limit is only 25 miles per hour when school is in session or there is a hospital on that street.

To conclude my discussion on how careless these illegal alien licensed California drivers are on California's streets and highways, I want to show the following other lawless acts of careless driving these illegal Mexican drivers are committing on our California streets: first, I want to point out that these illegal alien drivers often make their left hand turns at a 45 degree angle (This new way to make a left hand turn is now known as the "New California" left hand turn by California's legal citizens. These forty-five degree angle left-had-turns often lead to accidents on our streets because the Mexican/Hispanic driver making the left-hand-turn often clips the front fender or bumper of the other car waiting at the stop sign or light. I hate to say it but I can prove this last remark is true because I had one of these kinds of accidents this past year. Note: In case some Americans don't know the following facts, the California Hispanic or DACA Democratic controlled Legislature and Governor Brown passed a law in September of 2013 that allows Mexico's lawless invaders to get legal California (or American) driver's license, even though Americans have learned, through accident experiences that these Mexican people are not legit, or law abiding legal immigrants.

Finally, the Law Enforcement Officers (LEOs) of the Porterville area informed me that they have almost given up on enforcing "disturbing the peace" laws in this Central California county of Tulare. Although they told me that most cities and counties have disturbing the peace laws, they are finding the influx of Mexico's illegal aliens and other South American countries is growing so fast that they can't respond to all of the calls and complaints they get on weekend nights (especially in the summer months) in both the cities and county. So in the end, I have to say that these colonizing illegal aliens are getting away with breaking these types of civility laws when they have their parties in their backyards because there are so many of these parties on any given night. I want to also add the reason the LEOs of these area appear to have a hopeless or defeated attitude when it comes to trying to restore order and civility in our neighborhoods is because the live bands or DJs who play the overly loud Mexican music feel they don't have to respect the Individual legal rights of the few legal Americans still left in California. To add salt to the wound, or ears of these poor Americans, some Sheriff's officers told me they can often hear the music from over two miles away before they even get to the location of these parties they are going to try to control or shut down.

Oh, I want to add one more rude act these illegal aliens commit when they have these loud parties that usually get so big the guests that attend these overly large banquet type parties often park in no parking zones areas, school parking lots, in front of the neighbors homes, and many times they even block the neighbors' driveways, and finally, they also park on private property without getting city or county permits to use these facilities. I often wonder if the people paying for these parties even know what being a good neighbor means in their country, or have a name for a good neighbor policy, especially when their parties go all night and our children can't get to sleep. Since these huge, costly, loud, and alcohol infested parties go all night, any American family that has children often ends up with their kids crying all night because they can't sleep (happened to my family member and some of my friends living in Porterville, CA). I would like to add that our local legal American citizens have suggested that the city and county governments need to pass a new law that says any and all major parties with live bands or DJs that will have over a hundred guests must get an event permit, pay a fee, hire security guards, and can only have these parties in rented concert halls or licensed fairgrounds.

Now, to prove that these lawbreaking colonizing illegal aliens are being treated differently from America's legal citizens, I would like to present an example of what happened to some American college students when they had a party that got too loud so the neighbors complained to the police. Oh yes, I want to add what happened to these college students after the police arrived happened way before America had been invaded my Mexico's illegal alien mass invasion of America. Any way, I want to add that what happened to these college students' party, when compared to what happens to the current illegal aliens when their parties get to loud, was no joke. I say this because they almost got arrested. In fact, in my era, if some college students' party got too loud, the police or sheriff would show up and knock on the door and then either give the young men or women a choice of shutting down the party or getting a citation for disturbing the peace. But in these days of political correctness and bending over backwards to appease these illegal alien invaders, when these illegal aliens have an overly loud and huge party and the police are called to stop the party (Note: sometimes the LEOs don't show up at all), the police don't TELL these illegal partiers to turn the music down or off like used to do to Americans in the past, because these days the police instead ASK these illegal aliens if they would please turn down the music, which they do for about ten minutes or till the law enforcement officers are out of sight and then they just turn the music right back up because they know nothing will be done to them. My fellow Americans, this example I have just presented I feel shows America's citizens that these people are being treated better than Americans, and what is even worse, these illegal aliens are being handled with kid gloves when they break our laws or disrespect American's civil rights, all in the name of political correctness. Before I close this discussion on how California's government and LEOs are bending over backwards to accommodate or "fix" our laws to accommodate these trespassing and lawbreaking invaders, I want to remind my readers of how this government is also using a double standard to grant Social Services, cash aid, medical cards, and other cash aid so these colonizers can qualify for these taxpayer financed entitlements meant for America's legal citizens who might be down on their luck, or have lost their job due to outsourcing of their jobs to Mexico.

In the end, the sad part about these examples of lawlessness, that Americans are dealing with all over the Southwest in states like California, is that I feel these examples are only the tip of the iceberg of more bad things to come. I come to this conclusion because I feel that very soon these crimes will come home to roost all over America's states and cities because of the future uncontrolled growth and overpopulation by Mexico illegal alien invaders and Islam's alleged refugees who don't appear to believe in birth control of any type. The other sad changes I see coming to

America's cities can be found in small cities like Porterville where crime rates are climbing every year (Note: Porterville is considered a small city because it only has 50 to 60 thousand residents) and the majority of the violent crimes being committed in Porterville are being committed by our new illegal guests from Mexico and other South American countries' gang members (and even some non-gang members). On a sadder note, I hate to say it but the victims of these trespassing criminal killers should never have become victims of these killers because none of these killers have any reason to be in California because they never bothered to apply to enter America legally.

I want to add that the known criminals and gang members from Mexico and other countries that I wrote about in the last few paragraphs are known killers and have police records in their home countries. So, according to America's Immigration laws, these people should never have been allowed to enter America because they can never be allowed to be legal immigrants. I want to add here that the reason these illegal alien killers can never be allowed to be citizens of America is because US Immigration laws say they are considered undesirables and do not qualify to apply or receive green cards. In my book these killers, or Animals as President Trump described them in a 2018 interview, enter America as lawless invaders whose only intent is to commit crimes and terrorize America's legal citizens. And since these illegal alien criminals are wanted felons, I want to remind America's rogue Judges and the Democrat party, who often plead the cause of these so called "illegal immigrants," that America's immigration laws and military laws (because these people are invaders and not immigrants) say they are undesirables. And since US Immigration laws state this fact (and if these laws are not enough), I want to remind the our Rogue Judges and Democrat Party that these law breakers are attacking America's citizens so they should also be considered terrorists. To add salt the wound, although these wanted felons should be arrested as criminals before they ever enter America, no action is being taken by America's Government because the Democrat Party, our rogue Judges, and the other open border supporters keep pleading a case for these known gang members and ex-felons just like Fay Stender did back in the 1960s.

I hate to say it but America's Democrats, America's Rogue Lower Court and Supreme Court Judges, and America's Open Border Proponents appear to be clones of the now famous 60s ICON Fay Stender and the Democrat left wing supporters of that era who supported and protected the groups known as "the van guards of the Citizen's revolution" in America like the Black Panthers, the Weatherman, and Students for a Democratic Society who 'wanted to bring the war home' in the era of the Nam war. In case my readers don't remember Fay Stender, who I believe should be the poster child for leaders like Chuck, Pelosi, and the Democrat Party's Open Borders supporters, was the lady who helped many known killers serving prison terms get released because of racial profiling only to see these ex-cons kill again and again; to her surprise, one of these cons she helped shot her five times and she ended up a paraplegic for the rest of her life, so she took an over dose of pills while living in China for her protection from the very same killers she said were being racially profiled by American Society. The sad part of today's illegal alien criminals who are entering America is that (if America's government was doing its job) if these Gang member connected Mexican and other countries' invaders were arrested before they ever killed one American or got a chance to destroy America from within, I wouldn't have a reason to write this book. And! If our law enforcement officers were allowed to do their jobs, these killers would be arrested at the border and sent back to Mexico or other countries where they were wanted and never be allowed to return for fear of ending up in America's prisons for life. Heck, maybe Americans should demand these killers be put into prisons where they would pay back the Republic for their room and board by working for the United States at hard labor. I want to note that in many foreign countries, like Mexico, this is how these countries treat foreigners in their prisons who commit crimes in their country, or enter illegally.

To prove what I'm saying in this book is true, I want to now add that some Federal Prison Officers who are friends of mine recently told me that many California prisons and jails are so full of Hispanic and Mexican lawbreakers and terrorist Mexican gang members (as all Americans can see from the gang wars on the streets of Porterville and other Central California cities where these killers are terrorizing America's law abiding citizens) that the California Democrat DACA controlled Legislature is forcing Prisons to release these killers and terrorists early even before they've served out their full jail sentences. These officers added that they felt this kind of turn-style punishment was nothing more than a slap on the face of America's Citizens. Heck, who knows, maybe this turn style like or revolving door prison type of prison sentences are being allowed to happen in California because it allows California's government to keep these historically violent illegal Mexican colonizers in California so they can keep the jails full at all times? After all, if this is the plan, we Americans have to admit this plan is a great way to keep many of these taxpayer financed jobs open so Americans who have lost their jobs to overseas outsourcing can find jobs in this overpopulated state of California.

If my readers are wondering why I come to the conclusion that California's Government is allowing these illegal Mexican criminals to enter so they can keep our prisons full and create jobs for unemployed Americans, I want to add that my answer is simple. After all, prisons are "big business" and a great way to keep providing jobs for Americans who have lost their high paying manufacturing jobs to outsourcing to countries like Mexico, China, and other countries. If there are no manufacturing jobs in America, why not supply an endless supply of criminals from a country that already has their criminals operating in California so we can keep our prisons full. After all, my fellow Americans have to admit that by keeping California prisons full and open the California Government is able to provide high paying taxpayer financed jobs to the few real Americans left in this state. After all, the last time I checked on the cost of keeping these criminals in prison was something like around $48,000 per person per year. Don't forget America, this amount is what it cost per year. Another way to look at this cost is that these jobs are a taxpayer-financed investment on providing American jobs that keep feeding the businesses machine of America, and the US Government and the leeches known as American Politicians.

Before I close my discussion of why California has become such a lawless state and why someday America will soon end up being a lawless nation too, I think I need to point out that all the people from Mexico, the Middle East, and all the other undocumented and lawless invading nationals that are entering America at this time are coming from cultures that have a history of violence, poverty, ignorance, and want. I point out these very real and important facts because during my research I learned the facts I just mentioned do not work out well for the future of America's civilized and advanced culture. We Americans must not forget that our country's citizens have always had a culture that taught its children to OBEY America's laws and work hard so the will be able to live in a law abiding and American Constitution controlled Nation. Unfortunately for America's current citizens, some of America's and California's politicians and judges have decided to betray America's Republic (its legal US Citizens) by insisting that America's citizens accept and allow the destruction of America's sovereignty by giving any foreigner who enters America's Sovereign soil the same individual Constitutional rights that Americans gave themselves when they created their nation and decided to defend their rights by putting themselves under the control of the United States Constitution, criminal laws, and Immigration Laws.

I think Fredric Bastiat said it best when it comes to understanding how the American Constitution is supposed to work in the following statement that is found in his book The Law:

Frederic Bastiat (1801 to 1850) was a man who according to Walter Williams, "believed that the single greatest threat liberty was the government itself" [when it turns on its constituents and permits "legal plunder" of the laws the constituents created to protect themselves] (Bastiat, Frederic, The Law: The Classic Blue Print for a Free Society. Foundation for Economic Education: Hudson, NY, 2007). According to Williams, Bastiat proves this by making this statement, "See if the law takes from some persons what belongs to them, and gives it to others whom it does NOT (caps by me for emphasis) belong. See if the new laws (like Obama's Dreamer act) benefits one citizen (or illegal foreign citizens) at the expense of another (like US legal and Naturalized US citizens) by doing what the citizen can not do without committing a crime (as in entering the US illegally and then demanding the same rights and privileges as US citizens). This description, my fellow legal and naturalized, and green card US citizens is what Bastiat calls "legal Plunder." Doesn't this statement sound exactly like what the open borders US left leaning judges, open border pro illegal aliens politicians like Pelosi and gang, and states like California and their Governors like Brown and their legislature are doing by giving foreign law breaking so called illegal immigrants the same privileges, rights, and benefits as Americans in their quests to give so called Dreamers and their illegal alien parents a free path to US citizenship?

These acts of "Pro Legal Plunder" by American Left leaning Judges, politicians, and Democrat controlled American states are exactly what US legal American citizens should fear and be up in arms against because as you will soon see, according to Bastiat America is at a crossroad that he feels is a future of becoming a Socialist controlled country and NOT a Republic living under Democratic Rule. I think Williams says it best after he introduces Bastiat's definition of legalized Plunder that I mentioned in my last paragraph when he says, "With [Bastiat's] accurate description of legalized plunder, [one] cannot deny the conclusion that most government activities [that are being pushed by the left like Pelosi and her Democrat Party] are legalized plunder, or for the sake of modernity, legalized theft [of American citizens' right and privileges], and progressivism.

To make a long story short, Bastiat's conclusion on legalized plunder is that America's Constitution, her immigration laws, and criminal laws were (or are in these day an age too) instituted to only protect the people who instituted the American government for-and-of-the-people of the United States so that others could not enter the US and basically confiscate or lay claim too (as in illegals getting the same rights and privileges to live in the US with following US laws) their rights to life, liberty, property, and their pursuit of happiness that Americans fought for and earned, and set up to defend from those who would enter and also lay claim to these alleged God given rights. To explain my last statement, I think Bastiat says it best when he says, "What then is law? It is the collective organization of the individual right to lawful DEFENSE (my caps for emphasis)." Bastiat goes on to say, "Each of us has a natural right—from God—to defend his person, his liberty, and his property." (Bastiat, Frederic, The Law: The Classic Blue Print for a Free Society. Foundation for Economic Education: Hudson, NY, 2007).

Now that I've proven that this invasion is NOT anything that resembles "immigration," I think America's citizens have every right to be worried and upset that America's government is not listening to them and ignoring their voiced complaints and fears that writers like Charles Dickens and Fredric Bastiat understood in the past and warned us to keep our guard up. I point our Charles Dickens because I feel he took the time to warn mankind (and Americans in a round about way) to fear these kinds of scourges because they can and will destroy mankind's civilizations. After all, Dickens warns us to fear both "ignorance" and "want" in his famous story and book titled A Christmas Carol. I point this fact out because I thought of his famous words when I started to write this chapter. So what are the words that came to me? I found the scary words in the part where Dickens allows the Ghost of Christmas present to close with these chilling words to make sure Scrooge and mankind never forgets his warning: "These two children represent ignorance and want, but of the two, **fear ignorance the most**?"

Since ignorance and lawlessness appears to be the problem that someday may destroy America's lawful and Western European Christian Culture, that history says made her great, I feel Americans may very well "soon" have to make a stand and demand that America's government stop rewarding these lawless people that are infiltrating and invading American sovereign soil at such a fast pace that I feel America's culture may soon be dead.

Going back to my statement in the previous paragraph, I want to add that if America's legal citizens of this sovereign nation take the time to stand up to their government then maybe America will be able to weather this attack on her sovereign nation status and save America's law abiding Americana type culture and country. If we can take a stand, I really feel America can, and will, return to being a law abiding nation with high morals and high standards of honesty like it used to be in its early hay day when it was the most respected nation in the world: However! If we don't stop America's current direction, I truly believe America will end up heading towards what Emile Durkheim calls an "Anomie" culture. I want to add that An "Anomie Culture, according to Emile Durkheim, "describes the loss of direction felt in a society when the social control of individual behavior . . . becomes ineffective," very much like America and California have evidently lost control of Mexico's illegal colonizing invaders, their politicians, some of their citizens, and even some recent Presidents and current Supreme Court Judges. I make this statement because I feel America, like the state of California, is now headed to a state of high "Anomie Panic."

This Anomie Panic, according to Durkheim, results when a country that is suffering from this type of social behavior goes into "a state of normal-less-ness that typically occurs during a period of profound social change and disorder such as a time of economic collapse [(sound familiar?)]," or like when America and California went into a panic when Wall Street crashed. I feel America and states like California have been in this disorder since Savings and Loan companies and then America's banks stabbed Americans in the back and ripped them off. And! I hate to say it but we are still in this state of Anomie. To make matters worse for America's real citizens, I believe America's government has simply decided to throw in the towel and throw America's Constitutional, criminal, and immigration laws under the bus and push for a Socialistic type of government to try to prevent a complete collapse of America and to appease the political correctness world politicians. This pathetic choice, I'm sad to say, has only pushed America into a death spiral that will more than likely lead it to its extinction in the near future (Schaefer, T. Richard. "Durkheim's Legacy": Sociology. McGraw Hill: Boston, 9 Ed. 2005, pp 182-183.).

I want to note that, in my opinion, when America and California went into a state of "Anomie," pardon my words, all hell broke loose and that is why America and states like California are not only going broke under Democrat rule (like America was under Obama rule) but in a downward spiral towards a lawless, colonized, and out of control Socialized type of government (Note since President Trump was elected, America has started to recover slowly, but this could end if the Democrats ever take control of America's government again or impeach Trump.). I feel I can make this statement because America is not only dealing with the effects of Durkheim's Anomie, but it is also appears to be dealing with several dysfunctional cultures that include Islam's and Mexico's violent cultures that haven't changed in the past two to three hundred years, and they can't change because according to Edwin Sutherland's "cultural transmission" theory, "they are not capable of changing." The reason they can't change says Sutherland, "[is that both of these cultures have negative perceptions of America and they both continue to teach their children about America in this negative light which nurtures what] Sutherland calls 'a cultural transmission' of violence, anger, and hatred [for Americana that has been a part of both Mexico and Islam's cultures since their founders or leaders created and established these cultures]" (Schaefer, T. Richard. "Durkheim's Legacy": Sociology, McGraw Hill: Boston, 9 Ed.

2005, pp.182-183.) (Schaefer, T. Richard. "Cultural Transmission": Sociology. McGraw Hill: Boston. 9 Ed: 2005. P.183.).

As I completed my discussion of Durkheim's Anomie theory in this chapter, I also found that Edwin Sutherland added some facts that I felt added more credibility to Durkheim's theory by saying that "cultural transmission [helps define and describe how countries or nations (Iran for example, used as a country with an Islamic based culture) and some current violent culture have grown into what they've become in the 21st Century and why they continue on the same track to this day without a chance to grow or deviate from their past cultural norms. After all, Sutherland says, "cultural transmission" finds that "one learns criminal behavior [and religious intolerance of other beliefs] by interacting with others who believe this way of life is correct. These beliefs can include ideals like learning the "techniques of law breaking, [religious intolerance], [how to break into a car quickly and quietly, and how to use the word **infidel** to describe and attack non-Muslims in the world)]. Sutherland also says cultural transmission also influences a person's motives, drive, and rationalizations, which influences his or her violent behavior." If we apply Sutherland's theory to the Boston Bombers, I think my readers will see how the Boston bombers' justified their acts of violence on innocent Americans even though they were enjoying all of the benefits of America's Culture (Schaefer, T. Richard. "Cultural Transmission": Sociology. McGraw Hill: Boston. 9 Ed: 2005. P.183.).

The explanation I presented in the last paragraph unfortunately only goes to show how difficult America's politicians and judges make it on American citizens who try to Americanize, educate, or influence any of Mexico's illegal alien invaders or some (Note that I don't say all.) of Islam's radical followers. I really believe that if this political correctness crap was thrown out the door and Americans were allowed to try to influence some of these new comers to American soil by helping them become more Americanized (as many older US History books says was the norm in the past) maybe these migrants could be taught to become law-abiding and Americanized citizens that accept America's way of life and how her Western Christian Culture's morals and standards have work for the good of all in America for over two hundred plus years. Unfortunately, I just don't think this will happen in the 21st Century because of new laws like cultural sensitivity, inclusion, political correctness, and what I believe will be the killer of the Americana Culture DIVERSITY (which I feel is just a code word for killing off America's Americana culture that according to US History books saved the world in World War II).

Now that my readers understand why America is struggling with its own state of Anomie, I feel I need to point out that America's politicians, judges, big business corporations, big farm corporations and farm bureaus, and Wall Street bankers have all helped create this perfect storm by championing deals that brought Americans NAFTA, Open Borders, alleged under the table Mexican oil deals, Wall Street's collapse, and ex-President Obama's alleged attempted deal to help Egypt buy two German Submarines that has helped usher in a new era of social disorder and change in America. And unfortunately for America, this era of change and disorder has resulted in an American culture that I fear has America's legal citizens suffering from Post Traumatic Stress Disorder (PTSD) because they feel lost and angry at their politicians and Supreme Court Judges, and they feel they can't do anything to stop this downward spiral. I truly feel that America's drug use problem, violence, and so-called alternative life styles all have to do with PTSD. This downward Spiral is the one I have described in this book in various ways and sections of this book.

Unfortunately for my fellow Americans, this new dysfunctional and PTSD suffering America has itself spawned some dysfunctional subcultures of its own that appear to be self-indulgent, self-glorifying and me orientated people with visions of grandeur and riches that they feel the world owes them. One of these home grown subcultures that this PTSD suffering America has spawned is a young generation that has a "the world owes me" attitude towards life. Looking back at our current history, I feel this new subculture of self-indulgent people is becoming so large and prominent in America that America's companies are now aiming their commercials at them. To attract these people, corporate America is creating commercials with various young people that evidently its viewers are supposed to think that all of these young people possess earth-shattering skills of intelligence or IQ's that challenge Albert Einstein, have world class athletic abilities, and are smarter and better than their parents who served in Nam, changed the culture of music, invented the computer, marched in Selma Alabama and Washington for civil rights, confronted its own military and died on the grounds at Kent State, and put a man on the man. Gee, I guess the so-called "old-school" generation should have just sat back and been slackers like all this young generation so this generation could have done all the things their parents did in their life time.

Before I continue, I would like to add that there are some young people in this generation that are doing things the right way by working hard, studying instead of cheating, and contributing to society without expecting national television exposure or the world's adulation for their achievements. To these few young leaders of the future (I hope!), I say thank you on behalf of America's Patriotic Citizens, and I take my hat off to you for your humble and quiet way of helping America. By the way, I want to add here that I feel the "old-school generation" learned how to win and lose because we all didn't get rewards or participation trophies just for showing up and playing; we also didn't get A++ credits added to our GPA for showing up for a school event, didn't get A++ extra credit for a report on computers because we handed it in as expected, and extra credit added to our GPA for showing up for school so we could graduate with over inflated GPAs that show up in today's students' high school transcripts. The sad part of these over inflated grades is that really is no such thing as a 4.8 GPA in the real GPA system we grew up with and found on our transcripts and report cards back in the so called "old school" days.

Since I'm a retired California Junior College professor, I feel this bloated or "fixed" American high school GPA system that is currently being used in many of our American high school districts is a joke. America, although our high schools are using this over inflated GPA, I hate to say this but in reality there really is no such thing as a 4.8 GPA if we apply the real known GPA system that is used in higher education (colleges and universities). For those people who might have forgotten, the GPA system works like this my fellow Americans: A = 4.0 B = 3.0 C = 2.0 D = 1.0 and F = 0. My message to the American school districts that are using this "New" grading system is the following: I want to tell them to stop sending America's college professors your so-called honors students that in reality are not honor students because your bloated GPA system is only giving these students a false sense of achievement, which in the end adds up to about a 50 percent drop out rate after these students' first Semester in college (I saw this happen on my job at different junior colleges year after year.). If you will do the right thing, we college professors won't have to tell these students they belong in remedial English classes, remedial math classes, or remedial reading classes, and not in a university or college setting. My message to American parents who care about their child's education is that they force their school districts to use the real GPA system that actually helps show these parents how their student's education is really progressing.

Now that I've hopefully educated America's Republic as to who and what is pushing America towards its demise in the near future, I want to discuss a different kind of attack that is being used to attack American's value system of the past, and although this example points my discussion in a different direction, I feel this example is important because it provides concrete evidence that America's Americana culture is under attack by corporate America too. To begin, I want to point out a commercial that is currently being shown on American TV that I feel is aimed at America's young citizens who have bought into some of these new subcultures I'm talking about in this section of my book. This example comes to us from a company that is trying to sell energy drinks to these so-called young American geniuses (I want to note that I know there are some wonderful talented young students and adults who are still taking the right road to success by just working hard.) that I talked about earlier in my book.

This nationally shown commercial shows multiple ordinary young people doing so called extraordinary world class athletic stunts like skate boarding, surfing, jumping, and playing like world-class athletes, and it also shows them playing instruments like rock super stars and dancing like super stars just because they allegedly use this drink. The funny part of this commercial is that it is so far fetched that anyone who watches it should know it is a joke. In the end, the message is that any average American with average abilities can be a superstar just because they drink this famous energy drink or sports drink. What this commercial doesn't show my fellow Americans are all of the broken legs, arms, wrists, Head-concussions and deaths some of these alleged world class and no limits acts of stupidity cause every year to young people who are taken in by these types of commercials. I hate to say this to the parents of these young people, and the young people too, but reality says there are limits to what a real every day human can do in real life. And if the person doesn't understand the risks they are taking, they sometimes find out one major risk is called death by stupidity. And one more fact while I'm on this topic, reality also says there is no way to cheat this limit called death. My generation learned this fact as young people when we saw our brothers, friends, small town heroes, and our peers either come home in body bags, or come home in coffins draped with American flags from a war being fought in a far away jungle. I'm sorry to say this but the young men and women of my era did have "Fear," unlike the kids that wear their "no fear" T-shirts this days.

Not to shine my generation's apple, but! I want to remind my fellow Americans that my generation grew up in an era when people like common steel workers, truck drivers, telephone pole climbing workers, school janitors (like my Korean Vet Boy Scoutmaster who was a high school janitor), and even every day "school teachers" were the stars and heroes of my generation. These everyday Americans were the real superstars and heroes that we looked up to for guidance and role models, and I believe that is why this "old-school generation" landed on the moon, earned the right to vote at 18, and one of them (a Boy Scout Senior Patrol Leader) is writing this book to try to save his beloved American country from politicians and rogue Supreme Court Judges who are selling out America and her legal and rightful owners to a group known as progressives and a future United Nations controlled world government. Unlike today's modern generation that seems to live for money, the next fancy phone being offered for sale, driving carelessly because they're too busy using their phones to text, and making Gods of the Bling wearing computer assisted rappers or singers that sell fairy tale stories and sell fantasies using rap poems with stolen music (Sampling is not writing music, it's stealing in my book like plagiarism in writing.), or starts of singers with computer enhanced voices who I believe couldn't sing a cappella even if their lives depended on it, I am proud to say my generation didn't need any of these crutches to be good or great. In the end, I feel the reason America's old school generation never lived this way is because they had (and still have) lives and they were willing to serve and die for their country. My generation might not have had fancy cell phones, but we always respected our elders, respected (and still respect) America's laws, and were working by the age of 13 or 14 to earn money for school activities. My old generation might not have been cool by today's standards, but I feel we proved we were willing to take on our government if we had to save our country and get to vote if we were going to die in a war called the Vietnam Conflict. As for my generation, the only God we looked up to was a man who was sworn to poverty, never wore gold, never owned land but he did manage to walk on water and calm an angry sea.

Having made the statement above, my readers should understand why I find these types of (or kinds of) visions of grandeur commercials pathetic and without class, and I feel they have no redeeming value. I also want to note that the one thing I hate the most about these kinds of commercials is that they sell America's children and adults on the idea that the only way to be special in America, or this world, is to be rich or a super star, have an entourage, and have a job with fame, glory, and lots of money. As a man who grew up in America when Americans were among the hardest working, honest, and most honorable people in the world, I wonder how America's leaders managed to lead or guide this once great nation into the pathetic mess it is in the eyes of the world? I also wonder how our leaders got America so lost that just being an honest hard working American who earns an honest day's pay is considered a pathetic life in the eyes of most of today's young Americans. Is it any wonder why America's children don't respect their parents and their elders?

As I conclude this section of my book, I want to note there is one other new subculture that seems to be growing in America. This subculture that I see growing each year appears to include Americans who demonstrated and fought to try to clean up the 1960's mess America's Government created in their country back in the era of the Nam war, and it appears to be growing every year as America loses more and more control of her borders and sovereignty to the progressive and open borders movement that seems to be intent on establishing a Socialist type government on US Soil. As I observe these this new (OLD) sub culture that once fought for American freedom who appear to exhibit all of the signs of Post Traumatic Stress Disorder, I notice these "old-school" patriots have gone silent and appear to be giving up on America as they see more and more areas of America turn into suburbs of Mexico's Government, Muslim Nations, Puerto Rico, and other countries. And, as I watch these once patriotic fighters of the 60s give up and either move to other states or countries to get away from the growing influx of illegal so called immigrants, I find the worst part of this take over and is that it appears to be happening with the blessing of America's government, politicians, and both local and Supreme Court Judges.

To say that these Americans are suffering from PTSD (because they're seeing state after state become 50, 60, or even 80 percent illegal invader populations from Mexico other South American countries, and the world) would not be an exaggeration on my part, especially when I see so many signs that America's Government appears to be sanctioning this take over. In the end, I find it sad to see America's Government and each new Presidential Administration and Congress insist each new year that the only way to fix this mass open border like invasion is to allow the Government to gut America's Immigration laws and also end America's sovereign nation status so they can open up America's borders to the world's citizens (Note: In today's paper that was dated October 22, 2018, there was a story that said over 25,000 illegal Honduran aliens are headed for America's borders to enter without permission because they see Mexico's citizens do it and get away with it. The sad part is that the news also reported that Democrat Politicians were on the border escorting these illegal invaders across the border so the Border Patrol couldn't stop them. If this story is not proof that America is being invaded, then I what is it going to take America?).

In the end, I want to point out that because of the mess I mention in my last paragraph I feel these hopeless and lost Americans who are suffering from this open borders form of PTSD may someday snap, and if they do snap, Durkheim says, ["it might push these PTSD suffering] "people to be more aggressive and get more depressed, and this [will] result in both higher rates of violent crimes and more suicides" in the coming years. If Americans don't see a connection between the growing cases of addiction in America, the growing rates of suicides in America, and finally the growing acts of violence and shootings in our schools and on the streets of America, then I guess Durkheim and I are wasting our time doing all of our wonderful hard work and research, and providing Americans with all the facts I have just provided in this section of my book that I feel completely explains all of the horror and murders being committed by Americans killing Americans in this day-and-age.

From the discussion I just completed, I think (and hope) my readers should now be able to conclude that America's current political leaders must take the blame for all of the drugs, violence, suicide, and murders that have happened on American Soil over the past 47 years. I feel I can come to this conclusion because over the past 47 years not one politician, administration, or judge ever attempted to stop the flow of mass non legal or illegal migrants or illegal alleged refugees from entering US sovereign soil or even tried to enforce US Immigration laws, or create new ones like Japan's Government has to control illegal immigrants. The American government and its politicians have instead allowed the colonizing people of foreign countries like Mexico to enter American soil without legal permission, allowed them to ignore American Immigration laws, and have bent and twisted all of America's immigration and criminal laws to accommodate governments like Mexico (and her citizens) so this government could Colonize and be allowed to dump its poor citizens into America day after day without repercussions or sanctions of any kind. I feel America's leaders should also be blamed for making America into a lawless nation that is more anarchy than democracy these days. And as a result of their actions, these politicians have made things worse for America, her citizens, and her Western European Christian Culture that appears to be disappearing before our eyes as I write this book (Schaefer, T. Richard, "Durkheim's Legacy," Sociology. McGraw Hill: Boston. 9Ed. 2005. Pp.182-183.).

Since I've introduced the words "colonizing, colonist, and colonialism in this part of my book, I feel I need to define these words for my readers' edification and to clarify how these words are being used in the paragraphs of this section. And since I feel I've proved that some governments like Mexico's Government are in the process of re-colonizing America, I feel the word "colonizing" is a good definition to start with in this paragraph. I come to this conclusion because as you read in this section of my book I feel Mexico's goal is to not only dump their country's poverty problem on America's citizens, but I think we can all see Mexico appears to also be in the process of re-colonize America's Southwest states to reclaim it for their country. I think "Funk and Wagnalls Standard College Dictionary" describes Colonizing best because this dictionary describes it as an attempt "to set up a colony in [some country]"; settle [in a foreign country.] 2. To establish as colonists" (Colonizing." Def. 1-2. Funk and Wagnalls Standard College Dictionary. Text. Ed.1967.). The irony of these multiple and different core definitions is that they sound very much like what Mexico's illegal invading colonists are doing to America's Southwestern States and America's sovereignty as they pour across her borders with no end in sight. As for America's progressives, Democrat Party and ex-President Obama, I hate to tell them but I feel I just proved what is happening to America on he borders is NOT immigration, and it has nothing to do with what happened on Ellis Island.

Moving on to the next definition, I found the definition for the word "colonist" to apply seemingly nice in describing America's current illegal invasion mess because this word can be used to clarify and define the term colonizing (which I defined in the last paragraph) and even the word colony. But before I get ahead of myself and I define the word "colonist," I want to prove to my fellow Americans that the word colonist is quite volatile. I say this because as I will now prove, America's government passed a law in the past that warned any and all countries that the "America's" (both continents) were not available for colonizing by any country, especially by European nations like Russia or England, and even Japan. According to the law America's Government signed into law by President Monroe, "any attempt to colonize one of the Americas, including North America would result in the US taking 'necessary action (military) to stop what would be considered an act of aggression against the US" (Hofstadter, Richard, William Miller, and Daniel Aaron. "America Goes to War." The United States: The History of a Republic. Prentice-Hall, Inc. New Jersey: 1960, 6th ed.). This law, of course, is now known as America's Monroe Doctrine. And! Because the Monroe Doctrine exists, I can now show that this law even applies to any country (including countries like Mexico) that decides to swarm into a country like America and colonize it without the Republic's permission (Since America is a Republic this means America's Citizens decide who they want to allow to enter their country, and not the US Government.).

According to the Monroe Doctrine, the law makes any country's citizens that are part of a migrating force an aggressor or invader. To clarify this statement, I think we need to look in a dictionary and read the definition. When I looked up this work, I found Funk and Wagnalls book defines these invaders that enter America without permission as colonists in its definitions or senses: Colony: 1) a body of emigrants (note not Immigrants) and their descendants living in a land apart from, but under the control of, the parent country; 2) Any territory controlled by a distant state (think 10 major consulates in California and one in every major airport in CA), and "Colonist: a is a person who is: "A member or inhabitant of a colony [in another country" ("Colony" and "Colonist." Funk and Wagnalls Standard College Dictionary. Text. Ed.1967.). I should note that in most areas of America, where Mexico's illegal invading colonizers have decided to congregate and take over the area, these areas are always called "la Colonia," or "the Colony," so these invaders know they are here to stay and colonize and occupy America and are not here to immigrate or become part of the American fabric as US Citizens.

Finally, the last word I want to define in this section is the word "colonialism." I choose this word because I believe this word holds the key to what America's politicians, the past Obama Administration, and Mexico's government have either allegedly or agreed to allow to happen to America in some kind of deal or contract that has never been shown to America's citizens. And, I believe the contract includes letting Mexico's government and their citizens invade/enter the US without any kind of intervention from America's Government. Since this migration/invasion is being done with a "wink-and a-nod type of hands off fashion (because America's Government says they are needed to allegedly fill the need for farm hands and field workers in America), I think we now can see how or why so many Americans are not bothering to pay attention to the demise of America's culture and country. I guess these Americans are too busy being cool, progressive, or maybe just trying to survive to see the bad changes that are happening to America. From what I can see in our area, I think too many Americans are worried about the jobs that are disappearing and being sent overseas to China, Pakistan, Vietnam, Taiwan, Japan, and YES especially Mexico. By the way, if any of my readers ever get the chance to drive to the Mexican/American border, I really believe they will be shocked to see huge buildings, or manufacturing plants that belong to American corporations who have sent their industrial and manufacturing jobs across the border to Mexico and can be found in this area of the border.

In closing this section of my book, I want to note that I have been to this area and seen with my own eyes the large industrial complexes that are situated all along the American and Mexican border that are located on the Mexican side of the border. From what I saw in this area, and because there are so many huge manufacturing plants with hundreds of American jobs being done by Mexico's citizens, I decided to call these areas "Murder's Row." I call this area this name because this area has "taken and killed off thousands of jobs that Americans once held on US Soil." Having said this, I now see why I felt it was important for me to prove that Mexico is using colonialism to take over America's southwest and also take over American jobs. As for the definition for the word "colonialism," the word has this meaning: The policy of a nation [like Mexico] seeking to acquire [or] extend its borders"; In case you don't know it, Mexico has extended itself in states like California, Texas, Arizona, New Mexico, Nevada, Oregon, and Washington

("Colonialism." Def. 1. Funk and Wagnalls College Dictionary. Text. Ed.1967.).

I) MEXICO'S DECISION TO GO NEUTRAL IN
   WWI and WWII HELPS THE AXIS.

Educated men and women scholars have always known that history, or the past, holds the key to the future and that is why there is saying that makes the following point: "If mankind does not learn from their past mistakes, they are doomed to repeat them" (or something to that nature). The point I am trying to make here is that if mankind (or America) isn't careful and corrects the past mistakes it has been doing by allowing so called illegal migration to go uncontested over the past 40 plus years, this dangerous and costly mistake America and other countries in places like Europe are making (by allowing so called refugees to basically invade and migrate into their countries) will soon come back to haunt them and plague America and these countries with misery, pain, and civil wars. Now that I have my readers' attention, and I begin the final section of Chapter Two, I'd like to talk to my readers about some past historical events, or political actions, that Mexico's Government took (or committed) by turning on America's people and their American Government when "push-came-to-shove" during World War 1 and World War 2. I want to discuss these actions because I feel these acts were treacherous acts that must never be forgotten by Americans or America's Government and current politicians, yet today's American Politicians have swept them under the carpet. The treacherous acts I want to shed some light on ended up putting Mexico's Government and people on opposite sides (or against) of America's Government and citizens during World War One (WWI) and World War Two (WWII)) because Mexico decided they did "not" want to support (or contribute to the allies' war effort) America, her soldiers, or the allies that fought in these two world wars.

To make it simple to understand, my research found facts that prove Mexico and her Government failed to support America and her Allies' war effort to keep the world free from dictators during both WWI and WWII. According to the book <u>The United States: The History of a Republic</u> Mexico's Government made this choice twice because they were approached in each war by the enemies of Democracy, known as Germany and her allies, who asked Mexico to help them defeat America and its allies by simply not helping the allies or America during these wars. As I read the historical past in this book, I found that Mexico's Government evidently felt it was in their best interest to not help America or her allies during either World War One or World War Two, so they stayed neutral in both wars (Hofstadter, Richard, William Miller, and Daniel Aaron. "America Goes to War." The United States: The History of a Republic. Prentice-Hall, Inc. New Jersey: 1960, 6th ed.).

What I am about to report in this section of my book does not make Mexico's past and/or present government officials, their past presidents, or their citizens look good when their decisions are held under the light of historical facts of the world's history. I can make this bold statement because of what I learned in several historical books of the world. What I learned was that during WWI and WWII Mexico's politicians and its government decided to sit out each of these wars to basically see who would come out on top. As I read the facts in these history books, I felt Mexico's Government and Citizens made two very bad choices because they felt they might have possibly worked out a deal with America's enemies if America and her allies had lost in either WWI or WWII. Needless to say, I found this information disturbing and appalling when I read that on both occasions Mexico's treacherous Government chose to work against America in both wars. As I read these facts, I also had to wonder why Mexico's citizens backed their government's decisions completely both times? From the historical facts I am providing in this part of my book, I hope my fellow American compatriots understand that Mexico's government either never wanted to back the world, or America during the times of these major wars (that America fought to keep the world free), or they were just hoping to make a deal with America's enemies after each one of these wars ended (Note: In case America and her allies lost, I guess?). So from the choices Mexico's Government and its people have made in the past, I feel I can say that either Mexico has always prayed that America would fall so it could hopefully take back what they think is their land, or Mexico's government simply enjoyed being on the same side as any of America's enemies. Maybe, Mexico's Government made these choices just because they like being on the same side as America's enemies every chance they get. As a true blue American, I can only say that America needs to keep an eye on Mexico's actions even if its Government is holding the olive branch of peace in its hand.

If my fellow Americans and readers think about what Mexico's choices accomplished during both of these world wars, I think my readers will find that Mexico's sad and pathetic choices, during both wars, actually ended up providing support for the world's enemies that were "only" trying to destroy democracy and enslave the world's population in each war. And as pathetic and horrible as these facts appear to be, I think we can all agree from the facts I've presented Mexico's people and their government evidently didn't care who won these wars. What I feel is even sadder and more horrible is the fact that although I've proven (in this section) that Mexico's Government keeps choosing to have an anti-American historical past during major wars, and Several past Presidents that include ex-President Obama have kept themselves busy during their tenure asking America's citizens to give up their jobs, schools, sovereignty, and freedom to help Mexico's illegal invading and colonizing force of citizens to enter America illegally. These past presidents have also asked Americans to not complain or attempt to stop this invasion of America's Sovereign soil. Since I believe I have shown that Mexico and its people seem to enjoy betraying America's citizens and government, I think we need to look at some details in the next paragraph that I feel will show my readers how Mexico's people and government betrayed the world and America in the first World War and in the second World War (Hofstadter, Richard, William Miller, and Daniel Aaron. "America Goes to War." The United States: The History of a Republic. Prentice-Hall, Inc. New Jersey: 1960, 6th Ed.):

In the month of April, of 1917 and right before America entered World War One (WWI), I found facts in several history books that I used for references that stated "British naval intelligence . . . intercepted a coded message from German Foreign Secretary Zimmermann to the German Ambassador, who was living in Mexico at the time, informing him of the German decision to resume unrestricted submarine warfare [against the world and America]." Then, according to my sources "the message instructed Zimmerman to propose to Mexico that in the event of war between the United States and Germany the Mexican and German Governments should make an alliance and wage war Together [against America and her allies], and that Germany would support Mexico in an effort to recover '**the lost territory in New Mexico, Texas, and Arizona."** Lucky for America and because England intercepted the message and knew about the message Mexico's Government never responded to this message, but since there were many ways to respond to this message, the world will never know if the Mexican government ever did or did not respond to the German government in another manner. After reading this quote, I feel that maybe we Americans can now see that maybe this message is why Mexico's government decided to be neutral during WWI and NOT help the allies. I also feel we can say that this is why "President Wilson, "outraged at the terms of the note, at first hesitated to release it [(the facts in the message to the public)] to the public because he knew that it might inflame public opinion . . . [yet] on March 1, 1917, he [finally] decided to make it public . . . [and] American sentiment for drastic measures against Germany rose immediately," [but unfortunately not for Mexico? Why?] (Hofstadter, Richard, William Miller, and Daniel Aaron. "America Goes to War." The United States: The History of a Republic. Prentice-Hall, Inc. New Jersey: 1960, 6th ed.). I want to note that President Wilson did Mexico a favor in the way he handled this message because I feel that if he had released it right away Americans would have wanted to attack Mexico too.

I now want to add one more important historical fact that deals with World War Two (WWII) that again involves Mexico's government and its lack of support for America and her military soldiers who were willing to die to defend the world and Mexico's Government and her people against the evil Axis war machine that included Germany, Japan, and Italy. However, when push came to shove, Mexico's Government and its people pulled their support from America and her allies again, and they went neutral during the war. According the history books I used, they said that "although Mexico was included in President Franklin Roosevelt's famous "lend-Lease Bill," that was created by Roosevelt to furnish economic aid (and under the table arms) to the Britain, because England's resources were approaching exhaustion in their war against Germany, Mexico decided again to remain neutral during this war, so Mexico's Government refused to participate in the war effort." My sources added that during WWII America's politicians, again, never released information that told America's Citizens if Mexico's Government ever accepted this offer from FDR, or if they refused the offer and never became a part of the American allied group. By the way, according to these books, "In this Law Bill, Roosevelt proposed not to lend England money but to instead lend them arms, which were to be returned or replaced after the war was over. The Lend-Lease deal was set forth as a means of keeping the war away from America by strengthening the Allies." The sources I read also said, "Roosevelt included Mexico's government" in war effort law bill, but never said or reported if Mexico Government ever agreed to receive these arms. (One has to wonder why it appears that America's Government keeps covered for Mexico's Government in both wars?) (Hofstadter, Richard, William Miller, and Daniel Aaron. "America Goes to War." The United States: The History of a Republic. Prentice-Hall, Inc. New Jersey: 1960, 6th ed.).

Why Roosevelt included Mexico in this arms deal Americans will probably never know. I came to this conclusion because according to the history book you are now familiar with from my citations, "Mexico decided to become neutral during World War Two again and stayed out of the World War (like they did during WWI), and to make things worse, they allowed Hitler's German Government to hide documents in their banks, and Mexico never gave America access to these documents. I want to add that Mexico's Government also denied the allies and America their oil fields that would have helped the cause against the Axis." On this act alone by Mexico's Government and people, I feel I can say that Mexico never accepted Roosevelt's offer of weapons to help protect the Americas or to fight against the Axis. One has to wonder if Mexico's Government was maybe offered the same deal by Hitler's Germany that they were offered by the Kaiser's Germany during World War I and that is why Mexico and its people again decided to stay neutral and not offer the US or its allies any kind of support? I make this statement because I feel that Mexico's decision to "file for neutrality during World War II turned out to be a bad decision for the allies and America when gas and oil became hard to find during the war, and Mexico sat by and let their oil fields stay neutral too." In my opinion this choice by Mexico's Government was pathetic and a very grave decision for America and the World's military war effort against the Axis" (Hofstadter, Richard, William Miller, and Daniel Aaron. "America Goes to War." The United States: The History of a Republic. Prentice-Hall, Inc. New Jersey: 1960, 6th ed.).

As I end this chapter, I want to make sure my readers understand that I feel the facts in my research prove that Mexico's choice of going neutral during WWI and WWII ended up hurting America and her allies' war efforts; it also very likely cost American soldiers their lives because our military often found itself short on fuel that Mexico's oil rich fields could have provided, and Mexico's Government's choice of going neutral very likely prolonged the war and pushed America into using the "bomb" to end the war. To make things worse, my research I feel proves the point I made in my last sentence because US War History insinuates that Mexico's oil reserves would have come in handy during the war effort in the Pacific theatre because many of our military operations in the Pacific often found themselves short on fuel during their operations. Having discovered these facts during my research, I felt it was my duty to report them to America's Citizens in this book. My conclusion (and opinion) from all of the facts I found on this matter is that I found Mexico's government and its people to be mean spirited and treacherous towards America because on two occasions when Mexico could have helped America's military and America's citizens, Mexico's Government decided not to help America, and to stay neutral so they could allegedly, or evidently, wait and see who won the war and maybe cut a deal with Germany, Hitler, or the axis if they had won the war.

Chapter Three

A Journalist Deciphers the U.S. Judicial Systems' 14th Amendment Lie

(To ask the Holy Ghost for Guidance) I wish now to submit a few remarks on the general proposition of amending the Constitution. As a general rule, I think we would [do] much better [to] let it alone. No slight occasion should tempt us to touch it. Better not take the first step, which may lead to a habit of altering it. Better, rather, habituate ourselves to think of it as unilateral. It can scarcely be made better than it is. New provisions would introduce new difficulties, and thus create an increased appetite for still further change. No sir, let it stand as it is . . . The men who made it have done their work and have passed away. Who shall improve on what they did? (Abraham Lincoln 1848)

The US Constitution was written in 1787 by some of America's greatest leaders who were highly educated men. I want to add these men were not only leaders in the fight for freedom, but they had mastered their careers and they had also mastered the "other" English language that English Scholars call the written English language. I now want to add that they had mastered this written language through their education in England's Universities where according to British scholars, "proper English has always been taught and used." I want to add that among these educated men was America's future president George Washington who was a hero of the revolutionary war with England. The reason Washington was at this convention was because he had been asked to serve as the convention president for the writing of the US Constitution when the meeting was convened. According to Gary Rea, Washington served his country well at this convention along with "41 politicians and 34 lawyers who were mostly from the mercantile cities but [none] from the countryside" (How the Republic Died at Philadelphia in 1787.26 March 2010.Online Posting. http://worldpress.com). These men not only represented the 13 states that existed at that time but they also represented a political group that Gary Rea tells us were known as "Federalists" in the New America. Rea adds that these Federalist were people who wanted to abolish the states because of the 55 delegates who attended [the convention], 21 of these delegates favored some form of monarchy. So the end result was an essay that was written in proper English that used proper and correct English grammar rules that introduced the "rules" and "not codes of laws" that our modern day US Politicians and Judges now considers, or call, the law of the land of the United States of America.

This Constitution, to quote Rea, "[created] a government with no real checks and balances because the US Government [was supposed to] function as one entity" ("How the Republic Died at Philadelphia in 1787." 26 March 2010. Online Posting: http://worldpress.com.). If we think about the key fact that Rea just pointed out for us about America's Constitution, that our government is supposed to function as one entity, I think we Americans have to arrive at the conclusion that there are really no checks and balances in America's government as we were often taught in school and we are currently being told by our current politicians and U.S. Judges. Which leads me to think that this key point of the Constitution might be the reason why America's politicians and her government appear to enjoy committing white-collar crimes that go un punished by our criminal laws. These crimes against America that are often committed by current (and by past politicians too) politicians, unfortunately, almost always go unpunished because no law in America appears to be able to stop these illegal acts of crimes against the people. And even if these American politicians break Constitutional, immigration, and criminal laws, these politicians don't seem to care or fear the laws of America because history shows they have little to worry about if they are caught. And now, as I have shown here in this paragraph, I think we can all see why America's Politicians have nothing to fear when they go astray, or as I state in this book, "Go Rogue."

As I studied and researched America's Constitution in several older U.S. History books, I found my self thinking that my Research was telling me that the Constitution was drafted using an expository and process organizational writing pattern in the paragraphs of this essay because these highly educated men knew this style would help them present several detailed lists of subject matter that allowed them to explain and expound on all of the facts, principles, and ideas that they wanted to put into young America's Constitution. Yes, I am talking about the same Constitution that many of today's American Politicians enjoy beating up, tearing apart, and saying we need to ignore it because "it is too old for modern times." Unfortunately, I have to say to today's evidently illiterate politicians and rogue American Judges (that don't appear to understand the language of America's Constitution) that the men who wrote our Constitution knew that by using an expository and process writing pattern in their essay they would be able to persuade their readers of their century to accept their document, or the new Constitution. By using various types and styles of English writing that included an "argumentative" writing formula so they could convince and move their readers to accept the action taken in their written work, these educated men were able to sell their constituents on their idea for a Federal Controlled Government. After selling their constituents on their plans for America, they then (I read) used descriptive writing patterns to evoke a mood of friendship and cooperation between the newly created Federal Government and the citizens of the 13 States. I want to add here that the Expository and process organizational writing pattern was more than likely used to persuade the citizens to accept the US Constitution's principles or laws by informing, clarifying, defining, and explaining the principles found in the prose of this wonderfully written work. The final revelation I discovered during my research and analysis of America's Constitution was that America's Constitution does not use "legalese or lawyer's" terminology any where in the essay to explain the Constitution's workings, and I found there was a very good reason for this choice as I shall soon prove in the rest of the main section of this chapter.

From the aforementioned fundamental historical and grammatical facts I presented in the last few paragraphs, I hope my fellow Americans have learned that my research has taught them that America's Constitution is not a pamphlet or code book of laws as we are lead to believe by America's Supreme Court and Politicians, but it is instead a well written essay that was written to establish a Federal Government that would be owned and controlled by the legal members of the Republic that are known as legal US Citizens (Note: America was never meant to be owned or controlled by its elected or appointed leaders.). I should again note here that Fredric Bastiat states in his book, that I introduced earlier in this book, that America's citizens created the American Constitution to defend the rights they gave themselves from their own Government and/or any country or people that might come to America and try to lay claim to these rights by either force or thievery, and that the Constitution is not a set of rules that protect anyone who might enter America and demand or claim these rights for their own. Unfortunately for the drafters of the "Republic's Constitution," the US Government they elected into power in this Century appears to have gone rouge and decided they know what is best for America's Citizens and their country. I make this bold statement because during my research I found a pattern of facts that told me that from the ladder part of the 20th Century (about 1972) to the present day 21st Century this pattern of facts showed me that

America's politicians and Supreme Court Judges evidently, or to put it legally, decided to augment, twist, reinterpret, and ignore all of America's written laws. My research also found that our American leaders used this illegal decision to not only deny Americans of their God Given rights to their country and land, but they also decided to simply betray America's citizens and the states that they were supposed to be serving and protecting by giving away their rights to any foreigner who enters America illegally.

So how did these current and past American leaders betray America's Republic? According to my research, these leaders have betrayed America by interpreting America's well written Constitution (A great written essay that President Lincoln said should never be changed or amended) in some very creative and illegal ways that allegedly proved America's Constitution was not written as a defensive set of rules or laws that protect America's citizen's individual rights. I want to note that these Fredric Bastiat says America's Constitution was written by Americans for "themselves to protect their life, liberty, land, and citizenship from those who would enter the US and lay claim to US Citizenship by force or world law." And to tell my fellow Americans the truth, I found that as I read all of the wrongs these American Leaders were doing to America's Citizens, that included the creative and illegal interpretations these rogue American leaders were using, I felt a force inspiring me to write this book. I want to add that I will talk about this force in the next few chapters of my book. I want to also add that I've found the reason America's Federal Government and the Supreme Court are insisting in this 21st Century that America's Citizens have to keep trusting them to interpret the contents of the Constitution without any query or opposition. After all, these two powerful US government entities appear to also be telling America's citizens that the American Constitution is a book of law codes that America's citizens don't really understand so it should be left up to their Government and Judges to decide what is best for America's citizens. I don't know about you but this kind of reasoning and talk sounds a lot like the talk that past leaders like Hitler and Stalin used to take control of their people and abuse their Government's powers.

The problem with this US Government and Supreme Court Justices' request for Americans to trust them to do right is that I feel most readers with a good command of the English language don't need this essay (known as America's Constitution) to be interpreted for them. I came to this conclusion with complete confidence, when I did, because I feel most Americans can and do understand America's Constitution. And to tell the truth, I also feel America's citizens don't need any help from these rouge US government leaders to help them understand the Constitution because, thanks to the old school curriculum that was used in the past, my research says that Americans understand the Constitution very well on their own. In fact, I believe, the old methodology that was used to teach these "old-school" Americans when they were young worked so well that it only helped them grow up to create useless things like computers, radios, television, FM radio, plastic, and rockets that put man in space and on the moon, to name a few of their worthless contributions to mankind. Having provided these facts, I am sure I can say these Americans know how to find the main point, or thesis, of any basic essay like America's Constitution, thank you. I can also say these Americans more than likely also know that most of the time the thesis of an essay is introduced in the first paragraph of an essay, and like myself, my "old school" American peers also figured out that the thesis of the Constitution is found in Preamble of the US Constitution. For my fellow American peers from my era who did not have time to look into this fact, I (like my old school peers) found the thesis of America's Constitution in the Preamble of America's Constitution: "**We the People of the United States,** in order to form a more perfect union, establish justice, and insure domestic tranquility provide for the common defense, promote the general welfare, and secure the blessings of Liberty **to ourselves and our posterity, do ordain and establish this constitution for the United States of America." Yes, the Constitution's thesis is found in this part of the Constitution." Yes, my fellow**

Americans, the Preamble of the US Constitution is also the thesis of the Constitution.

Now that I've let the cat out of the bag and introduced the fact that the Preamble includes the thesis of the Constitution, I hope my fellow Americans will understand why America's Rouge Government and many politicians would rather keep us in the dark and tell us to trust them to interpret this "legal" document that is too hard for non lawyers or politicians to understand. For my fellow Americans who have been too busy to figure out this simple fact, I hope to soon prove to them that the Constitutions' Preamble holds the "key" and many answers to the many problems that are currently plaguing America and her sovereignty. I also feel, with the help of Fredric Bastiat, that I will prove the Preamble also provides some very important answers to many questions that America's Citizens are asking as they see America's borders overrun by masses of foreigners and their government doing nothing to stop it and the problems they are bringing with them to America's soil. Sad to say, the questions my fellow Americans are asking are only getting worse as they see their country falling apart before their eyes, their earning power and jobs disappear, and their country being overrun and colonized by a growing legion of lawbreaking invaders and alien colonizers from the Middle East, South America, Central America, and Mexico (note: In June of 2018, Fox News reported that this mass invasion had grown by between 300 and 400 percent.). The strange part about this invasion is that these so called immigration criminals and their lawless, colonizing actions are being championed by America's Judicial System and America's Federal Government that are the entities that are supposed to uphold America's laws and not allow this form of law breaking. Now my fellow Americans should see why I say America's Government has decided to go **rogue in the 21ˢᵗ Century and not protect America's Sovereignty or her vested citizens rights and Constitutional powers**.

From my experience as an American, I sense that the general consensus among modern day Americans appears to be that their elected government officials and appointed judges don't care about Americans or America's laws or her sovereignty. And to make things worse, I (like many of America's Citizens) sense that these politicians and judges have decided to ignore their citizen's pleas for legal justice, or their cries for help. These cries for help are not coming from alarmists or racist Americans but from every day Americans who see a trend of lawlessness taking over America so they are now demanding that America's borders be closed and protected better by their elected officials, and that these American Government entities protect America's sovereignty and citizen's rights now! Although history and historical records tell us that America's citizens have the real power in America's Republic, I sense that America's Government representatives (who are elected to represent their constituents) are not only ignoring their constituents' demands for legal action but they appear to have made the choice to protect and care more about the needs and demands of millions of lawless foreign trespassing alien invaders that keep rushing across our borders illegally. These elected official's choice (that I mention in the last sentence), I hate to say it, might be being influenced by the fact that many of them have taken money from lobbyists that represent groups like Corporate America, Farm Bureaus, and Big Business Farm (among others) Co-ops who need the cheap labor and ready made consumers to make huge profits. To conclude my thoughts on this topic, I want to point out the Declaration of Independence, says Fredric Bastiat in his book The Law, that contains a section that gives America's Citizens the right to dissolve America's government if it ever gets out of hand, as it appears to have done these days, or goes rogue and attempts to become the master of its Citizens also known as the Republic.

Many Politicians and Supreme Court Judges might consider the discoveries in the previous paragraphs as trivial or might say that I over simplified the US Constitution to arrive at my conclusion, but the fact remains that I can prove the Constitution is a wonderful written instrument and essay that has an introduction, a thesis, a body, and a conclusion that was left open ended in case it ever needed to be amended. Before I move on to explain and prove my conclusion, I want to add the fact that the "Conclusion" to America's Constitution can be found in Article VII and not the Amendments. As for the body of the Constitution, the body is basically all of the Articles grouped together, while the Amendments as we now know are mostly changes made to the Constitution to improve the protections written into the Constitution so they work better for America's vested and legal citizens.

So if my readers will indulge me, I think this part of the book is a good time to study the body of the Constitution for the good of America's citizens. If I include my readers on this study or analysis, I think we Americans will first learn and find that this essay was written using some very good principles of effective essay writing. After my fellow Americans understand this fact, I want to point out that this essay also uses accepted, established, and documented rules of English grammar that are still being used and taught all over the world to this day, especially in Japan. These grammar or writing rules I'm talking about here include establishing a thesis, or main point, adding needed paragraphs to support and develop the thesis (The main point in our Constitution's case, or the thesis that is found in the Preamble.), adding details and examples, transitional words, and finally an ending to complete the needed parts of this essay. Now that I've refreshed my fellow Americans' memories and added some new knowledge (or Schema) to my reader's memory banks of the basic principles of essay writing, I think it's time I helped them see how literary analysis and the rules of grammar and composition can be used to analyze America's Constitution so that they can see what I saw after I completed my work. I'm going to do this so I can prove to my readers the wrongs and misdeeds that are being done to our country's Constitution and her Citizens by what I feel are some very treacherous and Rogue Federal Government officials (I want to add that I feel California's government has also gone rogue and it is also committing the same type of offenses.) and Supreme Court Judges.

As I start this investigation on behalf of my fellow Americans, I want to say the following literary analysis of the Constitution I completed in this book should help me correct some invalid, illegal, and incorrect (mean spirited) interpretations that I feel have been purposely made by both elected Political and appointed Judicial members of current and past American leaders of current and past administrations. My analysis should then help America's citizens understand and appreciate the language and words that were used in the Constitution by its drafters. And later in my research, I hope to reveal the word tactics and Rhetorical Strategies the drafters of the Constitution used to convince the 1787 American Colonists to "buy into" the idea of having a United States Constitution instead of having individual state Constitutions that history tell us most colonists of that time wanted. My research will also allow me to show the cohesion, or wholeness, and the consistency that I found in the U.S. Constitution's Preamble and Body. I want to add here that I found the cohesion/wholeness of the Constitution is what holds the message together. Upon completing my research, I feel my readers will be able to better understand the context of the Constitution which includes the phrases, sentences, and passages found in the body of the Constitution that are closely connected to the nouns, pronouns, and words used in the Preamble so the correct message is delivered to the reader. This information I gleaned from my research I feel helped me find some answers that I feel helped the Colonists (and now my readers and myself) understand the meaning of the Constitution and why it was good for them and America.

Before I move on to discuss the results of my analysis of the American Constitution, I have decided to provide my readers an example of how our political leaders are bending over backwards and illegally interpreting the Constitution to get away with their lawless acts by simply ignoring the real principles of the American Constitution. To show my readers how America's politicians continue to ignore the Constitution, I have decided to use a news story from one of America's political events that happened during ex-President Obama's time in the White House. I'll do this so my readers will be able to better understand and see how (or why) America's politicians and even Supreme Court Judges' often use creative and very likely illegal interpretations of the Constitution to push their own personal agenda's or beliefs on America's Citizens. My fellow Americans should understand that these very creative interpretations often help these American politicians and Judges so much that they often use these creative and illegal interpretations to push their political party's views or beliefs on America's Citizens. Unfortunately for my fellow Americans, these politician's actions usually affect all of the lives of all Americans in negative ways.

To prove the statement I just made in the last paragraph, I will now present a news feature/story that involved one of ex-President Obama's presidential decisions that he announced during one of his speeches: I decided to use this speech as my example because in this speech President Obama used a literary trick called pragmatic rhetoric (This type of writing uses a persuasive rhetorical style to convince someone, like Americans, that Gadhafi had allegedly killed civilians in his country's civil war.) to explain and support his unsubstantiated need to disregard the "law of the land" so he could start a war with another country without Congress' approval (I feel he used this choice of Rhetoric to show his "means" could justify his "ends."). In the end, I found that ex-President Obama used this rhetorical trick in his speech so he could attack a foreign country that was not at war with America (a requirement that must be met when America attacks a foreign country) and convince Americans that he had this power because it came from his own interpretation of the Constitution. The problem with Obama's actions is that his interpretation was wrong and he broke Constitutional law, which is an impeachable offense. Since I feel I can prove Obama broke American Constitutional law, I will now show my readers how he broke Constitutional law.

As I said in my last paragraph, I feel I can prove President Obama broke Constitutional law in March of 2011 because on this day then President Obama basically declared war on a country that had not attacked America or had made any threats towards America. By declaring war on Libya's dictator led government without provocation or permission from Congress, President Obama failed to follow Constitutional law when he ordered America's Military to attack Libya's standing government without hearings in Congress, allowing America's Citizens to have an opinion, and without being at war with Libya. I hate to say it but because ex-President Obama's action failed to meet any of aforementioned requirements when he attacked Libya's Government; I say this because President Obama basically used the War Powers Act that is only reserved to be used in the Constitution by America's Congress: "The law I just mentioned, and I say again, is reserved for Congress in Article 1 Section 8." So when President Obama declared war on Libya and launched his attack without Congress' permission, he over stepped his Constitutional powers and he knew it. I came to this conclusion because Article 1 Section 8 of the Constitution states that, "The Congress shall have power . . . to declare war, grant letters of marque and reprisal, and make rules concerning captures on land and water [and] to raise and support armies . . . [but not the President]." So as I just said and proved, President Obama did indeed break Constitutional law and he got away with it without any kind of sanction or reprimand from the Democrat Controlled Congress.

To prove that I am right in my conclusion that ex-President Obama did break the law of the Constitution, I now want to present another story that I feel proves my statement completely because the story said that "9 liberal Democrats had broken ranks and had agreed with many of the Congressional Republicans' view that 'President Obama's authorization of military strikes on Libya, without congressional consent, [was] unconstitutional [and] and an impeachable offense" (Newsmax March 22, 2011, Meyers and Weil). To make matters worse for President Obama, Representative Dennis

Kucinich a Democrat from Ohio and big supporter of President Obama broke ranks and said in one of his many interviews (after Obama's ordered attacks) that "he was outraged over the President's decision to attack Libya without first consulting Congress" as is required under Constitutional law and his actions [were] Impeachable" (Liberty Counsel, Printed Hand Out. March 23, 2011.). Compare this illegal act that "was" an impeachable offense that was never acted on by the Democrat Controlled Congress to the current "unproven" accusation and investigation that President Trump and the Republican Party colluded with the Russian Government and I think you will see the double standard that exists in America.

Now that I have introduced and provided a current and timely example of how our elected politicians seem to ignore or simply make up their own interpretation of America's Constitution, and I think my readers will agree with me that it is time we backed up and completed an in depth discussion of the Constitution's Preamble that I introduced before I presented my example of how President Obama, like other American leaders, have been able to twist the Constitution's words to do their bidding. I will take this action so I will be able to support the discoveries I uncovered during my research and analysis of key areas of the Constitution. But before I move on, I'd like to point out this very important fact: While America's Political and Judicial System often look at the US Constitution as a legal code document (like for example California's Vehicle Driver's Code Book) that explains and provides the law of the land for their use, I am going to view and study the Constitution as a written prose work (or essay) that uses two genres (kinds or types) of writing that include "Descriptive writing" and "Exposition writing patterns." I want to note that I feel America's politicians use this wrong or incorrect interpretation (see the Constitution as a list of laws) so they can ignore the main thesis, topic, or point of the Constitution, which I will soon prove does exist and blows their interpretations out of the water and proves them wrong. To complete my task, I want how easy it was to find the thesis of the constitution when I analyzed key sections of America's Constitution. The ironic part of my analysis is that my results all pointed to the fact that the Constitution was a wonderfully written essay and not a list of laws.

To start my investigation, I want to start with a discussion of the writing methods/styles I feel the drafters of the Constitution used to write their great written work. The first fact I found was that our founding fathers used descriptive writing in certain parts, or areas, of the Constitution because by using descriptive writing patterns it allowed the drafters to clearly state for whom the Constitution was being written and why it was only being written for what they felt were the legal occupants of American soil of that time and all other future legal and vested Americans. The Drafters also used highly descriptive Expositive writing patterns because they knew they felt they needed to introduce and explain the directions and instructions of how to use their wonderful essay called the U.S. Constitution to both set up America's Government and protect the rights of this country's citizens. They knew that by using this writing method they would be able to better explain the process (a form of recipe that was needed to be followed) that was needed to form the new American government. To better understand these two methods of prose writing they used, I want to now show my readers two examples of prose writing that present how these patterns work. I first want to show an example of a "descriptive prose work," and then I want to present an example of an "exposition prose written work." I should note here that because of space limitations I only use two very short writing examples to prove my point. But, although my examples are short, I feel my readers will be able to see how these two kinds of writing styles were used to create or write America's wonderful Constitution that only belongs to legal American Citizens:

Note: The following paragraphs are examples of Descriptive and Exposition Writing Patterns or patterns that organize these essays for the benefit of the reader. These examples should help my readers understand how **descriptive** writing helps the writer present a clear picture using vivid words to describe something new: Like for example the Constitution's drafters used descriptive writing to introduce the Constitution and explain how it worked, and how **exposition** writing allows the writer to use a pattern to explain a process that either explains or creates something new: Like the Colony's delegates did in the body of the US Constitution when they drafted and explained the workings of America's Constitution.

Example 1. Descriptive Writing:

1) A descriptive patterned essay about a
   person or a classmate from college:

Bill stood six feet two inches tall in his shoeless feet. He wore beads, tie die shirts, and baggy bellbottom pants most of the time. When I first met Bill in college, the first thing I noticed was that he did not have an athletic body, but he did have good strength and was a bit muscular for not being an athlete. Bill and I met by chance in school because when we both arrived on campus both of us found out we did not have a place to stay. Although we both had set up our rooms in advance, the registrar had somehow failed to save each one of us a place in the college dorms. Since both of us were in hurry to settle down, we ended up renting a house close to campus. To make a long story short, Bill and I hit if off and had a great time just being good old college roommates, enjoying our first year in college, and our first year away from home.

Time passed by fast during our first year in college. We each knuckled down and studied hard, worked part-time jobs, and before we knew it half of the year had passed by for us. And then it happened, we met a girl that we both fell for very hard; I could tell we were going to have problems. As we both chased her and tried to win her favor, we found ourselves competing and drifting apart as friends. The other problem was that the young lady could not make up her mind as to which of us she liked better. In the end, I moved out of the house because Bill told me he felt I was playing dirty and telling the girl lies about him, which was not true at all.

Knowing things were only getting worse, I decided to stop talking to the young lady and to Bill so I could work on my grades and I could put the whole thing behind me. I also finally decided to move out and find my own place to stay. As I put the last few things in my car and gave Bill the key to our place, I told him it had been fun. The sad and pathetic part of this whole business was that in the end we young men had both learned that when it came to women sometimes friendships doesn't survive. The time passed by fast in school, and we soon found ourselves graduating from college. Since be say each other in school, we became friends again but not as close as we had been before the young lady came into our lives. I want to add that the last time I saw Bill, before we left college and parted ways, I noticed he had grown a beard and was still with the young lady. As he drove off with the young lady in his 1968 Pontiac Lemans, we both smiled and waved at each other and headed towards our unknown futures.

Now that I've introduced this short story and my readers have read this short prose work, I want my readers to first notice that I first introduced the topic of Bill and our friendship, then I used descriptive words like tall, shoeless, beads, tie dyed shirt, bellbottom pants, and I used the key component of restating or reintroducing the main topic of discussion through out my story (which is the friendship of the two main characters) so my reader could follow the main thesis or topic of this short essay. I want to remind my readers that the repetition of key words and descriptive words in this case help the reader know the details of the story. We should note the repeated detailed descriptive words help the writer keep reintroducing the main characters and the friendship of the two main characters, which is the key to the story. So, I want to note that the key points or components that are found in all descriptive pieces or written works are needed when a writer is trying to describe how a tool works, a research method, a story, or a sequence of events.

Example 2. Exposition Writing:

2) My example for Exposition pattern writing will be a short essay that explains a process, like making a specialty sandwich:

This sandwich was created early one summer morning when my family had run out of traditional breakfast staples like ham, potatoes, and ketchup to cook some ham, eggs, and hash browns with toast. Since I had some left over Salsa, some hot dogs, and eggs, I decided to see if I could create a breakfast sandwich to compete with something like our Local Mac eatery made, and thus was born my breakfast sandwich "the California Wedge":

To make the California wedge, that can best be described as a breakfast or brunch type sandwich that provides both good nutrition and a tasty snack, you will need the following ingredients/items and utensils: a fresh egg, black pepper, a pinch of salt (to taste), one cut up single hot dog, and two tablespoons of medium or hot tomato salsa sauce (to taste). You will also need a toasted sour dough English muffin and a microwave safe, small, round dish that will be sprayed with cooking oil.

This is how I make the California Wedge in my home: In a bowl combine the egg, salt, pepper, hot dog, and salsa and whip them with fork till well mixed. Pour the egg mixtures into the small round (microwave safe) cooking dish and cook the mixture in the microwave for one minute till done (time depends on the power of your microwave). To make the sandwich, put a small amount of Mayo on the toasted English muffin; put the cooked egg mixture on one of the muffin slices; add some more salsa to taste; top off the egg with a slice of Swiss cheese; make a sandwich, and then I hope you will enjoy your California Wedge sandwich.

In the short exposition patterned essay I presented above, my readers should notice that I first introduced the topic, which is how to make a certain sandwich. After I introduced the sandwich, I then started using key words that both described and explained what kind of key ingredients would be needed to make the California Wedge sandwich. Then, I introduced the process of how to use the ingredients to make and create the sandwich. This process type of writing I want to note here is exactly how the Preamble and the Constitution were written to work together. They were written in this manner so the readers of the Constitution would be able to understand and use the "detailed instructions, components, and methodology" that are found the Constitution's Amendments and Articles so the readers could set up and run the country known as the United States of America's Government. I want to also add one more important fact or point here that I feel proves why changing, misreading, or altering the key words or elements of the Constitution are wrong and should never be allowed. Let's say the person making the sandwich changes the process and the key ingredients found in my California Wedge Sandwich (like the changes I feel our politicians and Supreme Court Judges often make to the Constitution to serve their purposes). What would happen? I hate to say it but the California Wedge sandwich would no longer be the original sandwich, just like Constitution is no longer the Constitution when it's contents are misread or twisted on purpose. I want to note that I provided this simple essay to show that when the US Constitution is interpreted in creative ways by our current Supreme Court Judges and Politicians to serve their purposes their changes not only changes the meaning of the Constitution, but it also avoids the process found in the Constitution that is required to make any changes to the US Constitution that Congress must go through to amend the Constitution.

Now that I've introduced to the two forms of organizational writing patterns in the previous paragraphs, I hope my readers now have a better understanding of how these two prose writing patterns or organizational writing patterns were used by our founding fathers to draft America's Constitution and why I can prove the American Constitution was never meant to be read as a book of law codes. Now before I move on, I feel I need to review some key words and sentences that I presented earlier when I introduced my readers to a simple version of my analysis of the Preamble of the Constitution. Okay, if my readers are ready, I want to first re-introduce the simple analysis I did earlier in my book of the Preamble and take this analysis up notch so we can take a much closer look at the Constitution's Preamble and how it works with the body, or the Articles and Amendments. To start, I want to first introduce the Preamble again: "**We the people of the United States**, in order **to form** a more **perfect** union, (to) **establish** justice, (to) **insure** domestic tranquility, (to) **provide** for the common defense, (to) **promote** the general welfare, and (to) **secure** the blessing of liberty **to ourselves** and (to) **our** posterity, **do ordain and establish this Constitution for the United States of America**."

Before I go on, I want to remind my readers how I used the analytical tools or literary research tools to complete my earlier analysis. After I show my readers how I used these tools, I will help them remember and review the study that I completed earlier in this book of the key opening sentence that is found in the Constitution's Preamble, that is the only sentence found in the Preamble (Note: I'll be using these analytical tools or techniques on Section 1 of the XIV Amendment too to prove my point.). The first action I took to start my analysis (I want to remind my readers) included removing two key infinitive modifiers that included these two words: "in order." After I took this action, I then removed the prepositional phrases that all began with the "understood" prepositional (the word is not there, but the reader knows he or she must insert it into the sentence) word "to." I took this action so my readers could understand how each one of these "understood" prepositions worked in the phrases that included the "understood preposition "to." After adding the understood word "to" to the each of word phrases in the list of desired privileges and rights, I found the preposition "to" and the phrases formed a union known as a "prepositional phrase: These prepositional phrases created a list of (we'll say) desired results, needs, or privileges that included [to] establish justice, [to] insure domestic tranquility, [to] provide for the common defense, [to]

promote the general welfare, and finally [to] secure the blessings
of liberty to ourselves and [to] our posterity." After I removed
these prepositional phrases, so my readers could see what I was
saying or showing them about the infinitive and the prepositional
phrases, I then tried to help my readers see that what the reader
was left with was the famous introductory phrase, that our 1787
Colonial Constitution delegates wrote to open the introduction to
the Constitution. Hopefully my readers are not too confused and
will understand better in the next paragraph:

The famous phrase that begins the Preamble, I want my
attentive readers to learn now, includes the following key words
that start this famous sentence, "**We the people of the United
States.**" And since I took the time to analyze the words found in
this part of the sentence, I want to tell my readers that I was able to
discover that they not only begin the first and only sentence found
in the Preamble, but these words also serve to introduce the people
and subject, or topic of discussion, of the American Constitution
(which is the "PEOPLE" of the United States and no other nation's
people). This introductory sentence also includes some key words
that work as key modifiers for some very important nouns and
pronouns. I should add these key modifiers include a very important
prepositional phrase that helps this sentence describe and define
(or modify) the main pronoun "we" that begins this sentence. As
I analyzed this sentence, I found the word "**We,**" served as the
subject of this sentence and it was defined or described very well by
several modifiers that I will go into further later in this paragraph.
Together, these words create an appositive phrase where the subject
of the sentence "**We**" (this word was a nominative case pronoun)
is later complemented ("identified" or "defined") first by the word
"**the**" (an article), and then it is complemented (or modified) by the
word "**people**" (a common, plural noun), and finally, the drafters
used the "prepositional phrase "of the United States" to help modify
of the word "We," so the readers would know the Subject of this
sentence are the "People of the United States of America." After I
completed this part of my analysis, I found that when these words

were combined together they formed the introductory phrase which helped the founders tell us who the word "We" represented and to tell the reader America's Constitution was written to ONLY serve America's people because they were the ones creating or writing this Constitution for themselves. Or as Fredric Bastiat (the man I introduced earlier in my book) told us in the quote I provided earlier in this book: "The Constitution was written so that Americans could defend themselves against those who would attempt to claim the rights and privileges they created for themselves and put into their American Constitution."

Since my readers and I just learned the article "**the**" and the common noun "**people**" combine in the introductory sentence with the prepositional phrase "of the United States" to "complement or "modify" and describe who the key word **"We"** represents in this sentence, I hope my readers now understand how these words combine to describe or identify who the pronoun "**We**" represents in this sentence, which I feel was purposely used to help the lower educated colonists (or any reader of the Constitution) see that this word was being used to introduce the Subject or topic (and also serves as part of the thesis) of this introductory sentence that introduced their Constitution. I also want to note that in the end the Preamble and this phrase combine to form a sentence that introduces the "essay" known as the US Constitution. I also want to point out the "thesis statement" found in the Preamble does "not" include any words, terms, or other nouns like "the world's citizens," "the Mexican People," or any other nation's citizens in this introductory sentence known as the Preamble that introduces the US Constitution. I point this clear fact out because I feel this important fact proves that the US Constitution was written to serve only America's people on an individual basis as Fredric Bastiat states.

In a nutshell, I feel I just proved the American Constitution was written to only protect America's Citizens rights from the world's conquerors or invaders, like Mexico's illegal aliens. And since the thesis statement (and the Constitution) says that it only serves and protects America's citizens, I feel we learn the Constitution was written to only serve and protect America's legal citizens against those who would "try to lay claim the rights and privileges they created and wrote for themselves," and not any visitor, diplomat, illegal colonizing invader, squatter, or the illegal children of any trespassing illegal alien who finds himself/herself on US soil. In conclusion I want to add that it also insures that America's legal and lawful citizens are protected from being invaded or occupied by any foreign country or having to share their rights and privileges with any country's citizens, like Mexico's citizens, as Fredric Bastiat warns us in the quotation that I used earlier in my book. One more point I want o make here is that the American Constitution should never be changed to accommodate or include any of the people I just mentioned in the last sentence. I feel I am a lot like President Lincoln on the thought of changing America's Constitution. What did President Lincoln say on this topic? Mr. Lincoln made it quite clear in the following statement in one of his famous speeches: "This document (the Constitution) is perfect just the way it is..." So as far as I am concerned, like President Lincoln, the US Constitution should be left alone and never be amended again or in the near future. Unfortunately, for Americans who are reading this book, the written English language seems to be something foreign to our current and past leaders, Supreme Court Justices, and politicians because historical and current events show us that these people are currently interpreting America's Constitution in some very illegal and creative ways on any given day.

Moving on with my analysis and study of America's Constitution and her Preamble, I now want to point out again that the two key words **"the people"** were used to join the prepositional phrase **"of the United States"** which helped the founding fathers add more key information to the Preamble about the subject "We." Together, these words combined to create the phrase "We the people of the United States" which, as I said before, helped the Constitution's drafters clarify, identify, and describe the subject they were introducing in this phrase: "We the People of the United

States." The key to this phrase is that when it is added to the complete sentence it is able to advance the understanding "that the Constitution is being written for "the People of The United States of America and no other country, no other citizens, and no other world order." Since I feel I have just proved a key factor of who the American Constitution was written to serve and protect, I think I can honestly say the drafters of America's Constitution deliberately used clear, descriptive, and concise words so no one could alter the meaning of the Preamble or Constitution to serve their twisted or creative purpose to take away the powers and rights found in America's Constitution that were written to "defend" and "protect" American citizens' Constitutional rights that they wrote for THEMSELVES. By adding this statement I hope my readers now understand that this Exposition and Descriptive type essay known as America's Constitution was clearly written by American citizens to benefit and protect themselves and their fellow American citizens, **and no other countries illegal invading citizens. I am sure I can say here that the Constitution was never intended to serve or protect some alien country's citizens or world citizens' league of Nations, as the ACLU, America's current Politicians, and the present American Supreme Court Justices would have America's vested and legal citizens believe.**

Having established the subject of the Preamble's opening sentence, and in this case the only sentence found in this part of the Constitution known as the Preamble helps the drafters of the Constitution introduce the main topic of discussion or thesis, I then isolated the predicate (verb) of this sentence that included several verbs and its auxiliaries or helping verbs. I isolated these words to help me show this sentence had a very important direct object that had to be addressed in my analysis. After I completed my research, the first conclusion I arrived at was that the predicate of this sentence included the words "do ordain and establish," where the word **"do"** was used by the drafters as a helping verb for the main verb or the word **"ordain**." This discovery is important because this verb is followed by the word **"and"** which is a conjunction that I feel was used to connect or "join" the verbs **"ordain"** and **"establish"** **that were then used to guide the reader to the object of the verb.** Note: When these two words "ordain and establish" are joined together, they help the drafters create a compound transitive verb that helps them tell the readers that America's Colonial delegates felt they were not only establishing this important document for America's citizens, but they had been ordained (dictionary defines the word "ordained," as a word that means "willed or inspired by God") by God to establish America and her Constitution for **"America and its legal citizens"** (our quotations for emphasis).

Before I continue the review of my research of the Preamble and the US Constitution, I want my readers to note the word "Constitution" serves as the main object of the verb in this very important sentence (Note the word "very" for future reference) because it receives the action of the verbs. I decided to point this fact out because the object of the sentence that includes the two words "this Constitution" is then immediately followed by two prepositional phrases (serve as modifiers) that tell the reader who this Constitution was written to serve and protect, or as the sentence says **"for the United States of America."** To clarify what I'm saying, I want to add that this phrase serves as the object complement in this sentence because it refers, or directs, the reader to see that this sentence is talking about America's Constitution, or **"this Constitution."** More importantly, my analysis of this sentence helps me prove that this prepositional phrase also establishes and tells the reader who is **"Covered by America's Constitution,"** which are America's real legal Citizens.

To put it simply, We Americans are reminded again the American Constitution was being written to **"only"** protect and serve the people of the United States of America and no one else because no other country or citizens of foreign countries are mentioned in this introductory sentence that is the thesis of America's Constitution. In the end, if my readers don't quite understand all of the English grammar terminology I've just introduced, they don't need to worry about this problem because all they need to understand is that all of these words put together in this key sentence say that America's citizens that born to legal Americans, or to legally naturalized citizens, have the right to call themselves American Citizens according to their US Constitution and its laws, as Fredric Bastiat says or warns us. I want to add to my conclusion that no other country's citizens are protected or served by America's Constitution and this includes any foreign citizens who are visiting America, trespassing on US sovereign soil, or any of their children who might be born on US sovereign soil. In essence, because America's Constitution only protects and serves America's citizens and its rights and privileges were written to defend America's Citizens from those who would try to take or claim this rights, these means that there is no such thing as automatic US citizenship for any foreigner's child who might be born on US soil. I say this because they are NOT under the jurisdiction of America's Constitution or its laws.

Since I feel I have proven beyond a shadow of doubt that America's Constitution was written to only serve and protect America's citizens in Chapters two and three of this book, I think the time has come for me to prove that the results of my research and analysis of the Constitution's Preamble in this chapter can simply be proven by using a little grammar rule test that many students from my generation learned in the "good old days" when kids got a real education. This test my peers and I learned in school basically taught us to take the object and the object complement of a sentence, or this in this case the following group of words found in the Preamble **"this Constitution for the United States of America,"** and use them to create a new sentence that changes this group of words into the 'subject" of a passive voice sentence with a transitive verb. I bet my readers thought they would never hear this old trick mentioned in their lifetime again. Any way, getting back to my little grammar trick I am talking about, this trick tells us to take the object of the sentence and its modifiers (Note: For those who might have forgotten, the object in a sentence tells the reader who or what receives the action of the active verb in a sentence.), or in this case, the words the "US Constitution" and the words the "People of the United States" and use them to write a passive verb sentence. In the new sentence, I will take the object and its modifiers of this sentence (the words: 'this Constitution for the United States) and simply use them as the subject of my new sentence.

Before I write the new sentence I'm going to create, I want my readers to turn on their light of knowledge in their minds so I can blow their minds wide open. Okay, now that we are all ready, I would like to explain to my readers that in the old sentence the object and it modifiers ("this Constitution for the United States of America) received the action of the verbs or words "do ordain and establish" and completed the action of telling the reader who was covered by America's Constitution. In the new sentence, since I'm writing or creating a passive sentence, I will use the same words found in the object of the Preamble's original sentence to create my new passive voice sentence. The new passive voice sentence will include the object of the old sentence, which will become the subject of the new sentence. By using a passive form verb in the new sentence I will be able to write a sentence that will allow me to include the verbs "ordain and establish" from the original sentence, and the new sentence will look something like this one: "The US Constitution of the United States of America was ordained and established for the People of the United States of America."

As my readers can see in the new sentence, by using this little trick, I was allowed to show that the drafters of America's Constitution clearly "stated the Preamble's words and information were not only being used to introduce the body of the Constitution but they were also being used in the Preamble to introduce the thesis of the Constitution and to remind the readers that the Constitution was an essay that described who this document protected and served, which was ONLY America's citizens. Or, as Fredric Bastiat says, "the Constitution's Rights, Privileges, Principles, and Powers were written so that America's citizens could protect the privileges found in the Constitution for themselves." In short, these rights and privileges only belong to "the People of the United States of America and their legal children that "are natural born citizens" because their parents are already US Citizens. Before I close this discussion, I think my readers should note that no other country or other countries' citizens are included in the words of this sentence known as the Preamble (or the Constitution's body) and therefore they are not covered by America's Constitution. Yes my fellow American's, treasonous Supreme Court Judges, and treacherous American Politicians, the answer is that easy to find in America's Constitution, and it does require a law degree.

Now that I've introduced my readers to the real truth and facts found in the Constitution's Preamble, I feel I can say that America's Constitution clearly says that it only protects America's citizens and it empowers them to protect the country and their privileges from foreigners who might enter America illegally or by force and try to lay claim to the rights and privileges found in America's Constitution. I also feel these powers of defense can be used against any American government official who might try to take away these powers and give them to any foreigners or other people. Since the US Constitution was written or ordained to defend only the rights and privileges of "the People of the United States of America" and her legal naturalized Citizens, and not the world, I feel I can stake or claim this right for America's Citizens with complete confidence, because when the drafters of the Constitution discuss topics like citizenship, voting rights, birthrights, and the right to protect and defend these rights in any part of the Constitution's body, they are only referring to or speaking to the rightful owners of America's Constitution, known as the members of the Republic.

Before I move on, I want to point out the definition for the term (or word) **"ordain,"** which is one of the key transitive verbs used by the drafters in the Preamble, means (or is defined) "to be inspired by God." And since I noticed this interesting fact about the definition of this key word that I found in the Preamble, I feel the writers of the

Constitution felt their work had been inspired, or guided, by God's hand when they wrote this great historical document, so in realty they chose to not separate church and state in this sentence. Or to bring some professional people into my observation, I think Funk and Wagnalls dictionary says it best when it states the word "ordain has Biblical references in its definition that can mean 'to decree,' [that it is] said of God, and fate." Having introduced this very controversial discovery, I guess I can say my conclusion from this discovery is that the founding fathers (drafters) of the Constitution felt that God had predestined them to write the Constitution and that it was God's decree that they create America. Because I come to this conclusion, **I feel** this means the drafters felt they weren't just creating a document to create a new nation, but they were instead drafting a document for a country that God himself had predestined to be his nation, or as America's patriots like to call the American Nation, "God's Country." My conclusion from this discovery is quite simple: Although most modern day politicians and judges keep telling all Americans that God and our laws must be kept separate from America's Government, I just don't agree with them and here is my reason: After I discovered the facts I found in the dictionary about the word ordain, I felt I could say that in the eyes of the Constitution's drafters America exists on this earth because it was blessed and ordained, or founded, by the Lord our God with "His blessing."

To add more fuel to the flames of controversy I feel I just started, I want to now show that the drafters of our Constitution were so set in their beliefs in God that they included the term "ordain" in the "thesis statement" of their introduction of America's Constitution that is known as the Preamble. I feel they took this action because in their minds they felt they had to let the world know that America, her government, and the Constitutional laws of this new Nation had been inspired and created by God. By taking this bold stand, I feel the drafters of the Constitution basically stated or announced to the world that America had been founded and anointed as a Christian Nation by God himself. I know this statement is a bold stand to take, but I really feel the drafters used the word "Ordain" to remind any foreign citizen who might be thinking of becoming an American, or coming to America as a legal immigrant, to know that if they came to live in America they would be living in a Nation that had Christian values. So if these foreigners did decide to come to America, I feel the founding fathers were making sure these new immigrant knew what they were getting into when they decided to request permission to immigrate legally into America. To conclude, I also believe the drafters of the Constitution purposely included the word "ordain" in the Preamble to basically state that America had been "decreed by God" so that no American judge or politician would ever try to change the fact that America had been founded and was based on the Pilgrim's Christian Values. The Founding Fathers took this action, in my opinion, so that no American judge or politician would ever force America's citizens to take a back seat to any other religion, to atheists, to alternate life styles, or to Islam's alleged Religious Constitution. To quote a famous tuna-fish cartoon character we all grew up seeing on an old TV commercial, I want to say to America's Supreme Court Judges: ***"Sorry about that Charlie."***

While I know there will be many pro open borders supporters who will not agree with the conclusion I arrived at in my previous paragraphs, I feel happy to know that I was able to not only prove the results of my study, but that I was also able to formulate and explain some very precise and concrete facts in my review of my analytical research of the Preamble. And, I want to now move on to some other facts I found in the results of my analysis of the Constitution's Preamble that I feel helps me conclude and say America's Constitution's drafters intentionally used certain precise words in the opening paragraph of their Constitution to establish the key topics they were gong to address over and over throughout America's Constitution. I feel they used this type of writing patterns to make sure their readers knew America's Constitution had been written for themselves, or America's new legal citizens (and the future children of these legal citizens and legally Naturalized citizens) who were living in America at the time the wrote their Constitution. The deliberate use of precise words by these drafters of the Constitution became a pattern in the opening paragraph and it continued throughout the rest of the Constitution's body because this methodology allowed them to unequivocally establish that they were Americans and they represented their fellow Americans who, according to these drafters, were the only persons being empowered by their Constitution.

To prove the Constitution's main topic or thesis, and/or other key topics, are introduced in the Constitution's thesis and then are re-stated and re-introduced throughout the Articles and Amendments of the Constitution's body, I decided to use and introduce a book titled <u>The Harbrace College Handbook</u> as my reference guide to present some of the rules of effective writing that I used (and will use again) to explain the essay writing principle that are used in the Preamble's only sentence. To start, I want to first note that "the opening paragraph of an essay, as we all know, is usually where the thesis statement is found in an essay because the thesis helps control the subject matter of discussion that is found in the body or added sentences and paragraphs of the essay...[that help] support the topic or the main thesis [statement that is] always restated later in the essay as writer continues to expand on the main topic of discussion [where it is] usually reworded [and reintroduced] as the topic in many [of the] new sentences and paragraphs. This main topic is often clarified and verified throughout the essay as the main point or main topic... of the essay... [or in our case America's Constitution]" (Hodges, C. John and Whitten, E. Mary. Harbrace College Handbook, Harcourt Brace Jovanovich, Inc: New York. 1982).

Because I have just proved in the previous paragraphs that the Harbrace College Handbook explains very well that the main topic (or the thesis) is always repeated, reworded, and used over and over again throughout an essay (like in the US Constitution' main body that includes the Article and Amendments) to help the reader gain more knowledge on the topic being discussed, I feel my readers should now understand that each new paragraph in an essay reintroduces and refreshes the main topic or subject being discussed, so if America's Constitution is only talking about American Citizens, when a pronoun like "persons or people" is used later in a paragraph, the reader knows these people means America's Citizens, and not some foreign nation's people. This repetition helps the reader grasp the main point (or thesis) of the essay, or in our case the discussion of the principles and guidelines that are found in American Constitution. The repetition of the main topic also helps the reader learn to identify, define, or look back and find any needed antecedent for a pronoun that might be used in any future sentence that replaces the main noun or topic with pronouns that might include, for example, common nouns, collective nouns, or pronouns that are used to replace proper nouns like, as I said above, the words "American citizen." These common nouns, collective nouns, or pronouns can include a word like "they" that is used in the Constitution to replace the words "American citizens" in one of the Articles of the American Constitution. T

Continuing the discussion of repeating or reintroducing the main topics of discussion in an essay, I want to add that pronouns (like the word "they") and their antecedents (like the words "American Citizens") are often re-introduced and often repeated in various ways many new sentences and new paragraphs throughout an essay like America's Constitution. I want to remind my readers that by restating the topic of discussion by using words like pronouns, possessive pronouns, or common nouns the writer is able to reintroduce the main topic or topics throughout the written piece, or essay. By reminding my readers how the thesis' functions in an essay, and in our case the US Constitution, and how each future paragraph in the essay is used to restate the main topic of discussion by using pronouns or even common nouns, I hope my readers now remember how important the use of antecedents and the act of setting precedence is in an essay to a writer who introduces new sentences and paragraphs that might replace the main topic of discussion (that might be a proper noun like "Americans) with a pronoun like the word "they." I want to remind my readers that vague words like the common noun "persons" can include any vague general nouns, pronouns, possessive pronouns, or common nouns that the writer might decide to use in the body of the essay. If the drafter of the essay does his job when he uses a word like "their," the drafter will include an antecedent for this word so the reader will know that the possessive pronoun "their" (as in "their rights.") can be replaced by the antecedent that is the main topic of discussion that in our case might be "American Citizens' rights." As we can see, if the writer provides the reader an antecedent, the reader is able to define or understand that the vague possessive pronoun or vague common noun, like the word "their" (as in "their rights) that is being used in the sentence to represent, or take the place, of the main topic of discussion that might include the words "American Citizens' rights'.

I hope that by now my readers understand how simple a task it can be to find the thesis of a work like America's Constitution. As my readers can see, this task was not an impossible job to accomplish. So by now, I think my readers need to ask themselves why on God's Green Earth have so many so called highly educated Supreme Court Judges, Politicians, and federal lawyers failed to see or acknowledge the existence of this thesis that we can all see does exist in America's Constitution? Maybe these American leaders failed to see this key component of the Constitution because they simply decided to ignore it so they could continue to apply their sneaky little tricks like creating common laws to allow them to interpret the Constitution to do their bidding, like keeping America's borders open to the world's illegal alien invaders? I hate to come to this conclusion; but, didn't I just prove how simple it is to find that the Constitution is an essay with a full fledged thesis in it? So! Does it not make sense that our Supreme Court Judges and our current American presidents and politicians could have done the same?

Maybe the problem is not really a problem? Maybe these leaders knew all along what I have discovered but they decided to ignore these facts so they could continue to use America's Constitution in their creative ways to usurp the power it gives America's Citizens and that is why America now finds itself in such a mess in this Century? And again, Maybe If these American leaders had bothered to use the Constitution's thesis to make their decisions, America and her citizens could have avoided the serious problems that it is now facing in the 21st Century? They could have avoided problems like mass illegal migrants that are coming from all over the world and the hundreds of thousands of young children with no parents that are arriving at America's Southern Mexican Border that are forcing Americans to support them and take them in because they allegedly have no place to go in their homelands. I want to add that thanks to my discovery I feel all of these illegal migration and immigration problems could easily be rectified by utilizing the Constitution's thesis that is found in the Preamble, which says these foreign people are NOT part of America or citizens because they are not under America's jurisdiction. And, my fellow Americans, if these people are not under America's jurisdiction, then they are the problem of their homeland's government so they should be sent home immediately.

To continue the discussion of my discovery, I now hope my readers are able to see that if America's Politicians and Judges had taken the time to perform this simple act with a little research and analysis (in the past), maybe Peter Riesenberg might never have had to point out the following big error that he said America' Supreme Court Judges had made when they tried to justify their reason for inventing their own definition for the word "citizens" that is found in "Sections 2, 3, and 8 of Article "1" of the Constitution. To educate my readers, these sections are where the Constitution makes three references to the key word "Citizen." I want to note Peter Riesenberg pointed out the error because he found that according to his sources "America's" Supreme Court Judges, lawyers, and even politicians decided to create their own definition for the word 'citizens" in Article 1 because they came to the conclusion that "since the common noun "citizen" was allegedly not defined clearly, they [needed] "to look beyond the four corners of the Constitution . . . and create their own definition (Note: In my opinion this statement means these Supreme Court Judges decided to ignore the Constitution's thesis and prose, and its content.). Riesenberg also added that these judges, "decided to use a mix of ideas drawn from international law and natural law to define the word Citizen." Having pointed this fact out, I want to note here these American Judges (and those that followed) made this choice even though they were reading the same American Constitution that I read and analyzed and came to a complete different conclusion. And, contrary to their beliefs, I did find the word "Citizen" had indeed been defined by the Constitution's drafters by using antecedents that could easily be found in the introduction of the Constitution and other areas before this part of the Constitution, like for example the Preamble of the Constitution. Now, I want to again state the "Citizens" mentioned the Consitution are the people that are introduced in the Preamble in this phrase: "We People of the United States" (www.http:// Answers.com, Citizenship in the Western Tradition. Chapel Hill: University of North Carolina Press, 1992).

The sad fact is that (according the results of my research) these Supreme Court Judges' decisions appear to have been politically influenced and motivated even back in the days of early America. The other sad fact is that their politically influenced decision has been influencing Supreme Court rulings for over 100 years and hurting America's real citizens to this day. One other sad fact I learned during my research is that this and other tainted decisions made by America's Supreme Court Judges have been used by both right and left wing leaning Supreme Court Judges, like for example the late Chief Justice Earl Warren, to satisfy what my research found were political and special interest groups' needs. From what I learned during my research, I feel these damaging choices date back to the days of abolitionist and Suffragette eras. And according to my research, these politically influenced Supreme Court decisions appear to have constantly ignored the fact that the Constitution was an essay with a thesis that was (and is) self-contained. I often wonder if these politically influenced Supreme Court Judges' decisions don't go back as far as the 1860s?

To prove the conclusion I reached in the last paragraph, I think my readers and I need to look at an example from 1898 or the case of United States v. Wong Kim Ark: In this case, "the Supreme Court ruled that 'race, ethnic identity, or place of birth of a person's parents could not be used to deny citizenship to a person born in the United States," [but, I want to note here that these judges stopped there explanation abruptly and didn't add any more details to their decision. Having introduced this fact, I feel I can say that the sad part is decision is that they made this choice on purpose so they wouldn't have to clarify their decision, like for example if their decision only covered America's legal citizens or the world's citizens too, which many Supreme Court Judges now use in their ruling that states America's Constitution protects the world's citizens too (and their decision is what opens the borders for illegal mass migration with no stops). I want to note that since they failed to take this action, which I feel was on purpose, they were able to avoid putting these words in writing and avoid the slings and arrows their peers might have slung at them in that era. The fact that these judges left this door open back in this era is, I feel, what has opened the door for today's Supreme Court Judge to let any foreigner who enters American Sovereign soil illegally to be allowed to stay here without being arrested ("Citizenship: Oxford Companion to the US Supreme Court," Answers.com. Online Posting. http://www.answers.com/topic/citizenship.). Note: I feel I can come to this conclusion because of my discovery that proves America's Constitution does have a thesis that defines the word citizen, which means these judges failed to use the Constitution's controlling main point on purpose to make their bad and lawless decision. And when they made (make) this illegal decision, they very likely, and knowingly, committed treason against the Republic.

Now that my readers have some real solid facts to hold on to about the Constitution's Preamble and the Constitution's body, I feel I can better explain the problem with the decision these judges made when the decided to create their own definition for the word "citizen" using the world's interpretation for this word. As my readers can see from the facts in my previous paragraph, the problem with using this kind of logic is that the "Constitution" was an American idea and so were the facts found in the "thesis" of the Constitution known as the Preamble of the Constitution. Now that I introduced these facts, I want to add that the founding fathers made sure that anyone who read their draft would understand it was written to serve and defend their fellow American's "legal" citizens' rights to their Life, Liberty, and property, and the rights they created for themselves and their heirs (and naturalized citizens who went through the required, legal processes found in America's Immigration laws) as they proclaimed in their Constitution. I should note that all of these early Americans knew they had the right to defend their rights from the rest of the world because this power was promised to them in their Constitution. We Americans now know this because, as I stated here, it is introduced in the Preamble and completely explained in the body of the Constitution where these American rights are reintroduced throughout the US Constitution and individually explained in detail.

Having pointed out the key facts found in the Constitution that protect America's legal citizens, I now say with all due respect that Congress is legally bound to establish and enforce these God given rights of America's Citizens that are found in the Constitution because Section 8, Article1, of the US Constitution says they must take this action. The law I am talking about is known as America's law of the land, and it says Congress is required to obey and enforce all of these laws for the good of America's Citizens and no other nation's people that might enter US soil and try to lay claim to these American rights and privileges. I know I can come to this conclusion in my last sentence because there is no other written precedence in any part of the Constitution that gives foreign illegal citizens the same rights as America's vested citizens by name or insinuation, unless they have followed the law and become Naturalized US Citizens. Since I have just presented all of the aforementioned facts found in America's Constitution, I hope my fellow Americans will now be able to see that the Supreme Court erred completely when they made their bad decision and wrote their misdirected brief that I just proved was wrong. Instead of making this bad decision, I think these judges would have been better served to include the following fact or point in their decision that would have affirmed the principles written into the Constitution: "the parents or parent of any "Person" (or child) born in America must be legal or documented American Citizens (or the parents must have been in the United States as legal residents) for their child to be considered an American Citizen because this is what Section 1 of the XIV Amendment is really saying. By making the decision to only grant US Citizenship to children born to America's legal and legally documented citizens, their decision will then satisfy the Constitution's real principles and privileges that the Preamble says Americans reserved for themselves and their children. I feel I can write and make this statement now because America's Constitution makes this argument in the Preamble's thesis statement, and it arrives at this conclusion in the body of the American Constitution and Section 1 of the XIV Amendment, as my analysis shows.

One more point I would like to make about the word "citizen" can be summed up in the following facts: I feel I have proved that the Constitution was written to only serve and protect American citizens' rights and Constitutional privileges. And! I also want to note that feel I have proven that the Constitution was written so America's citizens could use it to defend the legal rights that they created for themselves and said as much in their Constitution (as Fredric Bastiat states). So to conclude, I feel my readers and I can arrive at the conclusion that the words "citizen" and "citizens" are being used to discuss America's citizens any time these words are used or mentioned in the Amendments and Articles that are found in the body of the Constitution because of the antecedents found in the Preamble. I also know these facts are true because the writers of the America's Constitution used the words "We the People of the United States" to define the subjects or people that they were writing about in the American Constitution, which is the antecedent for words like "people," "persons," or "their" that are used in the Articles and Amendments of America's Constitution. I know this fact is true because the thesis of the Constitution, or main point, begins with the words "We the People of the United States" in the opening sentence and paragraph that is the Constitution's Preamble. My readers should note that after the Constitution introduces the people who are writing this draft it then adds that the Constitution is being written for themselves, and only themselves, or America's people, in this part of the Preamble's sentence: [we] "...do ordain and establish this Constitution for the United States of America."

Now that I feel I have completely removed all of the alleged vagueness that so many Supreme Court Judges and American Politicians seem to find in the Articles and Amendments of America's Constitution, I feel these leaders and judges have no more excuses to create controversial common laws to settle some alleged vague statement they say exists in America's Constitution. So my dear Supreme Court Judges, Here are the facts that I found are in the Constitution that my fellow Americans and I now know because I proved them in this book: "When words like "citizen," "people," or "persons" are used in the American Constitution by the drafters of the Constitution, these words (for example common nouns and pronouns) are basically referring to America's legal or naturalized citizens that are introduced in the Preamble of the Constitution (with phrases like "We the people of the United States" or the people of the "United States of America").

Moving on, I want to now point out that the Preamble never mentions any other countries' citizens in the Constitution's thesis statement and that means, for example, neither Mexico's invading colonizers, other countries' invading aliens, or any trespassing Central or South American illegal foreigner that find himself or herself on US soil illegally have any legal rights to stay in America under the Constitution's principles. I can also add one more fact to strengthen the results of my research because I noticed that the writer's of the Constitution also used almost the same words at the end of the Preamble that they used to introduce the subject in the Preamble's only sentence. In short the writers used these key words to point out the Constitution was a document written to be used by Americans to defend their rights they created for themselves as written in the Constitution. Here are their exact words that were written and used in the Preamble: (Note: the understood words in brackets.)... [We" Americans]...do "Ordain and establish this Constitution for the United States of America." I think the writers used these very clear words because they serve as the subject and object of the only sentence found in the Preamble of America's Constitution.

I can't speak for "all" of the judges' poor judgment but I'm sure that maybe lack of research, political influence, or just plain laziness (a joke, maybe?) probably influenced these Judges decisions enough to ignore the fact that they should have thought about applying some English Grammar rules to the Constitution to see if it was an essay, or a book of law codes as they thought. If these judges had done their job, maybe this extra effort might have helped them avoid making the critical reading errors (that I feel they committed) that influenced their poor judgment and their ill-advised judicial decisions that very likely broke Constitutional law and criminal law. Maybe if these Supreme Court Judges had taken the time to study the English language's essay writing principles and had applied them to the Constitution like I did, they would have seen the weak logic behind their judicial decisions and they would have made better choices. I want to note that I am adding these suggestions and raising these questions because I sense that maybe these Supreme Court Judges' understanding of the English language was not as good as the men who wrote America's Constitution in 1787. After all, during my research, I found several studies that showed American's reading and writing abilities have been deteriorating to an 8th Grade reading and writing level since the beginning of the 20th Century (and has continued into the 21st Century). However, Unlike today's leaders and Supreme Court Judges, the 1787 drafters of the Constitution were highly educated men who had been educated in some of the best Universities England had to offer, for example like Oxford University. I don't I have to remind anyone that the British often remind us "the English have always been known as the keepers of the proper use of the English language." As for America, I believe Americans have mostly been known for butchering both the written and spoken English language.

Before I close my discussion on the poor and dangerous choices that America's Supreme Court Judges have made that started back in 1898, I want to note one more historical fact that I found interesting. What I found interesting was the time line of when America's modern day Supreme Court Judges made these types of damaging (and illicit) choices that changed America's Constitution for the worse by creating many new laws using Common law as their tool of deception. I want to note that the time line of these Supreme Court Judges' bad/illegal choices is important because during the time these judges served America, from the industrial age of the 1860s to the modern days of the late 1980s (and especially in 2013), America's Supreme Court Judges appear to have decided to do more damage to the Constitution than at any other time in American history by avoiding/ignoring the Constitution's checks and balances for writing American laws. I now want to go on record here and state that the damage that America's past Judges have done to the Constitution are currently being committed by today's Supreme Court Judges because they are not questioning any of these past judges' decisions. And to make things worse, I want to add these judges may not even know they are hurting or re-writing parts of the Constitution when they either accept these past decisions without question, or they write their own court briefs based on these ill-advised decisions.

I really hope that by now my readers are starting to understand and see why America's Modern day judges are making such poor, bad, misguided, and corrupted interpretations of America's Constitution. After all, for me to say or think that these judges are tainting their robes by making decisions that lean left or right and ignore the Constitution's real laws that they are supposed to enforce would be scandalous. But, I want to note here that the power brokers (who ever they are) who are brokering these damaging and illegal changes to America's Constitution, with the help of these judges, know exactly what they are doing because they waited over 100-plus years (changes were made between 1897 and 1974) to make many of these damaging interpretations and changes that are currently crippling (and have crippled it in the past) the US Constitution. As to my opinion on why these judges waited till 1897 to start making bad or illegal changes to America's Constitution, I think they waited this long because they were waiting for the drafters of the Constitution (and their immediate family members) to die so they would note be confronted by them in a public forum.

I would now like to move forward on my timeline of these judges' decisions that I feel have crippled our Constitution. I want add here that these major changes to the Constitution finally culminated between 1971 and 1973 because during these years the Warren lead Supreme Court forced America's states to grant welfare benefits to aliens and in doing so awarded illegal and law breaking foreigners (or non-citizens) many rights that the Constitution says were only reserved or written for America's citizens. I want to add that I found it interesting to read that the Warren lead court took this very illegal or treacherous (almost treasonous act) action during the Nam war era when antiwar rallies and demonstrations were the norm so no one was paying attention to the US Supreme Court's changes to America's law of the land. And, I want to note, the facts I just presented in the previous paragraphs basically means that the power-brokers that wanted to change the meaning of our Constitutional law and other US laws made sure that America's Citizens were too busy to see them change America's Constitution without the use of Congress or the laws found in America's Constitution. If my fellow Americans don't mind, I'm going to suggest that they follow up and find out how America's judges and the Supreme Court Judges can write their own laws using a little nasty trick called "common law" decisions, and that they also learn how "common law" decisions can basically change America's Constitution to help America's political parties push their agendas. By the way, the judges do not have to get Congress' approval to write these "common laws" and force them on America's Citizens.

Yes my fellow Americans, I truly believe these judges of the Warren era and other earlier eras knew they were corrupting or changing America's Constitution by saying they had the right to make decisions like saying illegal foreigners have the same rights to social services as Americans do, and they (America's Supreme Court Judges) have the right to say who is an American citizen. I say this because according to all of these so-called US Supreme Court Judges (who either were weak readers, or they knew they were breaking the law) they feel they have this right because according to them the Constitution was not "clear" about who was an American Citizen. And since they came to this decision, they feel or felt that it was their job to decide who can be called an American citizen. After reading this book that my readers are holding in their hands and learn the truth, I really hope my fellow Americans will able see and understand why I say and prove in this book that these judges were wrong and very likely broke US Constitutional law going all the way back to 1897. I also hope my fellow legal Americans are now ready to take action against America's corrupt judges because they now have the facts to prove that many crimes have been (and are being) committed against the Republic, and the US Constitution's laws by these rogue American Judges.

If my fellow Americans will allow me, I want to Return to my intensive study of the Preamble and key parts of the Constitution one more time (Which, I started in Chapter 3.) because I want to discuss the following key phrase that is found in the Preamble that reads as follows "in order to form a more perfect union." Next, I want to first note that in the English language the word "in" is often used to form either a prepositional phrase or an infinitive phrase. Having pointed out this fact about the word "in," I want my readers to allow me to yield to the principles of effective writing to find that in this case the word "in" is being used as part of a phrasal preposition. I know I can say this because there are more than two words in this phrase, which is a key requirement of a phrasal preposition. And, when I analyzed the Preamble, I noticed this phrasal preposition was being used to introduce a list of nonfinite verbs that all began with the understood preposition "to." These nonfinite verbs that I found were part of several prepositional phrases (as I stated earlier in this chapter) that included the phrases [to] "establish justice," [to] "insure domestic tranquility," [to] "provide for the common defense," [to] "promote the general welfare," and [to] "secure the blessings of liberty to our selves and our posterity." And, as I continued my analysis, I then found these prepositional phrases were used to modify the phrase "do ordain and establish this Constitution for the United States of America." To clarify the point I'm trying to make or describe here, I am saying this phrase restates the main topic or subject that is being discussed in Constitution, which says the US Constitution was being written for America's Citizens by American Citizens so America's Citizens could defend these rights and privileges that they had created for themselves from those who might try to stake a claim to their new Constitutional rights and privileges.

Moving on with my analysis, I now finally come to the action part of this phrase, which includes the required verb and/or verb phrase of the sentence that is needed to complete the drafter's thoughts. The verb or verb phrase I found in this sentence begins with the singular present tense and the helping verb "do." In this case, this verb is used to express or mean to "fulfill, to complete, or to accomplish something of importance," which in this case modifies the next term, "ordain." I now want to note, again, that the term "ordain" is a verb that according to Funk and Wagnalls

Standard College Dictionary (1967) means to "decree, establish, or predestine by God's will or fate." I would like my readers to now pay very close attention to the definition of this word, or term for future reference. My readers should play close attention to these results because amazingly in the 21st Century many government funded programs (like schools) and Americans are being attacked by the ACLU on behalf of Muslim Groups, Arabs, and Atheists in many of America's Judicial Courts for using the word God (Note: The same courts that amazingly use the Lord's Bible before any testimony with the words, "so help me God") or praying in Jesus' name at any government sponsored locations or programs. I guess I should remind the ACLU that the drafters of the US Constitution had the audacity to use the word "Ordain" in the Preamble of the US Constitution (because they evidently felt God had guided or helped them write the Constitution), and the word "ordain" has a definition or sense that says "ordain" is a reference to "being predestined by God's will or fate" ("Ordain." Funk and Wagnalls Standard College Dictionary. Text. Ed.1967.).

So as I wrote earlier in my brief introductory study of the Preamble, I feel the writers of the Constitution not only decided to say they were writing or drafting America's constitution for America's people, but they also overtly "insinuated, or pointed out," that they felt their creation of America and the Constitution had been predestined or created by God so they decided to use a word like "do ordain" as part of a key verb phrase that is found in the US Constitution's Preamble. By now my readers should see that even though many judges and lawyers keep telling us that America's religious past and her government must be kept apart or separate from the US Government, I feel my research just proved their point of view is wrong because the results of my analysis shows that the Drafters of the Constitution decided they wanted to praise the Lord for guiding them in their work by adding a reference to the Lord in the Preamble of the Constitution so they could honor their "Godly Ordained Constitution" they had just written. And as I move on to the next part of my analysis we Americans find that the conjunction "and," joins the verbs "do ordain" to the next key word "establish" that is also part of the Preamble's introduction. I want to note that I feel the reason the drafters of the Constitution used the word "establish" at this point was to make sure the colonist, or Americans of this era, understood the Constitution was being written to be a permanent fixture of America's Government, and most importantly that the Constitution was only being written for the Republic and to serve or protect America's citizens. I now want my readers to notice the English Dictionary says the word "permanent" is part of the definition for the verb "establish," as well as these two other key definitions: "to make secure, [or a] lasting institution." I want to also point out that in this sentence the drafters were making sure the words they used in their document all pointed to the fact that they were creating a lasting institution (government) that would be under the control of America's Constitution ("establish." Funk and Wagnalls Standard College Dictionary. Text. Ed.1967.).

Next, I want my readers to notice the next two words the drafters used in the Preamble's sentence, that were introduced after the controversial verb phrase "do ordain and establish," were the words "this" and "Constitution." My readers should note the word "this," is of course a pronoun that means or stands for "this thing presented here," which in this case is presenting the word "Constitution." The "Constitution" the drafters are referring to in this sentence is the one they were writing in 1787. And after the two words that read "this Constitution," the drafters then added the term "for" which is a preposition that told the reader who the Constitution was being written "for," or in this case to "serve" America's Citizens. And to make sure that anyone who took the time to read the Constitution knew "for" whom the constitution was being written (or who it served) the drafters added these final key words: "the United States America." I want my readers to note the phrase "the United States of America" serves as the object of the prepositional phrase that we are discussing in this sentence. These key words in this sentence use the definite article "the" to render the modified words "United States" as being special because "the

United States" in this era was known as the colonies that in this case, when they were grouped together, became the Republic of "America" or the United States of America.

Finally, when these words are all joined together, I think we Americans (and I should remind the ACLU and America's Judges) can all agree that each of these key words (for the United States of America) remind the reader that the Constitution was written to serve and protect "America's legal citizens." I can make this bold statement because this phrase also reminds the reader that America's Constitution is a legal tool that gives America's citizens the power to defend their Constitutional powers from those who would enter America and try to stake a claim to the rights and privileges that were written into America's Constitution for themselves. As my readers can see from the phrase "do ordain and establish this Constitution for the United States of America," the drafters opened America's Constitution with a thesis statement that included key words that told the reader who "this Constitution belonged to, which was America's vested citizens. The final realization I want my readers to understand here is that no other country, no other country's citizens, no visitors to America, and no undocumented colonizing or invading illegal aliens are ever mentioned in the words of this key phrase or sentence that tells the reader the following facts: "We the people of the United States, in order to form a more perfect union, establish justice, insure domestic tranquility, provide for the common defense, promote the general welfare, and secure the blessings of liberty to **ourselves and our posterity, do ordain and establish this Constitution for the United States of America."** After reading this key sentence that is know as the Preamble of the Constitution, I hope my readers now understand that the job of the Preamble is not only to introduce America's Constitution (a job it does well), but it also introduce the beneficiaries of these rights and privileges that are introduced and expounded on in America's Constitution. What other wonderful job does the Preamble do for America's Constitution? Well, the Preamble also does a great job of explaining the reason for the creation of the Constitution and it makes a point of re-stating, at the end of the sentence, that the Constitution is (and was) only being written for the "United States of America and its legal citizens."

Now that I've completed my discussion of the Preamble of America's Constitution, I hate to say it but I really don't know what else to say to convince my fellow Americans that America's Constitutional principles or laws were only written to serve and protect America's vested Citizens. In fact, If my readers don't mind, I want to point out to my readers that the Preamble sentence does not contain words or phrases like "people passing through America's states on vacation or on vacation in America," "all trespassers," or the words "any and all colonizing and invading aliens" in any part of the Constitution's Preamble, especially where the Preamble states who the Constitution was being written "for" or to "serve." This very valid point I just make here is very crucial to my analysis' results because I believe it proves the Preamble does create and sets the precedence (and some needed antecedents) that is needed later in the Articles and Amendments of the Constitution that help define and clarify any pronoun or common noun (for example) that might be used later in the body of the Constitution's the Articles and Amendments. A good example of this need is like when the drafters use various vague pronouns, vague common nouns, or any vague collective nouns that might need defining. Some examples of these so-called vague terms include words like "people" and "persons" that are used later in the Articles or Amendments of the Constitution. These two so-called vague pronouns are used to take the place of proper nouns or words like "We the people of the United States" or "for the United States of America that are introduced in early part of the Constitution so they can serve as antecedents (sets precedence) for these alleged vague words.

Now that I've presented this "eye-opening" conclusion in the last paragraph of this book, I want to make sure my readers understand that words like "people" or "persons" that are used throughout the Amendments and Articles of the body of the Constitution are great examples of the many pronouns, collective nouns, common nouns or groups of proper nouns (like We the people of the United States) that are used to repeat and restate the main topic or thesis that is introduce in the Constitution's Preamble and again paragraphs throughout the Constitution. The legal citizens ("the People of the United States") that the Preamble introduces in the thesis statement and repeats throughout the paragraphs of the Constitution are introduced so the reader knows and understands the Constitution's main topic of discussion is America's citizens and the rights they created to protect themselves (both natural born and naturalized citizens), their children, and their children that are heirs to these rights and privileges. **The other topics that are introduced in the Constitution include how the American Constitution's Articles and laws apply to these the legal vested residents of America, so Americans can use them to protect themselves from those who would attempt to illegally stake a claim to their written rights.** I believe these facts alone prove the drafters of America's Constitution never wrote or used any kind of Ambiguous words in the Preamble or attempted to use ambiguous words without taking the time to define them as any good writer would have done when writing this type of critical or difficult work.

Finally, I want to note that the delegates of the colonies, although some of them were lawyers, never attempted to use legal terminology to write the Constitution or the Preamble. I feel they took this action because they did not want to confuse their constituents that were living on colonial America on farms or in cities like 1787 Philadelphia at the time of the Constitution's drafting. These constituents, I want to clarify, were citizens that according to the online site www.digitalhistory.uh.edu included citizens like "wealthy Quaker American merchants, German-speaking farmers, African American slaves, and Delaware Indians." So by writing the Constitution in everyday commoner English, the drafters of this very important document were able to convince America's Colonial Citizens of 1787 to buy into defending and accepting "the idea of a new Federal Government and to let go of their ideals of having individual governments for each Colony, which many American citizens preferred in 1787, " and is stated in the on line historical web page www.digitalhistory.uh.edu.

As I conclude my analysis of these key areas of America's Constitution and its introductory paragraph that is known as the Preamble, I feel I have proven beyond any doubt that our Constitution is NOT some poorly written, or poorly worded, written work that needs to be constantly interpreted by America's politically influenced Supreme Court Judges, lawyers or politicians that often owe some lobbyist a favor for helping them get elected, or in the case of judges appointed. As a matter of fact, I'm sure that in the pages of this book I've proven that the US Constitution is very complete in-and-of-itself, and maybe this is the reason why President Lincoln once said in one of his many speeches that it should be left alone and not changed. In fact, I feel I can say America's Constitution explains itself quite well, if the reader takes the time to read it carefully and accepts it for the very brilliantly constructed essay that the drafters wrote. And to show I'm correct, I want to point out that Michael Meyer agrees with me when it comes to writing a complete essay, like the one I just wrote. I make this statement because Meyer says the following facts about writing a good essay in his book Thinking and Writing About Literature, (St Martin's Press, 1997, p7): "Whereas the topic indicates what the paper [(or essay)] focuses on [as in the introduction of the US Constitution that is found in the Preamble], the thesis or central idea [or main point] of the paper explains what the writers had to say about the topic, [again as written in the Constitution's Preamble]."

I now want to introduce a little trick I learned (and maybe some of my reader too) in school in the good old days when America's children didn't need a computer program to write well-constructed sentences. This trick that most of us "old school" students learned was used to find the thesis statement of an essay we had decided to write for our teacher. To find the thesis, my fellow students and

I learned we fist needed to write a sentence that began with the following incomplete thought process: "The main point (or my main reason) of my essay is." After we wrote this incomplete statement, we were than taught to complete the thought this way: "The main point of my essay is to "explain who the Constitution is going to serve, how it is going to work, and how it will be used to serve the people of America." The fact I present above is the reason I pointed out in my analysis that the Constitution begins with the words **"We the people of the United States"** which tells the reader that the Constitution was being written by Americans for themselves. I then pointed out key words like "in order to form a more perfect union," to establish justice, etc. (to explain this was the reason the Constitution was written), **and finally I pointed out that the Constitution ends with the words "do ordain and establish this Constitution for the United States of America." I want to note that by pointing out these closing words I was able to point out that America's Constitution was written to only serve America and its legal American citizens that are her vested and legal citizens. This writing trick I just introduced, I want to note, helps any writer isolate and establish what their main reason, topic, or thesis is going to be in their essay. Having proven my point, I want to again note that there is no mention of terms or words like "world citizens" or "Mexico's citizens" in either of these phrases that begin or end the preamble of America's Constitution.**

To conclude this Chapter, I want to remind America's leaders like ex-President Obama, President elect Trump, America's Congressional members, and America's Supreme Court Judges that they should notice and see that I've proven completely that America's Constitution was written to only serve America's legal and vested citizens and NOT illegal lawbreaking foreigners. The results or facts I just mentioned also apply to the Bill of Rights and the Civil rights Act of the 1960s because they are also part of America's Constitution that belongs to America's Citizens so they can use it as a tool to

defend themselves against those (including America's courts and politicians) who would try to lay claim or give away these rights and privileges that they wrote for themselves (As we are told and warned by Fredric Bastiat in his book <u>The Law</u>.

Chapter Four

Why Section 1 of the XIV Amendment does not Provide Automatic US Citizenship to "All" Children born on US Soil.

> (God's Country as He Ordained it) Step by unconscious step, a great nation—the mightiest, the most richly productive, and most gullible on earth—has been induced to renounce its military primacy as well as its constitutional safeguards . . .Credit for that remarkable, feat belongs to a working coalition of International Socialists, Communists, and [Islam fundamentalists], bent on capturing world power by stealth and deception and at the least possible cost to themselves.
>
> (Rose L. Martin 1973)

In Chapter Three, I established the best way to study and interpret several key parts of the US Constitution was to use Literary Criticism as my analyzing tool and the "grammar rules" of sentence construction and essay writing. These analyzing tools I used allowed me to analyze the Preamble word-by-word and phrase-by-phrase so I could explain how certain key words were used in the Preamble and the Constitution and how the preamble influenced the rest of the Constitution's body. Because I took the time to analyze these words and paragraphs, I was able to establish the grammatical function of these key words when they were used in the phrases and sentences of the Constitution's Preamble and its body. The results of my research established that the Preamble was more than an introduction for the US Constitution (as we were wrongly taught in school) because my research helped me prove the Preamble really serves as the Constitution's "thesis statement" that basically introduces the main topic and subject of discussion that is introduced and presented in the rest of the Constitution.

Since I proved the Preamble is the thesis statement of the Constitution and not just an introductory paragraph, I feel I can also state that America's Constitution is an essay whose content and prose are controlled by English Grammar essay writing rules that, when applied to the Constitution, help the reader understand the Constitution better and more clearly. Because my conclusion in the last sentence concludes that the Constitution is an essay, I was able to use this discovery to help me clarify and establish that the US Constitution was written to only serve and protect America's legal and Naturalized Citizens, and not some other countries' citizens that might enter America legally on vacation or illegally. So as I close this paragraph, I can also come to the conclusion that America's Constitution never says that it was written to serve and defend or protect the world's Citizens, Mexico's citizens, or Central or South America's citizens as America's Judicial system keeps trying to tell us.

Finally, in the last chapter (3), I established the importance of providing the antecedent of any pronoun (to define who or what the pronoun is taking the place of in the sentence), or difficult word, that an author might use in the sentences of a complicated written work or essay. Before I move on, I want to remind my readers that when an author takes the time to set precedence in an essay, and adds antecedents to his or her work, this act makes it easier for the reader to understand who is being spoken of in sentences that are found later in the essay or written work. I want to note that I'm pointing out this fact because many pronouns and common nouns that are often used in the body of essays (including the Constitution) often end up needing to be identified or defined by an antecedent so that precedence can be established and the vague pronoun or common noun can be identified or defined by the reader. The writer takes this action so the reader knows whom the common noun or pronoun is referring back to in either the sentence being read or the paragraph being read.

To continue my explanation, I want to point out the fact that according to the rules of essay writing the writer must provide precedence because the meaning of each vague pronoun or common noun must be clarified or defined for the reader; this task can be done either in the essay's thesis or in the introductory sentence of each paragraph that introduce a new topic or subject. When the writer provides a clear antecedent (which defines or identifies the vague pronoun or common noun) and therefore establishes precedence, the writer provides the reader a key word that either describes or identifies any vague word or pronoun that writer might introduce later in the essay or manuscript that is being written (or read). Some good examples of vague words would be the words "person" or "persons" that are often used later in a written work, as I feel it is done throughout the US Constitution's Articles and Amendments. Since I proved in Chapter three that the Constitution is an essay and the Preamble is its thesis statement, I think we can all come to the conclusion that it is time America's judges and politicians start looking at America's Constitution as an essay and not some list of laws, or list of law codes.

To make sure my fellow Americans understand the facts I just provided about essay writing and setting precedence in essays, I want to now add that if I have made it easier for my fellow Americans to understand how this procedure works I am sure my readers will be able to find the antecedents of any pronoun or common noun they might find in a long work like America's

Constitution. Having made this statement, I now want to show my fellow Americans how this rule works, or applies in different areas or sections of America's Constitution. If I can accomplish this goal, I hope to be able to end this so-called illegal immigration charade that America's Judges and Politicians are playing on America's citizens. And in case my fellow Americans are wondering why I took the time to both write this book and do the research, I did it because unlike current and past US politicians and American Supreme Court Judges who seem to enjoy inventing and creating their own definitions for vague words or pronouns that they find in America's Constitution, I want to know the truth. And later in this book, I hope to provide my fellow Americans the correct way to read America's Constitution that I feel is a brilliant and well-written essay type document.

If the written work I am discussing in this chapter doesn't sound like the US Constitution our current and past American Politicians and Supreme Court Judges keep telling us is a "poorly written and confusing legal" document (because it allegedly doesn't define words like "Citizen"), I think it might be because I have taken the time to identify and clarify many of the misconceptions these judges and politicians invented or created through out history so they could make America's Constitution do their bidding. I guess my next step is to show how often these leaders have misquoted or misread America's Constitution: on purpose? As my readers can see from my introduction of this chapter, I hope to not only show how often America's Judges have misread and misused the Constitution, but also provide my readers some solid facts that I discovered during my research of America's Constitution. By the time I complete Chapter 4, I hope to have proven that America's politicians and judges have not only misread and misused the Constitution, but they have also made some illegal mistakes (on purpose?) when they decided to add words or definitions to the Constitution. Finally! I'd like to add that America's Constitution doesn't protect the world's citizens because it never addresses this issue, these people, or mentions them in the Constitution's thesis known as the Preamble of the Constitution.

Before I move on, I want to say that maybe these American political, judicial, and other governmental entities always misread, altered, or changed America's Constitution because they owe (or owed) some powerful group or country a favor for helping them get re-elected or appointed, they are pushing their own political agenda or beliefs, pushing some political party's agenda, paying back some world wide farming Corporations favor, or they owe some Wall Street banker a favor. But make no mistake about this treacherous act because in the end, the altering or changing of the Constitution I believe comes down to good old payback for election favors and money in my book. After all, when America's Constitution is altered or changed, doesn't it always seem to help some powerful group, some political leader, or champion some new President's political agenda?

If my fellow Americans want to see a few examples of how I feel America's Judges are paying back their benefactors who helped appointment to their seats, I believe a good recent one from the last Administration was ex-President Obama's very open pro-Muslim agenda that put America in the middle of two civil wars that were not our wars, and according to the news ended up costing America's taxpayers billions of US dollars in munitions and man power to fight in these two Middle Eastern "civil wars" that had nothing to do with protecting America's citizens. And to add one more example from the last administration's political activities that went against Constitution law, I want to add President Obama's push to grant illegal Amnesty to 20 million colonizing and invading Mexicans and foreigners who are currently living in America illegally, and also his creation and illegal signing of a law that created the "Dream Act" that provided over 800,000 illegal Amnesty, and not one American Judge stopped him in either case. Maybe the reason America's taxpayer elected officials and entities work so hard for these foreigners is because they owe some foreign group or foreign governments a favor, or payback for a clandestine deal that was done behind closed doors? We can only guess why? Unfortunately, since I don't have super powers or a secret source to help me find the right answers to the questions I raised in this paragraph, I guess my fellow Americans and I will just have to guess why these American judges and politicians like to both ignore and change America's Constitution, that in the end keeps destroying and tearing away at America's Sovereign Nation Status and destroying her citizens' rights and privileges that belong to them.

Unfortunately for these lawless (my opinion) American taxpayer financed Government entities, Judges, and their supporters, and thanks to my research and the power of good old Literary analysis, I have found a way to prove that America's Constitution is a clear and concise written work of prose writing that any person with a good command of the English language (who takes the time to reads it carefully and correctly) can understand. I know I can say this because the exact meaning and purpose of the Constitution are all introduced in the Preamble of the Constitution. By now my readers should understand, I can make this bold statement because according to the facts I found during my research the Constitution presents its information in every day language that any knowledgeable person can understand. To prove my point, I want to note that my research proved the Constitution was written to serve America's compatriots or citizens (and only Americans and her naturalized legal citizens). Since no other nation's citizens or no other nation is introduced in the Preamble or is discussed in the body of the Constitution, I know we can say it was never meant to protect or serve the worlds' citizens, visitors in America, trespassing aliens, illegal Mexicans and their children, or any trespassing foreign colonizing citizen or invader who might decide to enter America illegally and demand these rights or try to take them by force or intimidation.

Now before I move on, I want to ask my fellow Americans to excuse me while I vent and give this message to America's Open

Border Proponents: Dear Open Border Supporters who want to destroy America's laws of Immigration and her sovereignty: I want to tell America's Supreme Court Judges, America's Politicians, the ACLU attorneys who might not agree with me, and all other open border supporters that (because the "Bill of Rights" are considered part of the US Constitution) the Bill of Rights and the Civil Rights we legal Americans fought for in the past were only written to serve America's Citizens. I know I can make this statement because nowhere in the Constitution do the words "world citizens," "Mexicans," or "other Nation's citizens" show up in its Preamble or the Articles or Amendments of America's Constitution. So, since these groups are not mentioned or addressed in the Constitution's thesis or in the body of the Constitution, I know I can say with deep conviction that the Constitution's principles and utilization concepts were written by Americans for Americans so they could use them to defend themselves from those who might try to take these rights from them by force, trickery, or treason, as Fredric Bastiat says in the quote I presented in this book from Mr. Bastiat's Book.

Now that I've shown I did my job in Chapter three and that I correctly and clearly explained the real purpose of the Constitution's Preamble (For those who might have forgotten, I want to remind them it introduce the thesis to establish the needed precedence that provides the needed antecedents that help clarify any and all vague words like pronouns or common nouns that might be found in the Constitution's body that are known as the Articles and Amendments.), I feel this is a good time to start discussing a quote I found in a chapter that had the title of "The Logic of Definitions." I point this chapter out because I feel it holds a key to the research and analysis that I completed on the Preamble and the key areas of the Constitution in my last few chapters. I found this chapter in a book written by two gifted and intelligent authors whose names are Jack Pitt and Russell E. Leavenworth. And! I decided to use this quote from their book because after I read Pitt and Leavenworth's book I felt I needed to add their ideas and recommendations to my research because their research helped solidify the results or conclusions of my research. I now want to show how their research helped me find some answers to several abused and ignored Articles and Amendments that are part of the Constitution. These abused and ignored Articles and Amendments, I want to add, have been incorrectly used and enforced so many times in American history that most American citizens don't' really know how these principles are really supposed to work, or if they are just too dated to be of use in the 21st Century.

In their book **Logic for Argument** (Random House, 1968) Pitt and Leavenworth make the following statement, "When we write or speak to some serious purpose [(Writing a Constitution for example)] it is our [(the writer's)] responsibility to be prepared to [write an] account for the meaning of the key terms we use" (Pitt, Jack, and Russell E. Leavenworth, Logic for Argument. New York: Random House, Fresno State College. 1968.): To clarify this statement for my readers, Pitt and Leavenworth are saying that when writers (or in my case the drafters of the Constitution) use vague or confusing words like pronouns or common nouns in complex written documents like for example the Constitution, they are supposed to be ready to define these words for clarity by making sure they provide precedence or antecedents that define or clarify who or what these pronouns or common nouns represent in the sentence or paragraph that might be found in the body of the essay or written work. My readers should note that I believe the drafters of the Constitution took this action when they included the "thesis statement" in the Preamble of America's Constitution which I proved earlier provides the necessary precedence (and antecedents) for future pronouns and common nouns found later in the Constitution's body. I also want to point out the thesis found in the Preamble, if read correctly, sets or provides the needed antecedence and precedence for the Constitution's body, and it even adds clarity to the body of the Constitution when the Preamble is read and used correctly.

I believe the precedence and antecedence the "drafters" included in the Preamble of the Constitution helped them define the key words and word groups they used later (like common and personal pronouns) in the body of the Constitution where the Articles and Amendments of the Constitution are found. As my readers continue to read this paragraph, I hope they will note that I am trying to establish Pitt and Leavenworth's principle that says "...Setting precedence in our essays or works (to establish clarity) is more than just providing an antecedent for a pronoun, because an essay's definitions (complex precedence) also provide the conditions for the use of certain words, or word, so the reader [(or readers)] knows exactly what the words that are being used mean," [or when the definition applies to any word, phrase, or clause, in question... this] simple distinction is important for it is the words or phrases that we define not the things, facts, or events which they stand for [that are important]" (Pitt, Jack, and Russell E. Leavenworth, Logic for Argument. New York: Random House, Fresno State College. 1968.).

Lucky for my fellow Americans and myself, I didn't have to look far to find an example or "condition" that allowed me to apply these writer's principles of writing and show how their principles work: I am of course talking about the US Constitution. As for the section of the Constitution that I feel I can use for the application of these two writer's principle? Well, I have decided to select Section 1 of the XIV Amendment because it is a perfect example of how important Pitt and Leavenworth's "defining for clarity" theory or rule is when writing essays that use many pronouns or common nouns later in the essay's body. By the way, in case my readers have forgotten how these two author's theory works, here is a refresher of how Pitt and Leavenworth's "defining for clarity" theory works. Their theory basically tells us "the difficulty of our essay's or written work's topic provides us (the writer) the 'condition' for the need to define any or all of our vague and difficult, or technical words that we might use in the [written] work or essay, and we take this action so the readers will know the meaning of all difficult, vague, or technical term used in the essay" (Pitt, Jack and Russell

E. Leavenworth, Logic for Argument. New York: Random House, Fresno State College. 1968.).

So now that I have added more information on their theory, I want my fellow Americans to look at an example that requires the application of Pitt and Leavenworth's "definition" theory that tells us to define vague words like pronouns and common nouns for clarity. As I said before, I didn't have to look to far because I found a great example in a sentence found in Section 1 of the XIV Amendment. This sentence in this section, as I soon prove, has constantly been so poorly interpreted and misread that I feel it now casts a dark cloud over America's legal and law-abiding citizens who keep looking for an answer in the 21st Century to this daunting problem that should have answered and to put to rest in the late sixties. So what is the problem that has put so many of America's citizens up in arms because it won't go away? The problem America's law abiding citizens see every day is a huge army of millions of illegal aliens running across America's Southern Border that divides Mexico and America. The problem is that these millions of lawless, invading, and colonizing unarmed citizens' armies from Mexico, Central America, and other Countries of the world are being allowed to stay in America and being given the same rights as US citizens by America's Politicians and Judges that have decided to betray its own citizens and ignore the true meaning and principles that are found in the Constitution. These lawless acts that are being committed by America's Government elected and appointed members are creating both daily and yearly anger and heated debates among America's legal and naturalized citizens because many of these Americans feel powerless and betrayed by these American Government Entities.

.

To discuss the anger of America's legal citizens, I feel we Americans have to come to the conclusion that maybe America's Judges and politicians are misreading and misinterpreting areas of the Constitution like Section 1 of the XIV Amendment on purpose so they can push an agenda that appears to be pushing America in the direction of a Socialist Government with no borders and no American Sovereignty. Now that I have taken the time to point out this very controversial problem, I want to also point out that as long as these treasonous judges and politicians keep getting away with their act of misreading and misinterpreting America's Constitution, Articles, and Amendments they will keeping pushing the envelope as far as they can to alter the meaning of America's Constitution and keep America's borders open to the world's citizens. In the end, I know these American leaders will keep trying to change or misinterpret the Constitution's principles and statutes illegally as long as they can get away with by finding alleged vague clause that they can manipulate like the one found at the beginning of Section 1 of the XIV Amendment: **"All Persons born or naturalized in the United States, and subject to the jurisdiction thereof, are citizens of the United States and of the state wherein they reside. No state shall make or enforce any law which shall abridge the privileges or immunities of citizens of the United States; nor shall any state deprive any person of life, liberty, or property, without due process of law; nor deny to any person within its jurisdiction the equal protection of the laws."** (Printed Scroll. N.P. Chicago: c. 1970).

Since the clause I introduced in the last paragraph (that's from our Constitution) appears to say that any or "all" persons born in America are citizens, even if their parents are not in America legally, or the parents are here on vacation, or are just entering America to have their child illegally to get their foot in the door (We all know this act as having an "anchor baby.), I felt this clause was a good one to use to apply Pitt and Leavenworth's clarity theory. After all, America's politicians, foreign governments, the ACLU, and America's court system have been using this clause as a law that they creatively "invented" (Note: They created or invented law according to them says that "any baby born in America is an American citizen.") to justify allowing millions of squatting or illegal aliens to stay in America just because their children are being born on US soil, or these illegal aliens manage to get into America and get a job before being deported. So, in defense of America, I decided to use Pitt and Leavenworth's clarity theory to show how illegal and wrong these American leaders' decision has been for both America and its citizens. If my fellow Americans (who I know feel angry and lost because they told me) will allow me to defend them, I think I can ease their minds and say fear no more my fellow American because I'm about to prove how wrong these agencies' interpretations have been for years and how illegal their actions have been based on their own decisions. When I apply Pitt and Leavenworth's writing for clarity theory to this section of the Constitution, I not only show the error these American leaders are making but I also prove the children of these illegal invaders or aliens, vacationers, and trespassing illegal aliens, or what ever you wish to call them are "NOT" American citizens just because they are born on US or American soil. And, Suffice it to say, I also prove that our founding fathers were smarter than any of today's politicians, judges, and American leaders who don't give them credit for writing a wonderful Constitution because they instead insinuate that America's Constitution was vaguely or poorly written so they have to augment it with their modern day brilliance. To tell my readers the truth, I surprisingly proved this fact to myself and learned that the drafters America's Constitution knew exactly what they were doing when they wrote America's great Constitution.

One more important point I want to make here is that both present and past "Open Border Proponents" or supporters are still using illegal and bad interpretations of this section of the Constitution and it's time I proved how treacherous these modern day leaders are in their decisions and actions. First, I want to note that although America's present day Supreme Court Judges and Politicians keep saying Section 1 of the XIV Amendment protects any and all newborn children born to illegal or lawbreaking American trespassing parents (known as illegal aliens who enter America for the soul purpose of having their child or children born on American soil so they can have an anchor baby), my research proves they are wrong. And, before I forget, I want to add that I also hope to show America's citizens that America's Politicians like ex-President Obama and our Supreme Court Judges, who keep insisting these colonizing trespassers' children are citizens, are simply using "white collar crime" principles that government and big business have always used to protect themselves from being prosecuted and sent to Federal prisons for their illegal practices that in my opinion are acts of treason. The reason these Government entities always make sure that their crimes fall under the "white collar crime" category is because they know that "White Collar and Occupational Crimes" are always prosecuted at very low levels of punishment (think Martha Stewart). So, even if they are caught and prosecuted, they all know they can depend on the principles of "white collar crimes to protect them from being prosecuted as real hard core criminals. I now hope my fellow Americans see why American political leaders from both sides of the political aisle and America's Supreme Court Judges are all willing to fight for the 20 Million and growing Mexican (and other countries) colonizing invaders by calling them "illegal" immigrants. If these politicians and judges know they have no fear of ever being put into real hardcore prisons, they know they can go about their dirty business without ever worrying about being prosecuted harshly for their illegal acts against the Republic.

After reading the last few paragraphs, I'm sure my fellow Americans now understand why Section 1 of the XIV Amendment is such a lightning Rod for America's Compatriots or her Legal and naturalized citizens who feel they've lost control of their Republic's Government and America's borders, which they know and understand belongs to them and not the Government's politicians or Supreme Court judges. I'm also sure my fellow Americans are now able to see why they feel that America's leaders and judges appear to deny America's Sovereign Nation status and enjoy ignoring America's Constitutional and Immigration laws instead of defending these two Icons of American law that were written to protect the rights and privileges of America's citizens from foreign nations who might decide to lay claim to these rights via collusion and corruption with America's Government. Since my fellow law-abiding American citizens are getting more desperate each year, I have noticed many of them are starting to believe that many parts of the Constitution were either written poorly or were bad laws from the start so some of them are demanding that these laws be changed or rewritten. Fortunately for them, I will soon prove they are wrong, and I will soon show them our immigration laws and our Constitution are perfect just they way they were first written if they are enforced correctly and justly according to the written laws. But before I prove these facts, I want to point out that President Lincoln warned us not to change the Constitution in several of his speeches because as he said, "it is perfect just the way it is written" (Note: I tend to agree with Mr. Lincoln completely.). After I'm done with this part of my book, I hope to prove that President Lincoln's was correct in his analysis of America's Constitution, and that in some ways, he gave us an omen of what was to come in this era.

Now that I've reminded my fellow Americans that both present and past Supreme Court Judges have been allowing any child born on US soil (including law breaking illegal foreigners) to become United States citizen illegally, I want to point out that I feel their actions are a crime and an act of treason against the Republic. Why do make these accusations? Well, let me explain that the actions our current American judges and politicians are taking are according to both Constitutional and Immigration laws crimes against the nation. To put it simply, their actions appear to be the main reason America's compatriots are feeling betrayed and powerless as they see their country overrun by Mexico's illegal aliens and many other foreign nation's army of invading citizens. America's Citizens also feel betrayed because America's Government and states like California are basically enticing these illegal by giving them rights and privileges that America's laws say belong to America's Citizens.

And because America's Government, Judicial System, and states like California are willing to provide these illegal hoards protection and special rights and privileges (that the Constitution says is illegal), these illegal aliens are living on American Taxpayer paid Social Services and cash incentives known as Welfare. And, unfortunately for America's Compatriots, since I once worked for California's Social Services welfare agencies, I know that the moment these illegal foreign alien invaders enter America and get their foot in the door they all apply and qualify for special US Government taxpayer paid Social Services programs that were once only meant to serve America's legal and naturalized citizens who found themselves unemployed or on hard times. And to add insult to the mental wound (that creates PTSD and triggers uncontrolled anger), after these illegal aliens arrive, they also qualify to have their U.S. hospital bills paid for or written off as a loss by American hospitals (who are going broke thanks to Bush's presidential mandate that he signed into power during his tenure), qualify for low income housing, qualify for free education and training for themselves and their children, and their children qualify for free breakfast, lunch, and after school snacks during the school year and free summer lunches and day care for their parents in the Summer.

I want to add that to complete the slap in the face of America's legal taxpaying citizens, these lawbreaking and invading or colonizing illegal aliens are left with little or no responsibilities for the care and feeding of their endless chain babies they have because they don't believe in birth control of any type because they say their religion does not allow it. Note: They all say they are Catholic, but almost all of them don't' ever go to church because when I attended Catholic services I seldom saw that many Mexicans in our church. By the way, I know I can make this claim because on Sundays I watch the men buy several 18 packs of beer and they sit around fires while they get drunk, play loud music, and their families just ignore them and stay home too. When I leave for church they are there, and when I return from church they are still where I left them getting drunk. This game, if we want to give it a name, happens like clock work every Sunday.

According to America's legal citizens and many politicians who want to close America's borders, the reason these illegal aliens are flocking to America has less to do with work and more to do with getting a piece of the millions of dollars in free taxpayer paid entitlements they qualify for the moment they enter US soil and set up their household thanks to some state's Democrat controlled legislatures. Although statistics show that many of these aliens break US laws and many have gang ties to Mexico's gangs, these law breaking illegal aliens continue to get rewarded by America's government and championed by a Mexican Government that is dumping its poverty and criminal problems on America's citizens. I'm sad to say but both the US and Mexican Governments are responsible for the growing flood of lawless non-immigrant and colonizing illegal invaders from Mexico and other countries that are following Mexico's foot steps as they slowly crush and destroy America's virtuous and once law abiding Western Christian Culture.

The sad part about this invasion (that might crush America's culture) is that America's culture and her citizens saved the world from oppression in World War I, World War II, and the Korean War. One more thing these Mexican and other foreign illegal aliens are destroying is the American Republic's once special sovereign nation status. Please note: I believes that since America's taxpayers are being forced to cough up the money to pay for illegal aliens' hospital bills, social care, their feeding, and their education the US government should write a law that says "any lawless invader who has had two children in America and has used American taxpayers services to pay for their children's birth, care, and feeding must have the woman's tubes tied. If the woman refuses, they should be given the choice of going back to Mexico (or country of origin) or getting to stay and getting their tubes tied, after the return to their homeland and start the process legally to apply for their green card to enter America legally (Remember, I proved their children are not US Citizens because there is no birth right statute in the US Constitution.).

So in the 21st Century, my fellow Americans find themselves living in an America that is basically being given away to the "worlds' citizens" and her Constitution's laws being giving away and used against them. Unfortunately for the American leaders who are behind these illegal actions against the Republic, Fredric Bastiat says these actions are wrong and they all break American Constitutional laws. And as I stated earlier, thanks to several ridiculous Supreme Court decisions, blunders, or wrong and lawless interpretations (which I will soon prove are wrong) America's Law Enforcement Officers now find themselves in an America turned upside down because many foreign and domestic criminal world elements are using the Supreme Court's "incredulous and ridiculous" decisions for financial gain by providing millions of illegal foreigners lawless entry into the US via the Supreme Court's "chain baby" mandate. The ugly part of these bad judicial decisions is that America's law officers can't do a thing about these bad decisions that protect these illegal aliens and their criminal benefactors because presidents like Obama use their Attorney Generals to prosecute these officers for doing their job.

Sadly, the blatant misuse of these damaging (and twisted) Supreme Court decisions by modern-day world criminals are now so common in America that one was recently chronicled in many of the United States' Newspapers as a feature article. This story was so shocking that it was even included in one of our local newspaper in the Central California city of Visalia. Here is sample of quote from the article that I believe says it all in black and white: "For Months, neighbors noticed a number of pregnant Asian women coming and going . . . .at an upscale townhouse development in suburban Los Angeles, they finally found out the home was being used as maternity center for Chinese mothers paying thousands of dollars to give birth in the United States so their Children would automatically gain citizenship, city [(LA)] officials said" ("Site for maternity tourists shut down." Visalia Times-Delta. 25 March 2011: 1A-3A.).

The Newspaper article I presented above not only showed the lack of respect foreign criminal elements have for America's Immigration laws and our law enforcement officers, but I feel it also showed how damaging the incorrect interpretation of Section 1 of the XIV Amendment has been for America and her citizens. I feel I can come to this conclusion because this bad judicial decision appears to have actually empowered the word's criminal elements to use their incorrect judicial decision for profit and to thumb their nose at America's Law Enforcement Agencies. And to make things worse on US Citizens, this damaging and misguided judicial decision and several other twisted Supreme Court interpretations and decisions (over the past 100 years) have made it easier for Politicians like ex-President Obama and leaders like Senator Reid, Pelosi, and Harris to label Mexico's invading colonizing armies as "illegal immigrants" instead of the "alien illegal undocumented trespassing invaders" that these law breakers really are in the eyes of America's Law Enforcement Officers.

The worst part of this charade is that even in the 21st Century ex-President Obama and the Democratic Party are is still asking America's citizens to accept these alien colonizers with open arms and to forget that America was once a respected Sovereign Nation that always protected its borders from mass invasions of undocumented migrants or world conquerors. Before I move on, I feel I have to remind these American politicians that birds, reindeer, and other animals migrate because nature tells them to do it. But when humans move into a new country without permission, this does not qualify as migration because humans must follow a sovereign nation's set laws and set time limits to "immigrate" into this nation because the world is now civilized. To add to the injustice being done to America's citizens, I like to note that past President Obama, many current members of Congress, and even the current Supreme Court Justices are continuing to push day-and-night to either write or pass a law that will reward these Mexican and other foreign colonizers with an illegal unconstitutional streamlined US government sponsored road to legal US Citizenship.

For those Americans who might not believe how brazen current and past American politicians and American Judges have been about forcing America's Compatriots to accept their decisions to let them give illegal and law breaking foreigners the same rights that Americans have under America's Constitution, I want to remind my fellow Americans that ex-President Obama, left leaning lower Court and Supreme Court Judges, Democrat and RINO politicians, and many current government employees that were appointed by the Obama Administration are still trying to use any means (legal and illegal) they can find to protect and help these illegal foreign citizens. These illegal means, I want to note, include ignoring and skirting US Immigration laws and Constitutional laws that I feel should be classified as a form of "occupational crimes" or "white collar crimes" (as described in the book Occupational Crime by Gary S. Green). In case my readers have forgotten, I want to remind them of the many social services and cash grants these illegal aliens qualify for and the fact that many Democrat Controlled cities and states have decided to become sanctuary states and cities so they can reward the over 20 million and growing illegal and law breaking alien colonists from Mexico and other countries by basically giving them illegal American citizenship status. Less I forget, I also want to point out that back in June of 2012, ex-President Obama used an executive order to allow almost "One Million" young, lawless, and invading colonizing 30 year olds and younger to stay in America by writing an Executive Order that was not legal because it was an "Amnesty Law" that only Congress could have written and passed according to the US Constitution. This illegal form of Amnesty (that in reality is not Amnesty but an illegal Pardon) that was provided by Obama gave these young invading aliens the freedom to snub their noses at America's Citizens, immigration laws, and America's Law Enforcement Officers because now they can stay in America without following America's legal procedures and laws and not be prosecuted or deported. Can we say these illegal aliens are getting preferential law breaking powers that America's citizens don't have, or have ever had, which we know has to be against the law and America's Constitutional laws!

Before I move on, I want to add that by giving these young lawless, colonizing, invaders permission to stay in America, as his personal guests, ex-President Obama really used his power to pardon on these invaders; however, unfortunately for ex-President Obama and these young illegal aliens, I will soon show all of America's citizens that our Presidents don't have this kind of power to write any laws, let alone immigration laws, and ex-President Obama was wrong to use his pardoning power on illegal alien foreigners like these young Mexican illegal aliens. I feel I should also note that at the time of this book's writing and printing, local TV news program announced that Congress had just accepted a plan to allow these law breaking Mexican colonists a "path" to citizenship, code words for a free pass to citizenship, courtesy of America's government without the Republic's (America's legal citizens) permission or input (Note: This law was not accepted or passed, so it was just a false alarm as we learned after President Trump was elected.)

The bad part about this news story is that ex-President Obama's Dreamer Act law is still with us, and all of the millions of now young adult Dreamers that Obama's law protects are getting closer to getting a free pass to US Citizenship. If this Dreamer Act law is left alone and not stopped during the Trump administration era, I believe ex-President Obama will have opened up a "Pandora's Box." I say this because this Dreamer Act law, to me, is more than likely only going to become an incentive for more millions of invading Mexican and South American colonizers to rush across our borders and enter America (Note: Although I wrote this sentence back in 2014, as I re-write this book in 2019, the news is reporting that there are anywhere from 5,000 to 20,000 illegal aliens from Central America headed for the Mexican/US border to enter America.). And, I also feel that when Obama signed off on his own created Amnesty Bill he broke several American Constitutional laws. And! When Obama took this action, he set himself above America's laws and the US Constitution and committed a "white collar crime." I want to note here that I truly believe that if this book does not stop this lawless invasion of America by the Mexico and many other nations, the actions of these illegal aliens will finally hasten the end of America's Sovereign Nation status. I come to this conclusion because a few more illegal actions by either another President or Congress will soon lead to a larger and more aggressive championed invasion of America's borders by either Mexico's historically corrupt government or by some other Southern or Central American country's invading citizen's army of illegal aliens. And when this happens, I feel this new invasion will pale in comparison to other historically reported invasions of other sovereign nations of this world. Less we forget, I remind my fellow Americans of the invasion of Rome by the Western Goths who invaded and colonized the Roman Empire in the 4th Century and how the Goths eventually conquered and destroyed all of the mighty Roman Empire.

Now that I've provided some hard facts that prove America's Supreme Court Judges and America's politicians are hurting America's Compatriots with their damaging judicial decisions and creative law bending, I hope this book will inspire America's politicians and Supreme Court judges to try to understand why they have failed America's legal and vested citizens. The sad part about this illegal invasion is that it could have been avoided if America's Supreme Court Judges had taken the time to review their past and present Constitutional law interpretations for possible reading errors, wrong or incorrect interpretations, or if they had questioned their own possible weak reading and grammar skills in the English language. If these judges had done their homework, maybe these American Supreme Court Judges would not have written their damaging court decisions or briefs, and they would not be enforcing these obviously incorrect judicial decisions. I truly believe that if these judges had taken the time to question their abilities and accepted their weaknesses before they made their damaging decisions they wouldn't have arrived at these damaging decisions that are causing America's Citizens and her Constitution so much trouble. To make things worse, I want to point out the fact that these judges and politicians have made these damaging changes or interpretations without ever asking for public input or having any kind of Congressional or public hearings to see if they were (or are) making the right decisions.

If I were to select a good example of a careless and hasty decision these judges have made in the past, I think I would select a critical decision that was made back in 1898 by America's Supreme Court Judges. In this bad or illegal decision, according to the information I found in US History books, America's Supreme Court Justices evidently either ignored or misread the true meaning of America's Constitution when they creatively ignored the true meaning of a sentence that is found in Section 1 of the XIV Amendment and they decided to augment its meaning. I add this comment because, according to the Oxford Companion to the US Supreme Court, these judges decided to avoid what America's Constitution said in Section 1 of the XIV Amendment so they could bestow US Citizenship on a young Chinese man who had been born on US soil to Chinese Citizens who did NOT have legal permission to work or live in America. According to several US History books I researched, in the case titled United States v. Wong Kim Ark, 169 U.S. 649 (1898) the United States Supreme Court ruled 6-2 that "a child born in the United States, of parents of Chinese nationality who at the time had a permanent domicile and residence in the US and were carrying on business...but were not employees of the Chinese government, automatically became a US citizen..."

The ruling I presented in the last paragraph that my research shows was written in a manner that left out, avoided, and ignored facts that showed their ruling was "WRONG," and unfortunately is still wrong and with us in the 21st Century. And, the sad part of their ruling is that this ruling has had a damaging effect on America's Sovereign Nation Status for the past one hundred years. And, thanks to this ruling from 1898, Americans in the 21st Century now find their country being invaded by the world's citizens (from various countries) who are mass migrating illegally into America so they can use this ill-conceived Supreme Court decision to their advantage. I should note that these invaders, or mass migrating illegal aliens, are basically occupying America and taken it over without firing a shot because of their anchor babies that the Supreme Court ruled was legal. I now want to add that this Supreme Court Decision is the corner stone of a huge disagreement over the precise meaning of the "citizenship clause in Section 1 of the XIV Amendment. I come to this conclusion because, as my readers will soon see, a professor of law and some other professionals all agree with me that these judges were wrong when they made this ill fated decision (Note: I will present this law professor's opinion, my opinion, and the other group's opinions later in this chapter.). By the way, I want to point out the fact that the Supreme Court Justices of this era said that the "citizenship language in the IXV Amendment encompassed the circumstances of this Chinese man's birth on US soil," which I will soon prove was wrong, and the results of my research prove this point, as well as the written results of several other professionals who weighed in on this bad 1898 Supreme Court decision ("Citizenship: Oxford Companion to the US Supreme Court," Answers.com Online Posting. http://www.answers.com/topic/citizenship.).

Before I present my results that prove how wrong these Supreme Court Judges were back in 1898, I want to point out this Supreme Court decision puts this critical decision front and center over the precise meaning of this area in Section 1 of the XIV Amendment that basically does not provide US Citizenship, but instead defines who is and who is an American citizen according to the definition of this part of America's Constitution. I don't want to get ahead of myself; however, I do want to point out that after my readers read my results and the results of a highly recognized law professor (and some other critics) who in a round about way completely agreed with my results. After I present these findings, I think my fellow Americans are going to see how wrong these judges were to arrive at their ill-conceived decision that is killing America's sovereign nation status and is pushing America towards its extinction. If my readers are ready, I will now present my discussion of this sentence:

The alleged citizenship clause that is in question, I want to note, is found in the first sentence of Section 1 of the XIV Amendment and it reads like this: "All persons born or naturalized in the United States, and SUBJECT TO THE JURISDICTION THEREOF, are citizens of the United States..." I want to now point out the error these judges made in their decision can be found in the fact these judges concluded (erroneously) that the words I put in capital letters were "Not talking about being Subject or under the jurisdiction of America's laws, but that it "...referred to being required to obey U.S. law," while living in America illegally or legally." So on this basis of this poor or badly interpreted phrase, and some borrowed definitions from other countries, these judges decided to interpret the language of this sentence that is found in Section 1 of the XIV Amendment in a way that "granted (and is currently granting all invaders too) U.S. citizenship to at some of the children born of foreigners because they were born on American soil: A concept that according to the Oxford Companion is known as Jus Soli." ("Citizenship: Oxford Companion to the US Supreme Court," Answers.com Online Posting. http://www.answers.com/topic/citizenship.) The funny thing is that today's Judges are ignoring one key part of this decision that to me sticks out like a sore thumb that has been hit by a hammer: I want my readers to note that these judges did not say "all" illegal children born in the us are US Citizens, but that "some of the children born of foreigners...were US citizens."

If I were to be asked to figure out how these allegedly educated judges, who were supposed to have mastered the English language and not just legal language, arrived at this pathetic illiterate like conclusion, I would have to honestly say the answer is beyond my educated mind. Since I earned and hold a Masters in English with an emphasis in Linguistics, TEFL/TESL, and Composition, I can honestly say (in reality, I have no idea.) that either these judges were possibly poor readers or they didn't have a complete grasp of the complexities of the written English language. I now want to add that either these two reasons are why these judges made this big ill-conceived blunder that is basically single handedly destroying America's Sovereign Nation status in the 21ˢᵗ Century, or another reason is that they were committing "white collar crime" because they made this decision to pay off a favor they owed some benefactor or benefactors. I honestly come to this conclusion because many open border supporters are using this decision to establish precedence for the illegal migrating hoards that are currently on their way to America via the Mexican border, or they are waiting at the border to enter US soil illegally to have their anchor babies and/or demand the same rights as America's vested citizens, or they are here to demand asylum from their alleged dangerous or poverty stricken country.

Since my research found there were some dissenting Judges in this land mark trial who didn't' agree with the majority, I guess this fact proves there were some Supreme Court Justices in this era who understood that the words "being subject to the jurisdiction of the United States" meant that these undocumented aliens had to be legal citizens or legal aliens living in America for there child to be a US Citizen, and that that these aliens had become US citizens and were no longer citizens of their original nation and therefore no longer "subject to any foreign power," as this sentence reads. Unfortunately for America, the judges who controlled the majority in this trial completely ignored this very correct and suitable conclusion because they decided to use and create their own definition and meaning for the word "citizenship," and, or, they decided to interpret this sentence to satisfy their ideals or political point of view. But if we fast-forward to the present, this book can prove these judges in the majority were wrong and more than likely broke the law. I know I can prove these judges of 1898 very likely committed "Embroilment because a professor of law from the 21ˢᵗ Century and an English Professor from the 21ˢᵗ Century have proven these judges were wrong to arrive at their incorrect decision. I want to also add I can also prove the dissenters in the minority in 1898 were right or correct in their argument that "subject to the Jurisdiction" means that this child (and today's children from illegal parents) were not under America's Government and laws jurisdiction because they could still be claimed or defended by their home country via "jus sanguinis," if they were threatened in any way by events on American soil.

If I add more details and facts to the last statement I just made, I know I can prove this law fact is true because these children inherit their citizenship from their parent's ties to their home country or land if the parents are still legal citizens of their home nation. And, If today's judges want proof for the conclusion I just reached, I give this fact in my defense: "If the illegal aliens in America are allegedly under US jurisdiction at all times, then why do the foreign consulates from countries like Mexico, Russia, and China always get involved in our legal proceedings when one of their citizens gets into trouble in America? These consulates get involved because these illegal and legal visiting aliens are not under US jurisdiction; however, these foreigners are under their home nation's jurisdiction and **not** "subject to the jurisdiction of the United States" as the Section 1 of the XIV Amendment says. Maybe the fact I just presented for your edification is why the Supreme Court Judges who were in the majority in 1898 decided to protect themselves from this legal fact by adding in their argument that they felt the drafters of the Constitution had not done a good job of defining the words 'citizen" or "citizenship" to their satisfaction. So, according to my research books and other sources, these Supreme Court Judges of this era said they decided to take action to change, or add their own interpretation by using "international and natural law" to define (of all things) the word "citizenship as it applied to America's Constitution. Unfortunately, I want to add, this Supreme Court Judges evidently forgot that America's Constitution and it laws were written by Americans to serve Americans; but, it was never written or meant to serve the world's citizens! To add insult to the slap on the face of America's Citizens, I want to now add that after these alleged American judges created their foreign language influenced definition for the terms " citizen and citizenship" they then used "their" definition to arrive at their judicial decision that I will now prove is crippling and dismantling America and her

Constitution ("Citizenship: Oxford Companion to the US Supreme Court," Answers.com Online Posting. http://www.answers.com/topic/citizenship.).

After I discovered America's Supreme Court Judges used "international and natural law" to define the terms "citizen and citizenship" to write their judicial decision in 1898, I found myself thinking their strange choice was very contradictory because, after all, the Constitution was written by Americans for the citizens of America and not for the world's citizens (or the United Nations). However, even after I looked over my research, I found the decision these judges made back in 1898 to be too hard to accept or believe. I therefore came to this conclusion that these American Supreme Court Judges evidently never bothered to have their facts checked or have an outside source check their conclusions to make sure their decision was a sound one for America's citizens and that it agreed with the thesis and premise found in the Constitution's Preamble (Note: Remember, I proved the Preamble is the Constitution's thesis statement). In the end, I felt I could make this accusation because of the facts I found on the web page titled Answers.com (topic, citizenship, 2/25/11) that I felt justified my criticism of these Judges' decision. My readers should remember that these judges used both "International and Natural Laws" to arrive at their incorrect conclusion that Answers.com says was wrong because "...the only justification they offered for making this damaging, [and what now appears to be an ill-fated,] and awkward decision was that "they felt the 'Constitution's Drafters' had not defined the true meaning of 'American Citizenship' in America's Constitution," [so therefore, they felt they had the right to make this damaging (and we soon prove illegal) decision]" ("Citizenship: Oxford Companion to the US Supreme Court," Answers.com Online Posting. http://www.answers.com/topic/citizenship).

To prove my conclusion in the last paragraph is correct, I'd like to add a few more facts to the revelations found in the last few paragraphs: Since America's Supreme Court Judges (both past and present) say Section 1 of the XIV Amendment gives them the legal power to grant citizenship to any world citizen whose child is born on American soil, I believe their decision about Section 1 of the XIV Amendment should be able to stand up to any literary analysis that I apply to their judicial decision of this section. After all, since the clause I am analyzing here was written in English and it uses English Grammar rules, I believe it should be able to stand up to any test or inspection that I decide to apply to their damaging decision. So, before I continue my analysis, I want to note that I found several problems with the Supreme Court's conclusion from the beginning. I can start my analysis this way because I found the following problem: Although America's Supreme Court Judges keep telling us that America's Constitution is like a "code book of laws," I can prove their decision is wrong by using the California Motorcycle driver's code book of laws to prove their choice is (and was) wrong and incorrect going all the way back to 1898. In fact, I feel I can honestly say and prove that America's Constitution is instead a wonderful work of prose writing that Grammar rules say is a well written essay. And since I can prove the Constitution is an essay, these means I can prove the Constitution falls under the guide lines and rules of English Grammar rules for essay writing, and it can be read and analyzed as an essay or written prose work and not some book of law codes like California's Motorcycle Driver's Handbook of laws.

But, before I prove these Judges were wrong to use "international law and natural law" to define the words "citizens and citizenship" in America's Constitution, I feel I need to ask my readers if they think we should accept these judges' (and politicians') poorly conceived conclusions? After all, from the information and research I've just presented, I'm sure my fellow Americans agree with me that this 1898 decision (like a few other ones I will soon discuss) seems to be one of the cornerstones that both "open border proponents and Mexico's lawless and land-grabbing colonizers are using to help millions of foreign illegal citizens invade America and then demand "American rights and privileges," that I should note Fredric Bastiat says they don't have. The sad part of this treacherous illegal act is that, as Fredric Bastiat" says, "America's Constitutional principles were written to only serve or protect America's legal citizens" [from Supreme Court Judges and American politicians who attempt to hand these rights to foreigners]. And since this action is taking place today, can we expect to see a Socialist state not far behind this act? (Bastiat, Frederic, The Law: The Classic Blue Print for a Free Society. Foundation for Economic Education: Hudson, NY, 2007)

Continuing my analysis, I want to add that I also found many US history books that also came to the same conclusions that I've presented in this part of my book. So, I now want to get back to this very bad and incorrect 1898 interpretation of America's Constitution that I feel is so bad for America and her citizens that it is allowing Mexico's and the world's citizens to invade America and conquer her without firing a shot. In short, because America is being invaded and America's citizens' Constitutional rights are being given to any foreign citizen who enters US soil, I feel America's Supreme Court has, and is, committing treason against the Republic. To show how bad this Supreme Court decision was for America and her Sovereign Nation status, in my state of California, these illegal citizens who cross the border via California's porous border and sanctuary state status are so embolden that they feel it is their right to tell Americans they have the same Constitutional citizen rights as legal Americans and America's citizens can't do a thing about it. And since America's Supreme Court Judges appear to agree with these illegal invaders, these none US citizen Mexicans current fly Mexico's flag all over California because they say California is now part of Mexico.

I now want to add that thanks to the "Dreamer" Mexican controlled California Legislature's two new laws that work together have given these illegal aliens California legal driver's licenses, and another law that works with this law allows them to register to vote at the time without being questioned as to whether they are legal residents or not (I want to note that if these illegal aliens get caught voting, this California law says the state takes the blame for it, or "mia culpa," so they can't be prosecuted.). To prove these laws are wrong, I wan to add that ccording to a newspaper article published in California on October 3, 2018 a record number of voters registered to vote for the mid-term elections: "California sets record as voter registration tops 19 million" (Associated Press, "California sets record as voter registration tops 19 million. No 196, page one. 10-3-2018.). The funny (ironic funny) part about this story is that in an early 2018 newspaper article it stated that millions of legal Americans are leaving California and are being replaced by illegal aliens at the rate of twice the amount of Americans who are leaving. So we Americans have to ask ourselves, who are these people that are allegedly registering to vote in a California that is becoming mostly illegal aliens? I know most Americans haven't seen these news stories on television or read about these new developments that I have introduced in this section of my book; however, since I have presented the dates and the newspapers these stories ran in this year (2018), I hope they now see that America's main stream media is not reporting all of the dangerous (to the Republic) news that is occurring in California and other Southwestern states, which are the epicenter of America's invasion. I also hope they now understand that what is happening in California will soon be at their doorsteps, if this invasion is not stopped before President Trump leaves office.

Now, before I move on, I want to ask my fellow Americans if they believe that Mexico's lawless invading colonizers should be given the same rights as law abiding American Citizens just because they've managed to enter America illegally? I also want to ask them if they believe our Supreme Court Judges (and politicians) are right to say these Mexican colonizers (and other invading citizens from other countries) are protected by America's Constitution and its privileges that belong to America's Citizens? I ask this question of my Compatriots because if Americans don't stand up and say no to America's Supreme Court Judges soon, then they better be ready to accept these illegal invaders' right to claim America and ignore

America's sovereignty in the next few years. However, if my fellow Americans don't agree with our Supreme Court Judges then maybe it's time all of America's citizens take the time to read my book from cover to cover so they can learn that their country is being handed over to the world state by state. If I can't convince my fellow Americans that it is time for them to fight for their Republic, I guess we Americans will just have to give up and let the world take over America and destroy America's culture. By the way, I don't believe the answer to America's growing problem of "an uncontrolled colonizing invasion" by Mexico's citizens and other countries can be found in a civil war in America, but I do believe the answer is going to require some very quick action and soon by her loyal citizens. And in realty, I think the answer is right under our collective noses, and I will soon prove it, if my readers will keep reading this book to the end.

If my readers are ready, I would like to continue my analysis of key sections of America's Constitution that I'm happy to say prove the answers to America's invasion problems can be found in the words, sentences, paragraphs, and thesis of America's Constitution that was created for the Republic's members by America's delegates. I'd like to now remind my fellow Americans that after I complete my analysis and research of the key parts of the Constitution I hope they will be cheering Section 1 of the XIV Amendment and a few other parts of the Constitution instead of asking for them to be changed or deleted. I also hope my fellow Americans will be cheering this book because I hope to show them how to use the results of my research to defend their Sovereign Nation's Status and to repel Mexico's invaders and other colonizers from other nations so they can stop the demise of America, stop their politicians and Supreme Court judges from continuing to give away US Citizenship to the world's citizens, and stop law breakers who enter America to have their children born in America so they can stay in America illegally. To begin, I'd like to introduce two sample sentences that have the same sentence structure as each other so I can compare and contrast them to show my readers a very important point they need to know. One sentence will come from Section 1 of the XIV Amendment and the other sentence is one that I wrote using the same kinds of words that are found in the sentence found in Section 1 of the XIV Amendment. I wrote my copycat sentence so I could use it as a comparative sample and to prove that US Citizenship is a birthright rule that was only meant to serve and protect the children of legal and vested American citizens that are known as US legal Citizens. After all, I did prove in Chapter 3 that the Constitution was written to only serve and protect America's legal citizens so they could defend the rights they gave themselves that are found in America's Constitution. And I remind my readers, these personal and individual rights that are found in America's Constitution were written by America's legal and Patriotic Founding Fathers, or authors, who did not write America's Constitution for Mexico's citizens, Central America's citizens, South American Citizens, or the "World's Citizens."

Since I stated that America's Constitution is a well-written essay of Exposition and Descriptive writing, and not a legal type book with law codes like for example California's motorcycle driver's code book, I'd like to begin my analysis by showing my readers an essay that allows me to present a copycat sentence that mimics the first sentence found in Section 1 of the XIV Amendment. After I analyze this essay and the key sentence that I put in this essay on purpose, I will first compare it to a "law code section" and some of the sentences that come from this law code book that I found in the California motor cycle driver's handbook. After I compare the motorcycle law code sample to my essay, I will then use my story and a sentence that I wrote that has the same sentence structure as the first sentence in Section 1 of the XIV Amendment to compare them and prove to my fellow Americans the Supreme Court Judges of 1898 were wrong. Note: By comparing and contrasting the three different types of written works I have selected, I feel I will be able to show and prove how wrong the Supreme Court Judges have been to say the Constitution was written so poorly they've had to interpret it themselves for the good of America, and they had to define key areas of Constitution and certain words used in some key areas of the Constitution so they could make it fair to the worlds' citizens.

The first example I present here is the sample essay or story I wrote to show several key facts that I want to point out about how the Constitution was written and why a key sentence in Section 1 of the XIV Amendment is causing so much controversy. To understand this controversial sentence, I decided to write a sentence that basically has the same sentence structure and wording as the first sentence that is found in Section 1 of the IXV Amendment. My new sentence I wrote to mimic the first sentence of Section 1 of the XIV Amendment, as my readers will see, has the same types of common nouns and pronouns that Section 1 of the XIV Amendment has or uses to present its information. To copy the Constitution's sentence structure of the IXV Amendment, I wrote my "copy-cat" sentence to have the same structure as the Constitution's sentence in that my sentence includes a requirement to establish precedence like the first sentence that is found in Section 1 of the XIV Amendment. By creating my copy-cat sentence in this manner, I feel I will be able to use its content to help my readers see and understand the mistake past Supreme Court Judges made in their judicial decisions, and the same mistake our current 21st Century judges are still making when they apply these alleged principles that they say exists in Section 1 of the IXV Amendment.

When I'm done introducing and analyzing my "copycat" sentence, I hope to have shown my readers the similarities between my essay's key sentence and the key sentence found in Section 1 of the XIV Amendment and why these judges made their mistake. If I can accomplish this goal, I know my fellow Americans will be able to see and comprehend the problem I uncovered during my analysis of Section 1 of the XIV Amendment. The other goal and job I hope to accomplish is the fact that Section 1 of the IXV Amendment does not include any wording that provides instant citizenship to "the world's newborns" who might be born on US soil, and I also hope to teach my fellow Americans how Section 1 of the XIV Amendment really works:

The Grateful Store Manager and the Children

Brian, Mary, and Sara had just left their school Pine Street Junior High, and since they were hungry, they decided to go to their favorite store that was on the corner of the same street they all lived on in their hometown. As they went up the stairs of the store, Mary slipped and fell on a lose board of the store and got hurt. When Brian saw Mary Fall, he decided to run into the store and get help from the Store-Keeper, but as a he ran towards the entrance of the store a local stray dog got scared and bit Brian on the ankle as he went by the dog. Since Sara was the only one not hurt, Sara decided to run inside the store to get help and call Mr. Calm the storeowner. The storeowner, Mr. Calm, heard Sara's calls for help and quickly ran to help Sara and her injured classmate. After Sara stopped yelling for help, she then quickly told Mr. Calm that Brian and Mary had been injured in front of his business.

Mr. Calm knew the children well so he quickly helped the Brian and Mary to make sure their injuries were not serious and then he called their parents to let them know what had happened. After taking care of the children's problems, and calling their parents, Mr. Calm then decided that along with taking care of the children's medical bills he would treat Brian, Mary, and Sara to free sodas for the rest of their middle school years. Since the children's parents had shown up and all had been taken care of, the children were told by the parents that they could accept Mr. Calm's gracious offer. So, as the children left with the first of many sodas to come, they all turned and waved goodbye to Mr. Calm.

As years have gone by, the children still go to Mr. Calm's store, and each time they go to their favorite childhood store, they get their free sodas for to enjoy with the snacks they buy at Mr. Calm's store. The Store Keeper, Mr. Calm, is always happy to see the children and is always nice to them because he knows that they will soon grow up and graduate and some day they will enter high school and then leave for college. Mr. Calm enjoys the children and he is very thankful for their friendship and that is why he waits for them to show up at his store at the end of each school day. Mr. Calm waits for the children to ask for their free sodas when they enter his store because of the deal he made: **All children who want their free sodas, and that come into the owner's store after school, are treated to their free sodas that they enjoy on their way home from school because Mr. Calm made them this offer.** These Children will always enjoy remembering Mr. Calm, even after they grow up and leave their hometown for college.

Now before I introduce the "driver's code book example so I can compare the code book to both my book and America's Constitution and how their structure is not the same," I want to make sure I remind my readers to play close attention to the sentence in the third paragraph of my "Store Manager's story that is written in bold type to make it stand out. This sentence is crucial to my analysis because it was purposely written to include the same type of wording that the first sentence in Section 1 of the XIV Amendment has in its structure. As my readers will soon see, my sentence is crucial to my analysis because it helps me prove that (from my research) both past and present Supreme Court Judges' interpretations of Section 1 of the XIV Amendment have been wrong. But, before I start my analysis of my sentence and Section 1 of Article XIV, I want my readers to first look at an example from California's motorcycle driver's handbook that I feel proves the Constitution and Section 1 of the XIV Amendment are "Not" written like law code statutes that are found in books of law codes:

Eye and Face Protection

"A plastic shatter-resistant face shield can help protect your whole face in a crash. It also protects you from wind, dust, dirt, rain, insects, and pebbles thrown up from the vehicles ahead. If you don't have to deal with these types of problems, you can devote your full attention to the road. Goggles protect your eyes, but they don't protect the rest of our face as a face shield does. A windshield is not a substitute for a face shield or goggles. Most windshields will not protect your eyes from the wind. Neither will eyeglass or sunglasses. Glasses won't keep your eyes from watering, and they might blow off when you turn your head.

To be effective, eye or face shield protection has to:

- Be free of scratches
- Be resistant to punctures
- Give a clear view to either side
- Fasten securely, so it does not blow off
- Permit air to pass through to reduce fogging
- Permit enough room for eyeglasses or sunglasses, if needed
- Tinted eye protection should not be worn at night or any other time when little light is available."

As my fellow Americans can see from the Eye and Face Protection legal code example I just quoted from the motorcycle law hand book, this legal section that has to do with head and eye protection does not read or look like anything that is found in Section 1 of the XIV Amendment or America's Constitution. Yet! Both American politicians and U.S. Supreme Court Judges appear to enjoy telling America's citizens that their Constitution is the same type of written work and this is why they say the Constitution should be read like a book of law codes and needs "legal" interpretation. Unfortunately for these Judges, I am about to prove how wrong they and America's politicians are about the Constitution, its Articles, and Amendments. By the way, I will be using the children's essay and my "copycat" sentence I wrote and introduced in the previous paragraph of this chapter to compare it to this driver's handbook and the Key sentence found in Section 1 of the XIV Amendment. As my fellow Americans can see in the motorcycle code book sample I just presented, the sentence structure of this written law tells motorcycle riders what type of face shield is a legal face shield, and it also tells the rider what is not considered a legal face shield when riding a motorcycle. This law is written in this manner that tells riders how they can be compliant in their choice of helmet and face guard and it also serves as a guideline for an officer of the law who might decide to pull a motorcycle rider over for possibly not having the required or correct helmet and face shield that the law requires for the motorcycle rider's safety. And, if the officer finds the helmet and face shield is not compliant with the written laws, the officer will then either cite the rider or give the rider a warning to get the right equipment to be compliant with the law.

Now that I've introduced how the motorcycle codebook of laws looks, works, and is applied in real life, I want my readers to notice the clear difference between the motorcycle code book's sentence and paragraph structure and the paragraph and sentence structure of my children's story that mimics and copies the sentences and paragraph structure found in Section 1 of the XIV Amendment. The first difference my readers should note is that the sentences and paragraphs look more like a list of points that must be met, while my children's story and Section 1 of the XIV Amendment are set up to flow as they add more and more details about the children, the store owner, and the events that created their lasting bond. The next comparison I want to make of these different types of writing styles is that the sentences found in my essay story only present simple narrative information that basically describes and presents the story of how the events of the story took place; while in the motorcycle law code handbook, the sentences are written in a truncated and choppy manner that only presents sentences that describe standards that must be met to meet the legal or required mandates of the laws found in this book. And, before I move on, I want to also note that my story and Section 1 of the XIV Amendment are both written to present the same type of narrative statements that use words that only present information and details about the topic being discussed.

Finally, although I only included a few sentences from a paragraph that is found in Section 1 of the XIV Amendment, I want to note that this narrative style paragraph presents the details and facts needed to understand how this part of the Constitution is supposed be used and applied to protect our American citizens' rights and privileges that we wrote for ourselves and no other county or its citizens. Therefore in simple terms, all my story and Section 1 of the IXV Amendment do is present narrative facts in a sequential sentence structure to provide the needed information of the written work, while the code book presents its information in a choppy, truncated, and point by point sentence structure that tells the reader how the requirements of this law can be met and how these laws will be enforced. To conclude my discussion, I want my fellow Americans to notice and understand that neither my story or the Constitution's narrative style sentences and paragraphs present any type of legal statutes that must be met, while the Motorcycle driver's handbook does present statutes and laws that must be obeyed and adopted to comply with the law.

To continue my discussion, I now want to remind my readers that we Americans can use the driver's book of law codes to test or prove either compliance or non-compliance of a required set standard or law we are reading. But in the case of the essay type written works I used to compare to this code book, the key sentences found in my children's story and the key sentences found Section 1 of the XIV Amendment do not require any kind of test to meet compliance because this is not goal of these two written works. I can make this argument because the key sentences in the Section 1 of the XIV Amendment and my story do not function as laws because they both simply provide narrative information that describes needed facts to understand the subject or topic being discussed. However, I do want to add that in the case of the Constitution and areas like Section 1 of the XIV Amendment the narrative information helps present needed information to understand how the principles of the new American Republic's Government apply and work to protect the rights and privileges of its citizens. As for my children's story, the narrative facts in my children's story are presented to inform the readers of certain important sequential information that is needed to both understand the story and to tell the story. Finally, I want to remind my readers that I did include a sentence in my story that was purposely written with the same type of words and style that first sentence in Section 1 of the XIV Amendment uses so I can use it to put an end to the misreading of this section of the Constitution by America's Supreme Court Judges in the 21st Century.

Not to get ahead of myself but now, I feel my next move must be to prove that America's Constitution does indeed tell us who an American citizen is in several sections of the Constitution. I also want to remind my readers that the sentence I wrote to mimic or copy the words used in the first sentence in Section 1 of the XIV Amendment include the following words: **All children who want their free sodas, and that come into the owner's store after school, are treated to their free sodas that they enjoy on their way home from school because Mr. Calm made them this offer.** I want to remind my readers that I wrote this sentence to help me completely shatter the premise that America's Supreme Court Judges have kept pushing to keep America's borders open. I also want to add that if I were to misinterpret my "copycat" sentence on purpose, like I feel our Supreme Court Judges and many American politicians keep misreading and misinterpreting the first sentence found in Section 1 of the XIV Amendment, I know I could prove the storekeeper in my essay or story should end up having to give free sodas to all of the children of the world. I make this statement because like the first sentence in Section 1 of the XIV Amendment my sentence also starts with the word "all" that is followed by a vague noun that doesn't tell us which children qualify for the free sodas. This means I could say that "all" of the children of America or the world could walk in to this man's store and demand a free soda, like the judges say that any child of an illegal who is born on US soil qualifies for instant American citizens status, or birthright citizenship because the first sentence of Section 1 of the XIV Amendment starts with two words "All Persons...etc."

But thanks to my example, I now feel that any American or any of these judges who decides to take the time to read this book will learn the truth, and understand the correct way to read and interpret both my sentence and the sentence found in Section 1 of the XIV Amendment. I can make this claim because my story's thesis (like the Constitution's thesis) states that this story is only about the three children and the storekeeper, and it does not include the world's children, while in Section 1 of the XIV Amendment, the Constitution's preamble or thesis of the Constitution states the American Constitution was written for "the People of the United States and the United States of America. By comparing introductory words found in my copycat sentence of my children's story to the introductory words (of the first sentence) found in Section 1of the XIV Amendment, I feel my readers should now understand why my copycat sentence proves that anyone with an understanding of English writing grammar rules should have understood that the first sentence (and first two words) found in Section 1 of the XIV Amendment should never have been misinterpreted to say that "all" children born on US soil should get instant US birth right citizenship automatically.

Now that I've introduced what I believe are the key facts that prove that Section 1 of the XIV Amendment should never have been misread, I want to ask America's judges and politicians, on behalf America's citizens, how can so many allegedly highly intelligent Supreme Court Judges and politicians (who were once lawyers) keep misinterpreting and misreading the first sentence in Section 1 of the XIV Amendment so poorly? Think about it my fellow Americans; how can these allegedly highly educated people keep misreading this section so badly that they are willing to give "any" child, who happens to be born on American soil (to illegal or trespassing parents) automatic American citizenship? What's even worse is that these allegedly educated people keep making this "bad or incorrect" interpretation every year without ever bothering to have an English language specialist or second party specialist analyze the wording found in Section 1 of the XIV Amendment so they can make sure they are making the right decision in these modern times of the 21st Century.

Okay, I now want to add one more very important fact here because, as my readers will see, I have just proven how easy it is to both understand the correct meaning of this sentence and how easy it to purposely misread and misinterpret sentences like the one I wrote for my children's sentence and Section 1 of the XIV Amendment, if one is careless or does to appease some benefactor. After all, if I can twist the sentence about the children getting free sodas to say that all of the children of the world can get free sodas, even though I proved earlier in my book the word "children" is controlled by the precedence found in thesis of my short story that says the "children in my story only include the three children found in my thesis statement, then I hope my readers now see how easy it is for some careless or indebted Supreme Court Judge to twist Section 1 of the XIV Amendment into a non existent law that hands out free US citizenship to any child of the world who is born on US soil. Since I just introduced several facts that say if the Constitution's thesis (that is found in the Preamble) is interpreted correctly and applied to Section 1 of the XIV Amendment correctly the only persons who get automatic citizenship are the people introduced in the Preamble of the thesis of the Constitution that starts with the words "We the people of the United States," I guess America's Supreme Court Justices and America's politicians better close America's borders and start sending back any and all illegal aliens currently living on America's Sovereign soil. Now that I've presented the needed facts and proof America's Citizens need to demand the removal of all illegal aliens from US soil, I now wonder why America's Supreme Court Judges have not been able to figure out the fact that America's Constitution has always set the parameters that tells the reader that "only children born to America's legal citizens are covered by America's Constitution?

To make things worse for America's citizens, I want to add that today's turncoat American Supreme Court Judges are still accepting the decision of the 1898 Supreme Court Judges, which makes no sense since I just proved how easy it is find real meaning of key sections of the Constitution. Since I just introduced a cartload of facts that prove the 1898 Supreme Court decision was wrong, I feel it is my duty to ask today's Supreme Court Judges why they are still failing to see (or take action) that the US Constitution is an essay and not a book of law codes? Is the reason they don't see the truth a lack of reading comprehension or is it that these Judges of the 21st Century really don't understand the English grammar rules of essay writing? Or maybe I should say, these Judges' problem is a secret desire to ignore the facts I have just described in this book because it makes it easier for them to twist this section to do their bidding so they can allow any child born on American soil free access to US citizenship so they can appease some benefactor?

After all, in Chapter 3 of this book, I proved the Constitution was only written to apply to and serve America's legal citizens and their children. And since I have proven that America's Constitution is an essay that has a thesis that says (as Fredric Bastiat wrote) the Constitution's rights and privileges were written so that America's citizens could use them to defend themselves from those who would try to stake an illegal claim to this rights and privileges (and to stop any government official who might attempt to give their rights and privileges to others that are not entitled to them), I'm sure my fellow Americans now understand why I make these claims based on the fact that the Constitution's thesis controls who the common noun "persons" refers to in Section 1 of the XIV Amendment, which, as I say, refers to the phrase "the people of the United States" that is found in the Preamble or the thesis statement of the US Constitution. So what is my summary of this conclusion? I think my fellow Americans will now agree with that the Constitution was only written to serve "The people of the United States" and not illegal aliens or their American born illegal children that might be born on US soil.

Now that I've presented several facts that contradict the Supreme Court's decisions and our politicians too (and I've proven beyond a shadow of doubt the US Constitution is "Not" written to be read like a book of law codes), I feel it's time for me to convince my fellow Americans that Section 1 of the XIV Amendment (as it is written) only covers babies born to America's legal and/or naturalized citizens by reviewing this facts and adding a few new ones. I can make this statement based on the fact that I can prove the common noun "persons," that is found in the first sentence of Section 1 of the XIV Amendment, can be defined by the precedence that was set by the Constitution's thesis (like my children's story) that I found in the Preamble during my analysis of this part of the Constitution. For my readers who might have forgotten, I remind them that I proved this fact in Chapter 3 during my analysis of the words and phrases that are found in the Constitution's Preamble.

And although I have proven the results of my analysis are correct, I know there might still be many American citizens, many American politicians, many American judges, and ACLU lawyers who don't care about the truth I uncovered during my research. I know I can come to this conclusion because instead of accepting the truth, these groups would rather ignore the facts and continue to attack America's immigration laws, criminal laws, and Constitutional laws by stating that America's immigration laws and Constitutional laws are outdated and cruel because they attack the "world's citizens who enter America illegally as illegal criminal aliens. Before I go further, I want to add that I feel these American leaders and citizens evidently either don't' care or don't have a clue as to what America's Constitution really says. And since I make this bold accusation, I want to add that maybe it's time we Americans accept the fact that maybe our politicians are attacking America's Constitution, America's immigration laws, and America's criminal laws because they either enjoy protecting the citizens of other nations who refuse to recognize America's Legal System and thumb their noses at America's Law Enforcement Officers, or maybe these Americans and leaders are simply working for some foreign lobbyist with deep pockets full of money that have been paying for their election campaigns and their political parties for years. And if this is the case, I guess we can all agree these parties owe the lobbyist a lot of BIG favors, including keeping America's border open to illegal aliens from all over the world.

Now that I've made some bold accusations in this section of my book, I think it's time for me to prove the results of my research by re-examining the results of my analysis of Section 1 of the XIV Amendment. To make sure my analysis is correct, I will be applying the same writing, grammar, and analytical tools that I used earlier in this book to analyze the Preamble and some key areas of the Constitution's body. If my readers will allow me, I want to remind my readers that the opening sentence of Section 1 of the XIV Amendment reads as follows: **"All persons born or naturalized in the United States and subject to the jurisdiction thereof, are citizens of the United States and of the state wherein they reside."** To begin my review, I think I need to remind my readers of the fact that I proved the common noun "persons" was used by the drafters of the Constitution to serve as the subject of this sentence and NOT the first word "All." If my readers will remember, I proved this point when I proved the "thesis" was introduced in the Preamble of America's Constitution by the drafters of our Constitution to help them control the precedence and subjects they introduced in the Constitution's thesis (for example in this case the common noun "persons" can be replaced by the phrase "people of the United States" that is found in the Preamble). I want to add these subjects (used as antecedents) were not only introduced in the thesis, but they were re-introduced throughout the Constitution's body (known as the Articles and Amendments) by the drafters by using pronouns, common nouns, or possessive pronouns that take the place of the topic or subject that was introduced in the thesis statement. The drafters took this action in the Constitution so they could add more details and facts about the main subject of discussion, which included facts like who the Constitution was written for, who the Constitution protects and serves, why the

Constitution was written, how America's Government was supposed to be set up, and finally how to run the new American Government and change it when it needed to be changed.

Incase my readers have forgotten, I'd like to point out that I feel I have proven without any doubt that the antecedents that are often included in the thesis statement to set precedence were always included to help define and clarify any vague words like pronouns and common nouns that might be used by the drafters in America's Constitution later in the body of the work. To prove my point, I want to note that one example of a common noun that has caused many problems for America's Citizens is the word "persons" that is found in the first sentence of Section 1 of the XIV Amendment. The reason this common noun is such a problem is that America's Judges have never accepted the fact that the antecedent and precedence for this word is found in the Preamble of the Constitution. I want to remind my readers that the antecedent for the word "persons" includes the words "people of the United States" in this sentence because the "persons" being discussed here are the "people of the United States" and no other citizens of any foreign nation of this world. I should add here that the seven wonderful words in the phrase "We the people of the United States" are what help me establish the fact that the antecedence for this common noun "persons" that is found in the first sentence of Section 1 of the XIV Amendment (as in "All persons born or naturalized in the United States...") is only talking about the children of America's citizens or the new born children of these legal American Citizens and not some illegal foreigner's new born child who finds himself or herself in America illegally. So, according to the English Grammar rules of writing, the new born children that are legally covered by the phrase "All persons born..." are the children of America Citizens because the antecedent for the word "persons" can be found in the phrase: "people of the United States." Please note that there is no mention of Mexico's citizens, Central American countries' citizens, South American countries' citizens, or the world's citizens in the Preamble or thesis of the Constitution.

Before I sum up the information I presented in the paragraphs above, I feel I should ask America's judges the following question: If I can prove the drafters were only talking about America's citizens when they wrote the US Constitution in a few paragraphs, then why do America's Judges keep telling America's Citizens the American Constitution was written for the world's citizens? Another question I'd like to ask these American Judges is why can't they see and understand that the thesis of America's Constitution's was written to create or set the parameters as to who is covered by America's Constitution? After all, these parameters, I should note, do "Not" include words like "the world's Constitution" or "Mexico's Constitution" anywhere in America's Constitution. So! Why don't they end this charade? Finally, I'd like to say isn't time America's Judges and Politicians end this charade? After all, I feel it's safe to say that I just proved America's Constitution was written or "ordained and established for the People of the United States of America" and no other citizens (that have not gone through the legal process of becoming a citizen of the United States of America). I also think it's safe to say these "set" parameters do not apply to any trespassing illegal alien invaders, their foreign born children, or their children that happen to be born on American soil illegally.

To recap, I want to remind my readers, again, that the main point of the Constitution's thesis is that it was "established" for "the People of the United States" by the people of the United States so they could use the statutes found in their Constitution to protect their newly created and established rights from anyone who might decide to either take them away or give them away to ineligible foreign citizens like our Supreme Court Justices do year after year by breaking Constitutional law. On these facts alone, I feel I have proven the Drafters did not, as we are led to believe, create a vague or loosely written "book of law codes," which America's judges say they did because they allegedly failed to define words like "citizens" or citizenship." In reality, to show the error of these judges, my research has proven the Constitution's Drafters were highly skilled writers with a high command of grammar skills and English writing skills who had the foresight to specifically say the Constitution was written for Americans by Americans, which again sets the precedence and antecedence for the Constitution's body that are known as the Articles and Amendments of America's Constitution. I hope by now that my readers understand the Constitution's "thesis" controls the central idea of America's Constitution and that "America's Constitution states emphatically that it was only written for America's Compatriots. In closing this very important paragraph, I want to add that I feel the Constitution's thesis also provided the drafters the words and phrases they needed to define all of the key pronouns, common nouns, or possessives they would use in the body of the Constitution to restate and reintroduce the main topics being introduced and discussed.

To help qualify the facts I just restated and introduced, I want to offer my readers the following very important information that I found in a chapter of Pitt and Leavenworth's book <u>Logic for Argument</u> that I feel helps me prove and qualify, as these two intelligent writers state, that the "setting of precedence" in our essays [(to establish clarity or define words as the Constitution's drafters did)] "is more than just providing antecedents or setting precedence for pronouns…" In fact, as I learned from Pitt and Leavenworth book, setting precedence and adding antecedence also includes the act of providing any needed definitions for different parts of an essay because "they provide the conditions for the use of a certain word or words so the readers know exactly what the words mean [(By the way, this is called complex precedence.)], or when a definition applies to a word or any word in question. [This] simple distinction is important; for it is the words or phrases that we define not the things, facts, or events which they stand for [that are important]" (Leavenworth, Russell E., and Jack Pitt, Logic for Argument. Random House: New York 1968.).

Now that I've qualified how important setting precedence and providing antecedents are to the readers of our essays, especially when our readers are trying to comprehend a complex written work, I think I should say maybe these judges should have done a little more research and their homework before they made up their minds and wrote their damaging judicial decisions that are currently destroying our nation's sovereign nation status. And maybe, I should say these Supreme Court Judges should have reviewed their interpretations of the Constitution for their own possible reading errors. If these alleged American Patriotic Judges would have taken the time to take these extra steps, had double checked their decisions, and had done their homework, maybe they wouldn't have made such poor damaging choices during the time they served as American Judges. Need I remind my fellow Americans that these Judges' decisions haven't just changed America's Sovereignty status during the time these Supreme Court Judges served, but to this day and age, their rulings and decisions have put America on track to be overthrown and colonized by Mexico Government, Mexico's citizens, and many other foreign nations that are following Mexico's lead. I make this damaging and incriminating statement against "all" of America's Judges because when I looked back at these Supreme Court Judges (and even today's judges) decisions I found that these almost all of these Supreme Court Judges either ignored or misread different sections of America's Constitution. And in retrospect, I hate to say it, but these judges' decisions have created an environment of lawlessness and disregard for America's laws and Sovereignty in the 21st Century that can only be rivaled by the lawlessness of the roaring 20's (and 30s) when gangs and their leaders like Al Capone ruled America and controlled whole cities like Chicago.

Although some people make think this accusation is too extreme, I remind my readers that the only justification these judges offered for making their damaging decision was that "they felt the 'Constitution's Drafters' had not defined the meaning of words like "citizenship or American Citizenship" in America's Constitution," or at least to their satisfaction. This problem that these judges allegedly saw in America's Constitution, according to these judges, gave them the right to write their own definition or meaning for American Citizenship by "using international and natural law" to define what "they" felt American Citizenship was meant to be in "America's" Constitution." If my fellow Americans don't see these judges' actions or decisions as strange, wrong, or out of the ordinary after I complete my research and analysis in the next few paragraphs, then maybe, they should think about the fact that I found it very strange and shadowy when I took into consideration the Constitution these judges were changing was "America's Constitution" and not the "World's Constitution." Having introduced these key facts, I feel we Americans must ask ourselves why these judges would decide to use **international law** to define the words citizen or citizenship to use in America's Constitution? ("Citizenship, Oxford Companion to the US Supreme Court." Answers.com Online Posting. http://www.answers.com/topic/citizenship.)

If my readers will indulge me to think out-loud for a minute, so I can answer the question I asked in the last sentence of the paragraph above, I feel the reason these Supreme Court Judges' made their strange, shadowy, and damaging decision was because they were influenced by some powerful outside political forces (that they were not supposed to be influenced by as Supreme Court Judges). I come to this conclusion because these judges first ignored the fact that they were answering a question that dealt with defining American citizenship, and second, they ignored the fact that the law they were dealing with was part of America's Constitution and not International law or some International Constitution. I can come to these conclusions because according to historians and Answers.com (who use the Oxford Guide to the US Government for their facts) "[these judges said they had to use] their Legal Power to safeguard 'world citizens' against depravation of American Citizenship." Not to rain on these judges' parade, but according to US Immigration laws "A person who wants to come to America as a legal applicant must meet the standards set in US Immigration laws by America's Congress or they do not qualify to be Americans." So in reality, not all of the world citizens, as they put it, qualify or meet America's

Immigration laws standards. And! I hate to tells these judges and today's judges but the reason these judges gave (so they could ignore the fact that they were dealing with America's Constitution) sounds a lot like today's American's kid's programs that award everyone trophies for just showing up to play or participate.

So, again, in realty and in the real world, I want to note that I feel the US Supreme Court Justices of the past (and many present Judges too) usurped the drafter's Constitution "thesis statement" by ignoring it, and then they inserted their own re-write or definition without having Congressional hearings or getting the Republic's (US Citizens) approval to change the Republic's Constitution that has opened a Pandora's Box. And since history tells us the changes these judges have made to the Constitution have caused Americans so much grief that I feel they suffer from PTSD, I think I now see why President Lincoln once warned us not to change the Constitution in any way "because its perfect just the way it was written." I want to note that when these judges made the US Constitution into an all-inclusive "World Wide" Constitution, they basically nullified or ignored the drafter's edicts, the Constitution's thesis, and the drafters' meaning of the US Constitution that was written to protect America's citizens from having their rights taken from them or given away by some rogue American political force. In the end, I sense this strange and very controversial decision by these judges appears to have been made to help create the current controversial "Anti-US American Constitution loop hole" (and legal mess) that ALL Open Border Judges, Politicians, Criminals, and Special Interest Groups from Mexico and other countries are currently using to side step America's immigration and Constitutional laws.

To make matters worse, I also sense that America's politicians, Supreme Court Judges, and lobbyists of today are using this turn of the century Supreme Court interpretation to attack American's Constitutional rights and privileges because America's Citizens keep demanding their borders be closed and all foreign trespassers or invading colonizers be sent back to Mexico or other points of origin of this world. I want to also note that while America's current Supreme Court Judges and US Politicians are allowing Mexico's illegal citizens, other countries illegal citizens, and alleged Muslim refugee religious followers to colonize America, an American by the name of James Monroe was so concerned with other countries colonizing the Americas (especially below America's Southern border) that he wrote a semi-law known as the Monroe Doctrine that warned all European and other Nations that "any act of colonization of the America's (this would include North America or America) by a nation will be dealt with by force," (including military action) because as the doctrine further states, "...we should consider any attempt on their part to extend their system to any portion of this hemisphere as dangerous to the peace and safety of America (Yet extending Mexico's Government or Sharia Law into America is not dangerous?)" (Hofstadter, Richard, William Miller, and Daniel Aaron. "Monroe and the World." The United States: The History of a Republic. Prentice-Hall, Inc. Englewood Cliffs: 6th ed. 1960.).

The ironic part (almost laughable) of this doctrine is that while this American president was creating a law to protect these Latin neighbors from being over thrown and colonized by other (mostly European) nations he failed to protect the United States of America from being colonized by the same Latin American countries he was protecting. I also find it ironic that President Monroe wanted to protect Mexico and all of the Latin countries to our South, but he failed to Protect America from being invaded by these same countries he was protecting. To make things worse, America's past and current Presidents appear to be falling all over each other to allow the invasion of America because they are giving these immigration lawbreaking colonizers the keys to America without putting up a fight. I hate to say it but this is not where our invasion problems end. I make this statement because I also find it ironic that the US Supreme Court, which appears to be Anti-US Republic, has decided to give any and all of these illegal invaders and trespassing aliens and their illegally born children (that in realty are colonizing invaders and not immigrants) the same rights as US citizens including automatic birthright citizenship for the new born children of these "foreign citizens," and no laws exist to allow them to take this action.

Well! I hate to say it again but these Supreme Court Justices are wrong! I can make this statement because in this part of my book I'm going to prove to the world and these Supreme Court Judges that their decisions (or interpretations) are wrong, dangerous, and illegal. Before I prove these judges wrong, I want to review a few facts that I found when I analyzed the Preamble by taking its only sentence apart to determine the functions of each word, phrase, and clauses. The interesting part of my analysis and research is that I was able to find so many answers to the questions these judges raised about the Constitution, and they were so easy to find and prove because the Constitution's writers made sure that whoever took the time to read the Preamble and Constitution carefully would find the answers with just a little bit of hard work. After I completed my simple analysis, I instantly found that they had used the plural form of the first person word "we" to establish the fact that the Constitution was being written for themselves and their constituents and not the world. They then added six terms to modify or tell us who the term or word "we" represented (that included a prepositional phrase) that helped them show the readers of the Preamble who the Constitution was written to protect and serve, which in realty is only America's legal citizens. After the drafters introduced the people they were addressing in the introduction of the US Constitution "We the people of the United States" they then added a list of infinitives that included phrases like "to form a more perfect union, (to) establish justice, and (to) insure domestic tranquility" to name a few of the infinitives they felt they needed to include to explain the reason they were creating this new Constitution for themselves and their constituents.

To continue my analysis, I next want to point out the infinitives I mention in the last paragraph were used to introduce promises or privileges the Drafters felt were needed to protect their new country's citizens from any foreign government or groups who might decide to stake a claim to these promises. These privileges and promises the Drafters were trying to establish for their fellow Americans were then attached to two possessive form pronouns that included these two words "ourselves" and "our" (as in "to ourselves and our posterity") so they could show to whom these promises or privileges belonged to in the Constitution. Since my fellow Americans now know the term or pronoun "We" represents "the People of the United States," or the persons being addressed/discussed in the thesis, I want to add that the words "People of the United States" were introduced by the American Constitution's Drafters to set precedence and provide antecedents to help define who the possessive pronouns "ourselves" and "our" represented in the Preamble and later in the body of the Constitution.

Now that I've proved the point I wanted to make in the last paragraph, I want to add a little more information about the list of infinitives found in the Preamble. I want to first say these infinitives are a list of what might be called "desired regulation codes" or "self preservation promises" that were meant to serve (or written to serve) "The people of the United States" or the legal members of the Republic and no other foreign country's citizens. And! Since the pronoun "we" represents or stands for the People of the United States, and no other country or its citizens, I want to say this fact means that when pronouns or common nouns, like the word "persons," are used later in the articles and Amendments of the Constitution (or the body) to re-state and reintroduce the main topic (thesis) of the Constitution we can pretty well conclude these pronouns or commons nouns are talking about "The People of the United States" and America's citizens, which are discussed in more detail in the body of the Constitution.

As I continue the review of my analysis of the Constitution's Preamble, I want to remind my fellow Americans that the drafters introduced the fact that they and their fellow Americans were to be the recipients of these "principles and self-preservation promises," and that these promises and principles were written so they could "secure the blessings of Liberty for themselves and their fellow Americans." After they introduced these promises they then add the predicate phrase "do ordain and establish" (transitive verbs phrase) to transfer the action of these verbs to the object of this sentence that in this case were the words "this Constitution." But! The Drafters of our Constitution knowingly then added a few more words, after the object of this sentence, to make sure the readers understood who these promises were set up to serve because they then added the prepositional phrases "for the United States of America" to make sure there was no doubt as to who America's Constitutional privileges, laws, and promises belonged to in the end. By the way, the phrase "for the United States of America was added to serve as the object complement to help identify or qualify the direct object of this sentence and to solidify who the Constitution served and who was being discussed in the Articles and Amendments.

To the eye opening information I've just introduced up to his point, I now want to add the fact that the drafters of our Constitution also had the for-sight to qualify, for any reader, that the most important part of America's Constitution was the fact that "the US Constitution" was only written to serve America's legal citizens **and themselves. And to these facts, I now want to add (and point out) that during my research I never found a place in the Constitution where it said that it was written for Mexico, the Citizens of the World, the children of the world's citizens, or for any of Mexico's children whether they were born in the US illegally or in their own country."** However, to show my readers that I am not racist or anti-immigration, I want to note that the Constitution can serve the World's Citizens if they are in America legally or are registered as Green Card Carrying foreigners because then these foreigners are considered either legal carded immigrants or naturalized citizens and therefore their children are considered legal US Citizens, if they are born on US soil. As my fellow Americans can see from the last statement I made, America's immigration laws do work and they are not outdated, if our politicians and Supreme Court Judges follow "all" of them and enforce all of them correctly. So! If America's officials, judges, politicians, or even some hired researchers are all willing to take the time to do their homework, I really believe they will find the same correct answers I found in America's Constitution and not some foreign definition or so called natural law.

Now that I've refreshed my readers' memories on how I was able to prove in Chapter 3 that the Constitution's laws, powers, and benefits were only written for America's citizens, I feel it's time for me to analyze one more crucial part of the Constitution that I feel is also being misread and misinterpreted possible on purpose. So as we stated earlier, I now want to continue my analysis by applying the same literary analytical tools I used in my previous paragraphs (and Chapter 3) to the first sentence that is found in Section I one of the XIV Amendment. Before I begin, I want to remind my readers that this sentence reads or starts as follows: **"All persons born or naturalized in the United States and subject to the jurisdiction thereof, are citizens of the United States and of the State wherein they reside."** The first thing my fellow Americans need remember about this sentence is that the term or word "all" is **not** the subject of this sentence because in this case, as I proved earlier in this book, it's being used as an Article (examples: "the," "a," and "an" are articles.) to introduce the common noun "persons" (Please note that the word "person" is not a proper noun.) which in this sentence, as I'll soon prove, is serving as the **subject** of the sentence and **not the word "all, which I'll soon prove is a none word."** I also want to remind my readers that I think past and present Supreme Court Judges have been interpreting this sentence to read that the word "all" is the subject of this sentence for the past 100 plus years and this is why the say that all of the children born to illegal aliens on US soil are US citizens automatically.

I also want to remind my readers that although the word **"all"** holds the position of a pre-determiner in the sentence I introduced in the paragraph above the word "all" is **not** considered a determiner or pre-determiner in this sentence because English writing rules say it is a none word (don't worry I will soon clarify this statement.). The reason I point this fact out is because the word "all," as it is being used in this sentence, is not considered a "real expression or term" as explained or defined by the English grammar rules of writing and Noel-Burton Roberts' book on sentence analysis. My fellow Americans should also note English grammar rules say a "determiner" basically informs the reader as to the "definite or indefinite" **inferred** knowledge of the word that follows a word like "all" that in this case is part of a noun phrase. To clarify this statement, the noun phrase that comes after the word "all" provides the needed information about the quantity or proportions that are being spoken of in the sentence, and "NOT" the word "all." So, since I just proved the word "all" is not being used as the subject of this sentence or a counting word, I want to happily tell my fellow readers that this conclusion allows me to prove/show the word "all" is being used as a non-determiner in Section 1 of the XIV Amendment, which means it has no value or position of importance and therefore non of the illegal alien children born to illegal aliens on US soil are American Citizens. So, again, this fact I discovered in the end allows me to prove that all of the children being born to illegal (un documented or illegally processed) aliens on US soil are not US citizens in any way:

To explain my conclusion I arrived at in the past paragraph better, I am now going to show my readers an example that reads like Section 1 of the XIV Amendment that I feel helps me explain the conclusion my sources reach to explain this rule: **All trucks with big truck beds can carry heavy loads.** In this sample sentence my sources offered to explain how this rule works, the word "all" is being presented as a zero article (or none article) because the word "trucks" is a mass noun like the word "persons" is in Section I of the XIV Amendment (Note: This fact is very important to this rule.). If my readers understand what I just said, then they I hope they will understand why Noel Burton tells us to understand that "Only **mass nouns (like mud) and count nouns in plural form (like the words "tables" and "persons") are analyzed as being determined by the 'zero article' rule (Note This statement means that words like "all" that begin the sentence have no value in these types of sentences.). I can make this statement because Noel Burton provides a clear example that I feel helps me prove the word "trucks" in this sentence and the word "persons," that is found in the first sentence of Section 1 of the XIV Amendment, are both considered the true count nouns in these sentences because they begin the sentence and are therefore the subject of the sentence."** (Roberts, Noel-Burton, Analyzing Sentences: An Introduction to English Syntax. Longman Group Limited. London: 1989, Pp. 139.). Before I move on, I want to restate that Noel Burton Roberts' research proves that the word "all" in the first sentence of Section 1 of the XIV Amendment and the truck sentence holds the position of 'ZERO ARTICLE' in both of these sentences because the word "all" has "no literary purpose." Roberts singles (notes) out this fact by using the letter 'O' with a line slashed over the "O" (like the "Ghost Busters" decal with the line through the ghost) to symbolize or remind the reader that this symbol means the word 'all' is not really needed or important in this sentence because the word "all" holds a null position, or is a zero article" (Roberts, Noel-Burton, Analyzing Sentences: An Introduction to English Syntax. Longman Group Limited. London: 1989.).

I want to note that Roberts also makes the following comment about applying this rule to pronouns (as opposed to nouns): "As for pronouns such as [the words] "him," "her," or "they," it is predictable that [theses] pronouns should not accept determiners because determiners are just a constituent part of noun phrases" [an example would be the noun phrase "her baseball bat and persons born or naturalized in the United States"] (Roberts, Noel-Burton, Analyzing Sentences: An Introduction to English Syntax. Longman

Group Limited. London: 1989.). Before I stop this line of discussion, I want to add one final bit of information about words/terms like "all," "this," and "some." I note here that these words can all become or function as pronouns or determiners (as in "all the kings men"); however in the case the truck sentence and Section 1 of the XIV Amendment, the word "all" does "NOT" serve as counting determiner (or pronoun) in either of these sentences because (as I established in the paragraphs above) in these cases the word "all" serves or functions as a "Zero or Null Article" (or non-word because it can be removed and the sentence is NOT affected).

What does the information in the last long paragraph mean to America's legal citizens that want to stop the birth-right citizenship error that is being applied to the children of any and all visiting and illegal trespassers who are coming to America to have their children so they can evidently colonize and invade the United States of America by getting their foot in the door illegally with an alleged "chain baby?" I'm happy to say this information and all of the facts I have just provided mean this English Grammar rule (which **cannot** be changed by any Supreme Court Judge who might be deficient in English grammar rules or reading abilities) reduces the word "all" to a null term or voided none-word that means it is "**NOT**" the Subject of this sentence that is found in Section 1 of the XIV Amendment. This conclusion or fact means the word "all" has no counting function here (because it does not have any value or function), and because it has no function (other than being part of the noun phrase), the sentence begins at the subject word "persons. Since "persons" is a common noun or pronoun type word, we can assume the drafters (of the Constitution) defined the word "persons" by providing an antecedent earlier in their prose work to establish precedence and to establish the word "people" represent people introduced in the Preamble as "the people of the United States" in this sentence. Again, I want to note the needed precedence and antecedence that helps define or identify the common noun "persons," or tells us who the common noun "persons" represents, can be found in the phrase/words "**people of the United States**" which are found in the thesis statement of the Constitution's known as the Constitution's preamble.

To put it laymen's terms, the examples and facts found in the previous paragraphs of this section all prove that the sentence **"All persons born or naturalized in the United States and subject to the jurisdiction thereof..."** does not literally mean "**all persons or people of the world who happen to find themselves born on US soil!**" I can conclusively come to this conclusion because this sentence, as I proved in the past few paragraphs, really begins with the word or common noun "Persons." So when I rewrite this sentence and replace the common noun "persons" with the word or phrase this word represents in this sentence, my readers and I learn this sentence is really making this statement: **"People of the United States ("who are) born or naturalized in the United States and subject to the jurisdiction thereof . . . etc are citizens of America." So by using the definition for the word "persons" that is introduced in the Preamble, I and my fellow Americans now can see that an American citizen is the only person who is under the jurisdiction of America's laws because they were born to (or were already) a US citizen."**

I can come to this conclusion in my last paragraph because the English grammar rules I used say that when a pronoun or common noun is used to describe a person, place, or thing the writer must set precedence by providing an antecedent to define any vague or difficult word that might be used in a complicated or technical written work, as in the US Constitution. And, since I can remove the common noun "persons" from this sentence and replace it with the phrase "people of the United States," I think this example proves the English Grammar rules I've just introduced and applied to this sentence are correct and the Supreme Court Judges' interpretations have been "WRONG since 1898." One more thing, my readers should note that the sentence "People of the United States who are born or naturalized in the United States, and subject to the jurisdiction thereof, are citizens of the state wherein they reside," really only defines who a US Citizen is, and it is does not have any thing to do with "birthright citizenship, or how a person can or does become a US Citizen.

Now that I have proven how wrong America's Judges were to arrive at their ill conceived decisions, I think I can safely say the introduction or preamble of America's Constitution states the Constitution was written to serve "the People of the United States" and not Mexico's or any other countries' citizens who enter America illegally. And! If these judges had done their homework or done a little more research, they would more than likely have found the precedence or antecedence rules of writing state that to define any vague words in a work all the reader has to do is find the thesis statement of the essay or work, or find a previous phrase, sentence, or paragraph that contains the needed noun or word that defines the vague word in question. I guess my example of the common noun "persons," which I prove can be found in the thesis statement of America's Constitution, is a good example of how this and other rules work.

Before I move on, I want to remind my readers that the drafters of the Constitution were not only brave men whose country of origin was England, but they were also highly educated men who knew exactly what they were writing on that fateful day. I should note here that England didn't just use the English language in their era. But, they mastered the English language in their great universities and they used it as a tool in their homes and business dealings just like the drafters of the America's Constitution did to write their wonderful Constitution (because some of them were more than likely educated in England). I want to add that I feel these universities were just as great then as they are now because they are still considered the cream of the crop in the world. In fact, in the 21st Century, there are many scholars, including myself, who would kill for a chance to study at one of England's esteemed Universities.

I hope the facts and discoveries I have presented in this chapter have started the blood boiling of every flag waving American Patriot. And if my fellow Americans are as mad hell like I am, I hope they will soon be ready to hit the road for Washington D.C. and start to plan some big demonstrations in the coming months to end this charade. When these demonstrations begin (hopefully in the near future), I hope these demonstrations will happen in front of America's White House and Congress' meeting hall. If my fellow Americans decide to take a stand for their rights and the Sovereignty of America, I believe we Americans will be read to send a message to America's Politicians and our Supreme Court Judges that their little game of playing with words and letting Mexico and other foreign countries and religions colonize America is over and DONE. Having drawn a line in the sand, I now feel I have to tell ex-President Obama and his party, all of our Congressional representatives, President Trump's advisors, and America's Supreme Court Judges your day of atonement is coming so you better be ready to provide some answers to our questions because Americans are tired of your BS and twisted lies. I hope I speak for the majority of Americans because I now say we Americans want our God fearing, flag waving, law abiding, so-called old-school country back now. I say this because "old-school is the best school" when it comes to enforcing all of America's laws. We Americans do not want some "new world, anything goes America" that has America looking more and more like a third world, trashed, dirty, and decomposing nation."

Now that I have shown my fellow Americans that Section 1 of the XIV Amendment is nothing more than a definition that explains or introduces to the world who or what an American is in this document, I think the best way to prove this conclusion and my results is by re-writing these sentence by replacing the common noun "persons" (which is the subject of this sentence) with the phrase or the words "people of the United States" so I can prove the point I'm making. I also want my fellow Americans to note that I will be taking out the null article or non-word "all" too to show this word is not needed to complete the message the drafters of the Constitution were making in this sentence. After I rewrite this sentence and make the changes I said, the sentence I would look something like this one: **"People of the United States born or naturalized in the United States of America, and subject to the jurisdiction thereof, are citizens of the United States and of the state wherein they reside."** As my fellow Americans can see in this new sentence that is created by replacing the common noun "persons" with the phrase "People of the United States, this sentence simply defines or describes an American Citizen, but it does not provide citizenship in any way,

There you have it my fellow Americans, and I really don't know what else I can say to show that a terrible and damaging wrong has been done to America's citizens because of some American Supreme Court Judges' decision. The terrible wrong that has been done to Americans is the fact that they are being force to accept and allow "any" foreign child born to any illegal foreigner on US soil to become a US citizen. If our current Supreme Court Judges want me to make my results clearer, I can also rewrite this sentence to read the following way too: **"People of the United States 'who are' born or naturalized in the United States, and subject to the jurisdiction thereof, are citizens of the United States and of the state wherein they reside."** If I rewrite this sentence from Section 1 of the XIV Amendment this way, I think we can clearly see the drafters of the US Constitution did indeed provide the needed definition that stated whom they considered to be American citizens. In the end, I feel this second sentence I just wrote alone proves my research and conclusions are right and correct. I also think I have proven that America's Politicians, Supreme Court Judges, and Presidents have all been committing crimes against the Union, and just maybe (or more than likely) treason against the Republic.

Since I know I have proven completely, and without a doubt, that no child born on US soil to any illegal alien or foreigner vacationing in America gets automatic US Citizenship under Section 1 of the

XIV Amendment because this function doesn't exist in this sentence (like America's Judges and politicians would like to us to believe it does), I now want to present two sources that also came to the same conclusion that I did, which is "the fact that "Birthright Citizenship just does NOT exist in the US Constitution either in print or by insinuation." The first source I present comes from an article that was published on October 15, 2015 in <u>The Valley Voice</u> on page 13 in their "Viewpoint Section." The article titled "Birthright Citizenship: Not Actually in the Constitution" was written by AG Peterson. This article included the following facts and conclusions about "birthright citizenship:

"John Eastman is the Henry Salvatori Professor of Law and Community Service, and former Dean, at Chapman University's Fowler School of Law. He is also the founding director of the Claremont Institute's Center for Constitutional Jurisprudence. The question of whether birthright citizenship should be abolished is based on the faulty premise that our Constitution actually mandates it." After this awesome introduction that matched my analysis and results, Peterson then introduced the first sentence of Section 1 of the XIV Amendment (like I did) and the article then added that "Eastman said, 'The text has two requirements for citizenship—that an individual is subject to the jurisdiction of the United States when born (Note; If my readers will remember, I proved all foreigners, including their unborn children inside of them or born in the US by accident, are not under US jurisdiction, and that is why Mexico has 10 major Mexican consulates in California—to protect **their citizens..**). Subject to the jurisdiction means more than simply being present in the United States. When the 14th Amendment was being debated...Senator Lyman Trumbull...stated that 'Subject to the jurisdiction of the United States means **Not** owing allegiance to anybody else. The drafters of the clause modeled it off the 1866 Civil Rights Act which grants citizenship to 'all persons born in the United States and **not subject to any foreign power...**Some advocates for illegal immigrants point to the 1898 case of the United States V. Wong Kim Ark, **but** that case merely held that a child born on U.S. soil to **parents who were lawful, permanent (legally, domiciled) residents was a citizen...**The misunderstood policy of birthright citizenship provides a powerful magnate for people to violate our immigration laws and undermines the plenary power over naturalization that the Constitution explicitly gives to Congress." Again, this article was published October 15, 2015 in The Valley Voice on page 13 in their "Viewpoint Section."

The second source that agrees with my conclusion comes from an article that I found on a web page titled GOPUSA.COM. In this article written by Bryan Fischer (OneNewsNow.com) on July 9, 2014 and titled "Birthright Citizenship is Flatly Unconstitutional, Fisher says, "A **correct** reading of the Constitution indicates that such children born on our soil are specifically excluded from citizenship...A plain reading clearly indicates that birthright citizenship is granted only to those who are 'subject to the jurisdiction' of the United States when they are born on American soil. Illegal aliens and their children, by definition, are not subject to the jurisdiction of the U.S. That's why they can be deported. Their children are no more subject to the jurisdiction of the U.S. than their parents are, and as little entitled to citizenship. The 'jurisdiction' clause was added to the 14th Amendment only after a lengthy debate. According to Numbers USA, Senator Jacob Howard of Michigan proposed the amendment because he wanted to make it clear that the simple accident of birth on U.S. soil was **not enough to confer citizenship...**Senator Howard said the jurisdiction requirements is 'simply declaratory of what I regard as the law of the land already,' an apparent reference to the Civil Rights Act of 1866.... In his debate, Sen. Howard said, 'This will not, of course, include persons born in the United States who are foreigners or aliens who belong to the families of ambassadors of foreign ministers accredited to the Government of the United States...'" Fisher then adds, "The logic is inescapable. If the children of foreign diplomats, who are in this county legally, are not U.S. citizens by birth, how is possible that children of illegal aliens could be?" http://.www.gopusa.com/freshink/2014/07/09/birthright-citizenship-is.

After reading the two other sources who completely agree with my findings in a round about way from my results, which all prove illegal alien's U.S. born Children are not automatically American citizens, I think I have proven the results of my analysis are sound and correct. After all my results prove this sentence is nothing more than a definition for the word American Citizen, so anyone who reads this Constitution will know what an American Citizen is in this Constitution. And, since I have shown my fellow American Citizens the truth and proven completely that the words "all persons" only applies to America's citizens and their children, I pray that my fellow Americans are now ready to shout the following fact from "sea to shining to sea": "Section 1 of the XIV Amendment is only a definition that describes who or what are American Citizens and it was not written to serve "any" child or children born to illegal or undocumented parents that happen to find themselves living on US soil because the parents are not under the jurisdiction of the US Government and neither is the child. If this is the case, then why are America's government officials and judges allowing Mexico to ten major Mexican consulates in California and many more small ones at entry points into California (and growing)? And! Why does Mexico's Government say it "Needs" all of these consulates to protect "their" citizens that are living in America and California? And! I should note that this fact alone shows these people are "Not" under the jurisdiction of America's Government and neither are their illegally born children (whether they were born in America or in Mexico).

To tell the truth, the only way these illegal "persons" or people (that the Supreme Court Justices and US Politicians protect by applying America's Constitutional law found in Section 1 of the XIV Amendment in an illegal way) fall under the jurisdiction of America's laws is when these illegal aliens break America's criminal or immigration laws by entering America without legal permission. I can say this because when they break US law they then do fall under the criminal jurisdiction of America's criminal and immigration laws. Another way to look at these law breaking "illegal aliens" is to call them invaders. Because if we call them invaders, they then fall under the jurisdiction of "America's war time and criminal laws. And, if we do assign these "illegal aliens" the status of being invaders, our state's police officers and Federal immigration law officers will then be able to do their job and arrest and send these illegal aliens and their children back to their point of origin. The legal laws found in America's criminal and immigration laws pull no punches when it is applied to lawbreakers because together these laws label these law breaking "illegal aliens" as undesirables, and when they become undesirables, they lose their chance of ever being allowed to enter America legally and become US citizens. I hope my fellow Americans get the point I am trying to make here for the sake of America's future and her PTSD suffering legal Compatriots or citizens.

Chapter Five

Conclusion: The End of the Beginning or America's Second Revolution

> Beware of false prophets [(or leaders)], who come to you in sheep's clothing, but inwardly they are ravenous wolves. You will know them by their fruits. Do men gather grapes from thorn bushes or fig from thistles?
>
> Even so, every good tree bears good fruit, but a bad tree bears bad fruit. A good tree cannot bear bad fruit, nor can a bad tree bear good fruit. Every tree that does not bear good fruit is cut down and thrown into the fire.
>
> Therefore by their fruits you will know them.
>
> Matthew: 7: 15-20

When I was a child growing up in my once upon a time "All American City" (my "hometown") of McFarland, California, I dreamed of going out into the world making my mark and then someday going back home to my little hometown of 6,000 American Flag waving and patriotic inhabitants of this city. Unfortunately, during the time I was growing up into an adult, a funny and sad little (ironic funny) thing happened to my small All-American hometown that I could never have imagined would happen to it. When I returned to enjoy my hometown of McFarland,

I found it had died and disappeared. In reality, what had happened to my hometown and childhood dream of going home to retire was that it became a illegal Mexican gang infested city with a crime rate that was off the scale when it was compared to other American cities of the same size in other states. The other fact I found out about my once peaceful and safe city of yesterday was that it had been completely settled by a foreign force of illegal Mexican citizens who didn't speak English. I want to note here that I came to this conclusion because many of the people I knew had moved out of McFarland to a city named Bakersfield and my home town was now occupied by thousands of Mexico's citizens who had never bothered to apply for permission to either enter America legally or had never bothered to apply for any kind of legal visa or permission to enter America. The other strange fact I learned was that these alien Mexican citizens were enjoying taking over my hometown with what appeared to be the permission of the California's state government, America's Federal Government, America's politicians, and America's Supreme Court Judges.

After doing some research, I found that thanks to America's government officials I wasn't ever going to be able to go home and retire in my once quiet "All American" city that had once been the home of hundreds of retired American war vets who had helped raise me and had defended the world and America during World War II and the Korean conflict. These great men, who made me proud to be an American citizen, taught me that honesty, hard work, playing fair, and loving my American flag and country was the way all Americans thanked their country for allowing them to enjoy all the benefits of being an American citizen. I also want to note that these brave men were citizens like "Gene Frediani a World War II vet I read about from South Park, Pennsylvania who served in the South Pacific from 1941 to 1945 as a radio operator. I want to note I learned about this great man from Nancy Paterline who wrote about Mr. Frediani for a magazine titled "Country People" that was dated November 2011. Another brave American Veteran citizen who I knew about was my Boy Scout Master Chuck Torres who served in Korea during the Korean War in the 1950s. The sad part is that almost all of the citizens I had grown up respecting and knowing in my hometown had all left the city of McFarland and moved to a nearby city named Bakersfield, California.

I want point out one important fact that I put in the last paragraph that might confuse some of my readers. Although Gene Frediani is not from my hometown, I wanted to mention this great real hero from WWII to show that these heroes were the norm in many of America's small hometowns like my McFarland heroes. These heroes were real men that we kids from the past looked up to in our lives. To tell the truth, men like Gene Frediani were such special men that most of the kids in America usually grew up hoping to be like these men when we grew up. The kids of my era always hoped we could grow up to be at least half the man these men were in our eyes. Unfortunately the heroes of my era, when compared to the heroes of this era, have fallen by the wayside in the eyes of today's young people. I say this because most of today's young people usually choose some rich athlete, some rich movie star, some rich politician, or some "bling wearing" wanabe rapper/singer that uses computers to enhance his or her voice for their heroes. I really believe that the heroes of my era wouldn't have even gotten a look or hello from today's kids.

The sad part of having today's kids look up to people like today's athletes, today's so called singers, and today's American politicians is that just when America's citizens start to trust let's say a famous politician, America's kids and citizens here that this politician was recently caught getting away with "insider trading (which is against the law) in America's stock market. As for the rich rappers who talk about killing for fun, using women like toys, and shooting some poor hard working police officer for fun, I hate to say it but Americans never hear about any of these rich rappers giving back to the "ghetto" kids that buy their garbage rap and make them rich (That is not until I wrote and published this book back in 2015; because in 2018, my fellow Americans and I heard the news that some rapper had given money to people in his community. I hate to say it but these kinds of charity acts are rare and often are used for publicity instead of coming from the heart, because the rapper's PR people make sure the world hears about this gesture.). Unfortunately when these rappers or other famous people do give to a community, they usually expect or demand free publicity for their donation. I hate to remind these publicity seeking famous men and women but they need to remember what our Lord Jesus Christ said in the Bible about "the old lady who gave her last two cents that she owned, without publicity or fanfare, and the rich man who gave a lot of money and then he yelled and drew attention to himself. As, the Lord said, which one gave more, I ask you?

The sad part about today's kids is that too many young kids, or modern day youth, often choose a local young street gang member who might have stabbed an "old lady" to prove he deserved to be a gang member to be their hero. To make things worse, America's gang members (like the killer I just pointed out) are being allowed to get away with being home grown terrorists in America by America's politicians and the Government because they say they are just "lost and have no chance of finding jobs in America's ghettos." I hate to tell these politicians and other soft on crime promoters but in my opinion these gangs members are getting away with terrorizing America's communities and keeping America's citizens in fear just like the world's terrorists do all over the world. I mean these gang members are killing innocent people and children. Yet! Our American legal system refuses to label these murdering gang members as terrorists. These politicians often say it's NOT politically correct to label American gang members as terrorists.

Having pointed out the facts about what is happening to America's youth, I now have to ask my fellow Americans what is the difference between these so-called American gang members who shoot up American neighborhoods (and whose stray bullets often kill innocent little girls playing in their homes--happened in Fresno this past year.) and terrorist group members who blow up bombs and kill Americans like they did in Boston and in Paris, France? From what I learned during my research, I hate to say it but there is no difference between these home grown gang member/ terrorists and real world religious or political terrorists who attack America's citizens and other countries' citizens. Having pointed out these hard facts, all I can add to what I just wrote is America needs to wake up and stop this run towards a lawless nation that both of America's political parties and America's Judicial System evidently seem to be intent on championing and pushing America towards in the 21st Century.

After reading my discussion about gang members and how these gang Mexican gang members have take over my "All-American" town of McFarland, my readers might want to ask me the following question: "So what is your little "All American" hometown like in this day-and-age"? Well to tell the truth, my ex-hometown of McFarland is now what appears to be an occupied town that has at last count about a 90 percent population of undocumented alien Mexican colonizers who broke US Immigration laws to enter America. And from the news reports and information I receive from "old-timers" who still live in this city, my little hometown now has nightly shootings, over 79 Mexican gang affiliates in the city of about 7,000 (Sheriff's department officer gave me this number), looks like a city you might see in Mexico, and has graffiti all over the city (see photos in this book) from gang member tagging. I want to point out the graffiti can be found almost all over the city including McFarland's road signs and the buildings of businesses that have left town. I also want to point out that McFarland has as many murders as most cities three or four times bigger than McFarland. To tell the truth, in a recent news story, I heard that Kern County's (the county where McFarland is located) homicide rate is currently running over four times higher than its usual average (2015). In fact, the city of McFarland is so dangerous at night that one of these lawbreaking Mexican colonizers was found guilty of shooting a 25 year-old two-year veteran of the Kern County Sheriff's Department in the face in 2008. Since this story was all over TV news, I still remember the sad details of this story and the children and wife this brave officer left behind. Note: Since California does not have the death penalty for murder, this man could come up for parole in 2023, or some time sooner because he's been rehabilitated.

I feel I can honestly say the city of McFarland has changed so much that when several graduates old-time graduate classes of McFarland High got together and had a class reunion a few years ago they were so shocked at what their hometown had become that they made up a little joke to handle the shock of their old once All-American city. These graduates who once lived in this city in the 60s and 70s, when their hometown was a wonderful and safe All-American town, created the joke that their McFarland had burned down and been destroyed. They did this so they could lessen the pain of seeing their town turned into what now appeared to be a third world city in Mexico. Since it hurt to talk about what they saw when they all went there to look around, their joke that their hometown of "McFarland had burned down seemed even more appropriate when they looked around the city. Although the joke helped lesson the pain of not being able enjoy their old hometown, the fact that they could never go back home was just too much so many left early and decided to not attend their ex-high school's homecoming football game. As the alumni of this city talked, they all came to the conclusion that the city where they had created so many fond memories had been crushed by this country's "Open Border" supporters like ex-President Obama and the Hispanic Dreamer laden California legislature that has opened the door to California for all illegal aliens and thrown America's laws under the bus.

Before I stop talking about my ex home town of McFarland, I want to note that after my book came out back in 2015 the open border people were not too happy with my book because the Disney Corporation decided to teach me a lesson and show the world I was not telling the truth. To prove to America and the world I was a liar,

Disney decided to write and produce a movie that showcased the children of these illegal aliens in a movie called "McFarland USA." Although the premise of this movie was that it had been written to allegedly tell the story of Mr. White the cross country winning team coach of McFarland High School, in the end, the movie ended up looking more like a propaganda movie that was meant to push how the children of these illegal aliens had risen from their poverty to become state small high school champions in cross country running. The movie also pushed the idea of how these children of illegal parents had overcome the problems of living in alleged poverty (I guess they ignored all of the Social Services and free lunches and after school free programs.) in a new county and then becoming "hard working athletic students in America.

The problem with Disney's film was that a year later, and after the movie came out, the two young men that had been pushed as the stars of the movie (that had allegedly made something of themselves in their new country) were both arrested for abusing their powers as law officers, and they are now serving time in California's Federal prison system. In case my readers want to know why these two ex-runners from McFarland High are now in jail, I guess the best way to shed some light on this topic is to tell the story of what happened to these two young men after they became adults in their "new American home." According to the news stories I watched on television and read in newspapers, both of these star runners went into law enforcement in Kern County, California. One young man became a Kern County Sheriff Officer and the other was hired by the Bakersfield Police Department in Kern County too. To make a long story short, one of the Mexican officers was arrested for pulling over young women and forcing them (raping them) to have sex with him to avoid getting tickets or arrested—fortunately for Kern County some of these young ladies were brave enough to come forward and he was arrested and found guilty. The other Mexican officer was arrested for making drug deals with the local drug dealers in Kern County and pocketing his protection or hush money.

I guess my research proved to be more accurate than Disney's research because my conclusion proves that America is not getting "good, honest, hard working illegal aliens" (like it did it the past when those people took the time to enter America legally) as ex-President Obama kept saying in his news bites during his tenure as America's President. One more scary point I want to make here before I end my discussion of McFarland is that if a powerful business like the Disney Corporation will spend millions of dollars to prove my book is wrong or not telling the truth, Americans should be very scared because this fact means that some very powerful and rich people are behind this "open borders" fiasco and the no immigration or borders movement. Oh yes, one more fact I want add here is that Disney went so far as to build McFarland High School a "college level sports complex, football field, and track to make this high school appear to be an "all-American school and prove my point of view point of McFarland wrong. Oh yes, the cost to Disney to prove my book wrong? Well, according to my research, the additions to McFarland High School cost over three million dollars, and this price didn't even include the cost to make the movie, produce it, and advertise the movie.

Another sad fact I found interesting and scary was that California's mostly Hispanic/Mexican legislature (that are second generation products of California's sanctuary state system for illegal aliens) appears to be so pro-Mexico's invasion that most of the recent laws they have passed appear to pat these lawless invaders on the back and give them more power than America's legal citizens to change California to look more and more like Mexico. And to make things worse, instead of filing criminal charges and passing new laws to stop the flood of illegal aliens that are coming to American or sending these colonizing invaders back to Mexico, the California legislature recently decided to pass a law that allows these invaders to get California, legal driver's licenses and even vote illegally in all of America's elections without any repercussions (if I have time during my updating of my book, I will add how this law works). So to repeat myself, this new law that the Hispanic California legislature just passed pulls no punches to the fact that it is meant to be pro-Mexico's illegal alien invaders of America and California because it was written to carefully ignore Federal Laws and make these illegal aliens eligible to vote in both local and national elections (which is against the law) without being held accountable. So why can't these illegal aliens, who might vote illegally, not be prosecuted? Well, if these illegal aliens are caught or "accidentally" happen to vote in America illegally. I should note that when this law was passed in 2013, the legislature included an escape clause that holds these illegal aliens blameless because California's Government takes the blame for the illegal voting by in a "mia culpa" manner. Before I move on, I want to point out again that this law gives Mexico' invading illegal colonizing citizens American driver's licenses and helps them register to vote, even though these people have broken Constitutional law, criminal law, and US immigration laws to enter American sovereign soil.

If my readers think that McFarland is the only American city that is coming to this kind of ugly end in California, they are wrong. Since I live California and I am watching first hand the end of many of these once All-American cities, I can honestly say that many cities in California are getting so dangerous that America's legal citizens are leaving California at the rate of "2-to-1." This fact was recently reported by one of the many newspapers in Central California in my new hometown. To clarify what I am reporting here, the articles I read in two of my local newspapers said that for every two new lawless Mexican illegal invaders who enter California, one US citizens decides to leave California and never return. In real numbers, this means let's say "for every 2,000 Mexican or other foreigners who enter California, some 1,000 US American legal citizens are making the decision to leave California forever." I want to add one more key point here that I read in these newspapers which said the US citizens that are leaving California are leaving California to either live in other American states or move to other countries (Note: I have my own plans to move to Japan if things don't change in the near future.). In fact, most cities in Southern California and Central California (known as the San Joaquin Valley) are running anywhere from 75 to 95 percent illegal Mexican alien invaders and these numbers are growing as I rewrite and edit this book in 2019.

So how bad are these dangerous, violent, and costly "illegal immigrants" (as our Democrat controlled state legislature and ex-President Obama like to call them) to America's infrastructure and her Americana culture? I guess the best way to show how bad these people are to America is by describing the negative impact this "illegal aliens" are having on California's cities. The first example of the negative effects these open border people are having on America is one that I witnessed first hand when I decided to visit one of my "old haunts" known as "Van Nuys Blvd that is found in the San Fernando Valley in Southern California near Los Angeles. On a lark, I decided to visit one of my once favorite haunts from my youth to enjoy some nostalgia from my past. Well to say the least, I was shocked to find one of my favorite areas now looked more like a third world, war zone, than a part of America.

The first thing I noticed about my once young man's happy cruise spot was that where once specialty stores, pizza stands, car lots, hamburger spots, and cruise nights were the norm from Friday night to late Sunday night there were now empty buildings, mounds of litter, dark abandoned streets, and many third-world-nation looking mom and pop shops with hand-painted wood store signs that were more than likely ignoring city ordinances of American building and sign esthetics. Before I move on, I want to note that this area was so special in the 60s and 70s that it was once considered the jewel of the San Fernando Valley for cruise nights. And! I want to add here that the "Royal GTO" car club of the 60s and 70s often made this street their weekend cruising center. The sad part of my visit is the fact that these ugly store fronts reminded me of the many new Muslim temples that are sprouting up in many American cities (like the one that can be seen from the 99 Freeway near Fresno, CA) that seem to tell Americans the "cultural genocide" of their Western Culture is close at hand. As for myself, or your author who was once an architect major, these buildings appear to be more of an eyesore than an addition to America's beautiful and esthetically simple once colorful Western skyline that was the norm in my youth (and the law, if I remember right).

Unfortunately for America and her citizens, I feel that America's Federal, state, and local community building code officers and engineers appear to be looking the other way when it comes to keeping America's skyline looking like America, like they did in the old days when protecting America's skyline and her Americana Culture was the norm. I should note that many home owners in America that own old homes for example from the turn of the century are often told that they can't touch their old registered National Treasure homes to make changes unless they get written permission from the building code officers that control the care and restoration of these "old National Treasure homes." If my readers will check the reason these homes are protected, I think they will find that the reason these civic leaders and code enforcers protect these historical sight homes is because they want to protect "these homes that are part of America's historical past and the natural beauty these homes provide to their neighborhood's skyline. Yet! These same civic leaders, who keep a tight rein on American owners all over America, now appear to not care if this new crop of alleged foreign refugees build gaudy and brightly painted buildings that are disfiguring America's skyline and sticking out like sore thumbs or warts on America's once Westernized and clean skyline. If Americans take the time to look at these buildings, they will first notice these buildings appear to have been built to evidently stand out and say we are here and we have conquered this nation. I make this statement because these buildings appear to have definitely been designed to be out of the local norm, and these buildings are not being designed to blend into any country that has a Westernized skyline or a Western like culture.

Although my opinion and twenty five cents won't buy any of my fellow Americans a can of beans, I am here to say that the next time my fellow Americans hear some news personality or some politician call these immigration lawbreaking Mexicans "illegal immigrants," or the alleged Muslim refugees America's new friends, they need to remember what is happening in the San Joaquin Valley, the San Fernando Valley, and my little hometown of McFarland. If my fellow Americans can't see what I am saying, I suggest they close their eyes and imagine what their hometown would like if it were a war zone instead of their safe American hometowns. After all, to call these illegal and violent colonizers (that one day decide to commit violent attacks like the Boston bombing or kill some poor lady to become a member of a Mexican street gang) "law abiding American immigrants," I think is nothing more than a big ugly political lie.

Why do I feel I can make this statement? I can say it because during my research I learned there is no such term as an "illegal immigrant." I came to this conclusion after I took the time to define this term correctly by using the English language dictionary. My readers should remember that I proved this point earlier in my book. And in case my readers forgot how the English dictionary defined these two words, I want to remind them that these two words put together mean or translate into the following meaning or definition: "a criminal immigrant." I also want to remind my readers the definition for illegal can also be defined as a "criminal" person. Now my fellow Americans should understand why I feel I can substitute the word "criminal" for the word "illegal." So in a way, when America's politicians and US judges allow these foreigners to break US Immigration and Constitutional laws, they basically condition these people to think that we Americans don't really obey or take our laws seriously so they can "ALL" be broken without repercussions. I want to remind my fellow Americans this idea is not a good one because of the old saying "spare the rod, spoil the child" conclusion.

Unfortunately for the "no immigration laws or open borders" groups that created the term "illegal immigrant," this term itself proves that all of these so called illegal immigrants don't have a legal leg to stand on (Constitutional or other wise) because according to America's Immigration, Constitutional, and criminal laws none of these illegal aliens can be given Amnesty or a route to US citizenship because of their law breaking actions. I can prove this fact because when these illegal aliens enter US soil by breaking the law they became "undesirable citizens" as written in America's immigration laws. The reason these illegal aliens became "undesirable citizens" is because they are considered "criminal immigrants" by their own acts and the definition found in the term that was given to them by their own supporters. Since these illegal aliens enter US soil as "criminal immigrants," America's immigration laws say they can never be accepted legally into America or given Amnesty or citizenship. So, I ask my fellow Americans why are America's Judges and Politicians tripping over each other trying to give these lawbreakers US Citizenship? And since they are really an invading and colonizing force, "criminal immigrants, and undesirables according to the Monroe Doctrine too, America's Judges and the US Government should really be repelling these "illegal aliens" by force. Since I've just proven beyond a shadow of doubt these illegal aliens are undesirables according to US Immigration Laws and Constitutional law, America's Law Enforcement Officers, America's citizens, and Americans who live in states like Arizona, California, and New Mexico do have the power to pass new laws to repel or push these invading colonizing illegal armies of illegal aliens back to the countries they call their roots by either law or force.

Now that my fellow Americans know why I can't go back to my hometown of McFarland to retire, which is one of the reasons I decided to write this book, I want to add a few other reasons that inspired me to write this book. As my fellow Americans can see and read in this book, I really didn't have much trouble finding shady American Government decisions or acts to inspire me to write this kind of book. I guess it also didn't help that one day, while I was driving down a street in my new hometown, I found myself looking at a huge Mexican flag flying over a house on the street I was on in Central California USA. I guess my fellow Americans can say that this sight was one of the first wake up calls (I have included several photos of some of these Mexican flags) for me. When I saw that huge Mexican flag flying over an American town like California, I felt like America had just been conquered by another nation and I knew something was wrong in my country and state of California. Since this huge Mexican flag (about 8 feet by 20 feet) was flying on this American street in my Sunshine state of California USA, I decided to start looking for other Mexican flags in my city and throughout my state when I drove around, and you guessed it: Mexican flags are now flying all over California.

I have to add that these flags are being flown from the city of Bakersfield (California) that is in the Southern part of the San Joaquin Valley to the city of Sacramento that is found way up in Northern California. What worries this Patriotic citizen is fact that these colonizing invaders are flying their Mexican flags day-in-and-day-out all over California and NOT the American flag that is providing them this new bountiful taxpayer financed life. From my point of view, I think these "illegal aliens" are telling us that they are here, they have taken over, and we can't do anything about it. Of course if my fellow Americans have read this far in my book, I think they know "now" that I have decided to prove these illegal aliens and their American Government treacherous supporters wrong. I think by now that my fellow American citizens know my book proves we have the power to send them all back home, and we have the power to stop their American Government treasonous supporters that support the illegal alien invasion of America. Finally I feel I have proven many of these US supporters have committed treason by allowing this foreign force to enter and occupy America, and Like Fredric Bastiat states in the quote I presented earlier in my book, I am telling my fellow Americans that America's politicians and America's Judges do NOT have the power to give away the powers written into the US Constitution that belong to America's citizens and their heirs.

Before I move on to complete this book, I want to tell my fellow Americans why I think the flying of Mexico's flag in our country by these illegal aliens is like telling us Americans they are here and we can't do anything about it. I came to this conclusion a few years ago while I was relaxing in my home. I start her because on this day a thick black smoke that smelled like burnt rubber came rushing into my home from outside through my cooling system. As I looked around for the smell of burning tires and loud road noises that were coming into my home, I found the noise was coming from just down my street. This noisy and dangerous sounding disturbance pushed me to walk outside and down my street to see what the problem was, or what the cause of all of the noise was on our once quiet American street. As I got closer to the smoke and noise, I saw a Grayish white truck doing donuts (circles) in the middle of the street while some adults and children were trying to avoid and walk around this truck on both sides of the road. When I approached the truck to see who was driving this dangerous way on our roads, I found a very drunk and non-English Speaking Mexican male sitting in the driver's seat that was almost passing out from drinking. I decided to tell him in my broken Spanish/English the fun was over because in America we had laws against this kind of dangerous acts on our city streets so he should stop before he killed one. I then pointed to the children that were trying to walk around his truck as he committed his reckless driving. I then added that I had called the California Highway Patrol so he had to wait for them to arrive because he was too drunk to drive.

After a short time of waiting, he told me he had to go, but by then I had managed get the keys out of the truck's ignition and soon the California Highway Patrol arrived and arrested him for drunk driving and impounded his truck. To make a long story short, the man was arrested and he was taken away. As they took him away, I reminded him that if this is the way he was going to behave in

America he should have stayed in Mexico where he could have more than likely gotten away with this kind of dangerous driving. His answer to me was a "million dollar answer": "I am here illegally and you can't stop me." He was wrong, as my fellow Americans can read in my book. Since this clown angered me so much with his remark, I decided to write this book to defend America's sovereign nation status that America's government and judges seem to be hell bent on destroying. As my fellow Americans can read in this book, I know we can force our government to do their job by forcing our politicians to take legal action and reminding them that they can be replaced if we find that our government has become corrupt and is committing treason against the Republic (note: The Republic is America's citizens) because the Declaration of Independence and the Constitution say we can take this action. Now that my fellow Americans know the truth, I hope they are ready to take action very soon so we can send all of these law breaking trespassing criminals back to their countries of origin.

I hate to say it but I know for a fact that this law breaking illegal aliens are the work of past Presidents like ex-President Obama, the Clintons, Pelosi, America's embroilment committing Judges, and all of the other "open borders" supporters who champion these lawbreaking aliens and keep telling them to keep breaking US Immigration laws because it's the new American way. The sad part of these insolent lawbreakers, like my reckless Mexican driver, is that they are just the tip of the iceberg of the growing lawlessness that is moving into California and America too. Now that my fellow Americans know why this legal and law abiding America citizen, like millions of other have done already, is planning to leave or move out of the state of California in the near future (if my book does not do its job), I hope my fellow Americans decide to fight for America instead of just suffering silently under the influence and mental anguish of PTSD that my research has taught me may be the reason some of our citizens are going out and shooting their own fellow Americans.

In case my fellow Americans don't understand why I just added this statement in my last sentence, I'm saying my research and studies in PTSD might have given me the reason we have so many mass shootings in America these days. And, this reason could be because Americans feel helpless as they see their country disappear before their eyes under the pressure of an open borders invasion that they can't seem to stop. And, I am also saying that some of the mass shooters that are committing these crimes evidently are being created by leaders like ex-President Obama and company and America's Judges who are championing the demise of America and her culture by pushing their anti-law attitude, pro-open border attitude, and allowing Mexico's citizens and government to colonize and steal our Constitutional rights and our country from the real owners of America's Constitution. As a news hound, I find the actions of leaders like past President Obama, Pelosi, and America's Judges dangerous and careless because their actions are turning America into a lawless society that looks at America's laws as guidelines instead of principles or laws that must be obeyed for the good of all of the Republic's members.

Since I wrote in this section that the reckless driving Mexican invader was just the tip of the ice-burg, I now want to clarify this statement by offering an example of pure disrespect these people have for America's laws. The act of disrespect for one of America's icons of American Patriotism happened during a Porterville Cinco de Mayo parade (Note: Cinco de Mayo celebrates a Mexican war victory, and sad to say no other minority race in America celebrates this kind of holiday in America.) that occurred a few years ago when many of the illegal Mexicans and a few Hispanics attending the parade decided to disrespect the American flag by hissing and booing as the America flag came by them on the parade route. The sad part of this act of disrespect for America's flag is that these kinds of acts of hate towards America's patriotic icons are becoming very common in the state of California. Although our local paper attempted to make light of this occurrence by only pointing out there had been complete silence during the passing of the American flag, the newspaper decided to not mention the other acts of disrespect the crowd had shown for "Old Glory." Our local paper did however take the time to mention that the same rude crowed of illegal aliens did cheer and whistle very loud when Mexico's flag passed by them. I want to note here that in retaliation to this display of hatred and disrespect for America's flag some American patriots decided to make a statement of their own by booing at the Mexican flag, which was of course was quickly drowned out by the mostly partisan Mexican crowd.

Since I don't want this book to be considered an angry anti-immigration or legal Mexican immigration (other legal immigrant) book, I want to note this book has nothing to do with anger and more to do with wanting to live in a Nation of laws like the one I grew up in when I was a young boy. I add this information because the next point I want to make in this final chapter is that I feel I've proven what is happening to America and her citizens is not any kind of legal or illegal immigration. I also want to urge my fellow American Compatriots that after they read this book they should start planning a 30 million American Citizens Patriot's march on Washington DC and the White House (to have some peaceful and loud demonstrations) to show these "open border" supporters that we mean business. This march and other marches that I hope will take place throughout America should be set up as soon as possible after this book comes out again. I want to add that unless America's citizens start to voice their contempt and anger America's current government officials and leaders will keep marching America towards a nation without borders and without Constitutional law. And, if these leaders get away these changes they will basically end American citizenship and America's Americana culture. In case my fellow American want to know who I think can set up these marches on Washington, I truly believe America's Tea Party can pick up the ball and start setting up these marches so Americans can show they are against a borderless nation. Why do I think the Tea Party and these marches will work great together? I think the Tea Party is great organization, and NO, I don't believe they are a white racist group because I'm one of their members, and I am a minority. I want to close this paragraph by saying that I believe America is at its best when everyone in America obeys and follows all of "America's laws" because no one is above the law, not even America's presidents, politicians, government employees, judges, law enforcement officers, or lawbreaking aliens.

I realize I have constantly pointed the finger at America's Supreme Court Judges in my book, so I guess it's time I clarified why I feel the Supreme Court and many of the lower court judges have not lived up to their responsibility. In fact, I know I can say these judges that serve on America's courts appear to keep breaking a very important Judicial Conduct rule that was written to make sure these judges based their judicial decisions on the written law and not their biased personal opinions. And, because I feel they've broken this rule that has the title of "Embroilment," I guess I can now disclose how these Supreme Court Judges and lower court judges are committing this wrong against the Republic. Note: Although the rule I'm going to quote comes from the California Judicial Conduct Handbook for judges, I am sure this rule applies to all of America's judges that appear to have been bought and paid for by those who politically handpick and appoint these left or right leaning judges for alleged life terms. But thanks to my research, I can now say that I have found an American law that says, "These judges can be removed from office by America's citizens" that are also known as the voting members of the Republic.

First, I want to point out that David Rothman says that judges who decide to influence their decisions with their own biases (which they are not supposed to do when ever they're hearing a case) can be found guilty of breaking a serious law that applies to America's Judges. Or as Rothman writes, "If one chooses the most common source of disciplinary trouble for trial [or Supreme Court] judges, it would be the danger of **embroilment.** For a variety of reasons, judges sometimes have difficulty maintaining the necessary professional distance between themselves...and the parties or the cause before them [because someone or something has already influenced their decision they will write in their decision]. Embroilment is the legal process by which a judge surrenders the role of impartial fact finder/decision maker and joins the fray. This act can manifest itself in (or by)...attempting to see to it that a certain result prevails out of a misguided perception of the judicial role ...or [a] simple loss of self control...We need not be reminded of the fragility of the rule of law when public confidence is shaken, nor of the degree to which public confidence in public institutions has deteriorated" (Rothman, David M. California Judicial Conduct Handbook. West Group. California: 2nd Ed. 1999.). I should note that since I have proven in other parts of this book how easy it would have been for America's Supreme Court Judges to hire someone to help them make the correct interpretations of the key Sections they completely misread or misinterpreted possibly on purpose, I feel that making the case of embroilment against America's current judges (both Supreme and lower courts) is not a farfetched accusation that can be proven to both taint and nullify these American Judges past and present decisions that are destroying America and her citizens' rights and privileges.

The reason I'm introducing the judicial rule of Embroilment at the end of this book is because I feel my research has proven America's Supreme Court Judges erred and made too many dangerous mistakes in the past and present that have hurt America and her citizens rights. After all, If we think back, I noted these judges created their own definition to state who they felt was an American citizen that I proved was an incorrect and misguided decision. And, I also proved these judges are now guilty of erring and making more bad mistakes in the 21st Century because they keep telling America's Compatriots that Section 1 of the XIV Amendment says "any and all" children born on US soil regardless of their parents' citizenship are US citizens, which I again proved in this book is "wrong because this Amendment is really just a definition of who or what an America is according to the US Constitution."

As for today's Supreme Court Judges, I feel they erred and made a huge mistakes, as established by the law code of embroilment, when they allowed ex-President Obama to hide his personal college records, grammar school records, and his place of birth records when he was elected America's President without allowing the public to have Congressional public hearings to hear the reason ex-President Obama should have this honor. I point this fact out because ex-President Obama was not crowned the King of America or the Dictator of America, so I guess we can say he is not above the law; however, he was elected as the leader of one of the most powerful free nations in the world that is known as the Republic by his peers or fellow American Citizens. And, this fact alone, I feel, tells us that his personal records became pubic domain when millions of America's citizens, who represent the Republic in the American Constitution (so they have the real power) decided they wanted to see his records. Since past President Obama became the leader of America, he should have known that his person life would become public domain, and if the people who voted for him wanted to know more about him, he should have known it was their right to demand to "know" who this man they voted into office was without any kind of suppression of his life history, his school years, and/or his college records. And since ex-President Obama is not the President of America now, America's citizens should now be allowed to see these records even if President Obama objects to this disclosure.

As I get to the end of my book, I want to add that I feel ex-President Obama should have been forced to prove who the heck he really is by being forced to show his past school and life records to America's Citizens that are known as the members of the Republic. Heck, if he had allowed Americans like myself to see his personal records that allegedly show he is a natural born Citizen, attended all the schools and colleges he says he attended, and that he indeed graduated from one of these colleges, I feel all of this talk of him not being a US Citizen would go away completely. So before another day goes by, I think it is time Obama's public life records and school records need to be made available to the American public. If the Supreme Court takes this action, ex-President Obama would finally be able to dispel any standing doubts or fears that America's government was breached or corrupted when he was elected America's President. After all, since a lot of America's citizens have raised many questions about Mr. Obama, doesn't it seem right that America's Supreme Court Judges should order ex-President Obama to provide access to all of his life records (not wealth records) so the public can peruse them? To close this discussion, I want to add that I really believe this act would not only clear up a lot of Obama's questions about his past, but it will also make many American citizens breath easier and feel comfortable with this man that was once America's President.

After all, wasn't ex-President Obama "elected" commander and chief of one of the most powerful and expensive militaries in the world? So because of this fact, I truly believe that forcing Mr. Obama to release "all" of his records is the correct way to proceed because of the way Article 2 Section 1 was written. I also believe it's right thing to do because his position controlled all of America's Government, and because this action would dispel any doubt about the veracity of this man that sat in the office of America's President. Having read my argument for the release of ex-President Obama's life records, I hope my fellow Americans now see why I say this is where the Supreme Court Judges erred, and why I feel they are more than likely are guilty of the charge of "Embroilment" for allowing this man to hide his past from his constituents. Now that my fellow Americans understand why I feel the Supreme Court should force President Obama to open up his life records, I want to add that I feel they committed the offense of Embroilment because they let their emotions taint their decision and because they felt they were doing the right thing by protecting the sanctity of the office and protecting America from being made a joke in the eyes of the world; but! As my readers can see from my argument, I feel they were (and are) wrong to keep these records closed to this day, and they are still wrong to stick to this decision.

To close my discussion of America's judges and ex-President Obama, I want to remind these Supreme Court Judges that when President Obama decided to become the President of the United States, or a famous public figure, he knew the price of fame and glory and that his life would become public record the moment he took office. I know I can come to this conclusion because I truly feel this country's voting constituents must always feel comfortable with any person who they elect into a political office that will affect their lives. And, although America survived ex-President Obama's presidency, like many other Americans, I still do not feel comfortable with this man's past because I still feel I don't know who this man Obama really is to my satisfaction. As a minority (with colored skin) male that has earned three Bachelor degrees, and a Masters (who considers himself a man of letters), I want to tell our weak reading (my opinion as an English Professor) Supreme Court Judges that I don't feel comfortable with their decision. As for his online birth certificate, I could care less if it's real or a fake, I want access to his private life records as both a member of the Republic (who has power over the government) and as an honored member of a group of reporters known as "Muckrakers." As a protector of the people of the Republic (or the man and woman on the street), I will not rest till I disclose this elected official's records to the masses for inspection.

Since I have found so many issues where I feel our Supreme Court Judges and politicians have erred in their interpretations of important documents like sections of the US Constitution and ex-President Obama's records, I feel that from this day forward all future Supreme Court Judge appointees and future political candidates should be asked to take a test like the GRE English Exam so they can prove that they have the ability to read and interpret old documents and laws that might be needed to do their job. I also believe that after they take the GRE English Exam they will need to get a passing score or higher. If these appointees and candidates pass the GRE Exam, I believe America's citizens will be more comfortable with these judges and politicians because they will have proven to America's citizens that they will understand what they're reading, writing, and voting on when they pass laws or reject new laws that might come before them during their time of service to America. In case my fellow American want to know why I think my request for this test is important, I think that any time a person is either appointed to a position or is elected to a government position these Americans need to know they are getting the best person for the job. I say this because any decision that these people make will affect millions of Americans and their country.

In the end, I think the GRE test is a good and important idea because many of America's old legal documents and past and current laws are not written in black and white legal jargon like today's legal codebooks that tells us what is legal and allowed in America, and what is not legal and not allowed in America under some old laws or new law codes. After all, we Americans know that most codebooks of American laws can usually be figured out by most intelligent Americans and even young adults, and these young adults can usually decide what is right or wrong when a law is broken. This fact about young adults should now help my fellow Americans see and understand why in some states a few 18 year olds have been elected to serve as local judges. Unfortunately for Americans, old documents have essays that require (as a famous justice that passed away in the last year of so said) analysis, textual criticism, and historical criticism applied to them so the reader can understand what the drafters were saying in the document or law that might have been written in the 18th Century. And, since these old legal documents are not written as law codes, my readers should now see and understand why I feel the GRE English Exam test is a good idea and needed to insure that any appointed judge or elected politician will be able to do his or her job and interpret these old documents and laws (or our new codebook laws better).

As I look back at the paragraphs I've written and the problems I've written about or covered in this book, I find myself noticing a trend in the problems I've written about in this book. The trend I noticed is that almost all of the problems I wrote about or discussed all fall under the area of poor ethics or a lack of ethics that seem to be the new way of life in America from the top to the bottom ("Ethics" and "class" are two things I feel America does not have anymore from its leaders down to the kids playing in our school yards.). Having noticed this lack of ethics trend that is growing in America, I decided that my readers and I needed to have a discussion on ethics as they apply to my book. I should note that I decided to add this discussion because the study of ethics often covers ideals like doing the right thing, following and obeying laws (American laws in our case), not asking others to give up their rights to get yours, or forcing your rights or religion on the majority because the courts and government feel a certain group is more important than the majority because of some so-called oppression that once existed in this group's country.

Since I've covered these kinds of topics throughout my book, I feel I need to look at the field of ethics to find out why America's government doesn't seem to value high moral standards or America's laws anymore. I also want to know why our Judges and politicians don't seem to want to enforce America's laws, and/or don't seem to value truth, justice, and the American way of life, which were once standards that Americans loved and were willing to die for in wars. Now, I want to ask my fellow Americans to think about what I just said, and I want to ask them this question: Doesn't it seem strange that America's new ideology of political correctness seem to say that America's government is anti law, pro ignoring laws, pro appeasing fringe lawbreaking groups, and pro putting the needs of fringe groups above America's Compatriots or legal citizens' needs? And finally, I want to say that I feel America's government appears to now be in the business of trying to use any means they can find to destroy the fabric of Americana culture, which is what made this country great and helped win World War II.

To begin my discussion on ethics, I feel I need to remind my readers that the field of ethics says when any group (or person) demands their rights for things like "free speech, livable wages, to marry members of the same sex, get free medical treatment, be allowed to break American laws, demand incomes without having to work, demand their country's religion and Constitution override America's Constitution, and demand their right to invade and colonize America and ignore American immigration laws and sovereignty, the law of ethics says these people can not force the majority to accept the demands of these minor groups at the expense of the rights of the majority. Having introduced this long list of wrongs that are currently trumping American's rights, I now want to advise America's Supreme Court Justices, America's politicians, and all political groups that think political correctness trumps the law or rules of ethics and American's Constitutional rights that they are wrong according to the rules of known ethics. The other bad news for these judges is that these small fringe groups who are staking a claim to the "200-year-old-rights and privileges" that belong to America's members of the Republic is that they again do NOT have the right to stake a claim to these American Citizens' rights. (Mabbott, J. D., An Introduction To Ethics. Anchor Books. Garden City, New York: Anchor Books Ed. 1969, pp. 41.).

And in case these groups and American Judges have forgotten, America's Citizens are the ones who created the successful Americana fabric and culture that is the envy of the world, and the reason these foreign groups of illegal world citizens are swarming into America so they allegedly can enjoy (and it seems to me, at the same time destroy America's culture) the Americana culture they envy. The sad part of these American Culture conquerors' quest is that it's stupid and wrong because when they destroy the Americana culture they will have destroyed the great Western Christian Culture that has always been the envy of the world and that saved the world during World War II (according to history books)! I also want my fellow Americans to remember that many America's Compatriots (legal citizens) feel they have the right to call themselves American Christian Baptized Patriots because their fathers, brothers, sisters, and mothers died and fought for this right over the past 200 plus years in two World Wars and many other foreign conflicts. To say it simply, according to the law of ethics, "when anyone demands their rights in America, they are basically telling America's proud and historically proven winning society and culture to step off the sidewalk and let a new way of life destroy the culture they have earned with their blood, sweat, and tears. To add more salt to the wound these American Judges have opened up, I feel the demands of these new illegal and so called refugee fringe groups are not valid because they have NOT paid the price for the rights they are demanding, or the freedom that they want America's citizens and Republic to give up, so they can make America look more like their homelands or points of origin. Do you hear me Supreme Court Justices and Open Borders politicians? I hate to break this bad news to you ego maniac American leaders but during my research I found your actions to basically be spelling or ushering in the "cultural genocide" of America's culture and nation.

Unfortunately for all these American leaders, illegal invaders (they are not immigrants as proven), and alleged refugee new comers to America, I believe they have all forgotten a very important part of the law ethics that I feel is the backbone of America's Constitution because I want to remind these groups that the laws of ethics says "with demands for rights come big some big responsibilities and a lot of reverse respect that must be (earned) acknowledged and then reciprocated back to the majority group." These laws of ethics and facts are correct because the world of ethics says that "when you make demands of others, you imply that you are willing to accept the hidden or unseen duties that include respecting others' [(or the majority's)] morality, accepting compromise, and obeying and accepting the laws of this majority," so you can enjoy the benefits and security that America's Constitutionally controlled Nation offers that are really not free because they have to be earned. (Mabbott, J. D., An Introduction To Ethics. Anchor Books. Garden City, New York: Anchor Books Ed. 1969, pp. 41.).

The aforementioned facts of ethics that offer safety and comfort, I believe, are the reasons that many of these foreign groups keep flocking to America. Unfortunately, the moment these groups arrive on US soil they appear to want to change and destroy the very fabric that made them want to come to America in the first place. Because these groups make this demand, I want to point out some very important facts that come from the rules of ethics. I want to point out these facts because unlike America's Supreme Court Judges who I feel tend to make "wishy-washy and embroilment" laced decisions to appease any and all new foreign groups who arrive on US soil legally or by breaking the law I tend to make my decisions based on facts and by reading and studying opinions that I find in historical books, law books that I then use to find some real concrete and fair answers. The sad part of the facts on ethics I presented so far is that America's Judges don't appear to take into consideration that their decisions should always consider the "principle of reciprocation" when they write their briefs or interpret laws correctly or incorrectly that lately have shown to weaken the earned rights and privileges these American citizens wrote for their own protection. So in the end, their decisions end up giving these new fringe groups rights that are now diminishing the accomplishments of America's citizens and the rights they fought for and earned through huge sacrifices.

To continue my discussion on ethics, I want to add that my research tells me that any demand for new rights by some foreign illegal fringe or refugee group always comes with a reverse or obverse set of reciprocal rules or demands that must be met and accepted by the new foreign group if they want to become a part of the American society or culture they have decided to infringe upon by legal and or lawless means. And, I also want to add that with these new set of requirements and duties that must be met, accepted, and paid for by respecting the host country's or host culture's new rules comes the gift of protection and the new home they seek. I say this to remind America's Judges that when they allow new foreign fringe groups to break or bend American laws or write new rights that allegedly protect these new illegal or refugee fringe groups they are taking away rights that were bought and paid with big historical sacrifices by America's citizens that are part of their Constitutional rights and privileges. In short, America's Judges are not only betraying America's citizens with their actions, but they are also taking away rights and destroying the American fabric of Americana culture with their pens every time they attempt to be politically correct and decide to allow some new foreign group the special privilege to break and ignore US laws, Constitutional laws, and criminal laws in the new politically correct Godless and lawless America of the 21st Century. (Mabbott, J. D., An Introduction To Ethics. Anchor Books. Garden City, New York: Anchor Books Ed. 1969, pp. 42.).

To prove the point I just made and introduced in the previous paragraphs, I want my fellow Americans to allow me to show them an important quote from a book on ethics that I used to study ethics in my ethics class. I use this book because I feel it has a very important lesson that I feel our American leaders need to learn because it discusses duties, demands, and rights of citizens that decide to "enter into a deal or accept any kind of contract that has to do with life on this world." So what does this book say about duties, demands, and rights of persons who enter into a business or life contract, like for example entering a new country and asking for permission to be part of this new country and its culture? This books says that "when a person decides to enter into a deal, like entering a foreign country to become a part of this country's culture and way of life (because this country is more successful and offers a better way of life than these people's original country of origin), this person accepts the fact that he or she is accepting the principles, laws, and traditions of the new country. And, although no actual paper contract is signed, the person that 'demands illegal' permission to enter and become part of this new country is in reality entering into an understood legal contract that says he or she is willing to live by the new country's laws, culture, and the country's social and moral standards, so when they are caught, they have to leave this country and return and apply to earn these rights correctly. This person also says he or she is willing to obey and accept both the cultural and legal laws of the new country and will not demand rights that he or she has not earned yet" (Mabbott, J. D., An Introduction To Ethics. Anchor Books. Garden City, New York: Anchor Books Ed. 1969, pp. 41.).

Now that my fellow Americans have allowed me to present some rules of ethics that I felt needed to be included in this book, I feel I need to show my fellow Americans what J.D. Mabbott says about the deals and contracts of life: "A man has a duty to pay his debts even if he regards the system, whose rules he sees, as inferior in its consequences to other possible systems [that are allegedly better], such as barter or loans [made] only on security. Hence the rightness of his payment cannot be derived from the superior good produced by the system, [(he decided to chose or accept the system without pressure)] . . . [Which means] the man himself accepted the system [or the new country's laws, culture, and constitution when he entered the new country], or when he incurred the debt, [so he has to pay the debt, and accept or obey the laws of this country that says he can not enter America illegally so he has to return to his country and apply the legal way of this country]." Mabbot also states that "a parallel case is that of a judge who enforces a law whose general results he deems to be bad, and because of the good done by the enforcement of the law in general, and because he accepted this set-up when he took up his appointment. [He has to enforce the law whether he likes it or not]. If he [or she] doesn't like the job, he [or she] can resign [his judgeship]" (Mabbott, J. D., An Introduction To Ethics. Anchor Books. Garden City, New York: Anchor Books Ed. 1969, pp. 41.).

As I come to the conclusion of my book, I find it sad to say that from what I see (or in my opinion) America's politicians, government, President, Supreme Court Judges, Corporations, and America's Big Coop Farm Operations and their Farm Bureaus (like the Tulare County Farm Bureau) all appear to enjoy rewarding

America's new lawless and law breaking new comers for breaking any or all of America's Constitutional, criminal, and immigration laws. So! I feel I have the right to say that America's businesses and leaders are all committing treason because these so called civic leaders are rewarding these law breakers by demanding that America's politicians, President, and Supreme Court Judges reward them with low income housing; free breakfast, lunch, and afternoon snacks and after school day care for the children of these law breakers; free EBT Debit Bank Cards that are taxpayer paid credit type cash or bank cards, and other rewards that include AFDC cash aid, medical cards, food stamps that provide fast food and entertainment options; and the right to avoid prosecution after breaking America's criminal and immigration laws. (Note: I want to add California's very left leaning state legislature and Governor have created two more cash entitlements and they are issuing driver's license to these lawless colonizing invaders that include the right to vote in all US elections without the fear of Federal prosecution because the state of California takes the blame if these illegal aliens are caught voting illegally.)

The facts I introduce in this last part of my book make me angry and sad because I feel our leaders are teaching Americans that hard work is a four-letter word that should be avoided and that obeying laws are a thing of the past because they are more like guidelines. As a child and young man growing up in America in the alleged "old-school" era, my parents and country taught me to respect my elders, obey those in authority, obey all of America's laws, obey the Boy Scout's laws I learned as a member of the Boy Scouts and Senior Patrol Leader, respect my teachers, respect my parents, and honor "Old Glory and serve my country if called upon to do my duty. Yet! These days the message the children of this new era are getting is completely different. The new message I hear from today's America appears to want to (especially from TV) break down the morals and culture of America. And to prove this statement, I want to point out an example that comes from television where commercials are teaching children that they are smarter than adults so don't have to respect them and not want to be like them because they are losers with pathetic 8 to 5 jobs. In rebuttal to this tasteless commercial, I want to note here that my parents taught me that good honest hard work never hurt anyone, even if it included working in the fields chopping cotton, thinning cotton, picking cotton, picking potatoes, picking watermelons, or picking grapes. I also want to add that in my era (when I was a young adult working in the fields for school money) the field crews often include White college kids, Black kids, Hispanic kids, Native American kids, and whole families. But thanks to unions like the United Farmer Worker's Union, the life or times I just mentioned can never happen again because farm worker unions control who works and who does not work in the fields.

Although my generation grew up respecting our elders and saying yes Sir, and yes mam, to older adults, today's youth are basically told by America's government officials, school officials, television commercials, singers and nasty word poetry rappers (who are not musicians or singers says this guitar playing musician), and America's new modern culture to ignore their elders because they are smarter than their parents and all adults. These members of today's modern culture teach today's children that unless you're rich and drive a Lexus you are no-body and a loser. I guess working for a living and supporting yourself is wrong in the eyes of today's politically correct American culture and we should all strive to be rich or on some kind of American Government entitlement program that supports us so we can all be equal in the eyes of what appears to be America's new Socialist Democrat controlled Government. I hate to disappointment our current leaders and big business but this way of life and message is unacceptable and proves my theory that America has lost the standards it once had, and it has also lost the special gift we called "Class" in my youth and era.

To show how strong this movement or culture of "living large" is in America, I hate to say it but I was starting to buy into this new American way of life without even knowing it. As to when I learned that I was starting to buy into the new American culture, I learned this lesson when I took a job overseas in Japan. Believe it or not, from the moment I arrived in Japan and started my new job in a beautiful Japanese University, I noticed that these people "all" gave one hundred percent when they were working on their jobs or attending a class in school. This attitude of working hard and giving it your best shot day-in-day-out didn't just apply to the Japanese people working in white collar jobs, and I want to note that I noticed this fact right away because I noticed that even the people working in blue collar jobs, hourly wage service jobs, and even simple entry level jobs all gave it their best shot day in and day out. I can honestly say I was impressed and found myself wanting to be like them when I was working on my job as a teacher at a private university.

In the end, I found myself retrained as an employee by these people, and the funny thing about my attitude change is that these people never knew what they had done for me. As I worked my job in Japan, I was reminded of my youth when my parents and America's culture also operated in this manner. I also found the Japanese people had reminded me of a valuable lesson I had learned during my younger days in the "good old days of America." So what was the lesson I had forgotten? I was reminded that any job, or good honest work, is good for you and your soul because it makes you a better person when you do it to the best of your ability for the good of all. As I worked alongside these hard working and honest people who always gave more than they got, I found myself working for the good of my students, my employer, my fellow workers, and the Japanese people but not for me. Finally, after I completed my contract, I found that I had learned how lost I had become as an American employee or worker because America turns its workers into "me oriented" employees, or "what's in it for me" employees. That is to say, I truly believe that I shed my poor work ethics I had picked up in America and I became a better person and worker by working in Japan.

Since I've shared the revelation I came to while working in Japan, I want to tell my fellow Americans that I feel Americans have lost the "class," or that special something we once had that made us a great nation. And unfortunately for America, the people of Japan now have the "class" that we Americans once had that made us the envy of the world. Since I feel our country needs to correct or rewrite America's work ethics, its good citizen ethics, and correct the message that striving to live a life of laziness, slacking of, living on social entitlement programs, and striving to be the star of your own reality show is the good life in America, I hope the message in this book will get the ball rolling and help America turn the corner so we can start going in a direction that will restore "American class and better life and work ethics." In case my readers have forgotten the "class" we once had, I remind them that "American class" included standards like "a hard day's pay for a hard day's work," "honesty is the best policy," and "your word of honor" is your "bond and the best policy." As your author, I really hope this book will be a catalyst to get the ball rolling in the right direction. And since the best place to start a project of this kind is in our own backyards, I have spent the past six years of my life writing and re-writing this book to hopefully restore and relearn the lessons of being a good and honest hard working citizen for the good of all Americans.

Now that I have committed myself to being a better American, I also have decided to do as President Lincoln told us to do in one of his speeches and start obeying all of America's laws and "swear by the blood of America's revolution that I will not stop till this country returns to being a country of honorable law abiding citizens and not allow anybody or person to break any American law." Don't worry my fellow Americans, I am not naïve enough to think America is gong to follow me and change over night because I know we have a big problem in America. I make this statement because America's Political and civic leaders in this day and age think nothing of ignoring and/or breaking immigration, criminal, and Constitutional laws to be politically correct or to appease the millions of foreign illegal groups that are rushing to our US borders. Finally, I want to add that I find it sad that America's illegal colonizers and too many US citizens are still being allowed to make welfare a way of life with the blessing of America's politicians. If you don't believe me, I can honestly say that a recent newspaper story said that in the State of California over 80 percent of the illegal aliens that live in California are "on some form of Welfare cash or food stamp aid program." The sad part of this story is that these "open borders" politicians continue to allow these illegal aliens to call good honest fieldwork "lowly jobs that nobody wants to do in America." I remind these politicians that in my era the young men and young ladies of my era worked in the fields every summer and on weekends to pay for their school clothes, their school dances, and to buy the cars we called "hot rods." And less I forget, the Japanese taught me that "all" jobs are respectful jobs because it's honest work that supports our families.

To prove my point that good honest fieldwork is "not bad or unwanted work," I'm proud to say that I will now prove that any kind of work is good work and "not" lowly unwanted work. And as I said earlier in my book, I grew up working (I was chopping, thinning, and picking cotton (and potatoes) by the age of 13 because this was the age that I was allowed to get a work permit in the 60s.) in the fields to pay for my school clothes and to pay for many of the school events and expenses that my single mother could not pay for during the school year. So my message to the political leaders and the field labor unions that currently control, support, and champion "open illegal borders" is this one, "Please stop saying that fieldwork and entry-level jobs are jobs that "no one wants" because you are wrong! From my experience, I think the real reason Americans don't want to do this work is because for millions of Americans know the pay is now too low and for others it's easier to be on welfare and not work. I also want to note that Mexico's scab workers that keep coming into America illegally by the millions are also keeping the wages of these jobs lower than they used to be in the 50s, 60s, and part of the early 70s because they will work these jobs for less and then simply apply for all of the special welfare, social services, and cash cards that they and their children qualify thanks to the Open Borders supporters in our Government and Mexican controlled legislatures like California's.

In case my readers didn't pay attention to what I wrote in my last paragraph, I want to say again that these illegal Mexican (and other countries) scab workers keep entering America illegally because they all know by now that they are eligible to sign up and get free taxpayer financed government cash and medical entitlements benefits that states like California and America's Federal Government enjoy giving to any person who enters US sovereign soil with their children. I think America's Politicians do this so these illegal workers will continue enter America illegally and work for any low pay that is offered to them. And! I want to add that I feel this army of invading colonizing workers is being allowed to enter America because America's Government wants to make sure that America's huge, greedy, farm coops won't have to pay livable wages like the small family farmers did back in the 1960s. And if my readers want to know why I'm ending this book with a discussion about fieldwork, I guess I can say it's because I read some very disturbing news in a local county farm bureau newspaper that was published by the Tulare County Farm Bureau. In this paper, I found two articles that really got my goat. To begin, one story was written by Kevin Rogers, a four-generation farmer from Arizona and the other story was written by Patricia Stever Blattler the executive director of the Tulare County Farm Bureau. I should note that each one of these "civic leaders" urged their farm bureau members to contact their local politicians like Congressmen Nunes, McCarthy, and Valadeo and remind them of the need for so-called immigration reform, which if you've read every page of this book basically means to first gut US Immigration laws and then provide more rewards and a free passes to Mexico's illegal colonizing force of law breakers so big farming coops can continue to get cheap and low cost scab laborers to reap higher profits.

Before I move on, I want to tell my fellow American that at one time local small farm farmers (not these huge corporations who keep forcing family farmers to sell their small farms) paid good and livable wages. The wages for farm labor in the 60s were so good that during the summer many of the big crews that thinned and chopped cotton, that I worked on, were made up of high school and college (white, black, Native, Asian, and Hispanic were all represented) aged male and female students and also the parents of these young people and other adults. Our local farmers were always happy to have these types of crews so they often allowed the young workers to carry transistor radios to listen to music while they walked the cotton fields and worked. Since the farmers knew most of the young people working in their fields, these farmers sometimes brought washtubs full of sodas and ice so the young workers could enjoy a cold drink during their lunch breaks. As my fellow Americans can see in this paragraph, the workers who worked the fields during my era never looked down on working in the fields or thought they were doing jobs that no body wanted to work. To tell my readers the truth, the majority of the young people working in the fields were very thankful that they could work a job that started at day-break (usually around 5:30 or 6 AM) and usually ended at around 2:30 in the afternoon because then we had the rest of the day to go play and have fun, or go on dates.

Finally, I think my fellow American need to hear about a discussion I had with some young men from this era who decided to try to work in the fields because none of them could find a job in my current home town that is located in Central California. In case my readers are wondering where these young men got the idea to work in the fields of Central California, I have to confess that I was the person who gave them idea because I told them that I had worked in the fields when I was a young man. To make a long story short, these young men decided to try to find work in the fields for some of the local farms in our area. After telling these young men how to find this kind of work, these young men all decided to see if they could get a job doing farm labor. These young men, I want to add, were all white and in their 20s so they were not some silly misguided young teens.

After a few days, the young men came back to talk to me again, and according to these young men, when they went out to ask for farm labor work (in 2013) in our local area (because they were desperate to find work and needed money for college), they were told by some English speaking Mexican men that only Mexicans were allowed to work in the fields of California because the United Farm Workers Union's controlled all farm labor. And! Since they were white, there was no work for them. All I can say about this event is that I feel the reason this happened is because it has to do with the fact that the UFW or United Farm Workers Union allegedly controls all field labor work in California. I also want to add one more thought on this subject as to why these young men were not allowed to work in the fields of California. I think the UFW has Governor Brown in its back pocket, and I feel Brown is the patron saint of Mexico's lawless invaders and the UFW because he protects this union like it was his pet project. I know I can make this statement because the UFW has been Governor Brown's pet project since he was elected governor back in the 1960s, and at that time he used California taxpayers' money to buy this union a microwave communication system that was state of the art in that era (Note: This was before the days of cell phones.). I hate to say it but so much for the statement that "only lawless and illegal aliens and Mexicans will take these field workers' jobs."

After I had this discussion with these young men, I found myself thinking about a discussion I had with my mother before she passed away a few years ago. During this discussion with my mother, she reminded me that many young students like myself often made enough money during the summer to buy cars, school clothes, pay for college fees, and even save enough money to pay for school events during the school year and that is why so many young Americans flocked to the fields of the Central California Valley to find good paying jobs. She also added that we young people were often allowed to work on the weekends during the school year because the local farmers knew most of the parents from our small towns didn't have the money to pay for extra costs like football shoes or cheer leading uniforms during the school year. According to my mother, the local farmers were good people who wanted to help the local kids succeed and stay in school. Thanks to my discussion with my mother, I learned that growing up in the small towns of the San Joaquin Valley was a special and wonderful time and gift for the young men and young women of our valley of that era. I should add here that at one time these small town local farmers were once the backbone of California's Central farming region throughout the Central San Joaquin Valley that is now known as America's breadbasket. I think the best thing I can say about these small farm farmers is that they cared about the people who worked in their fields. Unfortunately for America, most of these farmers are long gone into history.

Now that I feel I have educated my readers on what working in the fields was like in my area in the past, I want to add that if I could speak to the two "so-called farming civic leaders" that wrote the articles I reported on in this book I would give them an ear full of what I thought of their advice I read in their Farm Bureau paper. If I could, I would tell them that rewarding law breaking illegal Mexican aliens or colonizers with open borders and free citizenship is not the answer for Farm Laborer Reform, and it is not right or legal according to America's Constitution. I would also tell these farming leaders and their members that they should be ashamed of their unethical choices they are championing and pushing down the throats of America's Citizens. Finally, I would tell them that instead of demanding and asking for more cheap Mexican laborers they should be demanding that our borders be closed, our immigration laws be enforced, and that large farm coops be forced to pay real livable wages, provide health insurance, and retirement insurance instead of begging for more illegal Mexican cheap laborers to be allowed to enter America and destroy her culture and live on US taxpayer financed social services.

Since my readers now see that I believe good honest hard work never hurt anybody, because I actually worked in the fields from the age of 13 and up till I graduated from high school, I wish the media and these so-called illegal immigrants would stop putting down this good honest entry level farm labor work and saying it's work that nobody wants so illegal aliens have to do it. I hate to tell these people but if fieldwork paid an honest livable wage, offered health care insurance, and retirement insurance, I bet many Americans would do this work because they would know they could earn an honest living and not have to be on some form of Social Welfare to subsidize their income like 80 percent of the illegal workers living in California currently receive and use. Yes, my fellow Americans read this fact right because I verified this information from a story that read in our local newspaper this year (2018). Unfortunately for America's citizens, Mexico's scabs workers (and other countries' illegal aliens) only help these large farming corporations keep their wages down, and this reason they can do this is because America's taxpayers are forced to use their tax dollars to support these scab laborers with billions of dollars of financial, medical, and social services welfare aide that America's large farming coops should be paying.

Yes my fellow Americans, you read the information I just wrote right in the last paragraph right, and this is why I have always recommended that all farming companies or coops who hires these lawbreaking and colonizing invaders should be forced (by America's government) to become these so-called illegal workers' sponsors the moment they hire them. Since I have worked overseas in Japan, China, and other countries I knows that these foreign governments always force their companies who import foreign workers to be both legally and financially responsible for all of the worker's needs when they hire them. To make sure these foreign workers don't end up on their social services programs, these companies are responsible for these workers until their contracts and work permits expire. These countries take these precautions because they want to make sure the foreign workers will go home, or be sent home the moment their contracts end. I also want to add that no employer can hire these foreign workers in these countries unless the foreign worker has the required government's work permit in hand and their "in-country permit" to live in these countries and rent a home. These permits, I want to add, are always checked to make sure they have not expired, and if any company hires these foreign workers whose contract has expired with the old company, this new company must apply for an extension of the work permit and pay all of the required Government fees.

Since I've been writing about what appears to an American Government backed invading army of illegal low wage scab workers who keep coming to America by the millions, I want to conclude this book by discussing some American Government decisions that are only encouraging these illegal aliens to continue to ignore and break American laws. In case my fellow Americans are wondering what I am talking about, I want to remind them that their Supreme Court Judges and American politicians have done nothing to stop this flow of illegal aliens ignoring US laws, and they continue to give a free ride to any and all of these illegal aliens who break the law. And, because these Supreme Court Judges and American politicians continue to provide a stress free path to success by paying for free social services that are paid for with American tax dollars that come from the sweat American taxpayer dollars, I am sure that these illegal men, women, and children are only going to learn to be dependent on a welfare state provided services and entitlement programs for life because of these American Government freebees, which in my book is wrong.

To prove the point I made in the last paragraph, I want offer a very wise thought that Mark Burnett, the executive producer of the famous TV show **Survivor** said in his best selling book How to Survive and Thrive in the Game of Life: Dare to Succeed (Hyperion. New York: 2001): "Hardship is the only way they [(competitors or people trying to survive in the game of life)] can find out what they're truly made of—whether they'll back off when the going gets tough, or whether they'll find the courage to be bold and become their own hero in the process. It doesn't matter whether you win or lose [in the game of life], but how they play the game [(of life)]. I find the purity of that notion inspiring." I have to say that I completely concur with Mr. Burnett's assessment. And because I agree with Mr. Burnett's wonderful assessment of why he feels hardship is the best way to become a winner in life, instead of providing people unlimited social services and free money, I want to try to convince my fellow Americans, America's judicial leaders, and America's politicians that providing American taxpayer social services to these illegal aliens and letting them get away with breaking American laws is only setting these people up to be dependent on a "nanny state" type of government for the rest of their lives, and America cannot afford to this for ever because these actions are already undermining America.

I hope that by now my fellow Americans are starting to ask themselves why America's Supreme Court Judges and politicians are going out of their way to make sure these illegal aliens don't suffer any hardships or get deported, especially when we are told by men like Mike Burnett that when people like these illegal aliens are helped forever they never learn to become their own heroes or learn to fend for themselves in the "game of life." By helping these illegal aliens, Burnett feels these aliens are being set up for failure and dependency. Since I can't read the minds of our Supreme Court Judges or politicians, I can only guess that maybe these American public servants are taking these actions so they will be considered the heroes of these illegal aliens, illegal Mexicans, and the alleged Muslim refugee Colonizers that are now swarming into America. I can only guess that by helping these foreigners these American Government entities hope to get the support and votes of these foreigners for life so they can stay in power forever. Especially if these US leaders help these illegal and refugee aliens become U.S. citizens by working around or ignoring US Immigration laws. After all, if these illegal aliens and refugees eventually get to be US Citizens, these politicians and judges know they will have a legion of indebted followers at their command to support them and back them when they decide to take America in the new direction in the 21st Century that appears to be a "Socialist Democratic Nation," which we all know will not be good for America's real and legal citizens because the last Socialist Nation had a leader named Hitler.

I guess by now my readers can see that I agree with Mr. Burnett's philosophy of allowing people to suffer through their hardships so they can earn their way to get the things they desire like becoming a legal American citizen. By forcing these people to "work for the prize they want and force them to earn their prizes and goals they desire, I think these people will get more satisfaction when they achieve their goals, and that is why I agree Mr. Burnett when he says that "these people will feel good about themselves because they will have become their own heroes in the game of life." To put my ideals that agree with Mr. Burnett's theory in laymen's terms, I guess the best way to say it is that I feel any person who decides to come to America illegally should be forced to go back and apply legally for their right to live in America, be forced to earn their chance to live in America, and finally be forced to work earn the right to become a legal US Citizen by following and obeying America's immigration laws and Constitutional laws that are in the law books now so they will be given the chance to be their own hero. If America's Supreme Court Judges and America's politicians really want to help these illegal foreigners who want cheat and ignore America's laws, I feel these judges need to agree with me and force these illegal aliens and alleged refugees to be their own heroes and earn the right to become an American citizen by sending them home to start the legal process. I can come to this conclusion because I was raised by my parents and old America to earn my way and be my own hero, and I can honestly tell these American judges that if they decide to force these illegal aliens to earn their right to become legal American citizens the legal way, they will get better future American citizens who will not be takers because they will learn to be givers that will want to give back to America and succeed on their own guts and merit.

As for these lawless invaders that keep coming to America with their hands held out because they say American owes them (Note: This is how an old-school 1960s era Mexican "legal immigrant" friend of mine described today's new illegal Mexican aliens from this era.), I think it is time our Government officials grew a spine and started to enforce ALL of America's laws that are already in the books and stop ignoring the fact that they do exist. So without further delay, I want to tell President Trump, America's Congressional Republican and Democrat Representatives, and all of America's Judges that as a citizen of the Republic I am here to tell them it's time you American leaders started to grow a backbone and start to punish these illegal aliens/invaders by sending almost all of them (Note I say this because I feel about 20 percent of these aliens have earned a right to stay in America.) back to their homelands so they can be forced to enter America legally. By forcing these illegal aliens to enter America legally, I these aliens will learn that America is a land of laws and not the land of "guideline-like-laws" that anyone in the world can choose to either ignore or obey them if they feel like it.

I hate to tell America's President, Supreme Court Judges, and Civic and Business or Farming leaders but we Americans that are all members of the Republic known as the United States of America have decided that our Government's "open borders" policy is **not acceptable to us and it has to stop today!** I feel I can say this on behalf of America's Citizens because an "open borders policy" is not fair to America's legal citizens, and it breaks the Constitutional rights and privileges we Americans included in our Constitution to protect ourselves from you and those who would come to America and try to steal or stake a claim to these rights by force or ignoring US laws. I also want to note we earned these rights because we have sacrificed our brothers, fathers, and mothers in civil wars, world wars, and conflicts, and we have even suffered through stock market crashes so we could enjoy these rights and privileges that are written into OUR Constitution that was written to serve and defend American citizens' right and privileges. Unfortunately, thanks to these American politicians and Judges, we Americans now find ourselves losing our rights and privileges because they are slowly being taken away by these same elected officials who evidently enjoy giving away our Constitution to the world's foreigners or citizens. My dear American Judges and politicians I'm here to tell you that America's citizens of the Republic deserve better than what is happening to them and their country. Having had my say, I now hope America's leaders know why I decided to write this very controversial book that some of my friends tell me might cost me my life because it is going to anger many, many people. Well, my dear American politicians, Supreme Court Judges, and lower court judges all I have to say to this threat is that if it does cost me my life, I feel it will have been worth the cost because to borrow the great words of a great man I studied and admired in my youth, "I regret that I have but one life to give to my country." As for my fellow members of the greatest Republic in the world, I say to you, Happy Second Independence Day America, let's start taking America back starting today!

Appendix I

I have decided to add this appendix because I want to let my fellow writers and publishers, who I quoted in this book with respect, care, and caution to know that (because I'm a published writer and a Professor of transfer level English) I made sure this book stayed within the required guidelines that control scholarly research, criticism, and comments when I used a snip-it of their material from their published works. Since I have always taught my students to stay within the "Fair Use" guidelines or rules when using copyrighted material, I'm sure they will agree with me that all of the short passages or sentences I used in this book stayed within the frame work for quoting short passages for scholarly, scientific, and technical work as an illustration or comparison with the observations I made in this book. I also want my fellow writers and publishers to know that I have cited your books and short works so my readers will be able to find them and read them if they wish to learn more about your published works and your opinions on the topic that I quoted from in your well written and solid books and articles. I also want to thank my fellow writers and peers for their wonderful and intelligent writing, thoughts, and contribution to this work.

I next want to say that I've have heard that allegedly ex-President Obama is very thin skinned about being criticized on any topic. Well believe it or not, I think this weakness or possible flaw that ex-President Obama has sounds a lot like the one young King Solomon had when he first became the king of his people. Anyway, I feel it is sad that America has become a place where an entertainer can't make fun of an American president and this so called American leader can't laugh it off as a joke. In case my readers want to know why I think or believe young King Solomon sounds a lot like King, I mean President Obama (just a joke, lighten up), here is a short version of a story about King Solomon to show my readers why I feel Obama and King Solomon have a lot in common: "[He] had more than a healthy self-image. He had become bigger than life in his own mind. But this world-class greatness was not without significant cost. To fund his desires, Solomon, taxed the people to the point of economic exhaustion. When image is everything, no price is too high especially when it's, [the price], being paid by others. In addition to the misappropriation of national financial resources, Solomon was willing to tarnish the integrity of his office by violating divine mandates in an effort to advance himself" (McIntosh, Gary L., and Samuel D. Rima, Sr. Overcoming the Dark Side of Leadership: The Paradox of Personal Dysfunction. Baker Books, Michigan: 1998. 2nd Ed. Pp. 97.).

I hate to say it but doesn't this short story sound very much like the alleged thinned skinned ex-President Obama that ran America for eight years? If my fellow Americans want some examples that I used to compare with what was written about King Solomon to ex-President Obama, I want my readers to close their eyes and think about Obama's Billion dollar taxpayer financed nightmare called the American bullet train; think about Obama's use of the executive powers to get his way on so-called illegal immigration, even though I prove in this book that he broke Constitutional law; think about Obama's expensive Health Care program that he signed into power and that was finally rolled back when President Trump was elected into office; think about Obama's use of America's military that cost U.S. taxpayers millions of American dollars to allegedly topple dictators, but in the end, it only helped set up Muslim Cleric controlled nations that now control some of the riches oil fields in the world. The dangerous part of these results are that these oil rich Muslim controlled nations can now hurt America with oil embargos in the coming future if America decides to attack some Muslim controlled Nation and these Clerics don't agree. And finally, I want my readers to think about Obama's expensive vacations and alleged secret Social Security deal with Mexico's government that might some day cost America's taxpayers millions of dollars and push America's Social Security program into actual bankruptcy because it will divert US Social Security retirement dollars to Mexico for its citizens who might have worked in America illegally.

The next point I want to cover in this appendix has to do with the fact that the state of California has passed a law that forces both government and private businesses to translate everything they print into Spanish. Yes, that means anything that is sold in California must be labeled in both English and Spanish. As for government forms, again, anything that is published in writing or is announced in the news, on the radio, or on television must be presented in both English and Spanish. Having presented this new law, I have to ask my fellow Americans if they don't agree with me that America's Government and the Supreme Court are "out of control" in the land of the once mighty dollar bill that is quickly being over taken by China's currency? I use the words "once mighty dollar bill" because I think China's money will soon be the trading currency of the world and not the US dollar, and because I believe that our money will soon have to be labeled in English and Spanish and have both the words dollar and peso on it. This is my prediction and not a joke.

One more point I want to cover is the fact that the "cultural genocide" of America's Western Christian Culture and its end is getting closer and it will soon get out of hand. To prove this point, I want to point out the fact that California is slowly looking more and more like Mexico and it is slowly becoming a part of Mexico because more and more Americans are leaving the state on a daily basis because, as I was told a few days ago, "it's going to get worse before it gets better." To prove this point, I want to point out that a few weeks ago I took a friend of mine to the local county social services office to get some forms for his daughter who was pregnant. While I was in the office I noticed some interesting forms that were available to the public so I took some to read and boy did I get an eye full. As I looked these forms over, I found that these pamphlets were, I am sad to say, all published in so many foreign languages that I thought I was looking at fake or prank forms. In case my readers want to know how many languages were on these forms of American taxpayer paid social services, I can tell my reader that these forms had been translated into the following languages: Arabic, Farsi, Armenian, Portuguese, Punjabi, Tagalog, Ukrainian, Cambodian, Chinese, Hmong, Japanese, Korean, Lao, Mien, Russian, Spanish, Spanish Domh Nzangc, and Vietnamese just to name a few.

My fellow Americans I hate to give our State and Federal Governments some bad news but I really don't think that selling out the English language and replacing it with the worlds' languages is what tens of thousands of my peers and other America's citizens from different eras died for in wars to protect "America's freedom" and the "Americana" way of life. And! I really don't think these men and women who fought during the birth of America against England, fought the Kaiser during World War I, fought Hitler and the axes in World War II, fought North Korea and China in the Korean War, and fought China and North Vietnam in the Vietnam War sacrificed so much so that America's Government could basically just turn around and "GIVE" America away to the world without a fight. And finally, I don't believe these Americans were willing to serve and die for America so that Dreamer controlled legislatures in American states like California could quietly allow Mexico's and other foreign citizens to colonize and invade states like California. At the end of my research and this book, I found that this open borders' land grab of America appears to have the backing of America's politicians, Supreme Court Justices, big business, and large farming corporations whose bottom line only appears to be the act of making sure that their benefactors and stockholders get the huge dividends and tax breaks they feel they deserve while the cost and expense of supporting these illegal aliens and their children is passed along to America's Republic and the taxpayers who finance this country's Government.

Although California's (and America's) Government leaders might think they are wise and knowledgeable, I find it hard to believe that these elected civic leaders didn't take the time to research and read the California State Constitution to make sure all of their directives, laws, rules, or orders they recently passed (or re-wrote) didn't break state Constitutional law. And since California's state civic leaders, legislature, and California's state and County government administrators don't' appear to have bothered looking at or even reading the State Constitution that they are supposed to defend and uphold, I guess this is the reason they didn't read Article III Section 6 of the new California Constitution that still has some of the old laws in it. I come to this conclusion because if these leaders had bothered to read this section they would have learned that all of their current orders or laws basically all break California State Constitutional law:

Yes my fellow Americans, all of those Spanish only Billboards that are popping up all over California's roads and highways, all of the Spanish only laws, and all of the new rules that are being forced on California's state and county employees are not legal. How do I know this fact? I know it because I bothered to read and learn what California's Constitution really says, and here is what it says: "English is the common language of the people of the United States of America and the State of California. This section is intended to preserve, protect, and strengthen the English language, and not to supersede any of the rights guaranteed to the people by this Constitution; b) English as a right, English is the official language of the State of California; c) Enforcement: The legislature shall enforce this section by appropriate legislation. The legislature and officials of the State of California shall take all steps necessary to insure that the role of English as common language of the state of California is preserved and enhanced. The legislature shall make no law which diminishes or ignores the role of English as the common language of the State of California; d, Personal Right of Action and Jurisdiction of Courts: Any person who is a resident of or is doing business in the State of California shall have standing to sue the State of California to enforce this section, and the Courts of record of the State of California shall have the jurisdiction to hear cases brought to enforce this section" (The Senate, The Constitution of the United States of America and the Constitution of the State of California, Sacramento: 1997-98, p. 99).

Now that I've let the cat out of the bag and educated California's elected leaders, I hope some brave sole that has the time and money to correct these wrongs will soon sue California's State Government for failing to protect this law and the English language as the California Constitution orders them to do so by law (Note: I also hope all of America's state check their state Constitutions to see if they have this law.). Speaking of California laws, I want to add I also took the time to take a look at a few other California State Constitutional laws and I have to say that my effort was a real eye opener. I make this statement because I learned the new California State Constitution gives any person who enters this state the same rights as an American citizen, and it also has been rewritten to provide any person that is either a lawless invader of California (and America when they move on to another state) or a temporary visa holder broader rights than the US Constitution's Bill of Rights bestows on America's citizens. And! One more point I want to make here is that from 1964 to 1972 a hired committee of the state of California completely gutted and rewrote California's original Constitution so dramatically that I know this is the reason Mexico's lawless and invading citizens have been empowered to take over California. The California Constitution, I want to note, was changed by an alleged so-called hand picked commission that removed over 40,000 words from the original 75,000 words found in the original California Constitution (The Senate, The Constitution of the United

States of America and the Constitution of the State of California, Sacramento: 1997-98, p. 99).

After reading California's new rewritten Constitution, I tried to find a copy of California's old Constitution and learned that in my area there was only one copy in all of Central California. This copy I learned was only available to be seen or read on the Premises of the Central Library found in the city of Fresno, California, and only by appointment. I was told this means that anyone who wants to see or read this copy of the California's Constitution, and see what was removed from the old document, has to request a day in advance so the staff can arrange a day for them to come in a view it (so much for a free America). If they are lucky enough to get a convenient day and time to view this copy of the Constitution, take the time to travel to this city to view it and read it, they might get what they want. I decided not make the very long drive and take a chance wasting my time. Because as you can see, I found that it was too hard to set up a good time or day, and I was afraid this alleged copy my be just a shell of what the original California Constitution was in the first place. The kind of problems and road blocks that come with trying to view old documents of importance should now help my readers see and understand why I decided not to bother driving a few hours to this city that is known as a gang land strong hold of the Fresno Bulldog gang terrorist group. And to show how easy America's government has decided to make it for any invading force or colonizing force that wants to enter America's sovereign soil and take it over, I want to point out that when these foreign citizens break US Immigration laws by not asking for permission to enter US territory legally their offense is only treated as a simple **misdemeanor** infraction that any lawless or trespassing invader can either ignore or just work around it via our deaf, blind, and illiterate American Judicial system that is NOT protecting Americans or their Constitutional rights and privileges.

If what I have just reported in my book doesn't make Americans want to laugh or cry at how poorly America's Government officials and judicial system has decided not to protect Americans against those who would take over their country and their American Constitutional rights, then I guess I have not done my job. And! I guess when Russia's or China's Governments decide to invade and take over America these American leaders will only charge these countries with a misdemeanor crime too. Then I guess these America leaders will allow China's and Russia's "illegal immigrant" military forces to take over America because these American leaders will again use the excuse that these illegal invaders only want to live in America too and have better lives. I know the scenario I just painted in the last sentence shouldn't be taken lightly, but my fellow American have to admit that if what was happening to America is not a joke then why aren't America's leaders treating the invasion and occupation of America by millions of illegal aliens like a joke, or like these people are just migrating like birds and reindeer do in the animal world?

Continuing this thought, I want to say that since what I have written here is real and not a joke or natural migration, I feel we American have to admit that it appears that America's government has decided to give illegal aliens more power over America's citizens than the other way around. I guess this is the reason that the famous hamburger place with the golden arches is currently getting away with offering Mexicans and Hispanics 22 million US dollars worth of scholarships to "ONLY" Hispanic/Mexican students in America (Note: This is what the application says.). I should note here these scholarships are being giving to both lawless and illegal aliens and that is why I feel this fund is loaded with reverse racism. As a minority All-American patriot, I am going to go on record and say that if these types of scholarships were offered only to white American students these scholarships would be considered racist by all of America's minority groups and the Democrat politicians, and they would be screaming bloody murder. I'm also pretty sure that both Black and Hispanic students would be crying foul the moment they saw applications for only "white student" scholarships in any store!

I want to discuss one more important issue before I end this Appendix. And, the issue I want to discuss has to do with a postal advertisement I received in the mail that was sent out by a large farming company in Central California that was only written in Spanish. Since Spanish is not my first or second language, I decided to look up some of the words that I didn't know in a Spanish dictionary. What I learned was that this postal ad was an advertisement for any and all (both illegal and legal workers) farm workers to contact this large company in Central California to work for them. This ad boosted their pay was the best in the industry; they used only safe bug sprays to protect their workers, and all of their labor camps were located close to the work in the city of Kerman. This large Coop also added they offered work all the way till the end of November and that their packing sheds were designed for comfort. I want to note here that this ad could not have been read by people who only spoke English, and were field worker who might have been looking for a good job in California.

I guess my readers and I could say that these jobs were not being offered to all of America's workers, and this employer knew these jobs were not so lousy that no-one would want them. Yet, this ad that was written only in Spanish so only Spanish-speaking people would respond to it was note considered illegal. From what I read, I felt that only people living in America with Spanish/Latin surnames, like my father's Portuguese last name, had been sent these US Mail invitations to work in Kerman. By the way, I also noticed that this company's ad said "nothing about using e-verify to check their worker's legal status in America." But this company did brag that they have paid over $16 per hour since 2011. I hope my readers now see why the young white males that I wrote about in this book were willing to try to find jobs in this American farm job sector, that has evidently been closed to other nationalities by the United Farm Worker's Union. I can only guess that Caesar Chavez's United Farm Workers Union appears to only want to serve Mexicans and Hispanics living in American states like California and no other races. Hey, US Federal Government and California Government isn't this kind of act considered racist?

The final topic I want to write about in this appendix is to answer the question of what I feel should happen to these colonizers' property or belongings that they've accumulated using America's social services programs while working in America illegally by breaking Constitutional, criminal, and Immigration laws. I hate to say it but if I get my way and America's government begins to do their job and begins to repel this invading army of colonizers they will be able to find the answer by following the Japan's Governments most recent actions that sent hundreds of thousands of their illegal aliens home in one quick sweep and confiscated their property to pay themselves back because these illegal aliens had used many of Japan's services for free. The answer, I am happy to say is quite simple so read on my PTSD suffering legal Americans. The first answer to this problem, I am happy to say, would fall under the laws of "Forfeiture" that reads like this: "Criminal forfeiture is a punitive action by the Republic's government against any offender. Typically, it occurs as part of sentence following a conviction (like finding all of Mexico's colonizing, invaders and any other illegal colonizers in America guilty of breaking US immigration and Constitutional laws) of being found guilty of committing forced entry-without permission into America for the purpose of colonizing US sovereign soil 18 U.S.C. & 982, and by cross-referencing this laws with another law, it said it creates a framework of offenses and legal procedures governing this type of forfeiture, as does section 21 U.S.C. & 881. These statutes provides for the forfeit of "any property, real or personal, involved in such offense, or any property traceable to such property." In addition, Rule 32.2 of the Federal Rules of Criminal Procedure governs criminal forfeiture proceedings in federal court. Depending on the crime, U.S. Customs procedures from Title 19 may also control [this type of lawless action against the United States of America]" (Legal Information Institute, Online Posting: P. 2, Feb. 22, 2011, www.http://topics.law. cornell.edu/wex.forfeiture.).

The second part of my answer also falls under the law of Forfeiture and it takes the following action: "Property directly resulting from or that can be traced to, an illegal activity...[are forfeited.] Once a crime is identified, the government [(on behalf of the Republic or the American People)] may seize any property flowing from the activity (like working in America without legal permits or passports and not paying taxes by claiming too many dependents). In some cases, the government may seize property in lieu of provable criminal acts. I'd like to now point out that some illegal invaders who become famous, like that female singer so-called actress (our opinion) who bragged on national television that she'd had entered America as an illegal invading colonizer so she was an illegal immigrant (Note: Then she laughed at our laws.), should be forced to forfeit all of their property and wealth to pay America's Citizens back. This lady and others like her, as far as I'm concerned all need to be charged under the forfeiture laws, and the Monroe Doctrine because they all owe America's taxpayers financial restitution (and more than likely some incarceration and then deportation) for taking advantage of America's taxpayer paid programs and getting a free American education at the expense of America's tax payers. I am now happy to say that these types of lawbreakers should remember that according to criminal law, "[a claim of] statutory innocent owner defenses [might] provide a check on the seizure power, [but] . . . this burden lies with the owner, not the government," so she still needs to pay the piper someday soon. Finally, if this book does its job, and Americans demand restitution and declare war on these their own Government and these illegal invaders under the Monroe Doctrine that says, no nation in the America's can be colonized, I feel America's Citizens will have the last laugh (Legal Information Institute, online posting: P. 2, Feb. 22, 2011, www.http://topics.law.cornell.edu/wex/forfeiture.).

I want to add one more remark or fact about these law breaking illegal aliens that are working in America and their supporters that include many of America's politicians, many large farm corporations, some Supreme Court Judges, and some of America's

Presidents. The point I want to make is that I believe all of these supporters are guilty of "aiding and abetting" these invading illegal aliens so they really should be charged under this law because they are guilty of this offense. The reason these people are guilty of "Aiding and Abetting" these law breakers is because they all become "Accessories" to committed crimes every time they help these criminal illegal alien colonizers that commit crimes while working and living on America's sovereign soil. Some examples of these crimes include breaking American immigration laws when they first enter America illegally; the murders and rapes them commit in America, and the selling of drugs, and filing false tax statements to name a few. After all, this law states that helping law breakers requires this action by those who become accessories to a crime: "A criminal charge of aiding and abetting or accessory can usually be brought against anyone who helps in the commission of a crime, though legal distinctions vary by state. A person [(or group)] charged with aiding and abetting, or accessory, is usually not present when the crime is committed, but he or she [(or they)] has knowledge of the crime before or after the fact, and may assist in its commission through advice, actions, or financial support. Depending on the degree of involvement, the offender's participation in the crime may rise to the level of conspiracy" (Aiding and Abetting/Accessory-Criminal Law, Online Posting: P. 2, Feb. 22, 2011, www.http://criminal.findlaw.com/crimes/a-z/aiding and abetting _accessory.).

Now that I have presented some laws that can be used to prosecute the people that are helping these illegal aliens break America's laws, I am happy to say these supporter better be careful and ready to pay the piper now that this book has been re-edited, updated, and released again. Need I say more as to why I feel many of America's leaders and other government agencies, and justices are more than likely guilty of helping pass laws to aid and protect Mexico's and other nations' illegal alien colonizers of American soil? My fellow Americans there you have all of the facts and truth of the big lie that is being used against the owners of America's

Constitution. I have just proven these benefactors and the recipients of their help are all guilty of treason and conspiracy against the Republic, which are also called America's legal citizens.

To close this Appendix, I want to show how desperate America's legal citizens that live in California are getting these days: To show a spirit of defiance and solidarity, many of California's legal and rightful owners of both America's and California's Constitutional rights have started to fly the American flag every day of the year. These Americans flying these American flags are the few legal American hold outs that are refusing to give up and leave California and turn it over to Mexico's invaders (unlike the millions of America's that have left California for other states and countries). By the way, the flying of the American Flag night and day has nothing to do with 9/11 (although it did begin that way) anymore. Yes, we defiant Americans are flying the American flag night and day to tell our fellow Americans we're still here fighting the good fight and we refuse to give California to Mexico and its invaders. When I talk to my fellow obstinate and defiant legal Americans citizens about our flag flying, they often like to call our act of defiance our "Fort Apache Stand." We have decided to use this name as another act of defiance because we feel we are like the old Forts of the old west that were scattered outposts in the Wild West era of early America. So you visitors to California, the next time you see an American flag flying over a home in California, remember what it really stands for and that it is not for 9/11 anymore (or just 9/11). I know I can come to this conclusion because we California and American legal citizens are fighting a silent war that all present and past America's Presidents, Congress, Supreme Court Judges, and Occupied State Governments are turning a blind eye to because they appear to have all turned against the Republic. For those Americans who noticed my last sentence in this paragraph, YES, I know America is now an OCCUPIED NATION, and no one is going to convince me that it is not.

Appendix II

In this Appendix, I want to apologize for taking three years to write (and another two years to update, revise, and edit it again) this book and getting it into the hands of America's legal and law abiding real citizens that I know are now even more desperate to stop the decline and loss of America's Sovereign Nation Status. But since I lost most of the use of my right hand (yes, I am right handed) when I was injured while working for the US Government as part of Homeland Security, I sorry to say I can only type very slow because my left hand has become my dominate hand when I type on my computer. Please forgive me for letting you suffer under the oppression and occupation of Mexico's (and other nations' nationals) trespassing and colonizing invaders for the past five years while I wrote this book. Now that my book is ready to be re-published, I hope this book will soon free America from the yoke of our Government's oppression and a foreign country's occupation. My fellow Americans it is time for a second civil war of disobedience. I also hope my book will soon free us to be the "free and law abiding nation" that we once were meant to be in the eyes of the Lord. May God guide and use this book to help us in our fight and quest to free America from all of the rogue leaders who have betrayed this great Christian Nation and her legal members of the Republic, or America's legal and real Citizens.

Since I just let the cat out of the bag that I was hurt on the job, I want to take the time to talk about my injury because I feel my injury and the way I was treated by America's Government and its "Worker's Comp Program" employees, that hung me out to dry by ignoring my injury claim, made my injury worse and permanent because they denied my operation, which left my right arm crippled/injured for the rest of my life. I say they made it worse because like thousands of other American Government employees that get injured on the job while working for Uncle Sam, I was never treated or allowed to get treatment for my injury by this worthless program employees from the office called the "Office of Workers Comp." I want to add this program is run by people that get bonuses for denying as many injury claims as they can, and making sure the Government never gets billed for treating an injured American Government employee. Because I would need a compete chapter to tell my story, I won't go into the details of the lack of service and rude treatment I received and was subjected to by several employees of this Government entity that is supposed to care for and heal America's Government employees that are hurt on the job. Oh yes, my employer Homeland Security also hung me out to dry because they never tried to help me during my struggle with America's Office Of Workers Comp. I now wish I had never take this job and kept teaching college.

I don't want to say more about my injury here because this Appendix is not about me, but about the betrayal of America's citizens by its own government in so many ways; however, I am going to provide the following information about the OWC so my fellow Americans will see how their US Government does not treat or help its injured employees and their fellow Americans: I do want to say that if Americans want to help the thousands of ex and present US Government employees who are not being treated by this corrupt and heartless department known as the OWCP (whose employees I was told gets rewarded for making it so hard for injured US Government employees to get treatment that most these employees give up and just quit their jobs and file for

Social Security Disability financial help), they need to go on the web and read the following web page I found on the web: http://fedworkerscomp.net/linehan.html and learn what the OWCP is capable of and doing to their fellow Americans. After they read these posts, I hope Americans will take the time to write their Congressman or Congresswomen and demand that this Government program be closed and privatized, or revamped with all new employees that will care for the injured (Note: When I called this program, the man on the line laughed when I told him my problem.). The reason I want my fellow Americans to read this web page is because it is a report written by the American Congress on "Workers' Compensation Programs.

I want to note that the report is found on this web page was published by the Subcommittee on Government Management, Information and Technology; by Congressman Stephen Horn; and by the Hearing on Oversight of Customer Service at the Office of Workers' Compensation Programs. The testimony of James Linehan, lawyer on Tuesday, May 18, 1999, at 10 AM, in room 2154 Rayburn House Office Building, basically blew the whistle and top off how allegedly bad and corrupt this government program operates. This report will shock Americans! The other web page I have noted here can be found at http://www.fedworkerscomp.net/graham. html. This page is a running commentary of all of the complaints that have been filed against the OWCP by injured, maimed, and financially ruined past, and present, US Government employees.

Since I just said this book is not about me, I want to add some quotes about how the Office of Workers Comp currently functions or conducts its business, or in the case of these injured Federal employees does not function or take care of America's Federal Employees who get injured on the job. To prove the charge I make here, I am going to quote some statements written by injured employees that are on a web page that is trying to help these injured employees. And to show how poorly the Office of Worker's

Comp operates, I am also going to quote the recommendation that Congress and its chief investigator, James Linehan, made after they had a hearing to investigate the OWCP which was found to be a vicious, hurtful organization that was intent on not helping America's injured federal employees (and it still functions the same.): This first quote I want to present is from the web page, http://pogoblog.typepad.com/pogo/2004/10/winslow on waste. html. I found this web page on 2/17/2007 while doing research for this book:

The first injured employee's name is Teresa Crowe who posted her story on August 28, 2008: "I am an injured Postal Worker, suffering a massive rupture in 1997. I had a failed surgery with right leg nerve damage; it was deemed chronic and I have had re-occurrences over the last 11 years, 8 at work after doing heavy repetitive lifting, [instead of helping, they made] it look like I'm accident prone . . . They (OWCP) just want to get rid of people who are going to cost them medical fees that they never pay anyway, and make [you] look like the crook. My integrity stands, and that is a lot more than I can say for the OWCP." The second quote I want to present is from Sharon (no last name), who posted her injury story on July 18, 2008: "I too have been injured working at TSA, MSP, corruption at its best. The people in charge have no intention of helping. Their desire is to do everything to make injured persons quit, and many have, because of no help at all. My injury dates back to April of 2005, and I'm still waiting for help . . . [their job appears to be, or seems to be] trying to save tax dollars to make themselves look good at my expense . . .what a bunch of crooks..." (http:// pogoblogtyprdpad.com/pogo/2004/10/winslowonwast.html.). I want to note that this web page is full of stories like these that all have the same message. I feel that America's government is more interested in taking care of Mexico's and the worlds' citizens than America's injured federal employees who keep America running and safe so these invading colonizing aliens, the President, Congress, Big Business, and the Supreme Court Judges can all sleep well at night.

I now want to present a post written by James Linehan the lawyer who testified in front of Congress' Congressional Hearings that investigated America's Office of Workers' Comp because it had received so many complaints against this Federal Program. This quote is the Congressional Hearing's recommendations that were posted on line after they had done an intense investigation of the OWCP: "The present federal workers' compensation under the OWCP is a federal system without accountability to any court of law; a federal system that costs the private insurance sector millions of dollars annually; and a federal system of unilateral control with no incentive to assure that the effects of its actions are in the best interest of the federal employee. The OWCP is essentially a federal agency that has and continues to answer to no one . . . The Undersigned recommends that this Congress also act in the best interest of the thousands of injured, deceased or killed federal employees seeking federal workers' compensation for themselves and their families. The undersigned recommends that the most simple effective means of insuring that the OWCP acts in the best interest of the federal employee (rather than the OWCP) is to allow the federal employee a basic right of federal court review overseeing its actions (or non-action), the OWCP will have every incentive to act in the best interest of the injured federal employee rather than the best interest of the OWCP" (Linehan, James, Hearing on "Oversight of Customer Service at the Office of Workers' Compensation Programs," Washington DC: Congress, May 18, 1999: http://www.fedworkerscomp.net/linehan.html).

In the end, a Federal Court review board said the following in the recommendation: the "OWCP claims that the OWCP respond in a pre-set timely manner to federal employee's requests for information and action on their claims . . . Federal court review of OWCP claims will also assure that the claimant that in case of appeal she will have greater opportunity to be represented by legal council. In summary, by simply allowing federal civilian employees to appeal their OWCP claims to federal court review; the above noted problems of non-accountability and unilateral control of the

OWCP disappear. Without such court oversight, federal employees seeking compensation for their on-the-job injuries will remain subject to the whims and will of an essentially non-regulated agency" (Linehan, James, Hearing on "Oversight of Customer Service at the Office of Workers' Compensation Programs," Washington DC: Congress, May 18, 1999.) By the way, this quote came from this page: http://www.fedworkerscomp.net/linehan.html, 2/17/2007.

Although this Congressional Hearing sounds like it did something to stop the OWCP from its ugly and dark practices back in the 20th Century, this hearing accomplished **nothing!** The reason these hearing did nothing to help injured federal employees is because of the use of the word this group used to possibly make changes: "**recommends.**" Because Congress used the word "recommends," instead of the word, "**orders,**" Congress, again, left the OWCP with the power to continue the dark practices and ignore Congress' findings and "recommendations," because they were still left as essentially a **Non-regulated agency!**" So to conclude, these hearings, and Congress' recommendations were nothing more than a side show, smoke screen, or "much ado about nothing" so that America's citizens would think that they had corrected the underhanded ways the OWCP deals with injured, disabled, maimed, or killed federal employees who were injured on the job while working for America's Government, or even Congress. Do we get the picture as to why I say that Congress actually did nothing more than blow a lot hot smoke up the Republic's skirt? Yes, these Hearings were nothing more than the old "smoke and mirrors" BS that America's politicians are world famous for in good old Washington DC.

Before I stop talking about the new Federal Government programs that I learned about before my book went to print, I want to note one more new program that is being taught in something called "Diversity Workshops." These workshops, I want to note, are being forced on both private and government employees so that they can "learn more about the cultures that will soon overrun, destroy, and control America's citizens and their Constitution. Although the government is pushing these workshops as programs that create a bridge of acceptance for others (example illegal aliens, Gays, and the Disabled, to name a few), in my opinion as a minority male, these workshops are not for building bridges or a better America because to me they seem to be designed to force Americans to accept these cultures without complaints or backtalk because they have no choice in the matter. And, while these illegal aliens and new refugees do not have to accept or learn to like our American culture, our way of life, or the Americana culture, we Americans must accept the fact that we have to allow these new cultures to become the dominant cultures of America.

To conclude my thoughts on this topic, I want to also note that many of the American citizens who attended this workshops agreed with my opinion: I should note that many of the American Patriot who I talked me after they were forced to attend these workshops agreed with my opinion of the message these workshops are pushing. I want to add that many of these Americans who attended were too scared to tell the truth on how they felt about their "experience" at these workshops on the questionnaires they were given to fill out at the end of the workshops. The reason they didn't mention their disappointment with the message was because they feared retaliation from their employer's administration. After sitting through several of these workshops, I want to add that these employees and I also learned these workshops were not created to educate Americans about Mexico's citizens and other foreign illegal aliens that are now working in America, but to push the fact that America's culture, English language, and social culture should take a back seat to these alien's cultures. I end this paragraph with this statement because I feel we learned that in reality these workshops have the message that Americans "must" accept these new cultures and these illegal aliens that are being crammed down our throats without complaint.

To tell the truth, when I sat in on one of these Diversity lectures, I didn't hear message of bilateral acceptance, because what I instead heard was that THE Mexicans and Hispanics culture was the topic of discussion because it was a prized culture that should be put up on a pedestal. I also heard the message that nothing could be said about the Americana culture, the German culture, the Scottish culture, the Italian culture, or other cultures like the Native American culture because this was not the place or time. Evidently, as far as I'm (the Author) concerned, the message I heard was that the road to "celebrating diversity," the path to diversity, the tasting of diversity, and the accepting of diversity could only happen by stoning America's culture and accepting and learning that the Mexican or Latino cultures were better because America's Government had anointed this new culture as the king and dictator of America. Oh yes, the other message I got from these diversity workshops was that America's legal citizens can't do a thing about these illegal aliens and their cultures so Americans should shut up and accept it. Having come to this sick and ugly conclusion that I learned from attending these so-called diversity workshops, I want to say that as far as I am concerned "Diversity" is just another code word for killing-off and destroying America's Christian Western based Culture using "cultural genocide period!" To put it bluntly, Diversity to me is just another word for an American Government sanctioned "cultural genocide." I want to also add that I believe I can prove this fact because when someone in the meeting we were attending complained that their music was always played too loud in their neighborhoods, the leaders of the diversity lecture told us it was "part of their culture." I hate to tell these lecturers or leaders but when did rudeness, arrogance, and disturbing the peace of America's Republic become an acceptable and social moral standard? I never knew rudeness was an acceptable part of a peoples' culture.

In this Appendix, I want to now send a message to England, Austria, and especially to Japan and its people. I want to tell this countries that I feel these countries' law abiding citizens and their leaders need to read this book and internalize it, if they ever feel like they are also losing control of their sovereign nation status. Since I read a report that was filed by Mr. Sakanaka Hidenori, that in my opinion was not good for Japan, I feel it is my duty to personally address Japan's law abiding citizens and warn them that they need to start fighting the current "cultural genocide" war that is being waged against the kind citizens of Japan. This "cultural genocide" war is being waged by some world colonizing Powers that I feel want to colonize and invade Japan, like for example the French Govt. colonized Vietnam during the 20th Century. Since I have lived in Japan, worked in Japan, learned their language, and fallen in love with their wonderful culture that reminds me of my Native American culture, I hope they take the time to read this book and use it to fight their government and the foreign powers that are in Japan trying to destroy the Japanese culture that I love and respect with all of my heart. My dear friends and fellow natives of the land they love, I hope you listen to this man whose people had their culture, their languages, their traditions, and their land stolen from them and destroyed by using "cultural genocide." I want them to know that now is the time for all of Japan's legal and special citizens to stand up and fight for their culture and their homeland that they love. And, I want them to know that I stand with them in this book to defend their country, citizens, and their culture.

To continue the thought of defending a country's sovereignty, I want to tell Austria to stick to their "guns," (as we say in America when we tell someone to not change their mind on something that they believe is right and good for them). I make this comment because I read in a newspaper that in 2000 the European Union was threatening to politically isolate the country of Austria because they were or are anti-immigration, and I also read they have a party called the Freedom Party that is led by Joerg Haider who wants to make this movement official. Since I don't want to give the European Union any kind of publicity, I'm not going to say anything else about this group that as far as I'm concerned is no better than the people who arrived on our Indian land and killed and stole our land. As a Native American whose people lost their homeland, language, culture, food source, and are still under US Government occupation, oppression, and control (because Congress can take away everything we have at their discretion), I want to tell Austria they have my support for their stand and I hope that I read in the year 2019 that Austria has still not caved in or given in to the world's oppression of their indigenous people. After all some of these members are also some of the same members of nations that let Hitler walk in and take over countries like Austria (think The Sound of Music) without saying a word. I want Austria's leaders to know that in these times of a what appears to be a worldwide push for a World Wide Government, that would allegedly be controlled by the United Nations (that would very likely include destroying American and Austrian sovereignty), by groups like the European Union, America's" leaders, and many other nations Austria is smart not to let their country be overrun and colonized by any of these invading groups, religions, and cultures that are on the verge of destroying America's once great Western Christian Americana Culture.

As I continue this Appendix, I want offer my fellow Americans some wonderful and prophetic words that were written by one of my literary heroes who influenced my writing, Mr. Ralph Waldo Emerson. In his passage, Mr. Emerson tells us that he feels the job of a scholar (like myself) is to function in this world as a leader of change because of "the education this scholar provides by nature, by books, and by actions. It remains to say somewhat of his duties. The office of the scholar is to cheer, to raise, and to guide men, and [mankind] by showing them facts amidst appearances. He plies the slow, un-honored, and un-paid task of observation . . . But he, in his private observatory . . . must relinquish display and immediate fame. Worse yet, he must accept—how often poverty and solitude . . . and the state of virtual hostility in which he seems to stand to society . . . He is the world's eye. He is the world's heart. He is to resist the vulgar prosperity that retrogrades ever to barbarism, by preserving and communicating heroic sentiments, noble biographies, melodious verse, and the conclusions of history . . . This being his function, it becomes him to feel all confidence in himself and to defer never to the popular cry" (Van Dyke, Henry Comp. and ed. Select Essays of Ralph Waldo Emerson. New York: American Book Company, 1907.). This statement basically means that as a muckraker I will never get any news award from the Fourth Estate for my work, or be cheered and rewarded by those who would betray America or the Republic, and I could care less.

Finally, I want to remind my fellow Americans that the Declaration of Independence has always offered America's citizens, or the Republic, the right to make a change in America's government, if America's politicians decide to become a rogue government, as it appears to have gone in this 21st Century. This right to change America's government or to take it away from the politicians of this great country can be found in the second paragraph of the Declaration of Independence: "That whenever any Form or Government becomes destructive of these ends (to secure the rights of life, liberty, and pursuit of happiness), it is the Right of the People to alter or to abolish it, and to institute new government, laying its foundation on such principles and organizing its power in such form, as to them shall seem most likely to affect their Safety and Happiness . . ." Since this book has proven beyond a doubt that America's Government is betraying the Republic and its legal and vested American Citizens, I feel it is time for America's citizens to march on Washington DC and take away the power of running this government from our rogue politicians for 90 days so the Republic can establish and form a government that is willing to obey and enforce "all of America's laws." I offer this bit of advise because America's current government has become a non-law abiding or enforcing government that appears to be on the verge of destroying America's culture and its sovereign nation status by allowing Mexico and other South American governments to invade and occupy our sovereign soil, and I want to add that America's Government is also using its power to stop American Sovereign states from stopping this invasion and invaders.

I now leave my fellow Americans with some very disturbing numbers or statistics: I offer these very exact numbers, about what is happening to the state of California, as the invasion of America ramps up into high gear via California's gateway to America or "Azatlan's Mexica." Since I stated earlier in this book that California was being vacated by America's citizens who were being replaced by an unending hoard of Mexico's invaders, I want to provide these statistics for your education: "In Tulare County Hispanics (Code for mostly illegal Mexicans) made up 57.08 percent of the population . . . up nearly a full percentage point . . . Hispanics showed steady gains in population, increasing by an average of more than 8,000 residents **a year** . . . Whites meanwhile dwindled in numbers and now account for just 35.88 percent of the population in the county . . . Of the 58 counties, 48 percent experienced one or more years . . . of white population decline" ("California Department of Finance," The Valley Voice, Visalia, CA. April 16, 2009, page A10.). I want to add here that 4 out of 5 Old-School legal Hispanics, whose parents came to American legally in the 40's, 50s, and 60s, are against this "open border" form of so-called "illegal immigration" because they too feel these invaders should not be allowed to break US immigration laws, US criminal laws, and US federal laws because they feel the majority of these new Mexican (and other countries citizens) invaders enter America with their hands out saying, or demanding, "Dame' or Give me "free everything!"

Appendix III

In this final Appendix, I want to add some posts that I wrote and posted on my Facebook.com web page that was written to advertise the book you are holding in your hands. I feel these posts add a different dimension to this book that might help my fellow Americans understand the urgency of the problem that is facing Americans today:

A Civil War in America in the 21st Century, Maybe?

I was thinking out loud to myself today about the people in my state and other states that are ranting and yelling that they want to pull my state California out of the Union and go it alone like the Confederate states tried to do back during the Civil war era. They allegedly want to secede or withdraw from being a part of America because they don't want President Trump to be their President because they feel he cheated to win, or something to that effect. What these people don't understand is that there is no clause in the American Constitution for any state to withdraw from the union peacefully or through war. The key here is that in reality, according to what I studied to earn my History Degree, most states didn't exist as states till after they became a part of the United States of America and most of these states owe their existence to the United States of America.

To prove my statement I want to remind my readers that history books, especially a book by Edwin C. Rozwenc of Amherst College who wrote the book <u>The Causes of The American Civil War</u>, state that many states were just territories that were not recognized as countries and much of their power to exist was as a results of having a large dependence or connection to the original 13 colonies that were the United States of America. And! some of them, like California, owe their existence to the United States of America who paid other countries large sums of millions and millions of dollars to buy their freedom and their right to exist. So in actually, States like California were never independent states like they think. And if the United States wanted to call their bluff, it could ask these states to pay for their freedom at the current rate of exchange which would add up to billions or trillions of dollars.

If these secessionists want an example of what I am saying, here is a quote from Mr. Rozwenc book: "Our states have neither more nor less power than that reserved to them in the Union by the Constitution – not one of them ever having been a state out of the Union. The original ones passed into the Union even before they cast off their British colonial dependence; and the new ones each came into the United States directly from a condition of dependence, excepting Texas. And even Texas, in its temporary independence, was never designated a State. The new ones only took the designation of States on coming into the Union... Having never been States either in substance or in name outside of the Union, where did this magical omnipotence to 'State Rights,' asserting a claim of power to lawfully destroy the Union itself...?" The States have their status in the Union, and they have no other legal status. If they break from this, they can only do so against law and by revolution. The Union, and not themselves separately, procured their independence and their liberty. By conquest or purchase the Union gave each of them whatever of independence or liberty it has. The Union is older than ANY of the States, and in fact, it created them as States...What ever concerns the whole should be confided to the whole – to the General Government...

What is now combated is the position that secession is consistent with the Constitution is lawful and peaceful. It is not contended that there is any expressed law for it, and nothing should ever be implied as law, which leads to unjust or absurd consequences. The Nation purchased with money the countries out of which several of these States were formed. Is it just that they shall go off without leave and without REFUNDING? The Nation paid very large sums (in the aggregate, I believe, nearly a hundred millions of millions) to relieve states like Florida [and California (bought from Mexico)] to relieve Florida of the aboriginal tribes. Is it just that these States shall now be off without consent or without making any return...? Is this quite just to creditors of the world?" (Pp 44-45, The Causes of the American Civil War.)

Why U.S. Citizenship Privileges only
Serve the Republic's Citizens

In my recent posts, I have been providing my fellow legal or Naturalized American citizens facts that establish U.S. Citizenship according to America's immigration laws and her Constitution (when read correctly) that was written by its drafters who knew (because they were the founders or creators of these laws and rules that apply to Republics and Countries that establish Democratic Societies) how to write and establish the laws and rules as they apply to countries like France and America. Today I want to present an argument that I think my readers will find interesting because it's a call to arms of why America will not be here in maybe 20 to 30 years or in the near future if we keep moving forward in the direction America's Progressives and Socialist want America to move. But before I start, I want to warn my fellow Americans there is a trick to this post, but I won't disclose it till the end of this post:

"My fellow Americans, the name Americana Culture was given to the way all Americans lived and strived to live as Americans (even if they were new immigrants) once they found themselves legally accepted and given the title of American Citizen. This way of life that included the venerable patterns of American customs, holidays, and way of life that was dubbed Americana Culture was as much a part of America as Old Glory and the Pledge of Allegiance was (and has been) up until the past forty years. The reason I say up until the past forty years is because recently so called progressives and illegal aliens that have entered America have started to demand the same rights and privileges that were once reserved on an individual basis by America's U.S. Constitution to only serve America's legal Citizens. (Note: If you have read some of my past posts, you know that Frederic Bastiat a founding father and master of the laws of Republics and Democracies stated as such and even went so far as to warn all Citizens of Republics to be afraid when people like Progressives started to award the rights of America's citizens to any foreigner or person who entered America illegally.)

"For those who have studied the art of war, you will understand what I am about to try and teach to my fellow Americans, but for those who have never thought of war or paid attention to the ins-and-outs of war, I think the following thoughts will be a rude awakening. I want to start out by saying that Since days of old leaders have always preached the following thoughts on war: "Do not trust the enemy NOT to come; rather rely on your laws and defenses of preparation to keep the hounds of want and ignorance at bay; do not trust the enemy not to attack in both war like fashions or subtle ways; rather rest assured and hope that your preparations will prevent him from attacking; and to these thoughts, I want to add the following ones that I wrote to educate Americans: since America can not force its citizens to obey via intimidation, it must instead lead them towards a unified thought and culture that teaches love of country, its laws, its past history, culture, and past historical figures that created the nation they now call home.

As we loyal Americans that love Americana's Culture look upon America and see a country in turmoil, divided, and almost on the brink of civil war, I know we all see a country that once stood together falling apart into fragmented groups who only care about their self interests and not the good of the Country. To this statement I add that I find it sad to say but I see America as a patient who is barely escaping death from a usually fatal disease, so she is on life support. The patient (America) has not recovered and does not know how to recover, and since she now lacks a strong will to enforce, follow, and interpret her founding fathers' will and Constitution, she (America) is readily susceptible to infection from without.

Right now, foreigners with lawless ambitions threaten our borders; internally, evil doctrines flourish in the Halls of Congress and American State Governments. And because these facts are true, we must start today to go on the offensive and be on guard to defend America in any way that is needed. If the enemy is let in, ordinary people will conspire with him (foreigners and the enemy), officials will succumb to material desire in joint forces with him, and this country, as we can all see, will be lead and thrown into turmoil so that it will be easy to conquer. Those that have been tricked into joining forces with the enemy will say to us but we are America and have a wealthy nation and a strong army so why be afraid of these foreigners and enemy? Why be afraid, because at this very moment foreign enemies are focusing on our lack of unity, surreptitiously attempting to lure away those living in states that have marked themselves as Sanctuary states and aligned themselves with foreigners, their foreign governments and rich supporters and have captured their minds. Should the hearts of all Americans be won away, America will belong to the foreigner before the fighting even starts. Wealthy may America be, but this nation will NO longer belong to Americans. The results will be like giving weapons to the enemy and feeding thieves at our door. Surely, we did not work for two hundred plus years, fight two world wars, and build a wealthy nation and a strong army only to deliver it to the hands of thieves and bandits? I feel that any real red blooded American Patriot with the least bit of knowledge of realities will fail to see, and burn with indignation at prospect of what the future holds for America if we continue to proceed along the road that America is currently push towards by those who believe ignoring our laws and throwing away our culture and Constitution is what's best for America."

Now for the rest of the story: My fellow Americans, although I changed the words of this speech/verse to apply to America in this 21st Century, I have to confess here and say these are not all of my words. This speech was written in the 18th Century by a man/Patriot who was seeing his country go through what Americans are seeing their country go through in this 21st Century. The sad part is that his countrymen and countrywomen did not head his call to alarm and this man's country died about 20 or 30 years later because its leaders did not head his call. I leave you to your thoughts on what America's future will soon be in the not too near future if it continues on the road America's Progressive want to take her. This will be by last post for about three weeks, because I have a deadline to meet for two new books that will be out this Spring. I pray that this message will hopefully wake up some of the people who still think that open borders, no laws, Socialism, Progressivism, and sanctuary states are good for America's future. Sorry for the length of this post, but I needed the space.

Illegal Voting in California and America

Since many keep saying that many voters voted illegally during the 2018 midterm elections, I decided to do some research on my own state's new laws that were allegedly created to help more US citizens vote in my home state of California. The two laws I decided to research and study were written and passed in 2013 and 2015 during the Obama Administration's era and current Democrat controlled California legislature and Governor Brown's era. Although these law were allegedly written to make it easier for US citizens to vote in California, I found that these two laws were written to purposely work in tandem to basically, from what I gathered during my research, evidently ignore and circumvent Federal guidelines and laws that control the issuing of United States' drivers' licenses and protect the integrity of American elections.

In the end, I found what appeared to be purposely created loop holes that for some reason allows any illegal person who enters US Sovereign Soil to get a California license by simply either providing (for example) an alleged note from the (for example) their Mexican consulate that says they are in California legally to both get a US/California legal driver's license and/or just sign an affidavit (basically take their word on their honor?) that says they are in America legally. The kicker of these two laws is that if these foreigners are caught in a lie, they can not be prosecuted because the state of California takes the complete blame for either infraction because one of these laws has a "mia culpa" clause (that covers both new legislature laws) which basically puts the blame on the California's government and hold the alleged legal or illegal alien guiltless. You read my last two sentences right. These two laws forces US citizens and the Federal Government to accept any foreigner's word to both get a US/State driver's license and to vote in our Presidential and local elections because California's Government takes the blame for these aliens who break U.S. laws.

So who wrote these two handy laws that more than likely allowed millions of undocumented California residents to both get US/State driver's license that automatically registered them to vote in all US elections? The first law that started the disabling of these two Federal Laws that were written to protect the veracity of America was written in 2013 by a California legislator with the surname of Alejo. Mr. Alejo's law was dubbed AB 60, or "Alejo's Driver's Licenses eligibility required documentation." To save space and time, I'm going to just highlight the key areas that I found to be, to say the least, quite scary and meant to evidently "trump and ignore US Federal laws as they apply to the issuing of driver's license to America's citizens.

The first point of interest to look at is found in these words: "This bill would require the department to ISSUE an original driver's license to a person (note the key word here is person and not citizen) who is UNABLE TO SUBMIT SATISFACTORY PROOF that the applicant's presence in the United States is authorized under Federal Law IF HE OR SHE MEETS ALL OTHER QUALIFICATIONS for licensure and provides satisfactory proof (note here that later in Alejo's law we find that forms like the letter from the Mexican consulate is proof or a Mexican passport which is not a permit for US permanent residency.) to the department of his or her identity and California residency (in other words if an illegal has proof of who he or she is and is living in California, according to Alejo's law they considered American permanent residents because of Alejo's law and US Immigration laws be damned.) The bill would require the department to adopt emergency regulations, in consultation (This means the Department of Motor Vehicles can advise these PERSONS as to what they will accept as proof.) with appropriate interested parties as prescribed... The bill would provide the information collected pursuant to those provisions is NOT a public record and shall not be disclosed by the department, EXCEPT as required by law." So if we read this correctly, this bill does two things, one it allows the California to ignore US Federal laws as they pertain to issuing driver's license to US citizens so the state can issue licenses to ANY person in America, legally or not, and this law allows California to break US Federal Laws. And here is a great example of how Alego's law basically ignores US Federal Law: "This will would authorize an applicant who is unable to provide satisfactory proof that his or her presence in the United States is authorized under federal law to SIGN an AFFIDAVIT attesting that he or she is both ineligible for a social security number and unable to submit proof that his or her presence in the United States is authorized under federal law in lieu of submitting a social security number." Why is this statement in Alejo's law? Well, US Federal law states that ALL US state department's of motor vehicles require an applicant "for a driver's license to contain the applicant's social security number and any other number or identifier..."

Without going into the complete law, I think my readers should now get the idea of how illegal aliens/undocumented aliens are getting California license that intern allows them to get registered to vote because of our second law I decided to research that was dubbed "AB 1461, Gonzalez, voter registration: California New Motor Voter Program." Here is how Gonzalez's automatic voter registration works: We all know from experience the procedures we need to follow to register to vote in our area/country, but since the federal government decided it was a good idea to let ANY PERSON to be automatically registered to vote when they either apply for a driver's license or renew their state license, this law opened up a can worms in the state of California especially when the state's legislature, that is heavily loaded with both children who grew up in California that either came here illegally or were born here to illegal parents, is loaded with Hispanic/Mexican representatives who believe in open borders. Having said this, we should not understand why Gonzalez's law begins with this clause: "Under the program (AB 1461), after the Secretary of State certifies that certain enumerated conditions (These conditions advantageously can and evidently do come from Alejo's law.) are satisfied, the Department of Motor Vehicles WOULD BE REQUIRED to electronically provide to the Secretary of State the records of each person who is issued an original or renewal of a driver's license or state identification card or who provides the department with a change of address, as specified."

Here is the kicker: "The person's (again note the lack of the word U.S. citizen) motor vehicle records would then constitute a completed affidavit of registration and the person would be registered to VOTE, unless the person affirmatively declined to be registered to vote during the transaction with the department, the department did not represent to the Secretary of State that the person attested that he or she meets all voter eligibility requirements, as specified, or the Secretary of State determines that the person is ineligible to vote." Remember that in Alejo's law and this law no one can look at these records under penalty of law so only the state can decide who is legal to vote or to get a license in California, and the Feds can't stop them. And if an ineligible/illegal person does vote, what happens? Here is the final kicker that blew me away, nothing: "Section 2268 of this Gonzalez's law says, 'If a person who is ineligible to vote becomes registered to vote pursuant to this chapter in the absence of a violation by that person of Section 18100, that person's registration shall be presumed to have been effected with OFFICIAL AUTHORIZATION AND NOT THE FAULT OF THAT PERSON (In simple terms, oops, Mia Culpa says the state.). And to cover all the people who allegedly might have voted in 2016, "Section 2269 says, 'If a person who is ineligible to vote becomes registered to vote pursuant to this chapter and votes or attempts to vote in an election held after the effective date of the person's registration, that person shall be PRESUMED TO HAVE ACTED WITH OFFICIAL AUTHORIZATION and shall NOT be guilty of fraudulently voting or attempting to vote pursuant to Section 18560, unless that person willfully votes or attempts to vote knowing that he or she is not entitled to vote (wink, wink, again, oops "Mia Culpa.")."

Finally, I was watching network news this year (2018) after yet another alleged senseless mass shooting that took place in California, and after all of the analysts had their say, they all sort of came to the conclusion that "we would never know why these "normal Americans one day pick up a gun or rifle and commit these atrocious killings." To tell the truth, I think my book points out a key reason these Americans are "going mad" and committing these mass killings, and it can be found in the fact that they are very likely suffering from Post Traumatic Stress Disorder because they are seeing their European influenced America overrun and conquered by "illegal aliens, law breaking aliens, or armies of invaders invading and destroying the America they thought would never disappear." I say this because it is a fact that America's culture and Government will soon die in many ways and these weaker minded Americans are people that are basically losing their mind because they subconsciously "CAN"T HANDLE IT." To put in a scientific way, I feel Van der Kolk, McFarlane, and Weisaeth say best in their book Traumatic Stress: The effects of Overwhelming Experience on Mind, Body, and Society where they state the following facts that describe what many Americans are subconsciously feeling as they see "THEIR" America disappear by the uncontrolled invasion of law breaking foreigners that are Not being stopped by America's Judges or Politicians that are supposed to protect them:

"Christianson (1984) noted that when people feel threatened they experience a significant narrowing of consciousness, and remain focused on only the central perceptual details [(as in millions of invaders taking over America and their Americana disappearing))]. As people are traumatized, this narrowing of consciousness sometimes seems to evolve into a complete amnesia for the experience...'[Forgetting an event is] an exaggerated form of a general disturbance of memory which is characteristic of all emotions,' Janet (1909 p. 1607). [Janet] also noted that when people become too upset, memories cannot be transformed into a neutral narrative; a person is 'unable to make the recital which we call narrative memory, and yet he (or she) remains confronted by the difficult situation' (Janet, 1919/1925, Vol. 1, p. 660). This results in 'a phobia of memory' (Vol. 1, p. 661)...Janet claimed that the memory traces of the trauma linger as what he called 'unconscious fixed idea,' which cannot be 'liquidated' as long as they have not been translated into a personal narrative. When this occurs, they instead continue to intrude as terrifying perceptions, obsession-al preoccupation, and somatic re-experiences such as anxiety reactions...[Grinker and Spiegel (1945) noted that, 'Fear and anger in small doses are stimulating an alert to the ego, increasing efficacy. But, when stimulated by repeated psychological trauma, the intensity of the emotion heightens until a point is reached at which the ego loses its effectiveness and may become altogether crippled' (p. 820)."

The breaking point for all of those traumatized Americans that see their country slowly disappear a little more each day (as illegal aliens rush to America's borders every day), according to Horowitz, can be found in the fact that they finally break one day because of panic: "In Civilian trauma victims, Horowitz (1986) described an 'acute catastrophic stress reaction' characterized by panic, cognitive disorganization, disorientation, and dissociation," which I feel leads to the mass shootings America is now experiencing (Bessel A. van der Kolk, Alexander C. McFarlane, and Lars Weisaeth editors, <u>Traumatic Stress: The Effects of Overwhelming Experience on Mind, Body and Society,</u> The Gilford Press. New York, London. 1996. Pp. 285-286.). By the way, I feel these "automatism" acts of violence (that is not allowed by our courts as a defense in court for murder) are no different than when a veteran of a war like the Vietnam war goes off and starts to kill people because he flashes back to his days in Nam. Can we expect more mass killings as the Americana culture disappears from America and is replaced by the broken cultures these alleged refugees allegedly are said to be fleeing? I feel you can bet your life on it because of something called diversity, which I feel was created to destroy America's culture and replace it with these broken foreign cultures that belong to America's invaders.

Since I feel have proven that America is being invaded and is in a state of occupation by Mexico and other South American countries' citizens, I want to end my book by demanding on behalf of the Republic's legal citizens and voting members of the Republic that the Mexican Government recall all of its invading force that is currently occupying US sovereign soil immediately or the Republic will declare war because the Constitution says (without the consent of Congress) a state can . . . engage in war, **unless actually invaded, or in such imminent danger as will not admit of delay."** I want to add that if Mexico does not end its invasion of US sovereign soil that is outlawed under the Monroe Doctrine, the legal citizens of the Republic will more than likely have a reason to declare war on Mexico, its legal government, and its citizen army occupying U.S. Sovereign soil. I add this warning, because this book proves Mexico's invasion of America is **not** immigration. I also want to add the U.S. government will not be able stop Republic or America's citizens because America's government has failed to do its duty and defend America's States against an invader and aggressor as required in Article IV, Section 4: "The United States shall guarantee to every state in this union a Republican form of government, **shall protect each of them against invasion; and on application of the legislature, or of the executive [when the legislature cannot be convened] against domestic violence.**"

A MESSAGE TO THE PRESS

The message below was sent to our local paper and the San Francisco Chronicle the day after July 4, 2018 because a bullet hit the roof our home from illegal gunfire into the air. Luck for us no one was hurt:

From: One of your local minority male All-American men of color

To: The Mayor of Porterville and the City Council Members (Governor Brown and California's State Legislature)

Date: July 5, 2018

Reason: Last night's July 4 display of complete disrespect for local and state laws and disregard for public safety, which turned Porterville and the surrounding county area into a dangerous, disrespecting, lawless society that is only seen in third world countries.

I want to thank Porterville's Mayor and the Porterville City Council (and Governor Brown and the State Legislature) for making our city (an State) a Sanctuary city that allowed the city of Porterville and surrounding county area to become the home of thousands of new illegal neighbors who evidently have no respect for our state laws, no respect for their neighbors' rights, and no respect for America's July 4 celebration. I feel I can make this statement because last night our city in Central CA and, from what I saw on the news, the rest of California exploded in a flash of illegal air born fireworks and gunfire that basically made me and my neighbors feel like we now live in a lawless state and a lawless society. I often here that our new neighbors have come here to escape from the criminal elements in their countries but from what I saw last night the lawless element might be as close as these peoples' mirror and their reflection. Maybe it's time we outlaw all fireworks in Porterville and CA (or the State) and put up some stiff fines and jail time in the books for illegal fireworks and shooting a gun into the air. The bullets come down and the hole in my roof is proof of this fact. Is this the future of California cities and counties thanks to our leaders act to make California and our cities Sanctuary and lawless areas? I don't think I need to remind our leaders that have children that if you spoil children and let them do as they please you end up with disrespectful and disobedient children. This same rule applies to adults that you allow to break immigration laws, so they get conditioned to thinking that America's leaders are soft and don't care if people obey or respect American laws so it's okay to break all of them and NOT obey any of America's laws. Maybe it's time that Porterville and California outlaws fire works again and puts jail terms and hefty fines back into power for firing guns in the air for fun.

Sincerely, A fed up Porterville (and California) Resident who is tired of dodging people running lights, stop signs, and now illegal air born fireworks and gun fire bullets that hail down from the sky. Note: Now you see why so many Americans are leaving California for other states and countries. Yes, I plan to leave CA as soon as my wife and I retire from our long careers in once Law Abiding CA.

Happy Independence Day America's Citizens and let freedom ring; let's take America Back! One more thing, Since I feel God had a hand in the writing of this book, I want to now give our Lord Jesus Christ thanks for being my guide and inspiration as I wrote this book that I hope will save his country that we Americans have always called, "God's Country."

Recommended Reading

Belloc, Hilaire. The Free Press, IHS Press: Norfolk, VA. 2002.7-8.

Court says recess appointments to NLRB are unconstitutional." On Campus 32.4 March, April 2013: 11.

"Laird, Charlton." Ed. "Lutz, D. William," Rev. Ed. Webster's New World Thesaurus, "Funk and Wagnalls Ed. 1985.

Pitt, Jack, and Russell E. Leavenworth, Logic for Argument, P. 43-44.

California Senate, The Constitution of the United States of America and the Constitution of the State of California, Sacramento: California Senate 1997-98, p 85.

Welfare Spending Up 41 percent under Obama." Newsmax.com 23 April 2012. www.http://Newsmax@reply.newsmax.com.).

California State Senate, The Constitution of the United States of America and the Constitution of the State of California, Sacramento: California Senate, 1997-98 p 225.

312 *Reg. B. Two Stones*

House divided speech by Abraham Lincoln, Online Post: Oct. 15, 2011, P. 1, www.http://showcase.netins.net/web/creative/lincolnspeeces.

Cypresso. "United States is being invaded by Mexico—We need to be at war." News Public. 6 February 2011. <http://newspublic.com/index.php?

Landau." Funk and Wagnalls Standard College Dictionary. Text Edition: 1967.

Laird, Charlton and Lutz, D. William, Webster's New World Thesaurus: Funk and Wagnalls Edition. Simon and Schuster, Inc. New York. 1985. Pp. 374.

Hofstadter, Richard, William Miller, and Daniel Aaron. The United States: The History of a Republic, Prentice-Hall, Inc. New Jersey: 1960.

Walker, Brenda. Limits To Growth Page, 27 August 2012. http://www.limitstogrowth.org/WEB-text/aztlan.html.

Brown, Dee. Bury My Heart at Wounded Knee: An Indian History of The American West, Pan Books. London: 17th ed. 1983.

Cremony, John C. Life Among the Apaches, University of Nebraska Press: Lincoln and London, 1983.

Gelo, J. Daniel and Noyes, Stanley, Comanches in the New Southwest, 1895-1908. University of Texas, Austin. 1999.

Grilliot, J. Harold and Schubert, A Frank, Introduction to Law and the Legal System. Houghton Mifflin Company. Boston: 1989 P 357.

Dolan, F Edward, Jr. Amnesty: The American Puzzle. Franklin Watts. New York and London. 1975. Pp 3.

In Defense of the Constitution: Ending America's Occupation 313

Munro, William Bennett, Social Civics: Our Democracy in Action, The American School: Chicago, 1960. 3ʳᵈ Ed.

Obama, Barack. "Breaking the War Mentality." Sundial: The Weekly Newsmagazine. 10 March 1983

Cultural Genocide." Wikipedia: The Free Encyclopedia, 2 April 2012. http://en.wikipedia.org/Wikicultural_genocide.

Staver, Matthew, "ACLU puts Ten Commandments on Trial." Liberty Action. 4 May 2012. http://libertyaction.com.

Fox News. "Islamic Laws Influence in America a Growing Concern." Online Posting. Washington DC: Traditional Values Coalition. 2013.

Michener, A James, The Covenant: Volume 1. Random House. New York: 1980 p 28).

Photos That Changed The World: The 20ᵗʰ Century. Ed. Peter Stepan. Munich: Prestel Verlag, 2000

Brown, Tim. "Obama Administration Aids Muslim Brotherhood with $1Billion of Taxpayer Money for U-Boats." Online Posting. 11 Sept. 2012. http://freedomoutpost.com/2012/09/obama-administration-aids-muslimbrotherhood.

McDurmon, Joel. "State Dept erases religious freedom section from Report, hiding Arab Spring abuses." Online Posting. 13 Jan. 2012. http://americanvisionnews.com/3752/state-dept-erases-religiousfreedom-section-from-report-hiding-arab-spring-abuses.

Wooldridge, Frosty. "How Immigration and Multiculturalism Destroyed Detroit." On Line Posting 5 October 2009 http://newswithviews.com.

314 *Reg. B. Two Stones*

Laird, Charlton, and William D. Lutz, Webster's New World Thesaurus: Funk and Wagnalls Edition. Simon and Schuster, Inc: New York, 1971.

Schaefer, T. Richard, Sociology. McGraw Hill: Boston 9 Ed 2005.

McConnell, V. James. "Eron's Chicago Circle Studies," Understanding Human Behavior. Holt Rinehart and Winston: New York 5 Ed 1986.

Hofstadter, Richard, William Miller, and Daniel Aaron. "America Goes to War." The United States: The History of a Republic. Prentice-Hall, Inc. New Jersey: 1960, 6th ed.

How the Republic Died at Philadelphia in 1787." 26 March 2010. Online Posting. http://worldpress.com.

Hodges, C. John and Whitten, E. Mary. Harbrace College Handbook, Harcourt Brace Jovanovich, Inc: New York.

Citizenship in the Western Tradition, Chapel Hill: University of North Carolina Press, 1992

Meyer, Michael, Thinking and Writing About Literature, St Martin's Press, 1997.

Pitt, Jack, and Russell E. Leavenworth, Logic for Argument, New York: Random House, Fresno State College.1968.

Roberts, Noel-Burton, Analyzing Sentences: An Introduction to English Syntax. Longman Group Limited. London: 1989.

"(Rothman, David M. California Judicial Conduct Handbook. West Group. California: 2nd Ed. 1999.

In Defense of the Constitution: Ending America's Occupation 315

Mabbott, J. D., An Introduction To Ethics. Anchor Books. Garden City, New York: Anchor Books Ed. 1969, pp. 41.

How to Survive and Thrive in the Game of Life: Dare to Succeed (Hyperion. New York: 2001.

McIntosh, Gary L., and Samuel D. Rima, Sr. Overcoming the Dark Side of Leadership: The Paradox of Personal Dysfunction. Baker Books, Michigan: 1998. 2nd Ed.

The Senate, The Constitution of the United States of America and the Constitution of the State of California, Sacramento: 1997-98.

Berlitz, Charles. Native Tongues. Grosset & Dunlap: New York. 1982, Pp. 4.

Van Dyke, Henry, Ed, Select Essays of Ralph Waldo Emerson, New York: American Book Company, 1907.

Printed in the United States
By Bookmasters